THE F
RACKET STATE

Eva Richter
447-2954
NM

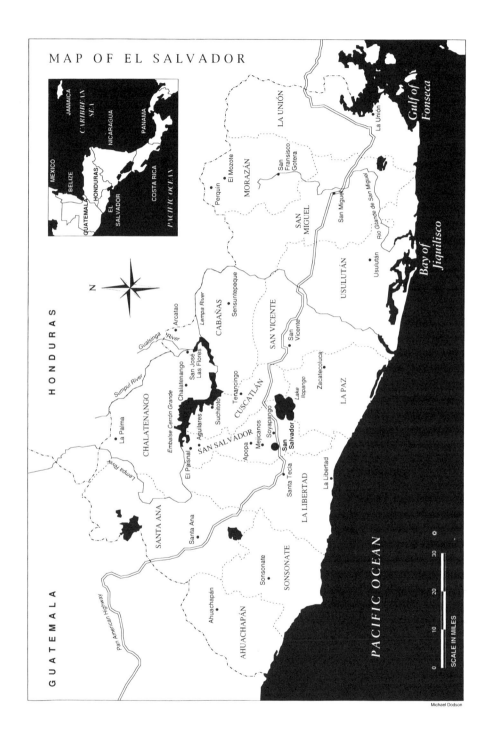

MAP OF EL SALVADOR

Michael Dodson

THE PROTECTION RACKET STATE

Elite Politics, Military Extortion, and Civil War in El Salvador

William Stanley

Temple University Press

Philadelphia

Temple University Press, Philadelphia 19122

Copyright © 1996 by Temple University
All rights reserved
Published 1996
Printed in the United States of America

Text design by Betty Palmer McDaniel

Library of Congress Cataloging-in-Publication Data

Stanley, William Deane, 1958–
    The protection racket state : elite politics, military extortion, and civil war in
El Salvador / William Stanley.
        p.   cm.
    Includes bibliographical references (p.   ) and index.
    ISBN 1-56639-391-4 (cl : alk. paper). — ISBN 1-56639-392-2 (pb : alk. paper)
    1. State-sponsored terrorism—El Salvador—History—20th century.   2. Death squads—
El Salvador—History—20th century.   3. Political persecution—El Salvador—History—20th
century.   4. El Salvador—Politics and government—20th century.   I. Title.
HV6433.S2S73   1996
972.8405—dc20   95-20998

For Segundo Montes

CONTENTS

ACKNOWLEDGMENTS

This book is based on field research conducted between 1987 and 1995 during repeated visits to El Salvador, Mexico City, Guatemala, Washington, D.C., and several other locations in the United States. The work would have been impossible without the generous funding provided by the Institute for the Study of World Politics, the John D. and Catherine T. MacArthur Foundation, the United States Institute of Peace, the Tinker Foundation, the Latin American Institute at the University of New Mexico, and the Gene Gallegos Regents Lectureship at UNM. This assistance allowed me to interview participants in El Salvador's politics, use archives in various locations, and observe events directly.

I offer special thanks to the students of the University of New Mexico and the taxpayers of the state of New Mexico, who pay my salary and provide the facilities that have helped me pursue this work. Like most professors at research universities, I am sometimes caught between my responsibility to my students and my responsibility to my research. Yet I believe that the depth of research and thought needed for a book of this kind, and the intensity of the work involved, make me a better and more empathetic teacher.

I have accumulated many personal debts during this project, especially to the many government officials, soldiers, diplomats, politicians, guerrillas, business people, United Nations officials, scholars, and journalists who generously allowed me to interview them. Because of the sensitive nature of our conversations, many asked to remain anonymous.

The document-based aspects of this research would have been impossible without the tremendous help I received from librarians, archivists, and colleagues in the United States and El Salvador. The staff at the National Security Archive in Washington, D.C., guided my exploration of their collection of U.S. government documents on El Salvador; the faculty and staff at the Inter-University Center for Information and Documentation and the Institute for Human Rights at the Central American University in San Salvador consistently facilitated my use of their resources; Olga Luck at the Department of State Freedom of Information and Privacy office was both courteous and helpful; Hugh Byrne of the University of California, Los Angeles, shared his cataloguing of U.S. government documents released in 1993 and 1994; and the Human Rights Project of El Rescate and Fundación Flor de Izote shared their extensive chronologies, weekly reports, and data base on events in El Salvador.

I began my research for a doctoral dissertation, which was supervised by Jonathan Fox (Chair), Martin Diskin, and Joshua Cohen. Peter Smith and

Brian Smith guided my initial conceptualization of the project. Their constructive and challenging input molded my working hypotheses, guided me through field work and the initial write-up, and pointed the way for many of the revisions that are embodied in this book. An anonymous reader for Temple University provided a stern and insightful review of the entire manuscript. Mark Peceny, Judy Bieber, Tom Gibb, Charles Call, and Elizabeth Wood also read and commented on the work. Mark wrote at least two sets of substantive comments on each chapter. Chapter Six, in particular, bears his mark. The final product includes as many of their insights and suggestions as I was able to incorporate. Karen Remmer, Linda Garrett, Carlos Chipoco, Tom Gibb, Frank Smyth, José García, Cynthia McClintock, Charles Call, Rafael Guido Véjar, Elizabeth Putnam, Kevin Murray, and David Holiday read and offered advice on individual chapters. Other friends and colleagues, including Chris Norton, George Vickers, Maggie Popkin, Jack Spence, Tommie Sue Montgomery, and Susan Kandel shared their insights and knowledge, provided an important reality check, and gave me the benefit of their far greater experience in covering Salvadoran affairs. I take sole responsibility for the errors of fact and interpretation that remain.

I could not have completed this book without the combination of patience, selective pressure, and sound advice offered by editors at Temple University Press. Doris Braendel supported the project from the outset and guided my extensive revisions of the original manuscript; Joan Vidal managed the copy editing and production process, working around my many delays and sojourns to Central America; and copy editor Jane Barry produced a final product that was much better than the one I wrote. I thank all of them for their professionalism and hard work. Thanks also go to Thomas Gentry, who prepared the index.

Throughout the several years of this project, I have been blessed with the support and encouragement of exceptionally good friends. Louisa Koch offered relentless hospitality in Washington, gave very convincing pep talks, and asked tough questions. My colleagues at the University of New Mexico, especially fellow Latin Americanists Ken Coleman, Mark Peceny, Karen Remmer, and Ken Roberts, have made Albuquerque a fun and intellectually rich place to work. My friends Chuck, Dylan, Suk, Anne, betts, Kathy, Jennifer, Sharon, Rob, Kent, Terry, David, John, Sarah, José Luís, and Carmen; my mother, Marjorie; and my brother John have offered talks, hikes, letters, e-mail, and companionship that have helped keep me happy and sane.

Finally I thank my companion, Judy Bieber, for indulging my academic obsessions (she has her own), for making life delightful in the midst of long hours of hard work, and for her sharp editorial pen, long talks about the state and society, and her encouraging way of saying, "You're almost done." Thank you, sweetheart.

THE PROTECTION
RACKET STATE

INTRODUCTION

In 1932, security forces commanded by General Maximiliano Hernández Martínez killed roughly twenty-five thousand peasants and workers in two rural provinces and a few towns in the western part of El Salvador. Five decades later, between 1978 and 1991, agents and allies of the Salvadoran government killed an additional fifty thousand civilians, from a population of roughly five million.[1] Victims included labor organizers, members of opposition political parties, priests and Catholic lay activists, teachers, and members of nascent guerrilla cells. Most of the victims were either poor people or people who worked with the poor.

Some were killed openly by the internal security forces, including the National Guard, the Treasury Police, and the National Police, during raids on communities that were suspected of harboring "subversives." More often, the killers were "heavily armed men in civilian clothes," usually driving unmarked vehicles. Such "death squads" removed people from their homes, usually at night, and took them away. Sometimes victims were killed summarily, but often they were tortured first. Bodies were then dumped along the highways or in well-known dumping grounds, such as "El Playon," a lava field northwest of San Salvador.[2]

The security forces embellished their killings to heighten fear. Victims were often beheaded. The names or initials of various death squads were carved into bodies, and the killers left hand-written notes warning that the same fate awaited other "subversives." Torture left unmistakable marks on cadavers: limbs, teeth, fingernails, eyes, tongues, breasts, and genitals were removed or lacerated; bodies were burned with fire or with acids that literally removed the features of victims' faces. In the capital city of San Salvador, morning commuters would find severed limbs, and even heads, at bus stops and on board buses. Lest anyone doubt the national scope of the death squads, families of victims sometimes found that their loved ones' heads and bodies had been dumped in separate departments of the country. Women victims were often raped; so, less frequently, were men.

As state violence escalated between 1977 and 1979, leftist popular organizations mobilized large numbers of new supporters to demand a stop to the killing and the release of leaders and members who were in prison or had disappeared. Guerrilla organizations of the left responded with an intensified campaign of assassinations and kidnappings. The state struck back, leading to a spiral of eye-for-an-eye retaliation by both sides.

Violence intensified in late 1979 and 1980. By the later months of 1980, government forces were killing civilians at a rate of a thousand per month (Socorro Jurídico Cristiano 1984). Uniformed troops carried out most of the killing at this point, eclipsing the work of clandestine death squads. Particular violence was directed against political leaders who advocated reform or moderation, or who negotiated solutions to the growing political crisis. The security forces, or death squads operating in close cooperation with government forces, killed the attorney general, the archbishop of San Salvador, and several reformist military officers. In November 1980, security forces killed the entire top leadership of the non-guerrilla left just hours before a scheduled press conference at which they were to present a proposal for a negotiated solution. Hundreds of other moderate, reform-minded citizens were killed. An army colonel who had been chosen to represent a reformist movement of junior army officers narrowly escaped two attacks on his life in 1980. Three of the reformist junior officers were themselves killed by hardline colleagues, and other military officers who favored reforms or had resisted orders to kill civilians were attacked or threatened.

The response to this onslaught was to some extent predictable. Mass popular organizations, which had been the primary form of organization by the left, broke up during the course of 1980. Many of their members either went into hiding or joined the armed struggle against the government. Moderate political opponents of the military who had been advocating reforms within the existing institutional framework began to align themselves with the revolutionaries. Meanwhile, the guerrilla organizations carried out a campaign to assassinate members of pro-government paramilitary organizations, killing over a thousand of them during the year. By late 1980, the opposition had committed itself to civil war. The disparate guerrilla groups unified to become the Farabundo Martí National Liberation Front (FMLN), which waged an increasingly successful military campaign against the government, nearly defeating official forces in the field by late 1983.

During 1981, government killing hit its peak. Government forces committed a number of massacres in which hundreds of civilians died. The military turned to indiscriminate violence against civilians in areas of the countryside in which the FMLN enjoyed support. In many communities no one was spared, as army commanders treated even children—born or unborn—as threats to the state.

During lulls in the combat, or in areas where the FMLN was less effective, government forces continued targeted repression against civilians suspected of favoring the guerrillas. Such killings were particularly intense in the western part of the country, where the National Police used the facilities of a meat packing plant to behead victims (as many as 34 per week were found beheaded in Santa Ana province alone), and in some cases to grind up their bodies so they could be washed down the drain.[3] Around sixteen thousand civilians died in 1981, the vast majority at the hands of the military (Socorro Jurídico Cristiano 1984).

Government violence gradually ebbed during 1982 and 1983, to roughly half the levels of 1980 and 1981. Thereafter, the killing declined dramatically, but to some extent killing was replaced by imprisonment and torture: horrible, elaborate tortures of civilians continued to be reported throughout the late 1980s. Moreover, government killing was never eliminated, despite intense international pressures. The bombings of a labor union and a human rights organization and the assassinations of six Jesuits and their housekeepers in late 1989 demonstrated that forces of the state were still inclined to murder, despite the international and domestic political costs of doing so.

In per capita terms, Salvadoran state terror was among the most severe in the hemisphere. The 42,171 killed by government forces during the six peak years of violence from 1978 through 1983 (Socorro Jurídico Cristiano 1984) constituted close to 1 percent of the population. The impact of the violence is even greater than this 1 percent figure suggests because deaths were concentrated among young people, especially men, increasing the likelihood that any given family has experienced a political killing or knows a family that has. In addition to those who were murdered, thousands more were "disappeared."[4] The only Latin American nation that may have matched El Salvador in the number of state murders per capita is Guatemala, where death squads and rural counterinsurgency sweeps killed between 50,000 and 75,000 between 1978 and 1985, and where the total death toll from thirty years of civil war has been estimated at 100,000 dead and 38,000 disappeared (Bowen 1987, 42; Brockett 1991, 59; Krueger and Enge 1985, 2; Simon 1987, 14).[5]

How can we account for mass murder by the Salvadoran state? Most readers will find it difficult to conceive of the mentality and spirit that enable individual soldiers to torture, slaughter, and mutilate defenseless civilians, whatever the ideological justification. Viewing the violence analytically, as collective behavior, it seems difficult to escape the conclusion that it was irrational. Though state terrorism clearly intimidated and suppressed some kinds of opposition at some points along the way, it just as clearly motivated many people to raise arms against the state, filling them with grim determination to take revenge. As David Mason and Dale Krane (1989) have shown, when state violence becomes sufficiently intense and random, it becomes entirely rational for individuals to take arms to defend themselves.[6] The state can create its own enemies, and by late 1983, the government of El Salvador had created so many that it faced serious risk of military defeat. Only massive U.S. assistance allowed the Armed Forces of El Salvador (FAES) to turn the tide and achieve a stalemate against the FMLN.

The conventional view in the social sciences is that state violence is a rational response to opposition. When social demands upon the state exceed the state's resources, or when opposition takes the form of violence and begins to threaten the state's control of society, then the state will logically respond with violence (Gurr 1986; Hibbs 1973; Jackson et al. 1978; O'Donnell 1978). This view has much in common with "realist" theories of international relations that focus on how and when states use force against one another: the challenge for the state lies in correctly calibrating its preparations for and use of violence to deter its enemies without goading them into making even more dangerous threats. By analogy to international relations theory, the domestic security dilemma facing the state is that failure to respond adequately to a threat may encourage its enemies; yet overreaction may produce more numerous and more radicalized internal enemies in the future (Hibbs 1973; Jackson et al. 1978; Mason and Krane 1989).

This analysis certainly fits well with some aspects of violence in El Salvador. State violence clearly increased in response to greater popular opposition. Moreover, it appears that in some ways, repression had the effect of deterring social opposition: when the opposition FMLN tried to trigger a mass insurrection in January 1981, after more than a year of intense state terror, they found that most of the urban population was too frightened to take part. Yet, just as clearly, state violence had the effect of intensifying opposition to the state in many rural areas, generating a popular base for the FMLN guerrillas, which kept them supplied with food, shelter, intelligence, and recruits, resources that, combined with international assistance from various sources, enabled them to fight the FAES to a draw in a prolonged war of attrition. Though successful at certain points, state repression in El Salvador was on the whole counterproductive.

One problem with applying a rational actor, opposition/reaction model to state violence in the domestic political setting is that this approach assumes a priori that the state has enemies it must deter with force. Why assume this? How would such a situation develop, and what measures could a state take along the way to prevent it from developing? States, even military or authoritarian ones, have choices between coercive and noncoercive responses to opposition, as illustrated by the Mexican state's alternatingly coercive and ameliorative response to the Zapatista uprising of January 1994. The Salvadoran military-led state of the 1930s through the early 1980s could have appeased the opposition, made concessions, allowed moderate opposition elements to take power, or at least attempted to channel popular mobilization into state-controlled (corporatist) organizations in which the popular sectors would exchange political freedom for socioeconomic benefits. Why was it so consistently coercive instead?

This question becomes especially salient with respect to El Salvador because state violence intensified most rapidly after October 1979, when a reformist coup organized by junior army officers removed the military president from office, brought reformist civilians into the government, and attempted to placate the popular opposition through major redistributive and political reforms. The junior officer corps, led by captains, strongly supported reformist measures, rejected the corruption and brutality of the past, and sought to bring change-oriented civilians into power. Their selection of junta members after the coup and the policies outlined in their "Proclama" were shaped by the Jesuit scholars from the University of Central America. Despite their reformist goals, despite their control of virtually all the barracks in the country at the time of the coup, and despite initially positive steps by the new government to implement reforms and regain popular legitimacy for the state, other state affiliates (the security forces and intelligence units) continued to torture, assassinate, and mutilate thousands of citizens, ensuring that a significant minority of the population viewed the state as so illegitimate that they would wage war against it.

This combination of policies was, to put it mildly, contradictory, and provides clear evidence that we need to avoid thinking of the state as a single, rational entity. Different elements of the Salvadoran state were working at cross purposes, and the elements that favored violence won the day. Moreover, state violence, directed against reformist officials within the state as well as against the population at large, played an important role in driving reformists from office and vetoing their strategy. The targeting of violence against civilian and military reformist leaders, against relatively moderate opponents who were seeking a nonviolent solution, and against beneficiaries of the socioeconomic reforms that were carried out in March 1980 all suggest that state violence was not only a response to opposition but also a means of competition for state power, a way of blocking reformist impulses and reformist leaders. All of this suggests that to understand why El Salvador suffered such atrocious violence, we need to look closely at the politics *within* the state, to understand why moderation died and how coercion became the state's predominant strategy.

One explanation for this bias toward coercion has to do with the economic and social structure of the country. A number of scholars have noted an elective affinity between economies based on export agriculture and internal repression. Repression is particularly likely to occur where modern export agriculture was established through expropriation of communal or municipal lands. Peasants displaced from their lands have little alternative but to work for low wages, helping to make production of export crops highly profitable for large landowners. The result is a highly stratified society in which rural workers are extremely poor and agrarian elites are extremely wealthy. Such elites have vested interests in continuing to repress and exploit rural workers and accumulate sufficient economic and political power to demand that the state continue to deliver the needed levels of repression while eschewing economic reforms (Brockett 1991; Carleton 1989; McClintock 1985a).

This structural explanation for state repression fits the El Salvador experience pretty well. Nonetheless, it is not fully satisfying for two reasons. First, this argument fails to examine *how* conservative economic elites impose their preferences on the state. There were, in fact, many junctures during the 1932 to 1979 period during which strategic elites within the military seemed poised to carry out major reforms in an effort to gain greater popular legitimacy and move away from coercion as a basis for governance. Yet these efforts failed every time, and reversals of reformism were accompanied by greater repression. Clearly the military state achieved little autonomy from social elites. The question is, why? How did social elites succeed in suppressing alternative models of governance favored by strategic elites within the state, especially when they held themselves apart from overt political participation?

Understanding the relationship between social elites and the military becomes all the more central when we consider the peace accords signed in El Salvador in January 1992, in which the civilian government of the National Republican Alliance (ARENA), representing the country's conservative elites, committed itself to radically reduce the legal powers and independence of the military, purge the military of violent and corrupt officers, dismantle the existing military-controlled internal security forces, exclude the army from responsibility for maintaining internal order, create a completely new civilian police force designed to safeguard the rights and safety of citizens, and incorporate the erstwhile guerrillas into the political life of the country as a legal party. These major reforms were accompanied by the creation of a new State Council for Human Rights (Procuraduría de Derechos Humanos) and modifications to the judicial system to make it more professional and less subject to political (and military) control. Taken all together, the agreements, whose implementation was supervised by an observer mission of the United Nations, greatly reduced the state's freedom to use coercion.

The decision to abandon coercion is all the more remarkable when we consider that the ARENA party originated in a conservative political movement that organized death squads and advocated a hardline response to leftist and reformist opposition. Why would a government of this party, funded by members of the conservative social elite who had resisted military reform for decades, sign away many of the coercive powers of the state? To reconcile this event with structuralist explanations of state violence, we must either show that the structure of the Salvadoran economy changed in some fundamental ways during the 1980s or consider the possibility that it was not so much the interests of social elites but rather the nature of their relationship to the state that generated the propensity for state violence.

To account for all of these anomalies, I find it helpful to disassemble the state analytically, examining state factions and their relationships with each other and with different components of civil society. A central theme of this book is the notion that the Salvadoran military state was essentially a protection racket: the military earned the concession to govern the country (and pillage the state) in exchange for its willingness to use violence against class enemies of the country's relatively small but powerful economic elite. To put it another way, state violence was a *currency of relations* between state and non-state elites. In the pages that follow, I trace how military leaders used conspicuous violence against civilians from the popular sectors in order to manipulate economic elites and preempt them from challenging the authority of the military. For almost five decades this strategy proved successful in maintaining civilian elite acquiescence to military rule. This strategy had costs, however. The mercenary relationship of some state agencies to economic elites and the use of violence for political manipulation cut both ways: private elites retained enough allies within the state to mobilize increased state violence at crucial moments, vetoing socioeconomic concessions by reformist military or civilian state elites. The state as a whole proved unable to break out of the protection racket model of state/society relations at the elite level because the leaders and agencies that were most involved in the violence developed vested interests in continuing a repressive strategy. This was to prove the military's undoing: by failing to achieve broader legitimacy and by using extreme and provocative violence against regime opponents, the military helped create an enemy that it could not defeat. In the end, the military forfeited its privileges, even those it had enjoyed within the nominally civilian-controlled governments of the 1980s, because it failed to defeat the FMLN.

This analysis points to a cautiously optimistic prognosis for Salvadoran politics in the short and long terms: the failure of military coercion, the development of the private sector elite into a political class (through the formation and electoral success of ARENA), and the institutional reforms achieved under the peace accords appear, in combination, to have broken the military's protection racket. Thus the inter-elite dynamic that helped fuel state violence and suppress economic compromise has been dampened, and the civilian economic elite has agreed to institutional reforms that compel it, at least for the time being, to rely on legitimacy rather than coercion to maintain power.

Many observers sympathetic to the FMLN have been puzzled that after a decade of civil war and thousands sacrificed to a revolutionary cause, the leadership of the strongest guerrilla insurgency in the Western Hemisphere would lay down their guns at the peak of their military power in exchange for institutional reforms—and relatively little else. Indeed, during the negotiations the FMLN placed greater emphasis on such reforms than on socioeconomic restructuring, a strategy seemingly at odds with the Front's historically Marxist ideology. Though the future remains uncertain, I suggest that the FMLN's strategy, whatever analysis and motivations were behind it, and whatever human and economic costs it imposed, may have achieved precisely the political changes the country most needed, breaking the protection racket through force of arms, then securing lasting change in elite civil–military relations through negotiated institutional reform. Ironically, the leftist FMLN has forced the creation of a liberal democracy more advanced in its political institutions than El Salvador's overall poverty and maldistribution of capital, land, and income would normally allow (Rueschmeyer, Stephens, and Stephens 1992; Seligson and Malloy 1987).

Any case study runs the risk of generating an elaborate argument that explains only a single, probably unique, case. Moreover, single-case analysis can focus too much on process and agency while overlooking structural constraints that would be more clear in a comparative analysis (Rueschemeyer, Stephens, and Stephens 1992, 32–33). In this book, I attempt to compensate for these drawbacks by maintaining "comparative awareness" and by examining a long time period, which helps make structural factors and sequences of events more visible. Moreover, my broader goal in writing this book is relatively immune to the risks of being too specific, since I am not attempting to generalize from El Salvador to the world. My goal is to illustrate, through the particularities of one case, a general proposition: that to understand state violence in most settings, we need to treat institutions of the state as actors with at least some degree of autonomy of interest and action; acknowledge that the state is not a unitary actor but a collection of competing groups, institutions, and factions, with different interests, perceptions, missions, and preferences; and recognize that under certain patterns of civilian–state and civil–military relations, the use of violence against civilians can serve the interests of military/state elites, quite apart from whether mass civilian opposition actually represents an urgent threat to the state. Rather than simplifying our understanding of state violence, I am trying to make it more complex, more nuanced, more sensitive to political and institutional context. I believe El Salvador provides an example of a set of factors that should inform theory and policy more generally.

The story of intra-elite politics and state violence in El Salvador is also a story of actively harmful measures by the United States. At several points the United States carried out institutional development projects that strengthened the agencies and factions of the Salvadoran military who were most invested in the protection racket. At crucial moments, U.S. policy makers, even those putatively motivated by concerns for human rights, acted as if they did not understand that different elements of the state were acting in contradictory ways, ignoring the violent actions of hardline agencies as long as structural and formal political reforms were under way. Part of the motivation for this book, then, is to urge international actors who involve themselves in helping poor countries develop state institutions, or who want to intervene against human rights violations, to operate from a finer-grained analysis of state institutions and politics, taking into account the role of violence as a currency of political competition among elites and state agencies.

The book opens with a theoretical chapter that examines existing literature on state violence and points to the importance of a state-centered approach. It proceeds with a historical narrative, a retelling of twentieth-century Salvadoran history with an emphasis on state politics and state violence. These historical chapters demonstrate that important characteristics of state violence, such as its intensity, targeting, and timing, cannot be understood without reference to intra-state and state–civil society relations at the elite level. In the process, the chapters make a series of specific arguments about the institutional characteristics of the Salvadoran military, about the role of repressive violence as a currency of relations among state and nonstate elites, and about the barriers to reform from within a protection racket state. Chapter Two examines the consolidation of military rule in El Salvador by means of the infamous massacre of 1932, then explores the features of the military regime that followed. Chapter Three traces the failure of the military to establish a reformist/inclusionary corporatist regime between 1948 and 1976, the ongoing use of violence against the public to legitimize military rule in the eyes of landed elites, and the failure of the military either to open the political system or to carry out substantive reforms that might have helped legitimize the regime even in the absence of free elections. Chapter Four traces the dynamics of violence and intra-elite politics during the government of Carlos Romero, whose provocative but inconsistent use of violence accelerated polarization and mass opposition to his regime. Chapter Five looks in detail at the reformist coup of October 1979 through the collapse of the first junta, showing how hardline elements of the military outmaneuvered reformists, in part by using massive violence against the popular movement to undercut the credibility of reformist elites. Chapter Six continues the work of Chapter Five, tracing the dismantling of the reformist movement in the military and the intensification of the hardline project during 1980. This chapter pays particular attention to role of the high command in operating a protection racket against members of the military themselves, the civilian right, and the United States. Chapter Seven examines how the FMLN's ability to resist defeat, combined with economic and political changes brought about by the war, helped undermine the military's protection racket and create conditions for antimilitary reforms built into the peace accords.

Chapters Four through Seven are based largely on primary sources, including interviews with dozens of Salvadoran military officers—among them most of the key participants in the 1979 coup and the majority of junta members—as well as civilian officials, party politicians, former guerrilla leaders, and United States officials. I also draw on hundreds of U.S. government documents released under the Freedom of Information Act, as well as two collections comprising thousands of State Department, Central Intelligence Agency, Department of Defense, and National Security Council documents declassified by the Clinton administration in 1993 and 1994.[7]

This book focuses on the actions and political strategies of the Salvadoran military. In the process, it says uncharitable things about many of its members and, most especially, its leadership, whose actions were in many cases despicable. The emphasis on the state's actions may strike some readers as inequitable in light of the fact that the FMLN killed thousands of people during the 1970s and 1980s. The emphasis on state violence is not motivated by a desire to ignore or apologize for the violence of the FMLN, which was in many instances pointless and inexcusable and under all circumstances regrettable. There is a need for a critical study of the FMLN and its use of violence. This is not that study. Rather, my goal is to provide a small initial step toward correcting the bias in political science scholarship toward studying rebellion and away from studying the violence of states. States command far greater resources than do rebels, particularly for killing. As Chapter One illustrates, states have killed far more people than have rebellions, yet we know little about the factors that influence state violence. I hope this book contributes to a better understanding of why states kill, rather than defend, their own citizens.

ONE

SELF-DEFENSE, CLASS OPPRESSION, AND EXTORTION: ALTERNATIVE VIEWS OF STATE VIOLENCE

Far more people have died at the hands of their own governments in the twentieth century than in war. Rudolph Rummel estimates the death toll from governmental mass murder of civilians at 169,202,000 — more than four times the battle dead for this century's international and civil wars up to 1987 (1994a, 2).[1] Rummel's painstaking and conservative estimates are intended to call attention to the magnitude of domestic killing by governments. While we are generally aware that the regimes of Stalin, Hitler, Mao Tse-tung, Chiang Kai-shek, Pol Pot, the Young Turks, and others have committed mass murder against their own citizens, we are seldom confronted by specific information regarding the actual magnitude of these crimes. Rummel insists that we cannot begin to grasp the reality and importance of state violence, much less begin to explain it and avoid its repetition, without examining its intensity, duration, and targeting (1990, 1991, 1992, 1994b).

Rummel's estimates, shocking and appalling in themselves, also point an accusing finger at academe, which has largely ignored the phenomenon of internal state violence. Our libraries are full of volumes on international war, its history, causes, prevention, and successful prosecution. International relations journals devote the bulk of their pages to questions of international conflict and cooperation. Meanwhile, scholars who study the internal politics of states (a field referred to as comparative politics) have focused on such relatively benign questions as transitions to and from democratic rule, comparisons of political party systems, bureaucracies, and methods of incorporating different sectors of society into the political system. The fact that many lives are at stake in the internal politics of nations has not been a focus of attention, at least not in the way that international violence has preoccupied international relations scholars.

To the limited extent that scholars studied internal violence prior to the 1980s, they gave most attention to rebellion, rioting, insurgency, and terrorism

(Gurr 1971; Paige 1975; Wolf 1969), even though the death toll from state violence has generally been far higher than that caused by regime opponents. The neglect of state violence as a legitimate research question began to give way in the 1980s as scholars finally began to explore both the magnitude of the problem and diverse ways of explaining the violent domestic conduct of states.[2]

Writings on state violence can be grouped into two broad sets, one derived from modernization theory and another derived from Marxism. Writings based on modernization theory tend to assume that states are legitimate. They therefore treat state violence as a rational and proportionate response to a threat to the security of the state. Questions of what the state is, whom it represents, or why it might face opposition are largely ignored. Writings based on Marxism view state violence as part of the broader phenomenon of class oppression. From this point of view, the state is a more or less closely controlled instrument of dominant class interests, and repression is simply a necessary mechanism for maintaining a system of class domination.

These two approaches, although ideologically opposed, have much in common. Both view state violence as a rational response to opposition challenges, treat the state as a unit, and see the state as an expression of underlying social structures. All three assumptions create serious problems when we attempt to apply these theoretical perspectives to real cases. First, state violence is often grossly disproportionate to the extent of opposition, contradicting the assumption that states apply force rationally. History offers many examples of states that have provoked rather than suppressed opposition through illegal, illegitimate, and indiscriminate acts of coercion. In such cases, state violence serves neither to defend a legitimate order nor to advance any conceivable dominant class project. Second, we know from studies of international relations and public policy that states are seldom unitary actors; rather, they include many components that follow different imperatives and frequently contradict one another. State policy is often made through the interplay of competing bureaucracies, rather than through some centralized, rational process. Finally, the structuralism of both modernization and Marxist perspectives tends to distance us from the concrete reality that states are institutions with interests and capacities. As I argue in detail below, the history of Central America illustrates that states have shaped the political arena, and even the nature of society, through their use of violence. It is unsound to treat states as merely an expression of society when they have the capacity to shape the nature of society.

This chapter, and the historical chapters that follow, are informed by recent literature that reasserts the importance of the state, its bureaucracies, and its strategic elites as actors in their own right, with their own interests and capabilities, which may be distinct from those of civilian social groups (Carnoy 1984; Evans, Rueschemeyer, and Skocpol 1985; Stepan 1978; Tilly 1975, 1990). The appropriateness of a state-centered approach seems obvious, given that agencies of the state are—by definition—the primary perpetrators of official repression. Yet this perspective has rarely been exploited to explain internal state violence.

I also draw heavily on insights from international relations theory. This may seem surprising, given that the topic at hand is *domestic* violence by states. However, on the sparse menu of relevant theoretical perspectives, international relations theories have the advantage that they at least deal with the question of why states engage in organized violence. A number of the general approaches within this literature can be adapted to a discussion of internal violence. Because much international relations literature focuses on explaining the behavior of states, there proves to be considerable overlap between insights derived from this literature and other state-centered writings.

My goal is to move beyond both modernization- and Marxism-based views to understand more clearly the incentives for state elites to use violence even in the absence of mass opposition or in situations where repression is not a rational response, or one that serves the interests of dominant classes. I explore the idea that states can operate "protection rackets," manipulating the appearance of mass opposition, or in fact generating it through inflexibility and brutality, in order to secure ongoing political and economic concessions from social elites. Drawing on the idea that state policy is often made through competition between bureaucracies, I explore ways in which violence against supposed enemies of the state can serve as a tool for competing factions or agencies within the state. Finally, I discuss in general terms the kinds of political and institutional changes, as well as international measures, needed to break a protection racket once it is established.

Among the specific propositions that I develop are the following. (1) While certain social and economic structures may provide a context conducive to state violence, state actors and social elites retain choices between alternative paths. (2) To understand the policies enacted, it is crucial to specify as accurately as possible how state and social elites interact with one another and to examine what role state violence has in maintaining that relationship. (3) Within the state, the nature and outcome of factional politics shape the policies chosen in particular moments. (4) Within elite social classes, the degree of political coherence and organization affects the propensity of elites to favor repression (the lower the political coherence of social elites, the more likely they are to depend on military institutions and coercive policies to advance their interests). (5) We can only understand the full impact of international and domestic political initiatives by evaluating their effect on the factional balance within the state and social elite. And (6) where agencies have the autonomous ability to use violence against regime opponents, this power can be used to secure the support of social elites and to scuttle reformist initiatives by other factions and agencies of the state.

Opposition/Reaction Models

It is perhaps not coincidental that while U.S. scholars ignored state repression, the United States was building political alliances with authoritarian regimes in the Third World as part of its strategic confrontation with the USSR. John McCamant (1984) suggests that political pressures caused researchers to steer clear of the topic. With or without such pressures, significant intellectual barriers to research on state violence were inherent in the prevailing theories of political development in the 1950s and 1960s. Even to raise questions about violence would place a researcher outside the intellectual mainstream.

The dominant theories of political development, referred to collectively as modernization theory, modeled the evolution of newly independent states on real and imagined aspects of Western European and North American history. A central assumption was that political systems were, by definition, legitimate expressions of the collective will of the people. People got the government they wanted and deserved (McCamant 1984; Shafer 1988, 51–56), a definition that left little conceptual room for illegitimate, abusive state conduct. Pluralist political theory treats the state as merely an arena of competition between interest groups, not as an independent actor with coercive capacity. Since the state was presumed to be the expression of the will of the people, any significant opposition was a sign of social deviance. Coercion was at most an occasional and temporary means of achieving compliance with the law. Pluralist scholars did not think to ask whether "coercive power could be used to shape the pattern of demands within the system" (McCamant 1984, 24). Structural-functionalist approaches, such as that of Gabriel Almond, considered "system maintenance and adaptation" to be key functions of government, but only communication and socialization processes were needed: "Not even a little arm twisting now and then would be necessary" (McCamant 1984, 24). The death toll that Rummel (1994b) documents in such developing countries as Turkey, Mexico, China, and Cambodia, makes these structural-functionalist reveries seem both negligent and incompatible with empirical realities.

The heroic assumptions of modernization theory have their intellectual basis in classical sociology. The classical sociologists believed that

> all institutions derive from the shared values of society, all are, by definition, legitimate and authoritative. . . . Thus, for Emile Durkheim, the state is "the collective type incarnate" and crimes are "acts universally disapproved of by members of each society [and which] shock sentiments found in all healthy consciences." Similarly, Tönnies defines the law as "nothing but common will" and declares that public opinion has "decided tendencies to urge the state to use its irresistible power to force everyone to do what is useful and leave undone what is damaging." The very exis-

tence of the status quo vouches for its legitimacy and reduces all differences with it to evidence of an unhealthy conscience. (Shafer 1988, 51)

Given the prevalence of this kind of thinking, most literature on internal violence focused on opposition, rioting, and rebellion—that is, deviance. Violence by states was not researched because it was viewed as unproblematic, as "what states do by right" (Gurr 1986, 45–46). Looking back on the research agenda of the 1960s, Ted Robert Gurr argues that the assumption that states were legitimate "confuses the contemporary global ideology of the state, in terms of which state managers justify their claims to authority, with the objective nature of the state." States may claim to be legitimate, in other words, but all we can objectively say about them is that they "claim to exercise sovereign (ultimate) control over the inhabitants of a territory, and . . . demonstrate enduring capacity to enforce that claim" (Gurr 1986, 45–46).

Modernization theory also neglected state violence in part because it viewed political turmoil in developing countries as a transitory problem on the way to pluralist democracy and full modernity. From this point of view, increased interaction with the modern world, particularly via international markets, would promote economic growth and modernization. Societies would move from traditional forms of authority to more rational, merit-based ones, a change that would advance both productivity and welfare. Modernization theorists recognized that problems were bound to arise along the way, since the process of economic modernization tended to mobilize populations through literacy, increased exposure to modern communications media, and migration from rural to urban areas. Rising expectations and instability produced by rapid mobilization could lead to popular demands that sometimes outstripped the coping capacities of states. Lucian Pye referred to these moments as "crises of legitimation" and "crises of development" (1971). In general, however, modernization theory assumed that states were predisposed to deal constructively with the stresses of modernization, and that they would resort to repression only when overstressed by popular demands (Huntington 1968; Packenham 1973; Pye 1971).

In one of the few empirical studies of these hypotheses regarding states' use of violence, Hibbs (1973) used events data to fit a multiequation regression model of mass political violence by both states and oppositions. Hibbs's working assumption was that "in nations where the burdens generated by social mobilization outrun the capabilities of sociopolitical institutions, political elites tend to resort to repression as an alternative means of social control" (181). The "burdens" resulting from social mobilization take the form of collective protest and internal war in varying combinations. The intensity of repression depends here upon the extent to which opposition takes the form of internal warfare; the timing of repression depends upon when mass opposition of either form appears.

Hibbs's empirical findings suggest that repression is an ineffective and sometimes counterproductive means of social control, especially when used against mass protest. "The reciprocal nature of these causal relations also demonstrates that Collective Protest and Internal War not only engender repression from elites, but that *the nearly instantaneous response to repression is most often more mass violence.* This is not at all surprising, for it is a common observation that meeting mass protest or rebellion with repression frequently only exacerbates the situation, at least in the *short run*" (182, emphasis in original). Not only does repression exacerbate both protest and armed rebellion, but the dominant causal sequence Hibbs finds "is one in which Protest is met with repression by elites, which produces in turn an escalated response of Internal War from its recipients" (182).[3] In other words, state repression turns protesters into guerrillas. Despite the short-run exacerbation of conflict, however, Hibbs concludes that repression deters internal war in the long run, probably because governments usually succeed in defeating insurgencies.

Hibbs's work is the most thorough and empirically grounded presentation of the opposition/reaction model, a model that informs many empirical or formal theoretical writings on state violence (see Duff and McCamant 1976; Jackson et al. 1978; O'Donnell 1978) and enjoys the status of conventional wisdom among scholars, international policy makers, and practitioners of counterinsurgency. For policy makers and scholars, the appeal of this kind of thinking is reinforced by its simplicity and by its similarity to "realist" theories of international relations (IR), which describe the world as an anarchic place populated by rational, sovereign states who pursue power and use force to deter potential enemies. The opposition/reaction model of state violence applies realist assumptions to the domestic setting. To the extent that states face internal threats, they depend upon force to deter their enemies. If their enemies are not deterred, states use force to conquer them. In this process, according to the realist perspective, states are acting rationally to protect themselves.

For states in the international system, there are risks associated with preparing, threatening, and using force. Preparing an excessively powerful military in an effort to deter aggression may produce the opposite effect, for instance, if other states perceive the build-up as threatening and go to war to preempt the first state from achieving superiority. A state that goes to war to protect itself may, in the process, frighten other states into forming alliances and building stronger militaries, or even going to war, to contain the new threat. The risk of creating enemies is known in realist IR theory as the "security dilemma." Steven Jackson and his colleagues (1978) see similar risks in the domestic arena, arguing that certain levels of state violence may actually trigger greater opposition rather than deterring it.

Just as realist IR theory is frequently used as the basis for policy prescriptions, particularly by political leaders, policy makers, and scholars who favor strong national defense measures, its domestic counterpart, which we can refer to as "domestic realism," is often used by leaders in militarized states and by counterinsurgency theorists as a basis for doctrine and policy for dealing with internal opposition. As with realist foreign policy, such internal doctrine emphasizes the use of force to *deter* opposition, or, if the opposition is committed to "aggression" against the state, to *destroy* it (see Lietes and Wolf 1966).

For a state to use deadly force against its own citizens raises certain normative and political problems, subjecting state elites to international criticism and even potential domestic criminal prosecution should a change of government take place. For state elites inclined to use violence, the blurring of international and domestic concepts inherent in "domestic realist" thought provides a convenient rhetorical cover. It enables them to justify their actions by redefining the domestic opposition threat as an international one, justifying the use of military force against citizens as if they were external enemies of the nation state (Ugarte 1990). This blurring of national defense and internal security concepts is evident in major writings in Latin American national security doctrine from the 1950s onward that describe internal opposition as an infection caused by foreign ideas, part of an ongoing Third World War against Communism and other threats to Western, Christian civilization (Lopez 1986). Such ideological constructs have been associated with some of the greatest atrocities committed by states against their own people.

Testing the Domestic Realist Model

Despite the dangerous normative implications of domestic realism, as an explanatory model it has intuitive appeal, plausibility, and parsimony. Whether one assumes that the state is a legitimate representative of the collective wishes of society, an instrument of the upper classes, or a semiautonomous actor defending its own interests, it seems reasonable to hypothesize that the state's use of repressive violence will be a proportionate response to the intensity of the threats it faces. When we hold domestic realism up to the light of empirical reality, however, problems quickly emerge.

Hibbs's research on the interaction of opposition and state repression, for all its methodological sophistication, is crippled by its dependence upon events count data. Events data are based on significant incidents reported in the press and therefore tend to undercount the most severe episodes and fail to reflect clandestine forms of state violence. States generally attempt to conceal mass murder by excluding and intimidating journalists, by using such mechanisms as "death squads" whose connections to the state are kept secret, or by "disappearing" people to prevent political murders from being recorded as such, at least in the short run. Even mass imprisonment and torture, as used in Uruguay from 1973 to 1980, are unlikely to be recorded in events data. Yet it is precisely such hidden measures that are likely to have the greatest terrorizing effect on a population. A study based on more valid indicators of the intensity of state violence in any given period would be unlikely to produce the finding that protest activities are unaffected by state violence, and might also reveal a more complex relationship between repression and internal war.

Unfortunately, accurate measurement of the intensity of human rights abuses in most countries has eluded the social science community so far. The clandestine nature of much state violence makes it difficult to document, as does the tendency of violent states to target human rights monitoring groups, impeding their ability to investigate abuses. Without detailed information on the acts committed by governments, most studies have depended on various ranking schemes, based on the presence or absence of certain qualitative indicators of repression or upon judgments by expert panels. Such rankings, though potentially more valid than events data, are still unlikely to account for very extreme conditions, as when an already highly repressive government begins committing genocide. The country's human rights ranking is unlikely to change, despite the fact that any informed person living there would perceive that conditions had become even more dangerous (Bollen 1986; Goldstein 1986; Stohl et al, 1986).

Rank order measurements also miss the politically significant, month-to-month interaction between repression and popular resistance familiar to anyone who has studied opposition sectors in authoritarian countries. As a result of these measurement problems, most quantitative studies on state violence (e.g., Hibbs 1973; Duff and McCamant 1976; Wolpin 1986; Banks 1986; Mitchell and McCormick 1988) do not recognize, much less explain, the extreme severity of the repression in Argentina in 1976–79, Chile in 1973–74, El Salvador in 1979–83, or Guatemala in 1978–85. Though more information is now becoming available regarding human rights abuses, through both strengthened international monitoring (Martin and Sikkink 1993; Sikkink 1993) and retrospective research by human rights organizations and post-transition truth-telling commissions, we are still a long way from having valid, reliable, cross-nationally comparable data on domestic state violence.

There is, however, sufficient evidence from individual cases to raise serious questions about the validity of the domestic realism view. State violence does not always coincide with opposition activities, nor do states that face comparable threats necessarily use comparable kinds or levels of violence in response. In El Salvador, as we will see in coming chapters, the state's use of violence was grossly disproportionate to the threat from the opposition at several points, beginning with the 1932 massacre of roughly 25,000 peasants and workers in response to an uprising that killed at most 95 people. Moreover, the timing and intensity of violence often bore no apparent relation to opposition activities. In Guatemala, the state killed about 10,000 people in the 1960s in an effort to suppress a band of 500 guerrillas. In the early 1970s, when the armed left operated mainly in Guatemala City and to little effect, state forces disappeared some 15,000 people (Simon 1987, 25). This violence helped consolidate the mass opposition that exploded into civil war in the late 1970s and early 1980s.

In Argentina, Brazil, and Uruguay, state violence sometimes flared up *after* the successful suppression of armed or mass opposition. Argentina's violence worsened during 1976 and 1977 and remained high during 1978, even though the guerrillas were virtually eliminated by the end of 1975 (Pion-Berlin 1989, 4–5). As it proceeded, violence came to be directed against a broad cross-section of society, far beyond the domain of active opponents of the regime. In Brazil, state violence, particularly torture, escalated following the military's declaration of the Fifth Institutional Act in 1968. The act was promulgated in a context of expanding popular mobilization, but the repression associated with the act catalyzed the development of a small guerrilla movement. That movement (with no more than 6,000 members in a country of 100 million) served as the pretext for a massive increase in the centralized power of the military (Moreira Alves 1985, 119). The rebels were quickly suppressed, yet state violence rose again in 1973–74 in the absence of a fresh opposition threat (Stepan 1988, 40–41). Similarly, the government of Uruguay quickly eradicated the Tupamaros and then went on to arrest, and in many cases torture, one citizen out of every fifty, even after roughly 10 percent of the population—many of whom presumably considered themselves at risk—had fled (Weschler 1990, 87–147). As Alain Rouquié puts it, the government's repressive machine became "an end in itself" (1987, 255–56).

In Colombia, a dramatic increase in state violence against civilians after 1984 coincided with the arrangement of a cease-fire between the government and guerrilla groups—an outcome that does not make much sense within an opposition/reaction framework. The Revolutionary Armed Forces of Colombia (FARC) had been active for over twenty years, augmented since the late 1960s and early 1970s by several other guerrilla groups. Disappearances and assassinations attributable to the military have not been unknown in Colombia, but they increased dramatically in 1984 after the government of Belisario Betancur arranged a cease-fire and allowed representatives of the guerrilla groups to participate openly in elections. Persons associated with the left-wing political coalition Patriotic Union (UP) were particularly targeted, along with human rights advocates and liberal professionals (Amnesty International, 1988).

Other states have responded very differently to equivalent military threats. After a brief insurgency in the 1960s, the Peruvian military carried out major reforms in an effort to placate and politically incorporate potential dissidents. The Venezuelan military used violence in a few zones and tortured suspected guerrillas in the 1960s but emphasized state service delivery in rebellious areas and political concessions designed to undercut the appeal of the insurgency (Blaufarb and Tanham 1984, app. H; Wickham-Crowley 1990, 204–7). In Central America the Honduran state responded to massive rural strikes in the 1950s with concessions and to later movements in the 1970s with a major land reform.

These contrasting examples suggest that some states are particularly prone to using force, even in the absence of credible internal threats. In some cases, state force provokes more violent opposition. Timothy Wickham-Crowley, for instance, notes that the Peruvian government's 1965 terror in Ayacucho produced what one observer called an "unbridgeable abyss" between peasants and the government, contributing to the subsequent formation of a particularly brutal guerrilla movement (1990, 235). In others, the repression has been effective but has eventually caused other problems for the militaries that perpetrated it, such as a risk of legal prosecution following the return of elected civilian rule. Moreover, even highly effective repression—such as that in Guatemala in the 1980s—does not necessarily deliver lasting stability: organized mass opposition in Guatemala has survived thirty years of state terror. On the whole, much of the internal violence by states in Latin America has been unnecessary, counterproductive, and grossly out of proportion to the actual challenge to the state's authority.

Repression as Class Oppression

An alternative tradition, which could be loosely labeled Marxist or dependency theory, sees internal repression as a by-product of underlying economic processes at work within societies positioned in the periphery of a capitalist world system. In contrast to modernization theories, which view interaction with international markets as positive, Marxist and dependency theorists generally argue that the mercantile relations between colonies and metropolitan powers and the subsequent integration of ex-colonies into the world capitalist market tend to produce economies, social structures, and political systems prone to stagnation, instability, authoritarianism, and repression (Carleton 1989; Carnoy 1984, 173–207; Jackson et al. 1978; O'Donnell 1978, 1979; Sheahan 1980; Weeks 1986).

In this view, economies on the periphery of the world capitalist system are generally consigned to producing commodities that are no longer profitable in core countries because of their resource requirements or labor-intensive nature. Several negative consequences flow from this kind of development on the periphery. First, countries tend to remain in extractive industries and commodity agriculture, where international competitiveness is highly dependent on maintaining low costs. When commodity-producing economies grow, they often do so by expanding the amount of land devoted to export production, or mechanizing existing production processes. Both have the effect of reducing opportunities for the popular classes to make a living. Peripheral economies tend to specialize in the one or two commodities that they can produce with competitive quality and at a competitive price; they lack the complex and diversified economies of core countries. While this may allow rapid aggregate economic growth and capital accumulation during good years, peripheral economies are highly vulnerable to price fluctuations (Carnoy 1984, 184–207).

In the long run, the growth of peripheral economies depends upon increased exports rather than domestic demand. Under these circumstances, economic elites have incentives to suppress wages and neglect social policies that might increase the buying power of domestic workers. The net effect is to create highly stratified societies in which the elites have vested interests in keeping the society stratified, while the subordinate classes find themselves highly vulnerable to unemployment resulting either from unstable international prices or from modernization and mechanization. Thus repression often becomes a structural requirement of continued accumulation in peripheral exporting economies.

Even when peripheral countries pursue industrialization rather than primary commodity production, development is likely to be accompanied by repression. Latin American countries attempted import substitution industrialization during the mid-twentieth century, developing national industries that produced for the domestic market behind protective tariff barriers. This form of industrialization initially created conditions for improved income distribution and a populist political alliance between workers and industrial capitalists, who shared an interest in improved purchasing power within the domestic market. Although the resulting regimes were not necessarily democratic, they tended to coopt the popular classes rather than repressing them. In most cases, however, such domestic industrialization formulas eventually stagnated, leading to the installation of more repressive regimes, which imposed austerity measures in an effort to attract additional foreign capital and "deepen" industrialization (O'Donnell 1978; Remmer and Merkx, 1983).

Just as modernization theory assumes that the state is a legitimate representation of the wishes of a society, dependency theories assume that the dependent state represents the interests of capitalist classes, both at home and abroad. As already noted, national social elites often develop vested interests in economic systems that can only be sustained through repression of labor. Andre Gunder Frank and Samir Amin add that demands from foreign capital for low wages and increased resource extraction also contribute to militarism and repression. As a result of these elite demands over the decades, both colonial and postcolonial states created coercive institutions, often aided by international assistance, which were exaggerated relative to other components of otherwise weak states (Carnoy 1984, 184–92).

While these societies develop strong states, their local elites find it difficult to establish ideological hegemony in the Gramscian sense. They tend to have little credibility as national leaders because they are known to be subservient to international capital (Carnoy 1984, 188–92). Moreover, as Alfred Stepan (1978) puts it, "The high degree of foreign ownership of industry reduces the relative size and power of the national bourgeoisie, while the national bourgeoisie itself often has a variety of credit, ownership, technological, and marketing dependency relationships with international capital. This, plus their frequent status as relatively recent immigrants, puts members of the national bourgeoisie in a weak political position to compete—in a nationalist environment—as an electoral force aiming at hegemonic acceptance for their position" (23).

Because dependent social elites find it difficult to persuade subordinate classes to accept the existing order, they tend to face mass opposition. Antonio Gramsci and Louis Althusser argue that forms of domination range from coercion to softer styles based on ideological persuasion. When the capitalist classes cannot win the consent of the subordinate classes through ideological influence, the elite will turn to the coercive capacity of states to preserve the existing mode of production (Carnoy 1984, 76–80, 110). In some particularly inequitable societies, popular opposition and state coercion become the norm, and the dominant social classes rely entirely on the coercive state apparatus, rather than attempting any degree of ideological persuasion, to promote their interests (Midlarsky and Roberts 1985).

Guillermo O'Donnell (1978) argues that the state's conduct during such moments of upper-class weakness will depend upon how serious a threat popular opposition poses. Where popular movements are strong and adopt a radical posture that threatens the capitalist order, states will impose extremely repressive regimes. O'Donnell posits that the more intense the threat, the longer it will take before the state permits a political opening. This may strike the reader as remarkably similar to the domestic realist hypothesis that state violence is a response to opposition. It is, in fact, the same argument as that of Hibbs, and remarkably similar to the "crisis of legitimacy" argument put forward by Pye (1971). Like the modernization school, it sees the state as reactive and defensive.

We can summarize the relationship between these two schools of thought by saying that the modernization and dependency schools disagree in their predictions regarding the structural relationship between development and repression, but agree regarding how states will behave during crises. Modernization writings view international market-driven modernization and development as positive forces that will eventually produce more rational, efficient, and harmonious societies. Along the way, however, the stresses associated with modernization will generate crises and popular opposition. During such crises, states will respond much as states in the international system respond to external threats, through rational, measured uses of force sufficient to defend the legitimate order. The dependency perspective differs in arguing that dependent economic modernization makes repression more, rather than less, likely. The conjunctural predictions of dependency, however, are essentially the same as those of domestic realism: dependent societies will undergo crises of hegemony during which the upper classes will depend upon the state to maintain order. The state does so primarily through repression, calibrated according to the intensity of the opposition threat. Both perspectives treat the state as essentially a unitary rational actor, defending either the "legitimate" order (in the case of modernization theory) or an upper-class project (in the case of dependency).[4] The next section will test these structural hypotheses in the context of Central America.

Economic Development and Repression in Central America

The structural relationship between economic development and repression in Central American countries proves to be more complex than suggested by either the modernization or the dependency perspective. Comparative evidence suggests that economic development based on export-oriented agriculture did not, by itself, generate repression, nor did it consistently produce harmonious modernization. The degree of repressiveness seems to be mainly a function of *how* export agriculture systems were established in the first place. Systems that were *founded* through coercive means tended to reinforce themselves, requiring escalating degrees of repression for their maintenance.

Agrarian capitalists in two countries in the region, Guatemala and El Salvador, have practiced what Barrington Moore (1968) calls "labor-repressive agriculture," meaning that they have depended upon coercive means, rather than market mechanisms, to guarantee the availability of labor. Such means include slavery, compulsory wage labor (vagrancy laws), or debt peonage. In both countries oligarchies derived their wealth from labor-repressive export agriculture and entered into alliances with national militaries to maintain highly exclusionary, labor-repressive, and antireformist governments that episodically murdered, tortured, and imprisoned many of their own citizens. Enrique Baloyra (1983) aptly labels this type of regime "reactionary despotism."[5] Though these "reactionary despotisms" have not been the only states in the region to use repression, they have done so with greater intensity and persistence than other authoritarian regimes. Political regimes in Honduras have generally been authoritarian in nature, but far less violent than El Salvador and Guatemala. Even the Somoza dynasty in Nicaragua never killed its citizens with the consistency and intensity of the Guatemalan and El Salvadoran militaries (Brockett 1991, 66).

The least repressive country in the region has been Costa Rica, which, though highly integrated with the world economy as an agricultural commodity exporter, has treated its popular classes with considerable toleration and flexibility. Costa Rican agrarian elites have depended predominantly on market mechanisms to attract agricultural labor, with the result that even landless laborers have enjoyed an adequate standard of living by regional standards. Moreover, the Costa Rican state, with the consent of its social elites, has provided a wide range of social welfare programs that have redistributed wealth and provided even the poor with education and health services unmatched in the region.

One obvious difference among these states lies in what they produce: El Salvador, Guatemala, and Costa Rica were major coffee producers since the nineteenth century, while Honduras and Nicaragua produced less labor-intensive crops. Were it not for the presence of Costa Rica among the coffee producers, one might conclude that coffee was the economic foundation of repression. Rueschemeyer, Stephens, and Stephens (1992, 163–65) have argued that in Latin America as a whole, coercion is more common in states in which labor-intensive agriculture makes up a predominant proportion of the economy, for the simple reason that plantation owners who require more labor are more vulnerable to wage demands and more likely to resort to repression to minimize their costs. Coffee is an intrinsically labor-intensive product, so the tendency toward repression in El Salvador and Guatemala fits the prediction, but the Costa Rica exception suggests that labor intensivity, in and of itself, is not a sufficient condition for labor-repressive practices to take hold.

To understand the linkage between systems of export agriculture and the repressive tendencies of some Central American states, as well as the contrasting consequences of commercial agricultural development in different cases, we must examine the mediating impact of class formation, geography, and the coercive role of states. Many scholars (e.g., Baloyra 1983; Brockett 1991; Weeks 1986; Williams 1994) argue that the manner in which export agriculture, particularly coffee, was initially established had a significant impact. Where coffee production began through forced expropriation of communal lands (as in El Salvador and Guatemala), labor repressiveness endured as a practice; where it began on small farms (as in Costa Rica), labor relations remained more harmonious well into the late twentieth century (Williams 1994).

The Costa Rican coffee industry began early, in the 1830s, using labor obtained through market mechanisms. Because of the country's low population density and the fact that almost all rural dwellers had their own lands in the early to mid-nineteenth century, wages had to be high to give peasants an incentive to work as wage laborers in addition to tending to their own farms. Within a few decades, international market price fluctuations and economies of scale generated a process of land consolidation. With land concentration, population growth, and the closing of the agricultural frontier, a landless proletariat began to form between the 1890s and 1930 (Brockett 1990, 73–74; Seligson 1980, 23; Weeks 1986, 40–41). Nonetheless, individual small farmers continued to make up a large proportion of the Costa Rican peasantry, and produced a significant percentage of the nation's coffee exports. According to Héctor Pérez-Brignoli, "Those who were initially the most successful in the coffee business formed a powerful ruling class whose wealth was based on a monopoly of coffee processing and the management of financial resources (credit, production financing, export). Even though these businessmen generally were also the largest landowners, their role in coffee production was secondary" (1989, 100–101). As a result, Costa Rica's coffee oligarchy could afford to forgo the use of repression to suppress wages. Since much of coffee production was in the hands of smaller producers, the elite became more accustomed to collaboration and compromise with subordinate classes and permitted the development of a more broadly based political system that became increasingly democratic during the twentieth century (Williams 1994).

In Guatemala and El Salvador in the mid-nineteenth century, most lands suitable for coffee cultivation were in the hands of indigenous communities (in El Salvador), the Church, or small-scale farmers (in Guatemala).[6] Liberals who hoped to promote new export products for the world market viewed noncommercial ownership of these lands as an obstacle to national development. Liberal governments therefore outlawed communal lands, expropriated Church lands, and abolished Guatemala's emphyteutic census, which had conferred perpetual renters' rights on tenants. The effect was to place potential coffee-growing lands under the control of entrepreneurs who could then develop coffee plantations. This process, which was sometimes enforced by troops, tended to produce larger holdings than were initially found in Costa Rica, as well as severe social dislocations as thousands of rural people were made landless (Browning 1971). The Guatemalan and Salvadoran states went on to pass agrarian laws prohibiting labor organizing in rural areas, supplemented by vagrancy laws that forced peasants to work a certain number of days on commercial plantations each year and inhibited them from finding other means of subsistence, such as squatting on unused lands, hunting, fishing, or gathering wild foods. Indigenous communities in Guatemala lost the legal protections they had enjoyed under past Conservative regimes and became increasingly subject to the coercive measures of both local and national officials.

Social class and political development in El Salvador and Guatemala was largely consistent with the sequence that Moore (1968) considered the road to fascism. Moore argued in general terms that countries with economic systems dominated by labor-repressive agriculture will end up with fascist governments if the urban bourgeoisie (that is, commercial, industrial, and financial capital based in towns and cities) subordinates itself, by choice or because of lack of independent strength, to reactionary agrarian elites. In El Salvador and Guatemala, economic development during the twentieth century produced a stronger, more diverse agrarian elite, along with a commercial and industrial bourgeoisie that was subordinate to the agrarian oligarchy. The expansion of cotton, sugar, and cattle production merely increased the breadth of agrarian interests opposed to land reform. Since landed interests dominated the financial system for the most part, little capital was available for industrial ventures. Even the efforts at import substitution industrialization under the Central American Common Market (CACM) were subordinated to the interests of export agriculture, as all the CACM members sustained the convertibility of their currencies (Weeks 1986, 44). As a result, economic modernization failed to create a combination of bourgeois elements and middle classes strong and independent enough to form an effective political coalition in favor of democracy and political incorporation of the popular classes against the resistance of the agrarian elite.

In the 1930s, low wages and unemployment resulting from the collapse in world coffee prices intensified conflicts between landowners and landless peasants. In this context, military regimes took power in both El Salvador and Guatemala and instituted increasingly severe repression, including the massacre of 1932 in El Salvador. Economies began to recover in the 1940s, bringing successive waves of agricultural development, including expanded coffee production as well as new products such as bananas, cotton, sugar, and beef. Each wave of expansion merely reduced the amount of land available to peasants for subsistence crop production, increasing landlessness and unemployment, driving down wages, and making rural populations more vulnerable to hunger (Brockett 1990). Thus, as agricultural elites expanded their operations and moved into new products, they simultaneously created for themselves an increasingly bitter class enemy whose potential for rebellion they feared. These pressures were greatest in El Salvador because it had the most severe land pressures, but were felt throughout the region—except in Costa Rica, where an expanding state sector, increasing social welfare programs, and higher wages ameliorated social grievances.

This evidence from Central America suggests a reflexive or dialectical relationship between the state and social classes. The state was instrumental in the development of the economic base for social elites in those countries in which repression was required for the establishment of the coffee economy. Once in place, these elites were able to maintain significant influence over the policies followed by the state, helping lock in conservative policies and related repression. Notwithstanding the understandable view of some analysts (e.g., Midlarsky and Roberts 1985) that agrarian oligarchies subsequently instrumentalized the state in Guatemala and El Salvador during the mid- to late twentieth century, we must acknowledge that states played a prominent role in the creation of these elite groups in the first place. Without the legislative and coercive powers of the state, the coffee economy might never have been founded in El Salvador and Guatemala, and without coffee there would have been a different and economically much weaker social elite. Throughout Central America, the upper classes were a heterogeneous and disunited group well into the twentieth century. Even in those states where liberals developed clear hegemony (El Salvador and Costa Rica, later Guatemala), the liberal "elite" was a hodgepodge of "landowners, merchants, middle-class urban dwellers, not to mention the many newcomers and quite a few newly converted Conservatives" (Pérez-Brignoli 1989, 94). These diverse individuals were able to enrich themselves in the coffee industry primarily because the Liberal reforms carried out by states helped "free up resources to develop the agricultural export economy and greatly broaden the economic basis of the new coffee producers. It might almost be said that the Liberal state 'created' its own ruling class" (Pérez-Brignoli 1989, 94).

Despite the considerable wealth that coffee elites amassed, the formation of anything resembling a dominant *political* class was gradual. Initially, "liberalism" was advanced by authoritarian rulers (even in Costa Rica) whose authority was often based upon command positions in the military. Military leaders were particularly important in the four northern countries in Central America, which had been embroiled for the first half of the nineteenth century in civil and regional warfare between Liberals and Conservatives, federationists and separatists. Thus, aspiring political elites in these countries established patterns of organizing armies for political purposes. Even as the states began to achieve monopolies over armed force within their territories, individuals with political ambitions needed to have military leadership skills to supplement their talents for electoral fraud, and changes of leadership often involved coups by military officers. Except in Costa Rica, the Liberal reforms required substantial force to implement land privatization and coercive labor measures. Both the Guatemalan and Salvadoran states established special rural security forces in the early part of the twentieth century to carry out these tasks.

Only in Costa Rica did the social elite convert itself into a political class capable of governing the country without dependence on military force delivered by the state. Though a series of elections were held in El Salvador, and the Meléndez-Quiñónez family managed to get its patriarchs elected president between 1913 and 1927, nothing resembling a coherent political class had yet developed. The fragility of "oligarchic" rule was made clear during the crisis of the world depression, when military strongmen took power in every country except Costa Rica, and the military played a predominant role in El Salvador, Guatemala, and Nicaragua. Aside from Guatemala's ten-year "revolution" from 1944 to 1954, militaries governed in all three countries, and intermittently in Honduras, for the next fifty years. Even the Guatemalan revolution was in large part facilitated by reformist leaders within the military, who permitted civilian elections to be held in the first place, prevented reactionary military coups against Juan José Arévalo, and provided the authority behind the sweeping land reforms of Jacobo Arbenz Gusmán in the 1950s. Arbenz, though elected, owed much of his political power to his stature within the military (Gleijeses 1991).

Patterns of development and state repression in Central America demonstrate no fixed relationship between the two. Growth led by agricultural exports has not consistently led either to repression or to balanced modernization and democracy. Nor have states consistently proven to be instruments of dominant class interests. In some cases, dominant social classes were largely created by the initiatives of states. Thus we need to view states as at least potentially autonomous actors in their decisions regarding repression.

Explaining State Choices

Clearly we need some more complete explanation of state behavior. We have seen that state violence is not necessarily a rational response to opposition or attributable strictly to the interests of dominant classes. During periods when Central American social elites were not politically cohesive, states exercised considerable autonomy in both their use of violence and their economic policies. This is consistent with a considerable body of Marxist writings on the state. In *The Eighteenth Brumaire of Louis Bonaparte*, Marx describes a situation in which no single, coherent political class is capable of dominating society, with the result that the state—in the form of the dictatorship of Louis Bonaparte—enjoyed greater power and considerable autonomy (Carnoy 1984, 52–54). Engels, too, sees the state as having greater independent power during "atypical," "non-hegemonic" periods in which there was no clear dominant class (Stepan 1978, 22–23).

Where state elites are highly organized and ideologically unified, and where civilian political parties are weak, state elites may be able to install relatively autonomous regimes. State leaders may be military officers or civilians, as in the case of corporatist regimes in Brazil and Mexico in the 1930s (Stepan 1978, 83–85). In either case, the question is whether the new regime, once installed, will establish a highly repressive or a more reformist style of governance.

In his discussion of corporatist regimes, Stepan differentiates between inclusionary and exclusionary strategies.[7] Inclusionary regimes attempt to preempt future conflict by constructing new class coalitions, organized by the state, to provide sufficient political support for the state to carry out socioeconomic reforms that run contrary to the interests of at least some social elites. In the process, states channel popular participation through labor unions, cooperatives, neighborhood associations, and other sectoral groups that are chartered and initially controlled by the state. Citizens voluntarily give up the freedom to associate outside official channels in exchange for anticipated material gains, though these may not materialize. In contrast, exclusionary regimes seek to demobilize broad sectors of civil society through repression, and tend to depend upon political support from upper- and middle-class groups.

According to Stepan, inclusionary formulas are more likely where political mobilization is relatively low and not highly polarized; where elaborate social welfare mechanisms are not already in place, so that the new regime can gain considerable legitimacy by implementing such reforms, and where the economic and symbolic resources of the regime exceed the demands it faces from mobilized popular sectors. Exclusionary regimes are more likely to appear when mass political mobilization and polarization have taken place, where popular demands exceed the regime's economic and symbolic resources, and where the regime has sufficient organized coercive capacity to suppress and demobilize popular opposition (Stepan 1978, 83–89).

As we have already seen, exclusionary regimes often use violence in counterproductive, provocative ways. Thus we need to explain not only the choice between inclusionary or exclusionary policies, but the degree to which policies are implemented in ways that are consistent with the purported goals of state leaders. Scholars encounter the same problem in explaining the sometimes irrational decisions of states to go to war or to avoid it: Some states miscalculate, others are irrationally bellicose, and still others are inconsistent and erratic. Some of the theoretical strategies of the field of international relations can be useful here. To account for nonrational conduct by states, we have to make modifications to the realist framework. One of the first steps is to recognize that policies can only be rational if policy makers have access to adequate information.[8] Moreover, to act rationally, state policy makers must accurately perceive international conditions. Factors such as cultural and educational biases and leaders' personal eccentricities can distort perceptions and lead to outcomes other than what realist theory would predict (Jervis 1976). Another modification we need to make is to recognize that "state" decisions are often the result of the interplay of competing bureaucracies, producing outcomes that reflect the relative political clout of different state agencies, not a rational policy-making process. The effects of bureaucratic decision-making processes can be compounded by the fact that the agencies that implement foreign policy often have standard operating procedures that diverge from the intent of central state authorities (Allison 1971).

To explain the foreign policies of democracies, we must take into account the fact that decisions are constrained by public opinion: state leaders cannot afford to pursue wars that their populations oppose. Citizens in democracies are rarely if ever willing to endorse war against fellow democracies, thus contributing to the scarcity of wars between democratic states (Doyle 1983; Kant 1983, 107–143). A new current in the literature of international relations suggests that domestic political constraints also shape state's international negotiating strategies, making pure realist assumptions inappropriate (Moravcsik 1993). Paul Joseph (1987) adopts a more class-based view of how domestic politics influences foreign policy. He makes a distinction between social elites (the capitalist class) who own and manage productive firms, and state elites (state managers) who are professional politicians, bureaucrats, or technocrats, both civilian and military, who actually make and implement state policy. Joseph argues that policy is shaped by competing currents of opinion among capitalist elites, which in turn interact with different "policy currents" among state managers within the foreign policy apparatus.

All of these qualifications can be adapted to explaining cases of internal state violence that do not fit the predictions of the opposition/reaction model. State elites' perceptions may be distorted as a result of ideology, training, education (or lack thereof), or poor access to information. For instance, state elites will find internal political opposition more threatening if they are unable to understand its basis and goals. Overreaction is particularly likely to occur in countries where state elites are highly dependent upon civilian social elites for ideological and political guidance. State elites who are strongly influenced by social elites are more likely to interpret social opposition to the status quo as threatening than state elites who have more independent means of forming their own political agenda (Stepan 1978). Input from social elites is more likely to favor repression in highly stratified societies, where elites see issues such as land distribution as zero-sum confrontations with the poor and pass these concerns on to the state. The propensity for repression in stratified societies is reinforced by the greater social distance between elites and masses, which leads state elites (acting on behalf of social elites) to feel fewer compunctions about killing people who protest or rebel. Social distance compounds state elites' lack of access to information regarding subordinate groups, contributing to misperceptions of opposition goals. The effect of social distance is greater if elites and the poor belong to different ethnic groups, as is the case in countries like Guatemala (Brockett 1991; Gurr 1986).

Gurr (1986) suggests other variables that may affect the likelihood that the states will use violence. One is past experience: repression is more likely in countries where it has been used previously with success. As Charles Brockett puts it, social elites who obtained and have maintained their economic privileges by using violence, and for whom the use of coercion is "reinforced by their subculture, would be more likely to believe violence an acceptable and effective response to any perceived threats in the present" (1991, 69). States that are heavily influenced by such elites are more likely to attempt repression, even in circumstances when it will probably not be effective.

Gurr (1986) and Brockett (1991) have observed that countries with larger internal security forces tend to use repression more frequently. In part, this is simply a matter of capabilities: states with strong repressive forces are better able to coerce their populations. It may also be a matter of resources: where state spending on repressive forces is greater than spending on public service functions, the state may lack resources to respond in any way other than repression. Not surprisingly, proportionately large security forces tend to be found in highly stratified societies in which social elites hold to rigid antireformist views. However, political pressures from social elites can be augmented by bureaucratic pressures from within the state. National guards, domestic intelligence services, "internal defense"–oriented armies, and secret police services, like any permanent bureaucracy, will tend to defend their budgets and institutional prerogatives. The stronger such forces are and the greater their prerogatives, the greater bureaucratic and political weight they will have within the state, and the more effectively they will be able to defend their interests.

Clearly, it is difficult to disentangle how these different factors contribute to state violence. Social elites tend to have more pro-repressive views in highly stratified societies. Such societies tend to have states that are heavily influenced by the views and political guidance of social elites, and also tend to have larger, more elaborate internal security forces. Within states, those agencies most involved in repression naturally develop vested interests in maintaining repressive policies. Where such forces are stronger, they will often have greater influence over state policy. Evidence from the case of El Salvador will demonstrate that internal security agencies can independently use their repressive capacity to influence policy. Moreover, there is obvious potential for a synergy to develop between reactionary social elites and repressive state agencies in favor of repressive policies.

All of these observations raise the question of how a country in which all of these factors are present can possibly move away from repressive policies, as El Salvador appears to have done with its peace process. Chapters Two through Six offer an analysis of how social elites and repressive military bureaucracies and factions manipulated each other to maintain a policy of repression and to suppress reformist, antirepression initiatives coming from civil society and from within the state. Chapter Seven explains how this synergy in favor of repression finally broke down as a result of popular resistance and international intervention.

Ideology and Perceptions

In domestic policy, just as in international relations, ideology can have a powerful influence on how state elites perceive their surroundings. In an authoritarian setting, the ideological outlook of a relatively small "strategic elite" can have an enormous impact on policy. Authoritarian regimes concentrate power in the hands of a few individuals who can choose and implement policies without being effectively challenged, at least in the short run. Strategic elites' views are influenced by their functional role within the state. A central bank manager will tend to develop a set of views distinct from those of the head of a social service agency, and both will differ from the views of an intelligence officer. Officials in different specializations have separate constituencies as well as social circles. They also function within different institutions. Military officers are accustomed to a rigidly hierarchical and secretive setting, while civilians are often acculturated to more open and flexible ones. These contrasting experiences can shape how state elites prefer to structure political life.

Education is likely to have a significant impact as well. State elites educated primarily at military academies will reflect the ideological perspective of those institutions. In Peru, for instance, Stepan (1978) found that the Center for Higher Military Studies (CAEM) had helped shape and disseminate within the officer corps a national security doctrine that called for a reformist, inclusionary corporatist strategy. This doctrine, and its broad acceptance, were crucial conditions for the military's installation of an inclusionary corporatist regime in 1968.

Unfortunately, the intellectual and educational work of other military academic institutions in the hemisphere has been more conducive to state violence. George Lopez (1986) examines the thinking embodied in the doctrinal statements of South American militaries and argues that versions of what he calls "National Security Ideology" (NSI) provide a framework for thinking about the state, national interest, the nature of security, and the obligations of state actors that justifies extremely broad and persistent use of state terrorism. NSI "reifies" the nation state as the unit of human society that must be preserved, strengthened, and built upon. The nation is seen as an organism whose individual parts are of subsidiary moral consequence. Aspects of individual security, such as freedom from arbitrary arrest, torture, or murder at the hands of the state, are simply unimportant in relation to the security of the state as a whole. The institutions of the state itself, and the military in particular, are of paramount importance because they are the actors of last resort for the preservation of the nation.

Lopez argues that a key component of NSI is its resurrection of geo-strategic thinking, which he links to the overwhelming concern of national security states with internal security. Under NSI, internal stability and the organic health of the nation are seen as vital to the nation's strength and its ability to compete and survive internationally. Under such an organic conception, security threats stem not so much from violent rebellion as from ideas and internal social forces. Any ideas or social movements that are not conducive to national economic development become threats to the state: "Under these circumstances, social science professors, union leaders, bank vice-presidents, and clergy who object to the economic policy of the state are viewed without much differentiation and are considered targets for suppression, if not outright elimination" (Lopez 1986, 86). With such a broad definition of the threats to security, an extremely severe and prolonged campaign of repressive violence appears to be necessary. It also becomes very difficult to define at what point victory over the "enemies" of the state has been achieved, with the result that state terror campaigns have been open-ended. Lopez' argument thus proves helpful in explaining not only the intensity of violence but also the breadth of sectors targeted by the state and the prolongation of violence even after the disappearance of armed opposition and significant popular mobilization.

Lopez is cautious about the claims he makes for ideology as an explanatory variable. He does not say to what extent NSI is an exogenous variable or merely an elaborate justification for actions that militaries want or need to take to promote their institutional interests. The reification of the state and its leaders under NSI would seem to suggest that this ideology is self-serving, yet there is a compellingly close fit between the actions that NSI logically requires and the actual conduct of several of the militaries that subscribe to NSI, suggesting that NSI either influenced or at least facilitated state violence.

Monetarism too has been linked to the propensity for state terrorism in Latin America. David Pion-Berlin (1989) focuses on this particular form of economic orthodoxy as an explanation for episodes of repression in Argentina and Peru after 1975 and shows that state repression and terrorism are associated, over time, with the ascendance of monetarist ideas. His explanation is that the content of monetarist thought made violence seem necessary to state officials. Monetary stability required an end to fiscal deficits (which were generally financed through expansion of the money supply). Balanced public sector budgets could only be achieved if the state could resist popular demands for state services and higher wages in the public sector. Thus, according to this logic, repression was required to eliminate one of the main causes of monetary expansion and (presumably) inflation. The rigidity of monetarist state elites was reinforced by their isolation from the political consequences of their views. Ensconced in central banks, they judged policies by technical criteria and depended upon international financial elites as their primary social and professional reference point.

Leninism, Stalinism, Maoism, the antiurban revolutionary purism of the Khmer Rouge, nineteenth-century Central American liberalism, and the "repastoralization" of Argentina in the 1970s have all provided ideological bases for massive acts of state violence (Buchanan 1989; McClintock 1985a, 1985b; O'Donnell 1978; Rummel 1994b). These episodes, plus the examples of monetarism and Latin American national security doctrines, suggest that certain ideas and projects can provide powerful rationales for prolonged, intense use of state terrorism, beyond what would be needed for the short-term suppression of opposition. Taking ideology into account helps us to understand cases in which state elites chose to use extreme repression under conditions in which the intensity of popular opposition did not seem to justify it. It also helps us comprehend the frequent occurrence of state violence that targets large numbers of politically inactive civilians and continues well past the point at which significant opposition, protest, and violence have been quelled.

If we agree that ideas and socioeconomic projects are important, we face the question of why a given military institution adopts a particular project or set of ideas. While the sort of NSI Lopez describes does in fact appear to have provided part of the rationale for mass state violence in several South American countries, the fact remains that militaries in these and other countries have over the decades chosen more reformist and populist paths. Even within those militaries that have most forcefully adopted and acted upon NSI, competing factions with very different preferences regarding types of political regimes or socioeconomic orders have operated.

One way to approach this problem is to assume that the adoption of a given ideology or project is the outcome of a process of political competition within a given military institution in which ideas, and leaders upholding particular ideas, compete for support among the officer corps. Just as the electoral success of political parties depends upon their ability to choose a platform that has broad appeal and minimizes defection from the party, the intra-institutional success of a given leadership group depends in part on its ability to choose political and economic ideas for which broad support can be built within the institution. A faction's ideas may assist it in gaining power, or a group may be able to take power for reasons that have little to do with its ideological predispositions.[9] Even in the latter case, the ideas adopted by a leadership group, whether before or after taking power, may affect their ability to maintain it.

This argument presumes that even within a formalized, hierarchical organization such as the military, advancement to the highest levels depends upon building "political" support among peers and subordinates. In more strongly institutionalized militaries, only the upper levels of the officer corps are crucial. In less institutionalized militaries, such as those of Mexico or the Southern cone up through the early twentieth century, or those of Central American countries more recently, the support of junior officers is necessary for a given leadership group to gain and retain control of the military.

As circumstances change, perceptions within a military institution regarding which ideas best support its interests may also shift dramatically. For example, an economically orthodox, politically repressive project may appear to maximize the interests of the military at one point by simultaneously dealing with perceived threats to the institution, increasing its organizational purview, and securing strong civilian support. The formula of repression and orthodox economic thinking espoused by the anti-Peronist faction around General Jorge Rafael Videla in 1976 was a potent combination in these terms. In a number of Latin American cases, such views have subsequently lost ground to alternative, liberalizing tendencies that promise to extricate the militaries from unsuccessful experiments in government. Reformist ideas can gain strong support within the military when the rigidities of the existing economic structures appear to be causing mass social upheaval, or when draconian methods of exclusion have become counterproductive. This type of scenario led to the development of reform movements within the Peruvian military in the late 1960s, the Honduran military in the 1970s, and the Salvadoran military during the late 1970s. Such reformist ideas, however, can (and did, in all of these cases) lose support if implementation proves more complicated or less immediately efficacious than expected.

The prospects for reformist and inclusionary approaches are reduced by the internal dynamics of states facing social and political unrest. National crises have both centrifugal and centripetal effects on strategic state elites. On one hand, a crisis may crystallize radically contrasting prescriptions for response; on the other hand, if the survival of the state as a whole is perceived to be threatened, many officials will want to present a united front. In the case of military regimes, internal polarization and the perception of threat can be heightened if (1) existing groups within the military seek out civilian allies, as happened in El Salvador during 1932 and 1979 (Anderson 1971, 95–97; McClintock 1985a, 107–111), or if (2) the civilian groups conspicuously court military factions, as happened in Chile in 1973 (Rouquié 1987, 238–248) and in Argentina in 1976 (274–76).

Under such circumstances, the simplicity and immediate practicality of policy prescriptions, and the extent to which they secure powerful allies for the military, are likely to be decisive. A military institution that is divided between reformist and conservative programs may quickly unify around conservative views if these appear to be the most reliable way of protecting itself.

Intra-State Politics and Extortion of Civilian Elites

The simplicity of hardline ideas may not be the only reason state elites tend to coalesce around violent, exclusionary policies. Stepan observes that corporatist regimes suffer from a "birth defect" that makes them tend toward greater repression: the fact that corporatist regimes are usually installed during crises and often use a degree of violence at the outset makes it difficult for them ever to achieve ideological hegemony in the Gramscian sense. Instead, they are likely to face ongoing opposition, even if only of a very passive, terrorized form, making it difficult for them to abandon overt coercion (Stepan 1978, 86). This argument does not fully explain the tendency of inclusionary regimes to decline in legitimacy and move toward more exclusionary strategies over time. An additional explanation may lie in the interests of state elites themselves: the tendency of corporatist regimes to beget opposition may be seen as highly desirable by some state leaders, particularly those positioned within the coercive apparatus of the state. Even latent mass opposition enhances their ability to claim greater power, resources, and prerogatives.

This is not a novel idea. In "War Making and State Making as Organized Crime," Charles Tilly (1985) argues that states may create "threats," or the appearance of threats, in order to legitimize greater demands on the resources of private capital. War making by states—picking fights with neighbors—amounts to a racket in which the state "protects" economic elites from external "threats" and thus justifies the construction of ever larger state institutions.[10] Tilly is referring to European states and specifically to conflict with external opponents. It seems plausible that Latin American states may have used analogous protection against *internal* enemies to increase their call on the resources of capital and strengthen the claim of militaries, rather than civilians, to control over the state.

Protection rackets may persist even in situations in which significant elements of the state apparatus would prefer a transition to a less exclusionary type of regime, either through elections or development of a more reformist set of state policies, such as those implemented by the military in Peru between 1968 and 1975. The problem lies in the capacity of elites within the repressive apparatus to resist such a regime transition by manipulating the appearance of threat or by *generating* a threat through repressive policies. Stepan notes that Mexico could easily have moved toward a more exclusionary form of corporatism had state elites chosen to follow such a path: "The polizarization variable was more favorable to inclusionary than exclusionary corporatism but in the revolutionary aftermath a victorious state elite could have at least neutralized the effect of this variable by 'creating' enemies to support exclusionary politics" (1978, 92n.). This comment anticipates a central point of his later book, *Rethinking Military Politics* (1988), in which he argues that a faction of the Brazilian state used intensified assassination and torture to create an impression of a greater popular threat, thereby impeding measures by moderate state elites to permit a political opening. Stepan asks, "Why, if the incoming 'military as government' began to plan the distensão in September 1973, did more than two-thirds of all 'disappearances' of political prisoners between 1964 and 1979 happen in 1973–1974?" (40). He answers his own question: "The extremists in the security community, fearing they would lose their autonomy, waged a new round of warfare against leftist organizations, both to eliminate them and to convince the 'military as institution' that the subversive threat was real and that distensão was a dangerous mistake" (41). The hardliners in the security community had grown accustomed to privileges, power, and considerable autonomy. They correctly ascertained that the sort of liberalization that the high command was promoting would harm their institutional interests. In response to this challenge, they exercised their independent capacity to carry out repression in an effort to signal the high command that liberalization was not advisable.

There is no reason to think that this practice is confined to Brazil in the early 1970s. On the contrary, the anomalies in patterns of state violence discussed earlier, in which repression seemed to increase after significant opposition was defeated (Argentina 1976–79, Uruguay 1973–80, Guatemala 1970–74, El Salvador 1932) or *preceded* significant armed opposition (Brazil 1969–70; El Salvador 1979–80) suggest that manipulation of the apparent "threat," as well as the generation of more militant opposition through repressive practices, may be widespread.

It is not difficult to imagine the political incentives for the kind of Machiavellian use of internal violence that these cases suggest. Conspicuous acts of violence against supposed internal enemies of the state can enable a repressive regime or coercive state agencies to develop and maintain a civilian constituency. By committing acts of repression, the coercive apparatus sends signals to social elites that threats from below still need a firm hand. This may help convince groups within the upper and middle classes who might otherwise become restive that they still need the services of a highly autonomous, authoritarian regime, thereby forestalling pressures for political liberalization. As in the Brazilian case, acts of repression may also be a means for hardliners to send messages to moderate factions *within* the state apparatus, convincing them that a threat still exists. Acts of repression can also effectively veto a controlled political opening or a transition toward a more inclusionary form of regime. Reformist state elites cannot expect to achieve a great deal of popular legitimacy while the coercive apparatus is disappearing, torturing, and killing citizens.

This fact presents a difficulty for reformist elites within states that have in the past engaged in exclusionary practices. Exclusionary regimes tend to grant their coercive agencies considerable autonomy. The means used to suppress opposition political activity and dismantle organizations of civil society are often illegal ones, and even where executive decrees and states of siege provide the formal legal framework for repression, state agents must consider the possibility that they may be held accountable for their actions following a future transition to democracy. Repressive regimes also need to consider the sensibilities of the international community, which since the 1970s has increasingly monitored human rights conditions and imposed sanctions on gross and systematic violators. Regimes attempt to avoid domestic legal problems and international political pressures by setting up special, highly secretive agencies to do the dirty work of repression. These are usually independent of significant government oversight of their budgets and operations, feature parallel

command structures separated from formal executive authority, and are sometimes organized in a cellular manner with little cross-flow of information between offices. Such institutions often obtained additional resources from the
United States, the USSR, or a combination of the two, as the superpowers
sought influence within the security forces of actual or potential client
states. These external resources further enhanced the autonomy of coercive
institutions from domestic political controls (Rueschemeyer, Stephens, and
Stephens 1992, 156; Tilly 1990, 217–24). In the Guatemalan and Salvadoran
cases, state organizations had close, organic links to civilian vigilante structures, an arrangement that deliberately blurred the boundary between state
and civilian responsibility while enabling state agencies to obtain financial
support directly from elite civilian clients.

Faced with such autonomous repressive agencies, even the best-inten-
tioned reformist state elites will find it difficult to shift state policies toward a
formula that will build popular legitimacy through greater responsiveness or
inclusion. Unless reformists can gain full control of the hardline agencies,
state-led reform efforts will be liable to subversion by antipopular terrorism
originating from within the state. This problem helps to explain why we seldom see transitions from exclusionary to inclusionary statist regimes: political
openings and reductions in human rights abuses seldom result from reformist
leadership within the state, but rather from a resurgence in the political power
of civil society and civilian political parties. This kind of shift in the balance
of power between state and society is most likely to happen when exclusionary strategies have proven ineffective in maintaining a workable social order;
where repression has been imposed on too broad a cross-section of society and
has created an antiregime civic movement that includes more powerful social
strata; where state economic policies or management harm the interests of social elites, triggering an organized effort among social elites to reclaim control
of the state; or where international political interventions have helped build
parties capable of achieving ideological hegemony and governing without dependence on repressive and/or corporatist mechanisms.

The following historical chapters show that all of these predictions hold
true in the case of El Salvador. Once the military took power on the basis of
repression and exclusion, repeated efforts by military elites to lead a transition
toward a more moderate, inclusionary, and popular form of governance failed,
in large part because of the veto power—in the form of repression—retained
by hardline factions and agencies within the state. The Salvadoran state could
not move away from military domination and governance by repression until
the armed forces failed to defeat a prolonged insurgency in the 1980s (thus discrediting coercive strategies), and until a political party of the right with heavy
assistance from the United States developed sufficient popular support and
ideological hegemony to govern without depending on brute force.

International Forces

The behavior of states is affected not only by their internal makeup and domestic social context, but also by their international context, which includes the international system of states, multinational institutions, regimes, and laws, and transnational forces, including markets, firms, production systems, and, increasingly, a transnational civil society. International factors may either worsen or moderate a state's tendency to use repressive violence. Gurr (1986) hypothesizes that connections to the international economy and to the world system of states tend to moderate domestic state violence, since repression is not acceptable to many states and institutions within the international community. As a given national economy becomes more heavily linked to international markets, it becomes more vulnerable to pressures to conform to international community standards, though the degree of this vulnerability depends heavily on the size of the national economy. Small states are likely to be more sensitive to international pressures than are large states such as the People's Republic of China. Large, powerful countries devoted to promoting democracy and respect for human rights can have a particularly positive effect. Samuel Huntington (1984) and Tony Smith (1994) view the United States in this positive light.

The ability of the international community to apply pressures depends greatly on the availability of information about internal state conditions. Kathryn Sikkink (1993) demonstrates that transnational "issue networks" of nongovernmental organizations, concerned governments, and international organizations such as the United Nations and the Organization of American States (OAS) have, by exchanging information and setting political agendas, made states more responsive to international pressures. One hypothesis is that a state that wishes to pursue closer relations with the international community will have incentives to abandon, or better conceal, its repressive practices. Incentives to reduce abuses will be particularly strong for small states for whom favorable reception by the international community is indispensable. This point is relevant to the willingness of social elites in El Salvador in the 1990s to move away from their dependence upon repression.

The influence of the international community is not consistently positive. In fact, the international system may actually increase the propensity of states to kill or abuse their own subjects. Noam Chomsky and Edward Herman (1979) argue that terrorist regimes in the Third World are the handiwork of the United States, citing U.S. encouragement for military coups and aid for post-coup governments, the U.S. role in providing weapons, torture equipment, and training, and evidence that U.S. intelligence and military operatives have participated directly in torture, assassinations, and other repressive activities. Though one may question Chomsky and Herman's polemical claim that the United States sought to establish a "client fascist empire," more methodical scholars (e.g., Rueschemeyer, Stephens, and Stephens 1992, 156) have concluded that U.S. military and intelligence assistance reinforced repressive tendencies at the expense of democracy. In studies of El Salvador and Guatemala, Michael McClintock (1985a, 1985b) finds that the United States, motivated by Cold War concerns, helped build up precisely those institutions within these states that were most prone to kill, most isolated from accountability, most heavily influenced by extremely conservative civilian elites, and most ideologically predisposed to see civilian regime opponents as enemies of the state, rather than as citizens expressing their needs. In effect, U.S. doctrines for how allied states should go about defending themselves against potential internal enemies dovetailed perfectly with the institutions and ideology of class oppression that were already in place in these societies. U.S. assistance merely gave more resources, and a reinforced rationale, to state institutions already inclined to torture and kill their own nationals.

The debate about the impact of U.S. involvement suffers from the fact that both sides ignore the simple proposition that we cannot fully understand a given state's policies without disaggregating the state into its component agencies and decision-making bodies. In examining how the United States or any other external actor affects the internal violence in a given country, we need to bear in mind the possibility that different agencies will have different impacts. Diplomatic and human rights agencies, for instance, may impose constraints on a foreign state's domestic violence at the same time that intelligence or military agencies are exacerbating the problem. Congress may be more (or less) sensitive to human rights concerns than is the executive. Policy may have mixed effects, and understanding its inherent contradictions may be vital to our judgment of an external actor's influence. This book examines in detail the proposition that even when outside actors intend to reduce state violence, they are unlikely to succeed unless they bear in mind the intra-state political considerations discussed above. Failure to take into account the interests and logic of protection racket institutions, as well as their capacity to shape the political arena by using violence, can completely undermine an external power's human rights policy, no matter how well intentioned. The Carter administration's human rights policies in El Salvador, discussed in Chapters 5 and 6, tragically illustrate this point. In the long run, the ability of the United States, multilateral organizations, or "principled issues networks" such as those described by Sikkink (1993) to check the internal violence of states will hinge on their ability to promote domestic state institutions that are inhibited from operating protection rackets.

TWO

🌾

ANTECEDENTS: THE *MATANZA* AND
THE ESTABLISHMENT
OF MILITARY RULE

Late on the night of 22/23 January 1932, several thousand indigenous and mestizo peasants in the western part of El Salvador attacked towns, police posts, and military barracks. Armed primarily with machetes but in some areas having a significant number of rifles, the insurgents took over several towns, overwhelmed isolated police posts, and indulged in looting, arson, and, in a few places, rape and murder. Most of the violence was directed against symbols of local oppression—the wealthy and their homes, mayors, and municipal offices (Ching 1995, 31). The rebels killed about 35 civilians and local police. Five Customs Police were killed in the attack on Sonsonate, and the National Police lost a total of 10 in Sonsonate and Santa Tecla. Nine National Guardsmen were killed and 10 wounded, and the regular army lost between 20 and 40 soldiers (Anderson 1971, 136).[1]

In response, National Guard and army forces from Ahuachapán, Sonsonate, Santa Ana, and San Salvador marched on the towns taken by the rebels and systematically defeated the insurgents. The better-armed government forces made quick work of the rebels, suppressing the last rebel band in Tacuba in just three days. With the military threat eliminated, government troops, with the National Guard playing the most prominent role, proceeded to massacre anyone in the western part of the country whom they suspected of having participated in the revolt. In practice, suspects included anyone who looked "Indian," dressed like a peasant, or carried a machete (as almost all rural workers do). Suspects were executed en masse by firing squads and truck-mounted machine guns. In many cases, people in the rebellious zones were told to report to neighboring National Guard barracks to receive safe-conduct passes. When they arrived, they were seized and executed. According to the account of Miguel Mármol (a Salvadoran communist who survived four bullet wounds from a firing squad):

From the barracks at Ahuachapán a stream of blood flowed, as if it were water, or the urine of horses. [Later] a lieutenant who was in service there would recall, crying, that the peasants who were being shot in groups in the patio would sing "Corazón Santo, Tú Reinarás" (Sacred Heart, You Will Reign, a Catholic hymn) and that in the pools of blood he and the soldiers in the firing squad had seen, clear as can be, the image of Christ and had refused to go on killing and protested to their superiors. The protest was made in such adamant terms that the Commander of the garrison ordered a temporary halt to the massacre. (McClintock 1985a, 114)

Corpses were piled in mass graves, in sulphur pits, and in the drainage ditches along the roads. Pigs fed on the human remains. In one case a church wall collapsed from having absorbed so many volleys from firing squads and machine guns (McClintock 1985a, 112–13). Though the exact extent of the carnage is unknown, in part because the government destroyed virtually all documents that could provide clues, at least eight to ten thousand were killed (Anderson 1971, 135). Other observers who conducted interviews in the area of the massacres put the number at around twenty-five thousand (Montes 1987, 191). The higher estimates would be equivalent to 2 percent of El Salvador's population at the time, and in the communities where the rebellions took place, up to two-thirds of the local population was eliminated (Paige 1994, 2). Whatever the number, the *matanza* ("slaughter") created enough fear that it effectively eliminated distinctive indigenous dress, languages, and other cultural expressions from western El Salvador. People were still afraid to talk about it 40 years later when investigators attempted to conduct interviews in the area, and the population of the western region has proven reluctant to participate in opposition politics to the present day (Paige 1994, 2).

The *matanza* was not confined to the rural west, though certainly it was most intense there. Large numbers of executions are reported to have been carried out in San Salvador and other cities, as government forces rounded up virtually anyone they suspected of being a leftist. The urban executions were so numerous that "the chief of the department of sanitation feared a major epidemic would result from the slowly decomposing bodies. By the end of January the number of deaths had risen to the point where burial became impractical, and the chief of operations ordered the incineration of bodies. Night after night San Salvador was disturbed by the rumble of military trucks carrying the captured into the city, and bursts of machine-gun fire as 'justice' was hurriedly rendered."[2] According to Salvadoran military historian Colonel Gregorio Bustamente Maceo, "Every night trucks went full of victims from the Dirección General de Policía to the banks of the Río Acelhuate where the victims were shot out of hand and buried anonymously in great ditches" (McClintock 1985a, 114). McClintock reports that "sometimes the killings in the cities were entirely arbitrary. Several accounts tell the story of a group of about 100 anti-Communist craftsmen who presented themselves at the garrison in San Salvador to offer their services as volunteers. They were invited in and then shot dead in the courtyard of the barracks" (1985a, 114). Such broadly random killing was hardly necessary to break the back of the communist movement, since the government had a nearly complete list of Communist Party members, who had registered by party affiliation (many against their own better judgment) in order to vote in the early January municipal and legislative elections (Ching 1995). Nonetheless, the killing went on for several weeks, until essentially all plausible targets had been exhausted.

The *Matanza* and the Consolidation of Military Rule

The rebellion and government massacre of 1932 took place in the broader context of what Everett Alan Wilson (1970) has called the "crisis of national integration" in El Salvador. The post–World War I period had seen rapid socioeconomic transformations. The coffee industry expanded vigorously during these years, displacing thousands of peasants from what little land had remained available, and finishing the work of the Liberal land reforms of the 1880s. These abolished the community lands (*ejidos*) generally used for subsistence crops in favor of the private ownership more conducive to export crop production. In fact, the extreme concentration of land ownership that is generally associated with El Salvador mostly came into being after the First World War. Whereas much of El Salvador's coffee had been produced by relatively small farmers prior to that war, by the 1930s 60 percent of coffee production was controlled by 500 of the country's 10,000 producers (Paige 1994, 4).

One of the primary mechanisms for land consolidation in El Salvador, as elsewhere, was the control by a relatively few powerful families of production financing and mortgages. Small producers faced usurious interest rates and needed only one bad year to lose their properties. As growing numbers of peasants lost their lands and had to seek wage labor, rural wages fell precipitously. In the mid-1920s, El Salvador's wages were among the highest in Central America; by decade's end, they were among the lowest. Thousands migrated out of the coffee zones to other parts of the country and, particularly, to the larger towns, where they swelled the ranks of artisans and construction and domestic workers. At the same time, the wealthiest of the coffee growers were achieving extraordinary fortunes. The reformist newspaper *Patria* editorialized that "El Salvador is becoming a monster with the head of a lion and the tail of a mouse" (Wilson 1970, 130).

Despite the growing wealth of the coffee sector, it is questionable to characterize El Salvador as having a national "oligarchy" during this period. The upper classes as a whole were a very diverse group, including established landed families from the 1800s, immigrants, and urban professionals, merchants, and bankers. Not all of the prominent families were involved in coffee production, as some very large holdings continued to produce indigo and other crops. The coffee sector itself was divided between producers and processors. During the 1920s, coffee processing and exporting had become increasingly concentrated in a few hands, resulting in a growing schism even within the coffee industry (Wilson 1970, 132–34). Non-coffee elites, members of the older landed families, tended to predominate within the state (Wilson 1970, 62).

Before the late 1920s, members of El Salvador's agrarian elite tended to be regionalized. Even the very wealthy remained on their properties, seldom traveled to the national capital (a difficult journey at best and nearly impossible from some locales during the six-month rainy season), and focused their social and limited political activities at the local level. Only a relatively small proportion of the national coffee elite belonged to the highest-status social club in the capital, the Casino Salvadoreño; the rest belonged to local clubs in their own provinces (Wilson 1970, 56–65, 135–36). This geographic fragmentation began to change once government investments in an east–west railroad link, combined with asphalted roads in some parts of the country, improved transportation and contributed to the formation of a national elite. Increasing numbers of prominent coffee producers found they could live in the capital city, San Salvador, and still control their plantations. They built ever more opulent homes in the capital, began to take a serious interest in national affairs, and in 1929 formed the Asociación Cafetalera (Coffee Growers' Association) to institutionalize and defend their interests (Wilson 1970, 139).

Although the coffee industry was beginning to produce a coherent national social elite, this group had not yet begun to consolidate itself as a political elite. Only a handful of families participated actively in national politics. The Meléndez-Quiñónez clan provided three consecutive presidents in the early part of the twentieth century, but the legitimacy of their elected regimes among the upper classes and the small emerging middle class (1913–1927) gradually eroded during the 1920s, just as Salvadoran society was becoming more stratified. As early as 1917, President Alfonso Quiñónez sought to broaden his political base by creating a labor organization called the Liga Roja (Red League). Subsequent governments sporadically opened greater space for trade guild organizing, which led to the formation of a series of labor federations, primarily among artisans. The governments' decision to permit such organizing was probably rooted in a corporatist impulse: they sought to recruit "auxiliary classes" to supplement their thin political bases, while keeping them from becoming a potential base of opposition (Guido Véjar 1980a, 68). The Meléndez-Quiñónez governments also sought to diversify the economic base of El Salvador through a variety of state initiatives to promote and subsidize new exports, develop industrial products, and experiment with new crops, such as cotton. A substantial loan secured from U.S. sources in 1922 increased the liquidity of the state and the relative weight of public spending in the economy.

The successor of the Meléndez-Quiñónez line, President Pío Romero Bosque (1927–31), opened the political system significantly. He exiled his predecessor to gain greater autonomy from the established political families, carried out an anticorruption purge of the government, unmuzzled the press, canceled the 13-year state of siege, reinstated constitutional rights, restored university autonomy, and declared an amnesty that allowed most political exiles of the past administrations to return (Elam 1989, 136). He also tried to improve public administration and earned the support of teachers and civil servants by ending the practices of payment with vouchers (*agiatismo*) and forced "savings." New laws favored the interests of clerical workers and professionals, both public and private, and increased the self-confidence and aspirations of these members of the small but growing middle class. In the municipal elections of 1929, political parties representing the emerging middle class did well (Wilson 1970, 197).

In the more tolerant atmosphere of Romero Bosque's administration, the Communist Party made advances and managed to gain control of important labor federations. But Romero Bosque, like his predecessors, eventually cracked down on the popular movements. Between August and September 1930, the security forces rounded up over 600 peasants in Sonsonate alone (Anderson 1971, 40). In December 1930, the National Police killed eight people at a demonstration in Santa Ana (Parkman 1988, 18), and between November 1930 and February 1931 around 1,200 activists were jailed (Dunkerly 1985, 22). The repression, however, did not effectively counteract the cumulative effect of presidential efforts to secure political legitimacy through tolerance of lower-class mobilization. A broad popular movement had formed by the end of the 1920s. After the worldwide crash of 1929, this movement, though internally divided, became a challenge to the socioeconomic status quo—a challenge that the conservative upper classes were not organized politically to counteract.

When Romero Bosque decided to hold genuinely competitive municipal elections in 1929, followed by a free and fair presidential contest in 1931, the nation's social elite was not well enough organized to take part. Despite a growing recognition that El Salvador needed a strong state and that it would matter who controlled that state, no single political party existed to represent upper-class interests (Astilla Carmelo 1976, 31). The several candidates who ran, supported by various hastily assembled parties, competed with one another for a relatively limited conservative electorate and lost. The victor in the 1931 presidential elections, Arturo Araujo, though himself a wealthy landowner, positioned himself politically as a social reformer whose Labor Party drew support from a broad cross-section of the increasingly organized middle and lower classes. His campaign platform promised better economic conditions for the poor, and some of his campaigners promised land reform, pledges that garnered Araujo considerable support and that he made no effort to contradict. Araujo won 47 percent of the vote, against 29 percent for the candidate of the old official party and 15 percent for a traditional liberal candidate. Although Araujo had to repay opposition deputies' campaign debts before the legislature would confirm his election by plurality, his victory was nonetheless a clear signal that the private sector elite was, despite its wealth, ill-prepared for the political forces unleashed by the 1920s (Astilla Carmelo 1976, 35).

One source of division within the social elite, of course, was the impact of the depression. As world coffee prices fell, growers became increasingly dependent upon and vulnerable to the decisions of a handful of banks, while bankers became increasingly cautious in providing production credits and aggressive about foreclosing on delinquent mortgages. The handful of processors and exporters who controlled most of the trade insulated themselves to some extent from the consequences of falling prices, passing on lower prices to producers and maintaining a profit margin for themselves (Guido Véjar 1980a, 65–80). While the full effects of the depression on the coffee industry had not yet been felt by the election of 1931, it is likely that material disputes among the wealthy impeded their ability to organize politically against the popular forces and those members of the elite, like Araujo, willing to mobilize those forces for political ends.

The power of the popular forces became abruptly apparent during Araujo's first days in office, when a massive demonstration of peasants demanded that he fulfill his campaign promises of land redistribution. The Salvadoran Communist Party (PCS), which had gained considerable strength among workers, peasants, and students, saw Araujo's reformism as an obstacle to their revolutionary agenda (Paige 1994, 17–18), and the party exploited popular disappointment with his failures to deliver immediately on promised reforms. Having used the vocal and mobilized popular sectors to gain office, Araujo subsequently depended on the National Guard and National Police to keep him there.

It is difficult to gauge Araujo's sincerity. He had an unusual background for a Salvadoran landowner, having studied engineering in London and worked there as an engineer, during which time he roomed with a union shop steward who belonged to the Labour Party. Upon his return to El Salvador, he distinguished himself as an unusually generous employer and became publicly identified with pro-labor causes. He was friendly with Alberto Masferrer, a distinguished writer, publisher, and editorialist, whose philosophy of the "vital minimum" argued on normative and practical grounds against the impoverishment of workers and peasants that had taken place during the 1920s. Masferrer's newspaper, *Patria*, had gone so far as to call for a reversal of the liberal land policies of the late 1800s and a return to the *ejido* system, under which communal lands provided for the subsistence needs of the rural poor (Wilson

1970, 117–18). Masferrer endorsed Araujo's candidacy and was initially supportive of his administration, as were other members of the reformist elite.

Yet Araujo's ability to implement reforms was limited. The depression had reduced the value of exports and thus the amount of revenue available to the government. Moreover, the government's ability to administer what little money it had was crippled by the decision of technocrats from previous regimes to abandon Araujo in protest against his reformist intentions (Parkman 1988, 18). Araujo dismissed many of those who were still willing to serve in order to make room for political appointees, who then proceeded to treat the state like a treasure chest. The extensive corruption of his administration, and his lavish spending on parties at the Presidential Palace, led many observers to see Araujo as an opportunist and demagogue.

Government salaries were soon in arrears, and Araujo gave the military no priority over civilians in the government. It is a measure of either his remaining idealism or his political naiveté that Araujo refused to favor the army, even though he depended on the military to remain in office. His vice president was Maximiliano Hernández Martínez, an army general, who had briefly campaigned for president on a reformist/populist platform before throwing his support to Araujo. Martínez' presence on the ticket had helped to ensure the loyalty of the armed forces during the tumultuous election and the postelection haggling in the legislature.[3] Martínez had considerable support within the armed forces and was able to deliver their support to Araujo, at least in the first few months of his administration. Perhaps in an effort to enhance Martínez' ability to deliver military loyalty, Araujo made him minister of war as well as vice president, creating a dangerous situation in which the commander of the armed forces was also the constitutional heir to the presidency.

According to McClintock (1985a, 103), Martínez was Araujo's "sole supporter in the Army high command." The U.S. military attaché said of Araujo in April 1931, "In most of the difficulties which have arisen he has relied on the Vice-President, General Maximillian [sic] Martínez" (McClintock 1985a, 106). Araujo's dependence on Martínez was exacerbated when his government announced its intention to seek a new foreign loan. Past loans had led to the regulation of Salvadoran national finances by a U.S. fiscal agent. The new foreign loan proposal triggered fears of more dramatic foreign intervention and anger over the expected misuse of the funds through corruption and extravagance.[4] The state employees whose lot had improved under Romero Bosque were sure that new debt would lead to a return to the IOUs and de facto payroll taxes of the past. Opponents of the proposed loans organized demonstrations, which turned into riots in San Salvador and Santa Ana. These were put down with force (Parkman 1988, 18).

Many of Araujo's decisions seem surprising in light of his increasing dependence on the military. First, he refused a reasonable request that military salaries be equalized across provinces of the country. Then he ordered all officers who were in professional schools or other nonmilitary educational programs either to withdraw from them or leave the military (Grieb 1971, 21–22). These actions sharpened the already intense dissatisfaction stemming from late pay, government corruption, and increasing disorder.

On 2 December 1931, revolt took place in several army barracks in and around the capital city. The conspirators were a heterogeneous group of younger officers who had organized their movement during the previous month. Army forces attacked the Presidential Palace, where they met tough resistance from the police on duty there. In the confusion, Araujo escaped to his private home, then on to the National Palace in the center of town, where he attempted to rally the forces that remained loyal. Unfortunately for him, the National Guard at that point cast its lot with the *golpistas*, leaving the loyal cavalry and police hopelessly outnumbered. Araujo then set out for the western part of the country, hoping to organize a counterattack with loyal soldiers there. Before leaving the city, he made a final telephone call to the Artillery barracks, the headquarters of the conspirators, and found himself talking with General Martínez, who claimed that he was a "prisoner." Araujo left San Salvador still wondering why a "prisoner" was answering the phone (Anderson 1971, 60–61).

Martínez and the Military in 1931

The Salvadoran military at the time of the coup was not a particularly impressive institution. There had been some efforts at professionalization during the first three decades of the century, and Salvadoran forces were generally viewed as the best trained and organized in Central America. It was, nonetheless, a rudimentary force, comprising three main elements: the army, the National Guard, and the National Police. All together the three forces numbered only 3,500 men. Individual units were very small: for instance, the First Infantry regiment based in the capital city, which was an important player in the coup, included only 120 men. Of the three forces, the National Guard, modeled on the Spanish Civil Guard, was the most "elite" in the sense that its troopers were paid three times as much as army soldiers and were far more likely to reenlist, whereas army troops were generally conscripts who served only one tour. The National Police were also more likely to be careerists rather than conscripts, but they were more lightly armed than the National Guard. The differences between the army and the security forces would become clear during the course of the 1930 peasant rebellion, when army officers had to disarm their troops to prevent them from siding with the Communists.

Of the forces, the National Guard was the most closely aligned with major coffee growers. The Guard, formed in 1912, had served particularly to enforce the 1907 Agrarian Code (Ley Agraria), which prohibited trade union organization among rural workers. It also took on various administrative functions helpful to local landowners, such as keeping lists of names and descriptions of agricultural employees, as well as law enforcement tasks such as arresting people for gathering firewood, picking berries, or otherwise harvesting any food without the landowners' written permission. Local Guard units were often given supplemental salaries and other perquisites by landowners, making their relationship essentially a mercenary one.

Despite cordial relations with elites at the local level, it was by no means a foregone conclusion that Martínez and the military would remain in control of the state. Some elements of the private sector elite were "disconcerted" by Martínez' bid for power (Salazar Valiente 1981, 92), in part because of his posturing as a populist during the 1931 presidential campaign. Martínez was, in addition, from humble and mestizo origins, in contrast to the largely white, wealthy criollos who had governed El Salvador in the past. He was also known for holding unusual religious views, having published several books on theosophy and the occult prior to assuming the vice presidency in 1931.

Some of Martínez' nationalistic policies, though they later proved beneficial to the stability of the economy, were initially greeted with skepticism by wealthy coffee growers. In one case, "the president was forced to suffer through a rough meeting with representatives of the cafetalera, led by Francisco Dueñas, the greatest of the coffee barons. These men demanded repeal of Araujo's monetary decrees of October prohibiting the shipment of gold abroad, on the grounds that the bankers were using the tight money situation as an excuse for not making loans to the coffee growers. But Martínez refused" (Anderson 1971, 90). Martínez' policies ultimately favored coffee producers at the expense of bankers, as we shall see, but the concern of the Cafetalera is understandable insofar as the military had not yet established itself as a corporate political actor. (Although two military officers had run for the presidency in 1931, Martínez himself and Antonio Claramount, they were not "candidatos militares but rather militares candidatos" [Wilson 1970, 200]). The upper classes had little reason at the outset to have faith in Martínez' vision and policy-making skills.

Another question mark hovering over the future of a Martínez-led government was the extent of U.S. opposition to him. U.S. foreign policy at the time required denial of recognition to any individual taking power as the result of a coup d'état. Senior levels of the State Department intended to apply diplomatic pressures, in keeping with U.S. support for the 1923 Washington Treaties, under which Central American nations had agreed to discourage revolts by denying recognition to governments seizing power through force. Though not a signatory to the treaties, Washington had supported these terms to encourage stability in the region. Up until 1931, any government in the region that the United States refused to recognize fell. Moreover, because of the crisis in El Salvador's public finances and the likely need for renegotiation of debt payments, "the position taken by the United States meant, literally, the death sentence for the new government" (Astilla Carmelo 1976, 50).

Washington's position was quickly undermined, however, by the incompetence or willfulness of its minister in El Salvador, Charles Curtis.[5] Curtis apparently favored Martínez' taking power after the coup, in large part because he distrusted the junior officers on the "Military Directorate," whom he characterized as "little more than half witted" and "utterly irresponsible youths," having "no capacity and no fixed plan beyond getting rid of the present government" (quoted in Grieb 1971, 155). Curtis' hostility to the Directorate continued after Martínez was named as provisional president, because he believed that the young officers had retained Martínez as a figurehead merely to satisfy domestic and foreign opinion, while continuing to exercise power themselves (Grieb 1971, 155).

Despite explicit and repeated instructions to make the U.S. Policy clear to both the directorate and Martínez, Curtis focused unsuccessfully on getting the Directorate to resign and neglected to send the signal that the U.S. would not recognize Martínez. In fact, he recommended recognition to the State Department.

Curtis' actions succeeded only in buying Martínez some time, as Washington quickly sent a special envoy, Jefferson Caffery, to evaluate the situation. Caffery found that the "better elements" (that is, the upper classes) were now supporting Martínez, "as for the moment he offers a stable government and they very much fear that any change in the situation might bring renewed disturbances." He advised applying pressure to oust Martínez before it was too late and replacing him with a provisional junta (Grieb 1971, 160). When this proved ineffectual, Caffery pressured the younger officers of the Directorate to ask Martínez to resign in favor of Colonel José Asencio Menéndez, who had been at sea at the time of the coup and was thus recognizable according to U.S. policy. But events intervened: "just as Martínez' replacement appeared imminent, a series of so-called 'communist-uprisings' swept the country" (Grieb 1971, 162). The rebellion had an immediate political effect. On the second day of the uprising, the Military Directorate, which U.S. diplomats had been trying to coax into replacing Martínez, instead transferred full executive power to him (Elam 1968, 31). For its part, the United States abandoned its efforts to oust him, since removing him would jeopardize the unity of the military.

The Politics of the *Matanza*

The government had ample advance warning of the rebellion. During 1931 Communist-organized demonstrators and the security forces had engaged in increasingly frequent and violent clashes. Dozens of demonstrators were killed, yet the peasants' militancy seemed undaunted. General José Tomás

Comm. Party

Calderón (grandfather of President Armando Calderón Sol) reported to Martínez on the "ostentatious disrespect and lack of fear of authority" on the part of demonstrators and recommended reinforcements for the garrison in Sonsonate (Anderson 1971, 76). The Communist Party also viewed the combativeness of peasants in the western part of the country with alarm. In correspondence sent to the Comintern in Moscow, PCS officials complained that western peasants were moving too fast, demanding that the party participate in the January 1932 municipal and legislative elections. The party had only the beginnings of an organizational structure in the west, and feared that participating in elections would accomplish nothing while exposing the party's membership to repression. Pressured by peasants who wanted representation at the local level, the party reluctantly agreed (Ching 1995). When the government committed blatant fraud in the elections, and when Communist protests were met with violence, the party's Central Committee issued orders for the formation of a Revolutionary Military Committee to prepare for armed action.

As with participation in the elections, the decision to rebel went against the better judgment of most party leaders. One PCS official wrote to the Comintern that "we can't stop the revolutionary wave . . . the masses have a thirst for blood and are under the illusion that with their machetes they are ready to carry out a movement of this kind" (Ching 1995, 30). The party knew they lacked the weapons, training, and organizational structure to defeat the government. Yet faced with the intense militancy of the classes they claimed to represent, they perceived no choice but to provide some leadership and coordination for the explosion that was about to come (Ching 1995, 31). First, though, they made a final effort to avoid armed conflict by sending a delegation to meet with the president. Refused an audience with Martínez, they warned his senior aides, "The peasants will win with their machetes the rights you are denying them." The war minister replied, "You have machetes; we have machine guns" (Anderson 1971, 85–92).

By this point, the military had collected, through informants, detailed information regarding the preparations for revolt. The Communists' planning was so slipshod that the military had little to worry about. There was, essentially, no military plan. The rebels simply hoped to overwhelm the military with sheer numbers, ignoring the difference in weaponry. Most rebels would be armed only with sticks and machetes. The only significant number of rifles available to them were ones cached in the west by Araujo loyalists planning to invade El Salvador from Guatemala, though they hoped to receive additional arms from sympathizers in military barracks.

The government dealt a crippling blow to the movement by capturing the party's top leadership just a few days before the revolt. The Ubico government in Guatemala captured Juan Pablo Wainwright, who had been preparing to lead the forces from Guatemala. Shortly thereafter, on 18 January, the National

[Handwritten margin notes: peasants mung & quick / wanted local reps / when the gov't comtd blatant electn fraud / a revolut. milit comm. prepared to take armed action]

[Handwritten margin notes: communists had t real military pl. no weapons / sticks + machetes / plan was to overwhelm milit. w/ their great #s]

[Handwritten note at bottom: Wainwright (leader of comm. revolt) captured by Guat.]

Police captured Augustín Farabundo Martí, the de facto head of the party, along with two of his key lieutenants, Alfonso Luna and Mario Zapata. Prior to his capture, Martí had issued orders for the revolt to take place on the 22 January, and the uprising went ahead, despite the arrest of the leadership and Communist supporters within the military. In the words of a Comintern report on the disaster, "The CC (Central Committee of the PCS) was effectively nonfunctional during the insurrection. (There was no) CC to direct the masses . . . no central leadership, no national command, just a series of local insurrections" (quoted in Ching 1985, 31). As Miguel Mármol remarked, "We did it too late, like assholes, we did it after the enemy had begun his repression and delivered devastating blows to our leadership apparatus, to the basic military nucleuses, putting us totally on the defensive" (quoted in Paige 1994, 20).

The "military nucleuses" to which Mármol referred were conspiracies among the soldiers in several army barracks to rise up in support of the rebellion. The Communist Party had circulated pamphlets in military barracks arguing:

> Above all, the soldier is a worker or a peasant whom the rich exploit in factories, shops and fields. When he is still a youth he is taken to the barracks where he is forced to bear arms in defense of the wealth which he has produced for the rich as a worker or peasant.
>
> The discontent which the soldier feels in the barracks from the oppression by which he lives is the result of the fact that a soldier, enduring the lies of chiefs and officers, feels that they are his enemies, because these same chiefs and officers belong to the same class which exploited him in the factories, shops and fields. (Elam 1968, 38)

• Comm. party infiltrated the military

•/ class rhetoric

• milt. resp by killing officers

The next circular was even more direct: "COMRADE SOLDIERS: Don't fire a single shot at the revolutionary workers and peasants. Kill the chiefs and officers. Place yourselves under the orders of the Comrade Soldiers who have been named Red Comrades by this Central Committee" (Elam 1968, 39). The conspirators in the army were uncovered when enlisted men reported suspicious activities to their superiors. The discovery of these plots precipitated a state of siege in 6 of the 14 departments (Elam 1968, 39). An entire company of the First Cavalry was executed by firing squad. There were similar executions in the First Infantry Regiment and the air force. The U.S. legation reported at the time that nearly half of the soldiers in the regular army were "dismissed" in January 1932. On 16 January, a week before the rebellion, officers disarmed, arrested, and shot many members of the Sixth Regiment of Machinegunners (McClintock 1985a, 119). Though easily suppressed, these rebellions reduced the effective numbers of the military and may have contributed to the determination of the officer corps to use extreme measures, since the Communists had committed the sin of carrying "the class struggle into the heart of the armed forces" (Rouquié 1987, 247).

The extent to which the government was prepared in advance for the revolt has led many observers, both at the time and since, to suspect that Martínez deliberately let the revolt go forward in order to make a dramatic show of putting it down. Mario Salazar Valiente wrote that "the martinista government premeditatedly permitted the communists' plans to go forward" (1981, 92). Anderson found a widely held belief "among informed persons in El Salvador" that Martínez actually sought to provoke the insurrection in order to gain legitimacy in the eyes of the social elite and the United States. According to this view, the announcement of January elections in which the Communists were invited to participate, and the subsequent exclusion of the Communists from effective competition in the areas most prone to insurrection, were part of a diabolical scheme to provoke a reaction. Some historians argue that in the weeks prior to the rebellion, Martínez gave the Communist leadership more freedom of movement in the hope that they would successfully catalyze a revolt (Guido Véjar 1980a, 24). There are even reports of direct incitement to rebellion: the Salvadoran historian Mauricio de la Selva wrote that Martínez sent "army recruits back to their home villages to spread the word that the acting president wanted reforms, but the rich would not allow them unless a campesino demonstration changed their minds" (cited in Anderson 1971, 85).

On balance, the evidence of premeditation is incomplete. Despite good intelligence on the rebels' plans, Martínez failed to redeploy greater forces to the west (in fact, small National Guard units were removed from towns that were likely targets of the rebellion, rather than being reinforced). This suggests that, at a minimum, Martínez was confident of the military's ability to handle the situation: he could afford, in military terms, to let the rebellion go forward. Whatever degree of premeditation was involved, the military's success in suppressing the rebellion, and the slaughter that followed, were extraordinarily beneficial to Martínez' political position, both domestically and in relation to the United States.

The evidence is compelling that the *extent* of the slaughter was dictated by political calculations rather than internal security. The intensity of the violence, the random selection of victims, and the prolongation of the slaughter until there were no more targets (or until coffee growers became concerned that there would be no one to harvest the crop [Wilson 1970, 267]) are most consistent with an effort to demonstrate the usefulness of the armed forces to the social elite and foreign observers. Extreme repression helped create an impression of extreme danger. The U.S. minister in Guatemala in 1932 declared that the uprising had been "greatly exaggerated and used for political ends" (quoted in Anderson 1971, 150). A member of the U.S. legation at the time wrote, "The de facto regime is undoubtedly keeping up the fear of communism for practical reasons in order to make it appear that General Martínez is indispensable and cannot step aside at the present time" (quoted in McClintock 1985a, 121).

harsh + prolonged violence as deterence tord future rebellions

The prolonged, random violence is also consistent, of course, with a decision to prevent future rebellions by exacting a horrible price for this one. Such an explanation, however, presumes that Martínez was thinking far into the future in the midst of a very fluid political situation in which his tenure in office was highly uncertain. Though his actions had the effect of preventing further revolts for decades, it seems more plausible that Martínez was acting in accordance with his short-term political interests, which were best served by convincing the social elite and the United States that they needed him.

strategy — convinced social elite + U.S. the they needed him (Martínez)

The Salvadoran social elite was easily convinced. The 1932 rebellion fulfilled their worst nightmare—a mass revolt by the "Indians" whom they had oppressed, and depended upon, for so long (Anderson 1971, 17). Prominent coffee growers had been expecting trouble for some time: Wilson quotes the coffee magnate James Hill as saying, "Bolshevism? . . . It's drifting in. The working people hold meetings on Sundays and get very excited. They say, 'We dig the holes for the trees, we clean the weeds, we prune the trees, we pick the coffee. Who earns the money then? . . .' Yes, there will be trouble one of these days" (1970, 136–37). Yet, remarkably, the upper classes did virtually nothing to prepare themselves before the rebellion. Members of the elite in the western part of the country made virtually no effort to arm themselves or to take refuge. Though a civilian Guardia Cívica was formed once the rebellion began, this was a military initiative rather than a civilian one. The unreliable *Cívicos* played almost no role in the fighting or the massacre, but were consigned, instead, to manning posts in secure towns while the National Guard (and, in the cities, the National Police) did the dirty work.

he did + the elite branded his military — so grateful they elected him const. pres. (happy he kept comm. under control)

Documents released by the government after the rebellion began helped reinforce the upper classes' fear and willingness to support the military and Martínez. Among these were the orders that Farabundo Martí himself supposedly sent on 16 January, which instructed the rebels to use against the bourgeoisie "the most opportune means, that is to say: shoot immediately or kill them in some other way without delay. . . . Do away with all of them, saving only the lives of the children" (quoted in Anderson 1971, 92–93). The upper classes' fears gave Martínez an opportunity to extract resources from them: he set up a Council on Public Order, which included representatives of five leading families, to coordinate the collection of funds, ostensibly to strengthen security arrangements and pay the troops. The council collected about U.S. $200,000 for the campaign against "the Indians," though a Canadian naval commander who observed its activities, V.G. Brodeur, noted, "Just how much of this sum eventually found its way into the soldiers' pockets is a doubtful point" (quoted in McClintock 1985a, 119).

The political consequences of the upper classes' gratitude to Martínez were almost immediate. "Under pressure of the emergency," Parkman reports, "the National Legislative Assembly on February 5, 1932, elected him constitutional president to finish Araujo's term, and leading liberals joined his government. Having established himself with the oligarchy and much of the urban population as their savior from the horrors of Communist revolution, he launched his career as El Salvador's last, and perhaps greatest, *caudillo*" (1988, 20).

International Legitimacy

Even though Washington had been moving away from military intervention in the region and was on the verge of removing the Marines from Nicaragua, it would not have been unreasonable on Martínez' part to suspect that the United States (or other powers) might intervene, especially since the State Department in Washington took a dim view of him. In reaction to the 22 January rebellion, U.S and Canadian warships rushed to Salvadoran waters and offered to land troops if needed (Anderson 1971, 129–30; Grieb 1971, 163). Understandably, Salvadoran officers were not keen on permitting a Yankee military intervention in view of the unsavory history of such actions in Honduras, Nicaragua, Santo Domingo, and Haiti. They made a point of demonstrating that they had the situation well in hand. General José Tomás Calderón sent a message to the captains of four ships anchored off Acajutla that the Communists "had been totally beaten and dispersed" and would be "entirely exterminated." He reported on 29 January that "already 4,800 of them have been liquidated." According to one account:

> Commander Brodeur went ashore to pay his respects to the General, and to "verify . . . in a general way" the report of 4,800 killings. On shore, he was enthusiastically embraced by General Calderón, invited to lunch in Sonsonate the next day, and to "witness a few executions." The commanding officers of the Canadian ships *Skeena* and *Vancouver* accompanied General Calderón and an aide to Sonsonate, and "given an exceedingly good lunch . . . they were shown five Indians who were about to be shot, but did not witness the actual execution as this was thought to be inadvisable." (McClintock 1985a, 116)

Calderón came to regret his announcement of the 4,800 "liquidated" Communists, as this received prominent and not entirely favorable treatment in the international press. He subsequently clarified that by "liquidated" he had meant "broken and dislocated" (Anderson 1971, 130). In view of other evidence, however, and his clear intent to dissuade the U.S. forces from landing, it is likely that he meant what he said the first time.

Anderson concludes that in committing the *matanza*, "Martínez may have been trying to pose before world opinion, especially that of the United States, as the champion of anticommunism" (1971, 134). U.S. attitudes toward

Martínez indeed shifted markedly following the *matanza*. Although the State Department continued until 1934 to hold that he could not be recognized, the tone of U.S. communications with his government changed, and the United States halted active measures to unseat him. The State Department sent the following message to U.S. Chargé William J. McCafferty: "You will of course make it clear that the Department as it has already stated is not (repeat not) motivated by any unfriendliness against General Martínez for whom it has great regard" (Grieb 1971, 165). McCafferty's communications began to reflect a new tone of moderation, referring regularly to the "efficiency" of the new government. Once Martínez was officially "elected" to office, the United States found a means of recognizing him.

His success in preventing U.S. intervention further reinforced Martínez' credentials with the Salvadoran civilian elite and contributed an additional dimension to subsequent right-wing political ideology. El Salvador had always enjoyed greater economic independence from the United States than its neighbors. With the *matanza*, El Salvador became one of the few countries in Central America and the Caribbean to survive a major internal upheaval without suffering U.S. military intervention. This independence became a point of nationalist pride and a source of friction between civilian rightists and the military when, in the 1980s, the Salvadoran military aligned itself closely with the United States at the expense of upper-class interests.

The Protection Racket

During the crisis of 1931–32, it was unclear whether the military or some reconstituted regime of the social elite would end up governing El Salvador. The political disunity of the upper classes, combined with the high level of popular mobilization, presented an opportunity for Martínez and the military to expand their political power. Yet both the Salvadoran upper classes and the U.S. government were skeptical about Martínez. The 1932 rebellion gave him the opportunity to establish his political legitimacy through mass murder of opposition peasants and workers. Neither domestic political forces nor the international community (aside from negative news coverage) provided any significant incentives for restraint. In fact, the risk of invasion by U.S. forces provided an incentive for a conspicuous demonstration of will and capacity to maintain order, regardless of the human cost. Clearly, the upper classes, with their fears of rebellion and their general interest in a frightened, unorganized, and low-cost workforce, favored harsh measures. To the extent that Martínez hoped to win their acceptance, he had good reason to deliver the kind of coercion that they would prefer.

But Martínez was not simply an instrument of landowners. He was in a position to manipulate elite perceptions of threat through the kinds of measures he chose to use in retaliation against popular unrest.[6] This enabled him to establish, on a national scale, a protection racket under which he offered to defend them from a threat that he either provoked or made to seem greater than it was. Moreover, he was able to extend this racket to influence U.S. policy makers, who shared the Salvadoran social elite's concerns about the purported Communist threat and were thus manipulated into recognizing Martínez despite official policy to the contrary.

Although Martínez was a personal *caudillo*, he represented the military as an institution. Thus his increased control over the state signified, from the beginning, an expanded and enduring role for the armed forces in the politics of the nation. "By dealing successfully, if brutally, with the question of disorder," Elam observes, "Hernández Martínez had acquired the right to advance the process of militarization" (1968, 45). According to Rubén Zamora, militarization meant not only "a hypertrophic development of the repressive apparatus of the state, but also a constant shift in our political life, lasting until the present. This act [the repression of 1932] has been the base upon which there has taken place the development of an increasingly autonomous state, which has not only grown quantitatively and qualitatively, but has also developed a greater capacity to act *politically*" (1976, 518, emphasis in original).

The durability of the events of 1932 as a basis for militarism resulted in part from the nature of the rebellion and the lessons that elites learned from it. As Jeffery Paige points out, "The fact that El Salvador's only experience with social reform and popular mobilization ended in insurrection led by sectarian followers of the Communist International profoundly influenced popular and elite attitudes toward reform and social change" (1994, 22). From the point of view of the elite, reformists had created political space for opposition, and the result was a Communist-led rebellion. Thus most wealthy Salvadorans learned from the events of 1931 and 1932 that reformism and organized opposition opened the door to revolution. The political implication of this was that the only way to prevent revolution was to deny any political space for either elite-led reformism or popular mobilization. The perceived need for political exclusion made the upper classes more willing to leave governing in the hands of the armed forces, reversing their tendency of the late 1920s toward greater participation in national political affairs. It also provided historical precedent that justified, in the eyes of the Salvadoran upper classes, a self-serving political dogma of resolute opposition to any socioeconomic reforms.

Over the next 50 years, the elite sometimes found that support for militarism contradicted their own opposition to reforms, particularly when military leaders sought to attract greater popular legitimacy or promote development models different from the *laissez faire* liberalism the social elite preferred. Working through allies within the military, the elite ended the Martínez regime, blocked political openings and economic reforms in the 1960s and 1970s, and contributed to a policy of mass murder by the armed forces in the late 1970s and early 1980s.

From Violent Rise to Nonviolent Fall: The Martínez Regime

Often characterized as little more than a reinstatement of "oligarchic" rule, the Martínez regime was actually a considerable departure from previous regimes in El Salvador, marked by elaboration and strengthening of the internal security apparatus, state intervention in the economy, an expanded administrative role for the armed forces, and personalism. The first three developments proved to be lasting; the personalism of Martínez' rule became his undoing. His struggle to remain in office catalyzed elite opposition, and his response to that opposition—populism and repression against the elite—directly undermined the basis for his rule, which was his ability and willingness to protect the privileged and suppress the rebellious poor.

Shortly after the _matanza,_ Martínez established new mechanisms of state control throughout the country, but with particular impact in rural areas. The most important of these was the requirement that all persons carry an identification booklet known as a _cedula de vecindad,_ a type of internal passport that enabled authorities to more closely track the travels and places of residence of rural citizens. These measures, combined with laws outlawing the Communist Party and prohibiting publication of all doctrines deemed "anarchic and contrary to public, social and economic order," helped to institutionalize the security state established initially through the terror of the _matanza_ (Gordon 1989, 66).

The essential role of the "protection racket" in legitimating the Martínez regime came to the surface whenever a serious challenge arose to his position. During the brief provisional presidency of Colonel Menéndez, which provided the formal discontinuity in power that allowed Martínez' "election" and recognition by the United States, the security forces miraculously uncovered a new "Communist conspiracy," strengthening the enthusiasm with which the Salvadoran elite and the United States welcomed back the "savior" (Parkman 1988, 151). As both elite and mass resistance to a fourth Martínez term began to grow in 1943, an opposition pamphlet "accused Martínez of pinning the 'Communist' label on the campesino uprising of 1932 and perpetrating the massacre to secure his own position, asserting that he was plotting another 'Communist revolt' for the same purpose" (Parkman 1988, 49). Even after Martínez' resignation in May 1944, student organizers of the civic strike that had brought him down caught members of Martínez' secret police attempting to provoke a group of peasants into looting stores in San Salvador, presumably to create a pretext for the dictator's return (Parkman 1988, 88).

When the protection racket was in full force, however, Martínez had an unprecedented freedom to maneuver in state economic policy. While the

Meléndez-Quiñónez governments had talked about state economic measures and carried out a few small experiments, Martínez acted boldly to protect the country's coffee industry, in the process not only violating the *laissez faire* norms of most of the country's elite but expropriating the assets of Salvadoran and foreign creditors. Shortly after taking office, Martínez decreed the Ley Moratoria, which suspended the payment of all domestic private debts, reduced the interest payments on them by 40 percent, and prevented further foreclosures of mortgages on land (Anderson 1971, 149). Given the depression conditions faced by many coffee producers, this measure, though obviously harmful to the bankers in the short run, preempted the foreclosure of hundreds of coffee properties, including many small to medium-sized farms, and thus prevented massive additional concentration of land. In 1934, Martínez established the Banco Central de Reserva (Central Reserve Bank) and took away the right of the private banks to issue their own paper money. In the same year, he established the Banco Hipotecario (Mortgage Bank), which was charged with providing production credits for commercial agriculture. Not surprisingly, these measures were greeted with caution and even opposition by members of the liberal economic elite because they expanded the economic role of the state. By the mid-1930s, however, their utility for the coffee economy as a whole was recognized, and Martínez won the "unqualified support" of the civilian elite (Elam 1968, 57). Even after the worst effects of the depression were past, Martínez continued to expand the role of the state: The new constitution of 1939 "for the first time gave the state the exclusive right to regulate the coining of money, mail, telegraph and telephone services, and radio broadcasting, and increased the number of enterprises that might be operated as state monopolies" (Parkman 1988, 21).

Several of Martínez' ventures, including the Banco Hipotecario, were partnerships of the state and the economic elite. The Companía Salvadoreña de Café (Salvadoran Coffee Company), established in 1942, attempted to stabilize prices and make production loans. In the late 1930s, the Banco Hipotecario branched out into marketing and warehousing activities for crops and handicrafts.

Martínez' interventions broke the dominance of the private banking sector in production financing. Moreover, the main civilian partners in the Banco Hipotecario were major coffee and cattle producers themselves, rather than financiers. The Asociación Cafetalera (Coffee Growers' Association) and the Asociación Ganadera (Cattle Producers' Association) between them owned 95 percent of the stock in the Banco Hipotecario (75 percent was held by the Asociación Cafetalera alone) (Parkman 1988, 37). In the process of establishing these quasi-statal financial institutions, Martínez intertwined state and private interests. While these banks served private interests and supported the key productive sectors of the economy, they also served the personal interests of state officials. The Banco Hipotecario, for instance, played a prominent role in mortgage lending to military officers (Gordon 1989, 72).

Guido Véjar (1980a) depicts the Martínez regime as an *expression* of the restored dominance of the coffee growers, but the sequence of events suggests that Martínez' policies made the growers' recovery and relative advance possible. The state under Martínez, in other words, exerted considerable initiative of its own. Martínez chose actions that were in the interest of, though often initially opposed by, the coffee growers. Combined with the protection he offered, his policies transformed the growers into key supporters of his government for almost a decade.

Martínez was similarly assertive in dealing with foreign creditors. In 1932, he defaulted on El Salvador's obligations to U.S. creditors under the 1922 loan agreement, canceled numerous contracts with U.S. corporations, and nationalized the utility companies, many of which were foreign-owned (Astilla Carmelo 1976, 61–62; Wilson 1970, 256). His confrontation of U.S. creditors proved to be well-timed: the new Roosevelt administration preferred to avoid unseemly interventions and therefore did little more than provide its good offices to help the New York bankers renegotiate payment schedules for bondholders. A first agreement on rescheduling (struck in July 1932) provided for El Salvador to pay between 15 and 20 percent of customs revenue, rather than the 70 to 100 percent of the original agreement. Martínez later suspended even this reduced rate of payment, and negotiated a new agreement in May 1933 that lasted until 1935. One more suspension of payments (1936) achieved a still lower interest rate (Astilla Carmelo 1976, 116–18).

Aside from the fun of testing U.S. resolve, brinkmanship toward U.S. creditors gave Martínez considerably more public revenue to work with, and he devoted much of it to programs for the poor. In 1932 he created the Fondo de Mejoramiento Social (Social Betterment Fund) and an agency to administer it, the Junta de Defensa Social (Social Defense Board). Mejoramiento Social was used to transfer a limited amount of land to landless peasants: "Great estates were turned into Haciendas Nacionales and divided up. Roads were run between the small parcels, so that they could not be reunited" (Anderson 1971, 150). Relatively few people (less than 2 percent of the peasantry) benefited from the reforms, and the new farms were not economically successful. Large-scale growers complained about the deterioration of formerly productive plantations, but the reforms went largely unchallenged, especially in comparison with the growers' strenuous reaction in 1976 when President Arturo Armando Molina attempted smaller-scale land reform. In the mid-1930s, coffee producers were still beholden to Martínez for the 1932 crackdown and for economic policies that were helping them to weather the depression. They were therefore unwilling to challenge him, even when his social policies cut directly against elite ownership of land.

This willingness to give Martínez the benefit of the doubt disappeared during the latter part of his period in office. When he sought a third term as president in 1939, many of his cabinet officials resigned.[7] All were below the level of minister, but they were the highest-ranking *civilians* in the government, since military officers controlled most ministries. The civilians had been an important source of technical and administrative competence for Martínez' regime, and their participation in his government had signaled the support of the economic elite. Their departure left Martínez surrounded by military advisers, incompetent civilians, and yes men, and vulnerable to the sort of administrative collapse that had undermined his predecessor, Araujo.

The main reason for the resignations was constitutional. As Parkman puts it, "Alternation in office was one principle of the Constitution of 1886 that had been consistently honored in practice, and Martínez' assault on it threatened to do away with "the last vestiges" of El Salvador's liberal institutions and traditions" (1988, 30).[8] In addition, Martínez' economic nationalism and bias toward the coffee producers was impeding the development of new industries, particularly cotton. In response to increased international demand during World War II, entrepreneurs had begun growing cotton along the coastal littoral—with considerable success, except that import restrictions made it difficult to obtain the machinery and chemicals needed for more efficient production. Cotton growers began to organize among the professional staff of the Banco Hipotecario and played an important role in galvanizing opposition to Martínez (Gordon 1989, 75).

As elite support dried up, Martínez turned increasingly to a popular base. Beginning in 1942, he tolerated rudimentary forms of labor organizing, and in 1943 tried to make the cause of labor and land reform his own, harking back to the themes of his 1931 campaign for the presidency. "His speeches to the weekly Pro-Patria assemblies in early 1943 attacked the concentration of wealth in the hands of the few, while expounding on the virtues of cooperatives and Mejoramiento Social's land distribution program" (Parkman 1988, 35). This strategy of seeking broad popular support as elite support dried up was parallel to the strategies used by the Meléndez-Quiñónez and Romero Bosque governments before him, as well as the military governments of the 1960s and 1970s. Martínez' flirtations with pro-labor politics were not entirely successful: the concrete benefits were meager, and workers remembered the events of 1932. His efforts to find popular support, however, did galvanize elite opposition. Members of the upper class became concerned that Martínez might proceed with social security legislation, a minimum wage, and, worst of all, reforms to the tax system that might make it effective in collecting revenues from the rich. They were also concerned that Martínez' initiative to create industries under the umbrella of Mejoramiento Social might generate unwanted competition for existing firms (Parkman 1988, 35–36).

These fears were well founded in the sense that Martínez did move aggressively to wrest more money and more political power from the agrarian elite. In 1943 he fixed cotton and coffee prices, raised taxes on cotton and coffee, and passed laws that allowed the state to interfere in the management of the cattle and coffee associations. Since these associations controlled the Banco Hipotecario, controlling them would allow Martínez to take over the bank and its resources, even though the bank's funds had originally come from largely private sources. Opponents suspected that he intended to make the bank a patronage machine for his Pro-Patria Party.

To understand the nature of the Martínez regime, it is crucial to follow the sequence of its unraveling. The economic elite's initial objections to Martínez did not stem from his policies, but from a perception that he had worn out his legitimacy by trying to perpetuate his own power. Particularly within the middle classes, opposition stemmed mainly from his repressiveness and flouting of even minimal standards of constitutionality. U.S. Vice Consul H. Gardner Ainsworth noted that the middle classes had "almost no direct economic grievances against the government" (quoted in Parkman 1988, 55). Martínez had inserted an economic dimension into his conflict with the elites by directly assaulting their core interests. He tried to rally the military to him with populist talk, telling officers that the "capitalists were against him" and that "all his plans for social betterment and economic improvement—including higher pay for the Army—[were] being blocked by the selfish and uncooperative attitude of the wealthy class" (quoted in Parkman 1988, 52). At the same time, he attempted to shore up the protection racket by reporting to the oligarchy that he had discovered a major Communist conspiracy to exploit any openly contested elections. His ability to pose as a protector, however, clashed with his need to control elite-led political opposition. He took to arresting members of the elite, and by 11 January some 40 were in custody (Parkman 1988, 53).

On 25 January 1944, the Constituent Assembly revised the Constitution to give itself the power to elect the president, and proceeded to do so. This had been expected. What was not anticipated was a series of laws that allowed Martínez to establish a monopoly of any "services that may be beneficial to the community and which the laws may determine" (Parkman 1988, 54). These laws basically gave Martínez the power to nationalize or socialize any aspect of the economy, and they galvanized opposition to Martínez among the upper classes. U.S. Vice Consul Overton Ellis polled the leading 24 families in the country and found that 20 of them were anti-Martínez, 2 supported him, and 2 abstained from expressing an opinion (Parkman 1988, 57).

The core of opposition to Martínez was an organization called Salvadoran Democratic Action, created in 1941 by many of the officials who had resigned from Martínez' government. Forced underground after only two public rallies, it became "the general staff of a conspiracy to frustrate Martínez' fourth-term aspirations" (Parkman 1988, 42). The moving spirit of the conspiracy was a coffee grower named Agustín Alfaro Morán, former auditor general in Martínez' government, founder of the Companía Salvadoreña de Café, and president of the Asociación Cafetalera. Alfaro Morán clearly represented the sentiments of the coffee producers: these elites were flirting with the idea of governing the country.

The upper-class conspirators had middle-class allies, particularly among professionals, whose political ideas and expectations had been heavily influenced by Allied wartime propaganda about democracy and self-determination. A charismatic physician named Arturo Romero emerged as a champion of reform and attracted additional middle- and even lower-class support. He was known, among other things, for his generosity in treating indigent patients. The movement as a whole, however, depended on upper-class bankers, merchants, and the coffee elite for leadership and financial support. U.S. consular official Overton Ellis reported that the Alvarez family, which owned the world's largest coffee mill, was a key supporter, as was the most prominent citizen in Santa Ana, Francisco Alfaro (Parkman 1988, 44).

Meanwhile, a parallel conspiracy developed within the military. Army officers' reasons to oppose Martínez had little to do with his conflicts with the upper classes. The main grievance stemmed from his favoritism toward the security forces—the National Guard and National Police—over the regular army. The security forces had always received much better pay, but after 1937 Martínez allocated them a growing percentage of the budget, and they received new weapons. Promotions too tended to favor officers in the security forces (McClintock 1985a, 127–28).[9] Within the army, promotions were based not on merit, but rather on personal loyalty to the dictator. During the 1940s, Martínez replaced commanders of internally strategic posts with officers who had risen up through the ranks, removing those who had been trained in the academy or abroad. His personal secret police constantly surveilled officers, and he created a civilian militia using members of his Pro-Patria Party, a move that violated the military's monopoly on armed force. These grievances cut across the ranks (Elam 1968, 108–9), but most of the conspirators were younger, academy-trained regular army officers. A high proportion were lieutenants; most were in their twenties, Parkman reports. One informant told her that 70 to 80 percent of the army supported the revolt (1988, 58).

The civilian and military committees joined forces in early 1944, and on 2 April they struck while Martínez was out of the capital. Two army brigades in San Salvador and the Second Brigade in Santa Ana rebelled. However, the First Artillery barracks (called El Zapote), the National Police, and the National Guard held out against the rebels, who prematurely announced over the national airwaves both their anticipated victory and which units had refused to join the revolt. Hearing on the radio that the security forces' barracks had held,

Martínez managed to work his way, apparently without resistance, to the National Police headquarters. The rebels were soon defeated, with considerable casualties. En route from Santa Ana to the capital, a convoy of army troops (and probably armed civilians) were ambushed by the security forces, who killed 53 and wounded 134 (McClintock 1985a, 130; Parkman 1988, 60).

The execution of 10 alleged conspirators chilled many Salvadorans and led ultimately to Martínez' downfall. Twenty other officers were sentenced to death in absentia, along with nine civilians from the Democratic Action committee.[10] Dr. Romero was captured, wounded, and taken to a hospital in San Salvador, where he remained under a death sentence. Popular revulsion against the sentences provided Martínez' elite opponents with the opportunity they had been looking for. Democratic Action called a general strike that was so complete that the dictator left office one week after the strike began.

Though clearly a popular action, the unprecedented effectiveness of the *huelga de brazos caídos* ("strike of fallen arms") depended in large part on support from the elite. The strike was led by students from the university, most of them from elite or middle-class families, with organizational and financial assistance from businesses, banks, and wealthy citizens. Individual businesses and families contributed as much as 5,000 colones (U.S. $2,500). Business owners and bankers paid workers, taxi drivers, and bus drivers to cooperate and provided some with safe houses to protect them from reprisals during the strike.

Organizers attempted to avoid large demonstrations, which might give Martínez a pretext to use violence. In the end, however, a number of large demonstrations took place, and Martínez showed restraint. His regime, if not the state itself, was in grave danger; yet despite his imprisonments and executions, he did not use widespread violence as he had in 1932.

The explanation for his passivity is that mass killing could no longer serve to legitimate his government before the economic elite. They were, after all, paying people to participate in the strike. Repressing demonstrators would not have made them feel better protected; moreover, since they were playing an important role in mobilizing popular opposition, there was, at least for the moment, relatively little risk that the movement would go beyond the immediate goal of ousting Martínez. The dictator was therefore no longer in a position to manipulate the perception of threat; on the contrary, his increased use of repression against members of the elite in the months leading up to the strike, including the police shooting of a youth from a wealthy family, had made Martínez himself a threat. When secret police agents failed to provoke the looting that might justify a crackdown, Martínez found that he had run out of leverage. His only choices were to violently attack the social elite or to leave office. He chose to go.

1944–1948: The Transition to Institutional Rule

Before he left the country in 1944, Martínez managed to impose an officer of unswerving personal loyalty, General Andrés I. Menéndez, as his successor. Surprisingly, instead of attempting to establish *martinismo sin Martínez*, Menéndez announced his intention to hold free elections and even permitted the civilian liberals who had mobilized against Martínez to reorganize Democratic Action into a new political party, the Democratic Union Party (PUD). He also tolerated the formation of a National Workers' Union (UNT), which quickly enrolled 50,000 members. Surviving cadres of the clandestine Communist Party were the top and mid-level leadership (Elam 1968, 76; Gordon 1989, 75).

The electoral campaign got under way during June and July 1944. The PUD quickly established an overwhelming popular advantage, in part because its presidential candidate, Arturo Romero, was widely viewed as a hero of the confrontation with Martínez. Opposing the PUD was a reincarnation of the old *Martinista* party, Pro-Patria, renamed the Unification Social Democratic Party (PUSD), whose candidate was the hardline General Salvador Castañeda Castro. PUSD had the support of sectors of the armed forces that were hostile toward Romero.

While the popular PUD and the military's PUSD campaigned against each other, the economic elite of the country was in political disarray. Some planters and members of the financial elite belonged to the PUD; others supported the military. Two splinter parties, the Salvadoran Agrarian Party and the Social Republican Front, had elite support. Both put forward candidates who were divisive and transparently self-serving, and garnered little support. The relatively low quality of the economic elite's electoral effort and candidates reflects the fact that, despite their distaste for Martínez, they had grown accustomed to working through the military rather than competing directly for political power. They lacked the political will to build a unified party and compete against the more radical agenda of the PUD. This failure made a democratic outcome unlikely and a return to military intervention almost inevitable.

From June through October, popular mobilization shaped the political campaign. Mass demonstrations forced the Assembly to reverse a decision to make an old-guard *Martinista* the first designate of interim President Menéndez. The assembly then renounced Martínez' 1939 constitution and reinstated that of 1886, which provided greater confidence in future elections. Meanwhile, whatever commitment may have existed within the officer corps to observe the results of the coming election quickly eroded. Arturo Romero's PUD joined forces with members of Democratic Action and the UNT labor federation to form the United Democratic Front (FUD), creating in the process a mass-based political party in which the PCS was known to have considerable influence (Gordon 1989, 75–76). The FUD laid out an ambitious agenda, including a "complete economic and social overhaul of the country" (Elam 1968, 82). The liberal press in San Salvador joined in attacking the military as antidemocratic, corrupt, and abusive. Faced with the prospect of handing over government to a group of civilians who "had no record of respect or sympathy for the entire concept of armed institutions" (Elam 1968, 93), the divided military began to reunify in opposition to the elections and the civilian liberals, leading to attacks on Romero and his followers, searches, insults, arrests, and occasional shootings throughout the country (79). The various factions of the social elite did not trouble themselves to reunify: they stood back and let the military deal with the situation.

Military opposition to the electoral process eventually took the form of a bloodless coup d'état against Menéndez, led by the director of the police, Colonel Osmín Aguirre y Salinas. Aguirre had been the director of police in the early years of the Martínez administration and had been one of the principal architects of the *matanza*. Not surprisingly, he justified his coup in the language of the protection racket: "The seriousness of the moment in which I have acted has not escaped me; a man aware of his responsibilities. Anarchical ferment has kept the country in constant peril during the last few days, seriously threatening the institutional life of the Republic. The Salvadoran family has been divided by a flood of passion and we men of conscience could not help but be alarmed by the proximity of chaos" (quoted in Elam 1968, 97).

Aguirre delivered the protection expected of him. The evening of the coup, leaders of the PUD, Democratic Action, and the UNT were arrested and slated for deportation. In the next week, hundreds of liberal opponents were jailed. The university was closed down by its own adminstrators; and the two main liberal newspapers in the country also succumbed to pressure to close.

Aguirre appears to have been opposed by the commercial and financial sectors of the elite. As businesses and banks throughout the country closed following the coup, the military took over and informed employees that they would be dismissed if they did not show up for work (Elam 1968, 99). Using such means, Aguirre headed off the kind of general strike that brought down Martínez.

Meanwhile, FUD leaders who had been deported to Guatemala formed a government in exile and received international recognition. An invasion force of some 2,000 FUD militants, with some support from junior and mid-ranking army officers included Oscar Osorio, who was to become president in 1950. Like the Communist insurrection of 1932, the force was "untrained and undisciplined," and depended on the success of a series of planned uprisings in army barracks (Gordon 1989, 76). When support failed to materialize from within the army, the invasion force was quickly overwhelmed by Aguirre's forces. Four hundred and fifty of the rebels were killed, as were 150 government soldiers (Elam 1968, 103). Though demonstrations still occurred, the defeat of the FUD invasion removed the last serious opposition to the military. The high command could once again claim to have saved the country from communism and chaos.

On 14 January 1945, military rule was confirmed with the essentially uncontested election of General Salvador Castañeda Castro as president. Despite efforts to sideline Aguirre and other factional competitors within the military, Castañeda did not succeed in reestablishing a personalistic regime comparable to that of Martínez. In fact, his policies created the conditions for his removal only three years later by a movement of "progressive" officers who sought to renovate military rule, carry out substantial reforms, and govern on an institutional, not personalistic, basis.

The threat posed by the PUD and FUD during 1944 had caused the military to pull together across generations, professional backgrounds, and ideologies. The brutality and conservatism of the Castañeda government, however, and the absence of an immediate threat to the military as an institution, weakened once again the glue that had temporarily held the various factions together. With the basic principle of military governance firmly established, junior and middle-ranking army officers with internal, institutional grievances and a more populist socioeconomic philosophy decided to put the *Martinista* old guard out to pasture.

Their project was facilitated by the fact that, despite his repressiveness toward the civilian community, Castañeda did not attempt to build a system of personal control within the military as had Martínez. He allowed, in effect, a political *apertura* within the military institution. He also enhanced the relative power of the regular army by bringing the National Police under the control of the Defense Ministry, rather than the Ministry of Interior (Elam 1968, 123–24). Castañeda committed the error of simultaneously providing junior officers with an easier context within which to organize and giving them reasons to act against him. He decreed a new law that regulated the number of officers at each rank; its impact was strongly in favor of existing senior officers, leading to the expectation that many junior officers would be dismissed. He then proceeded to send reformist junior officers out of the country for training.

In December 1948 Castañeda took extraconstitutional steps to prolong his term by two years, triggering a coup against him organized by a group of army majors. Once in control, the *golpistas* held a meeting of the entire officer corps in which three officers and two civilians were chosen for a Revolutionary Governing Council. The vote was held without regard to rank, with each officer having an equal vote, which favored the more numerous junior officers. The new council forced the retirement of all officers above the rank of lieutenant colonel, effectively eliminating all of the officers with close ties to Martínez. They then appointed a cabinet made up of middle-class civilian professionals. The council promptly abrogated all inconvenient constitutional provisions but promised to hold elections for a Constituent Assembly and a new government in 1950.

The "Revolution of 1948" sought to establish a new model of military rule based on regularly held elections, expanded social services, and increased state intervention in the economy, particularly in the form of investment and support for industrialization. By expanding state intervention, they hoped to shift productive resources out of agriculture into industry and commerce, reducing over time the economic and political preeminence of the agrarian elite and softening the acute distributional inequities in Salvadoran society. By involving the entire officer corps in decisions, they sought to ensure that the role of the military in politics would be an institutional commitment, rather than the project of a single individual such as Martínez. Yet during the 30 years of institutional military rule inaugurated in 1948, the military never escaped the narrow confines of the protection racket he had established. Like Martínez, post-1948 military presidents failed to build a genuine base of mass political support. What independence they did demonstrate on political or socioeconomic issues triggered elite opposition, usually in the form of conspiracy with conservative factions of the armed forces. Military presidents repeatedly found that staying in office required them to retreat from major reforms and demonstrate their usefulness through repression. The resulting model of rule, despite its reformist and corporatist pretensions, ultimately collapsed into what Enrique Baloyra (1982) has called "reactionary despotism," setting the stage for revolutionary war.

THREE

THE FAILURE OF
INSTITUTIONAL MILITARY RULE

With the Revolution of 1948, the Salvadoran military put itself forward as the one institution capable of distinguishing the national interest from the particular interests defended by the liberalism of the nineteenth and early twentieth centuries. In order to carry out its national development project, the military set itself apart both from strict accountability to the population (though elections would be held and popular policies enacted) and from the upper classes (though they would be allowed representation in areas of the state that regulated economic activity). The military, as the institutional heart of the state, intended to balance the conflicting demands in Salvadoran society; it would neither turn the state over to a civilian mass public that had proven itself prone to leftism, nor act merely as an instrument of an oligarchy whose selfish pursuit of private interests would impede national development, stability, and the ability to resist communism.

This ambitious program set the stage for disaster in El Salvador. The military proved ill-suited as an institution to implement the corporatist project that the Revolution of 1948 proposed. Successful corporatist politics generally depends upon an implicit agreement by poor and middle-class sectors to channel their political demands exclusively through official parties, unions, and associations, with the expectation that the state will respond effectively to some of those demands (Schmitter 1974). For their part, strategic sectors of the upper classes must be willing to defer to the state out of a recognition that their long-term collective interests, if not their short-term particular interests, are best served by an autonomous state.

Between 1948 and 1976 the Salvadoran military state failed on all of these dimensions. It proved unable to deliver enough socioeconomic benefits to maintain its legitimacy in the eyes of the country's poor majority. Until the 1960s, it failed to organize its own rural base of support, depending on conservative agrarian elites to deliver rural votes. When the military did begin to organize that base (initially the Democratic Nationalist Organization, ORDEN), it engaged more in intelligence gathering and repression than in political action. At the local level ORDEN tended to serve agrarian elites and was organized and maintained by the most conservative sectors within the military. Though it eventually involved tens of thousands of members, it never served as an effective means for channeling demands to the government and more often gave local elites an instrument to repress labor activists. Those discontented with rural conditions had to look elsewhere for political expression. In urban areas, the military's official party failed to consistently incorporate middle sectors, intellectuals, and liberal politicians, while official labor unions lost ground to illegal, more militant organizations that were better able to secure benefits for their members.

Lacking both the organizational structures and the ability to deliver material benefits, the military adopted a very inconsistent posture toward political competition, sometimes encouraging it to gain greater legitimacy for its own electoral victories, sometimes resorting to blatant manipulation of the electoral system, and, in later years, overt fraud. This combination contributed to opponents' alienation and, eventually, their shift toward armed opposition.

The political and development strategies of the military during this period were not the work of a rational unified state responding to its environment, but rather reflect the conflicting impulses within the military, influenced by a variety of external forces. Repeated political crises generated divergent tendencies, as competing groups of civilian elites sought supporters within the military and as officers themselves sought a workable formula. The result was factional strife. Some officers wanted the institution to abandon its role in government and permit a genuine democratization process. Others wanted the military to remain in power but deepen its commitment to socioeconomic reform. A third current favored a Martínez-style crackdown. Reformist officers carried out coups in 1960 and 1972 that sought to transfer power to civilians. Both were defeated by more conservative countermovements, and though the military appeared to redouble its commitment to delivering material benefits to the population in the wake of each of these coups, it ultimately failed to earn popular legitimacy. The final chapter in this saga was the military government's attempt to carry out a land reform in 1976. Private sector opposition forced the military to back down, leaving no alternative but repression. Unwilling or unable to chart a course that conflicted with the core interests of agrarian elites, the military effectively shifted the costs for maintaining military rule onto the population, preferring, in the end, to kill large numbers of its own citizens rather than bear the costs involved in challenging the more conservative faction of the oligarchy.

The reasons for the military's failure lie in institutional characteristics of the armed forces, their political strategy, and their political and financial relationship with economic elites. Basic institutional problems complicated the creation of a more responsive and sustainable form of military government. First, the high command placed a high priority on misappropriating money. During the period from 1948 through 1976, the military steadily expanded the state sector and colonized new agencies with its officers, creating magnificent opportunities for profiteering by the upper ranks. These new sources of profit combined with the more traditional practices of renting out soldiers as private security guards or day laborers, for which unit commanders received commissions. As it colonized ever more lucrative posts within the state, the military turned to the *tanda* system of career advancement and distribution of spoils, in which officers from each military academy class (*promoción* or *tanda*) rise together through the ranks, regardless of individual performance. Combined with the nonrenewable six-year presidential term, this system provided each *tanda* with a period of access to lucrative top command positions. Though probably more stable than the personalism of the Martínez era, this system created some unfortunate incentives: since state policy was made primarily by top officials enjoying their brief time at the trough, they tended to adopt short-term political strategies rather than the bolder initiatives needed to create a sustainable corporatist system. Since presidents generally chose their successors, officers from the *tandas* next in line had reasons not to advocate more radical policies, even when it was clear that the long-term viability of military rule required them. Conversely, senior *tandas* who were likely to be forced into retirement during the next presidential succession provided fertile ground for conservative conspirators seeking to catalyze military coups or interfere in the selection of the official presidential candidate.

The result of this system of spoils was a consistent failure to take the political initiatives and risks needed to establish a workable single-party system managed by the military. This problem was compounded by the factionalism of the military and its openness to conflicting civilian influences. Top officers were "hardly immune from the various forms of suasion available to the wealthy" (Webre 1979, 17). Presidents who were too reformist would lose the support of agrarian elites and be challenged by more conservative elements within the military. At the same time, junior army officers, who were mostly of lower- and lower-middle-class origins themselves and not yet benefiting from the "suasion" of the wealthy, tended to favor policies that would benefit the poor majorities and harbored a certain hostility toward landed elites. Junior officers were responsive to overtures from liberal civilians calling for an end to military rule, corruption, and repression. Hardline presidents risked being overthrown by their younger, more reformist subordinates.

As a result, all of the military presidents from 1948 to 1977 maintained an uncomfortable compromise between reform and repression, and between political openness and exclusion, responding, as necessary, to the most imminent threat to their tenure. Though presidents were vulnerable to pressures from hardliners and reformists, neither of these tendencies could sustain power: the hardliners lacked any basis for popular legitimacy, and the reformists were generally young, politically inexperienced, and unable to convince a majority of officers either to join with politically mobilized civilians or forgo the antic-ipated privileges associated with continued military rule. The resulting system was highly profitable for its top echelons but fundamentally unstable in the long run and prone to considerable violence along the way.

The persistence of practices and ideology that had become institutionalized under the Martínez protection racket impeded more reformist or democratic strategies. These views and practices were embedded in the agencies of the military dedicated most directly to internal security—the National Guard, the Treasury Police, the National Police, and domestic intelligence networks de-veloped during the 1960s and 1970s. These forces tended to maintain close mercenary relationships with landowners and business elites and shared with them an intense, self-serving anticommunism. Their members also enjoyed supplemental pay and other perquisites as a reward for defending upper-class interests from union organizers and other menaces. The ties were most inti-mate at the local level, but high-ranking officers within the security forces con-sistently aligned themselves with the most conservative civilian interests at the national level, providing reactionary agrarian elites with a reliable source of conspiratorial allies within the armed forces. Thus, while the military high command sometimes tried to distance itself from civilian elite interests, por-tions of the military remained heavily invested in the protection racket. For the security and domestic intelligence forces, major reforms designed to re-solve social conflicts were not attractive.

The persistence of these institutions of the old system took on greater im-portance because they played such a central role in organizing what should have been corporate structures to support the project of 1948 in rural areas. The National Guard and later the National Special Services Agency (ANSESAL) played an instrumental role in organizing and maintaining ORDEN, corrupt-ing whatever incorporative function ORDEN might have had.

As Baloyra points out, by justifying its role in politics on the basis of anticom-munism, the military handed private sector elites an ideological advantage in their dealings with the military itself: "The military's efforts to defend its reforms on the basis of anti-Communism only made it and its reformism more vulnera-ble to attack by the oligarchy, which continued to monopolize the proper vo-cabulary. Thus military reformism could always be castigated as hasteful, dem-agogic, and dangerous and injurious . . . to some basic pillars of Salvadoran society, such as the right of property and the free enterprise system" (1982, 21). This ideological trump card was to prove an especially important factor in the instability of reformist movements within the military, who struggled with the in-herent conflict between their perception that reforms were necessary and their inability to shake off the concern that reforms (or electoral competition) could give rise to the communism that was their institution's most basic enemy.

The porosity of the military to civilian elite influence might have been less harmful to a corporatist project if a significant portion of the civilian elite had been willing to support reforms affecting the agrarian sector. The military's economic development policies favored banking, commercial, and industrial interests in order to help create a new industrial/commercial elite that would be politically autonomous from agrarian interests. Support from urban business elites had been crucial to corporatist experiments elsewhere in Latin America. Although the military's statist initiatives did promote industrial development, much of the investment in this sector represented diversification on the part of existing agro-export elites, which strengthened their economic base without changing their core interests or political values (Gordon 1989, 57–60). Commercial and industrial interests would have benefited from land reform or legalization of rural collective bargaining, either of which would have placed more buying power in the hands of a broader cross-section of society. Portions of the commercial and industrial sectors remained under the control of families whose primary economic interests were in agriculture, while those families which specialized exclusively in the more modern sector remained far weaker economically. The few members of the urban business elite who dared advocate agrarian reform suffered threats and intimidation by the agrarian elite and their allies in the security forces, and therefore never provided a significant base of support for reformist policies by the military.

Thus military governments frequently found themselves under pressure from the landed elites to use greater violence to ensure control over land and labor. Just as Martínez had established his legitimacy with elites by means of the *matanza* and periodically reinforced his position through conspicuous "protection" of elite interests, subsequent military governments found repression to be a crucial element of their formula for governing. Anticommunism provided the rationale for government actions ranging from reforms to electoral exclusion to mass murder. Even governments that began with either economic reforms or political opening found they needed to use conspicuous repression to appease disgruntled civilian elites.

The impact of the elites' opposition to reform was compounded by fact that their main avenue of political expression was to conspire with conservative elements of the armed forces. Since right-wing challenges usually took the form of intrigue involving hardliners in the security forces, military leaders found it expedient to give these forces *carte blanche* to carry out crackdowns, thereby defusing tensions within the military and lessening the likelihood of a coup.

The First Phase: 1948–1960

When Oscar Osorio took office in 1950, his administration began what appeared at the outset an unprecedented process of replacing economic liberalism with statism. The Constitution of 1950 provided the state with powers to intervene in the economy to "ensure all inhabitants of the country human dignity." It also restricted economic liberty "where it should conflict with the social interest." Even the right of private property, virtually a religious icon to the agrarian elite, was constitutionally protected only as long as the property served "social functions" (Gordon 1989, 78). The state asserted powers to regulate work days and minimum salaries as well as labor relations. After imposing higher taxes on export earnings, the government established a variety of programs designed to promote industry and reduce the cost of urban living through housing programs, public health (Seguridad Social), and food subsidies (Gordon 1989, 79). Good coffee harvests and prices augmented state revenues for these projects. Perhaps the greatest emphasis of state investment policy, however, was in infrastructure development, including ports, hydroelectric projects, and roads.

The government combined these developmentalist and populist measures with some preliminary steps toward corporatism. It created an official, highly regulated sector of organized labor, confined to urban industries, and an official party, the Revolutionary Party of Democratic Unification (PRUD), which sought the kind of vertical integration of different classes and interest groups characteristic of the Institutional Revolutionary Party (PRI) of Mexico, where Osorio had lived for four years following his support of the ill-fated PUD/UNT invasion from Guatemala in 1944.

The PRUD failed to achieve either the revolutionary legitimacy or the rural organizational structure that strengthened the Mexican Party, however. It never developed a permanent party structure, essentially disappearing between elections and leaving citizens with no local party mechanisms through which to channel their political views and demands. Many of the PRUD's core organizers had been associated with Martínez' Pro-Patria party and continued to be ineffectual in building a genuine mass political following. What legitimacy the PRUD initially enjoyed was quickly squandered, as Osorio's government earned a reputation for corruption and unresponsiveness to popular demands despite its ostensibly reformist posture. In a remarkable gesture of political hubris, Osorio manipulated the Central Electoral Council (CCE) to ensure that there was effectively no competition in the 1952 elections: from 1952 until its dismantlement in 1961, the PRUD controlled all seats in the legislature, excluding the opposition Renovating Action Party (PAR), which had originated in the movement against Martínez in 1944 and had commanded a respectable 43 percent of the vote in the 1950 presidential race (Baloyra 1982, 38; Webre 1979, 18). In 1952 Osorio cracked down on the left, jailing hundreds and exiling most of the known leaders of the underground Communist Party (PCS). Simultaneously, Osorio pointed to the communist threat in neighboring Guatemala and argued that moderate reforms were necessary to avoid widespread popular discontent. This argument persuaded the social elites to tolerate the PRUD's taxation and developmentalist measures, and even to go along with policies permitting urban labor organizing (Elam 1968, 147).

As early as the mid-1950s, therefore, a basic dilemma for the Revolution of 1948 had become evident. The military could not maintain broad popular support without providing socioeconomic benefits, and it could not deliver these without jeopardizing its support among elites, unless they were carefully justified on anticommunist grounds and accompanied by measures demonstrating the government's commitment to its protective role. Yet such crackdowns further eroded popular support, undermining the military's hopes of establishing an autonomous base of incorporated political support.

By the end of his term, Osorio was discredited among both the elite and the general population, having satisfied the expectations of neither. The next president, Colonel José María Lemus, continued the same uncomfortable balancing act. He promptly installed prominent lawyers affiliated with the agrarian elite as his ministers of exterior relations, justice, economy, interior, and labor (Castro Morán 1989, 208–10). Yet the need for broader political legitimacy moved Lemus to counterbalance the upper-class orientation of his cabinet with a political opening that allowed exiles to return and permitted freer labor organizing. As with past openings, popular organizations quickly filled the available space. Communists exiled by Osorio returned and resumed their activities. The General Federation of Salvadoran Workers (CGTS), coordinated by the PCS, emerged as the leading and most militant labor organization in the country. Hardships brought on by low coffee prices in 1957 and 1958, combined with rising prices for staples, fueled large demonstrations (Gordon 1989, 83). The Cuban revolution in 1959 prompted even greater militancy as movements of the left began to contemplate the possibility of revolution, though at this point there were no preparations for armed struggle.

Unfortunately, Lemus had exhausted the range of reforms that could be carried out without a major confrontation with upper-class interests. He had already damaged his relations with the coffee growers by intervening in the coffee market in 1958 and 1959, when he forced producers to reduce their output in an effort to shore up falling prices. Unwilling to incur the wrath of the economic elite by going further in the reformist direction, Lemus cracked down, ordering troops to fire on demonstrations and arresting hundreds.

Rather than cowing the opposition, Lemus' repression catalyzed a broader mobilization. Middle-class groups, students, and Communists formed the April and May Revolutionary Party (PRAM), whose name recalled the months of rebellion against Martínez. Osorio, who had continued to be active within the PRUD, broke with Lemus and formed a splinter he called the Authentic PRUD. Subsequently, a new movement called the National Civic Orientation Front (FNOC) brought labor, civic groups, the old PAR, and the PRAM together in a broad opposition front.

This intense political confrontation created deep divisions within the military. On 26 October 1960, a reformist movement supported by junior officers, Osorio, and the FNOC overthrew Lemus in a bloodless coup. The *golpistas* and their civilian co-conspirators chose three civilians from the National University with connections to FNOC to serve on the junta, along with two colonels and one major. The combined leadership evoked a supportive demonstration of more than eighty thousand people (McClintock 1985a, 136), but it frightened the civilian right and significant portions of the officer corps, even officers of relatively moderate views. The successful *golpistas* had to go from barracks to barracks, explaining to their colleagues the reasons for the coup and their plans for reestablishing constitutional government. The questions raised during these meetings showed that many officers wanted reassurance "that military supremacy in national matters would continue" (Elam 1968, 157).

The new government was vulnerable to charges that it was opening the door to communism. The three civilians on the junta were linked with organizations in which Communists had a considerable presence and had personal contacts with Communists active in the National University.[1] One of them, Fabio Castillo, had worked with PCS leaders in the 1944 movement against Martínez (Harnecker 1993, 48). U.S. embassy cables from the period, perhaps affected by the high-level Communist influence in the Arbenz government in Guatemala, referred to the new junta as "a triumph of 'infiltration' by subversive forces into the highest levels of government. Under their direction, 'a Castro/Communist takeover . . . loomed large'" (McClintock 1985a, 200). The United States refused to recognize the junta, reducing support for the junta within the military. In the wake of the Cuban revolution, the Salvadoran officer corps anticipated that they might need some help in dealing with leftist elements. The popular organizations that had continued to grow during Lemus' administration, despite repression, now flourished under the more lenient policies of the 1960 junta. Radical labor and political leaders exiled by previous governments returned. The junta's ties with mass organizations of the left, and its stated intention to hold open civilian elections, alarmed the more conservative sectors of the military, to say nothing of the upper classes.

The Second Phase: 1961–1972

On 25 January 1961, the reformist junta fell in a countercoup led by a group of middle- and upper-ranking officers. In response, a crowd marched to one of the barracks still holding out in support of the junta and asked for weapons. When the officers declined, the crowd marched across town to the barracks where the counter-coup was being coordinated, planning to demonstrate their opposition. En route, the crowd was fired upon (Harnecker 1993, 26). When supporters of the junta threatened a general strike, leaders of the counter-coup called out National Police and National Guard units to disperse the crowds, and roughly a hundred people were killed by gunfire. Former members of the junta were arrested and exiled. As in 1948, an assembly of the officer corps met to elect the post-coup leadership, and settled on Lieutenant Colonel Julio Adalberto Rivera and Colonel Aníbal Portillo as initial members of the new Civil-Military Directorate. Three conservative members of the civilian elite were added to it (Elam 1968, 161–62).

The initial cabinet of the government was, in the words of former president Osorio, "ridiculously rightist," perhaps in reaction to what was seen as the excessive leftism of the 1960 junta. Yet considerable reformist sentiment persisted within the officer corps, even among those who had opposed the 1960 experiment (Castro Morán 1989, 217–23). This sentiment came to the fore in February 1961, when the army issued a *proclama* that declared the military's solidarity with the population and set forth a reinvigorated reformist program reminiscent of 1948. This *proclama* triggered the resignation of the two most conservative civilian members of the directorate, but the government survived.

The actual policies of the new government were more or less in line with what the *proclama* promised. The main reforms enhanced state control over the economy and improved the government's ability to raise revenues. The government restructured the Salvadoran Coffee Company to better protect smaller coffee producers from larger growers who controlled processing and marketing facilities. It reorganized the Central Bank once again into a publicly controlled Central Reserve Bank. It imposed new taxes on the export of shrimp and other products, and put stricter controls on contraband and other "customs fraud." The popular dimensions of the directorate's program challenged the agrarian elite's interests only at the margins: laws raising the minimum wage, requiring paid Sundays off, enhancing pension benefits for commercial employees, and protecting small businesses. None of the measures threatened the agrarian elite's core interest—control of land—and in any case landowners often managed to undermine the intent of the laws, evading the minimum wage law, for instance, by paying more but ending their previous practice of giving workers two free meals every day (Anderson 1971, 155).

Overall, the policies of the directorate reflect considerable continuity with both the Martínez era and the 1948 model: the new government first established its "protection" credentials by cracking down, then proceeded with reforms intended to legitimate it to a broader audience and ameliorate some social discontent. Yet the reforms were basically peripheral to the causes of unrest and would ultimately prove unsuccessful in incorporating large sectors of the population as supporters of the government.

The transition from the "ridiculously rightist" cabinet and harsh repression of January 1961 to the reformist program that followed was not a conscious policy but rather the outcome of expediency on the part of military leaders. The civilian right agreed to join the government in the wake of the repression used at the time of the coup. They then abandoned the government when it advanced a reformist agenda. The reformist impulse came from junior officers and was resisted, at least initially, by the more senior ranks (Castro Morán 1989, 221–23). The fact that the upper classes abandoned the government was not sufficient to cause its collapse; it was a strong enough warning, however, to ensure that the "reformist" officer corps avoided radical policies that might trigger active civilian elite opposition.

The United States immediately recognized the 1961 directorate, satisfied that it represented more "responsible" elements of both military and civilian leadership. The new government benefited from increased aid levels under the Alliance for Progress, including soft loans totaling $25 million in 1961 (Webre 1979, 41). U.S. State Department cables predicted that the new government would carry out the reforms promised by the more anti–United States 1960 junta, but viewed it with greater confidence because it was outspokenly anticommunist (McClintock 1985a, 149).

In 1962, Colonel Rivera, an original member of the 1961 directorate, was elected to the presidency. He ran unopposed as the candidate of a new official party, the National Conciliation Party (PCN). Though it tightly controlled the 1962 election, the military also appears to have recognized, in the wake of the mass mobilization of the late 1950s, the fall of Lemus, and the 1961 protests against the directorate, that it needed to make greater efforts to legitimize its rule to a broader cross-section of Salvadoran society. One indication of this concern was that "Rivera campaigned as hard as, or perhaps harder than, he would have had he been opposed" (Webre 1979, 47). Once in office, Rivera began a process of political liberalization, pushing through a new electoral law that provided that future legislative assemblies would be based on proportional representation, allowing a broader range of political parties to obtain seats in the unicameral body. Though these measures would subsequently cause great problems for the military, they were politically expedient for Rivera in the short run, since opposition parties would need time to exploit the new political space. In the meantime, Rivera had to "discover a way to keep his opponents out of the streets" (Webre 1979, 48). The electoral opening served that purpose.

The main beneficiary of Rivera's reforms was the newly formed Christian Democratic Party (PDC), whose platform called for structural economic reforms within a capitalist framework, and genuine democratic competition. The PDC quickly replaced the nearly moribund PAR as the main party of opposition. The results of liberalization were optimal for the PCN because it now had a credible electoral opponent but had nonetheless retained majority control in the Legislative Assembly. The more important event, however, was the election of the Christian Democrat José Napoleón Duarte as mayor of San Salvador. Duarte renovated the city's public services and set up Communitarian Action to promote community development services on the basis of organized self-help. Duarte's early reputation for effectiveness, sensitivity to popular demands, and grass-roots organizing activities gave the Christian Democrats the core of a mass following, which would in the long run pose a threat to the PCN's dominance.

The PDC acted cautiously in the 1967 presidential elections, holding Duarte in reserve for nearly certain reelection as mayor of San Salvador and running party Secretary General Abraham Rodriguez for the presidency against Colonel Fidel Sánchez Hernández. The PAR had by this point been taken over by the Communists, forcing its more conservative elements to form the Salvadoran Popular Party (PPS). The PAR candidate was Fabio Castillo, the former National University rector who had served on the short-lived 1960 junta and who had been one of the main targets of U.S. charges of "Castro/Communism." The PPS ran a retired army major and coffee grower, Alvaro Martínez, a shrewd choice that threatened to draw away two of the main constituencies of the PCN (Webre 1979, 93–94). The main strategy of PCN candidate Sánchez was to play up the PCN's role as protector of the country from communism, focusing on the threat posed by PAR candidate Fabio Castillo (Webre 1979, 97). The press reinforced the PCN strategy by giving extensive coverage to the Castillo candidacy and running a special feature series on the uprising of 1932, which it blamed on communist manipulation of the ignorant peasantry. By allowing the PAR to remain in the race, the military "heightened the value of the Red scare issue to the PCN" and at the same time managed to enhance its image as a force for democracy (Webre 1979, 99).

The PCN's electoral strategy started to backfire in 1968. The PDC had 78 out of over 200 municipalities under its control after the 1968 elections, and the 1968–70 session of the Legislative Assembly saw the PDC team up with members of smaller parties and mavericks from the PCN to change committee rules and pass reformist legislation. These activities brought increasing rightist pressure against Sánchez, particularly after he declared at the opening session of a congress on agrarian reform that such reform was a necessity (Baloyra 1982, 45). This kind of talk was seen as all the more threatening since the Rivera government had quietly distributed plots of land to some thirty-five hundred families near the end of his presidency (McClintock 1985a, 152).

As a counterweight to his reformist rhetoric, Sánchez took actions that signaled his concern for oligarchic interests: he assigned Colonel José Alberto "Chele" Medrano, who was politically allied with agrarian interests, to command the National Guard, the most powerful command within the security system and the position most concerned on a daily basis with the suppression of rural labor organizers. In late 1967, President Sánchez and Colonel

Medrano pressured the agrarian elite to finance an expansion of ORDEN, claiming this was necessary to fight communism and was "consistent with El Salvador's own historical experience," a statement that was, in this context, a reference to the events of 1932.

The Security Apparatus

The electoral loosening of the 1960s was accompanied by reinforcement of the internal security apparatus, with U.S. assistance. The stronger security system reduced, rather than enhanced, the military's autonomy from civilian elite influence, contributing to political closure and reversal of reform efforts in the 1970s. The United States must bear a measure of responsibility for creating conditions that undermined any possibility of successful military-led reformism. As in many other countries in Latin America during the 1960s, U.S. reformist rhetoric and aid for schools, hospitals, and other benign public institutions under the Alliance for Progress were accompanied by material, financial, and technical assistance for internal security institutions.

The first U.S. measures followed the massive demonstrations against Lemus in mid-1960. The U.S. embassy requested aid for the security forces, and Washington responded by sending a two-man team from the Office of Public Safety of the International Co-Operation Administration. The team detected a growing threat due to infiltration of arms, "subversive materials," and commercial contraband. They saw the National Guard as the linchpin of the security system and as probably one of the most efficient police forces in Latin America, but concluded that security arrangements were nonetheless deficient and that "the internal security situation in El Salvador may soon develop into one of extreme urgency" (McClintock 1985a, 198).

After the overthrow of Lemus and the January 1961 countercoup, the embassy became extremely preoccupied with the fear that former junta members might organize subversion from outside the country and cabled Washington about "reports of clandestine movements of personnel and arms across El Salvador's frontiers and coastline" (quoted in McClintock 1985a, 199). In retrospect, these reports seem somewhat exaggerated. Following the 1961 countercoup, the PCS formed the core of an incipient *foco guerrillero* structure, which was called the United Revolutionary Action Front (FUAR), and a politicomilitary school, both under the direction of Schafik Hándal.[2] These efforts went no further than gathering a few pistols and learning to use them, distributing propaganda, and adopting some innovative self-defense strategies to protect PCS and other popular leaders at demonstrations. The school was broken up by the police in 1962, and no significant military actions were ever taken (Bonasso and Gómez 1993, 24–27; Harnecker 1993, 24–29). Not until the 1970s did splinters of the PCS and radical PDC groups again form active armed organizations.

Meanwhile, the United States had increased military aid and, more importantly, initiated and supported the development of a countersubversion intelligence network, based on local informants and integrated at the national level. Regular military aid did not amount to much, despite the hyperbolic language about the communist threat: some seventy vehicles, plus radios and a few thousand carbines. The intelligence assistance, however, was both more extensive and politically far more important. The first step was to improve the intelligence section within the National Guard. Throughout the rest of the 1960s, the Office of Public Safety (OPS) provided law enforcement training and assistance in El Salvador. Its teams regularly included "investigative advisors" who were operatives of the Central Intelligence Agency and who "spent virtually all their time with the intelligence agencies, to the neglect of Public Safety's own, more conventional work," and much to the irritation of the regular OPS staff (McClintock 1985a, 61). Several of the Salvadorans who were involved, such as General José Alberto Medrano, were on the CIA payroll, worked closely with U.S. Army Special Forces ("Green Beret") advisors, and received prominent recognition for their anticommunist services. Medrano was personally awarded a silver Presidential Medal by President Lyndon Johnson "in recognition of exceptionally meritorious service." Medrano later claimed that Johnson had told him: " 'I know all about you, Medrano. You're doing good work. I know your pedigree'—like I was a bull!" The United States sent Medrano on a three-month tour of Vietnam to observe U.S. counterinsurgency techniques (Nairn 1984, 23).

Medrano began his work by forming a small, elite intelligence-coordinating agency known as the "Security Service," which had a staff of at most fifteen men. This was later reorganized and expanded as a presidential security agency called the Salvadoran National Special Services Agency (ANSESAL). The agency did not initially engage in routine intelligence gathering; it relied on the reinforced National Guard intelligence section for that. The Security Service's main accomplishment was to form the nationwide, grass-roots network of informants known as ORDEN (the acronym means "order"). Most of the members of this organization, at least at the outset, were recruited from among soldiers recently discharged from military service, since they had been drilled, observed, and politically indoctrinated, making it easier for officers to select "reliable" candidates (McClintock 1985a, 204–7). ORDEN members, most of whom were tenant farmers or small landholders, got easier and cheaper access to agricultural inputs, personal loans, health care and education for their families, and immunity from prosecution for minor offenses. ORDEN members were also permitted—even encouraged—to carry sidearms (Cabarrús 1983, 43, 260). Their primary responsibilities were to local landowners, who also virtually controlled the many National Guard posts that were located on estates. The intelligence network that ORDEN served, however, was more centralized.

By the late 1960s, ORDEN had become increasingly public, serving as a sort of mass rural auxiliary for the military's official party, the PCN.[3] This meant that ORDEN members were known as such, and participated prominently with the army and National Guard in civic action projects such as building schools or repairing bridges. ORDEN also continued its spying role, identifying and reporting on possible subversives. This information was routed through local National Guard commanders to departmental intelligence centers, and then on to the San Salvador National Guard intelligence center. As ORDEN became more public, it also served increasingly as a paramilitary force, providing muscle and sometimes deadly force against organized labor and other "threats." In its intelligence and goon squad roles, ORDEN was effectively an extension of the National Guard and Treasury Police and, like these agencies, formed close political ties with local elites, from whom ORDEN members received favors and material rewards. This tie with the oligarchy was to become important in 1971 when Medrano stepped forward, with the coffee growers' backing, as a presidential candidate *in opposition to* the army's official PCN candidate. In this contest, portions of ORDEN provided manpower for Medrano's campaign, reinforcing the oligarchy's ability to challenge the military politically.

ORDEN's goon squad role became more prominent in 1968, when the radical National Association of Salvadoran Educators (ANDES) went on strike. The trigger was a new law that increased the number of years of service before retirement from 30 to 40. The government saw the ANDES strike as particularly threatening because it was accompanied by large rallies and demonstrations attended by a broad cross-section of regime opponents, and triggered a series of sympathy strikes by the Communist-controlled Salvadoran Unitary Trade Union Federation (FUSS) (Gordon 1989, 113–14). As strike actions spread into other sectors, the ORDEN members and National Guard forces beat and imprisoned ANDES leaders and "disappeared" two teachers, whose "almost unrecognizably mutilated" bodies were found much later (McClintock 1985a, 207). These actions, which brought a halt to the ANDES strike as well as strikes in other sectors, further enhanced the prestige of the National Guard, ORDEN, and their commander Medrano in the eyes of the conservative civilian elite.

The net effect of U.S. security assistance was to reinforce the factions of the Salvadoran military with the closest ties to conservative agrarian interests. Counterinsurgency doctrine and technical assistance, delivered by U.S. "temporary duty" advisers and army Mobile Training Teams (MTTs) in the 1960s, helped restore a secret police structure that had atrophied in the years since Martínez was ousted in 1944. Ironically, this institution-building effort, though successful in its own terms, was probably unnecessary, given the absence of a real guerrilla threat in the 1960s. Moreover, it created institutional and political changes that undermined the ability of the army leadership to carry out the kinds of reforms that might have prevented violent political conflict in the future.

The 1969 War

President Sánchez received a reprieve from the growing tensions between his government and the civilian right when El Salvador went to war with Honduras in 1969. The war resulted from mutual recriminations regarding the balance of trade within the Central American Common Market (CACM) and the presence of hundreds of thousands of Salvadoran migrants in Honduras. Underlying stresses existed because El Salvador had industrialized more successfully behind the tariff protections of the CACM, leaving Honduras to buy more expensive Salvadoran products in lieu of items previously imported from the United States and Europe. Honduras found itself using scarce foreign exchange revenues to fund its trade deficit with El Salvador and in 1966 resorted to a boycott against Salvadoran goods (Bulmer-Thomas 1987, 171–99).

The trigger for the war was the 1969 expulsion of thousands of Salvadoran immigrants. Salvadorans had begun migrating to Honduras as early as the turn of the century, and the flow had accelerated during the 1920s and 1930s. In the 1950s and 1960s, small tenant farmers lacked access to land.[4] In a sense, immigration to Honduras was a warning sign of the underlying agrarian problems that would contribute to conflict within El Salvador by the mid-1970s. As commercial agriculture expanded, and particularly as landowners shifted into activities like cotton, sugar, and beef production, which use more land, the rural poor found less land to rent. Previous tenancy arrangements, such as the *colono* system, under which major landowners provided subsistence plots to their permanent workers, were phased out. At the same time, the mechanized techniques used for cotton and sugar production meant that there was little demand for farm laborers. Although similar processes were under way in both El Salvador and Honduras, lands were taken out of subsistence production faster in El Salvador (Anderson 1982; Durham 1979; Ruhl 1984). By 1969, Salvadorans made up 19.8 percent of the estimated 427,000 agriculturally active persons in Honduras, and the 300,000 total Salvadoran immigrants made up 12 percent of the population of Honduras (Durham 1979, 125).

By 1969, just when technological changes in the banana industry were leading to layoffs in the north coast region, poor tenant farmers in Honduras were having difficulty finding arable land to rent. This combination led to increased popular pressures on the Honduran government to carry out further land reform. In response, the government ordered the eviction of all Salvadorans who were farming federal lands. The conventional interpretation is that the government was responding directly to specific popular demands to expel Salvadorans. Durham's (1979) analysis of the origins of the war, however, based on household surveys in Salvadoran and Honduran communities, suggests that for the most part Salvadorans were *not* resented or seen as competitors by poor, rural Hondurans; instead, most Honduran small-holders and tenant farmers saw them as allies against large landowners who were progressively (and frequently illegally) expanding their holdings, driving small farmers off the land. Most of the political pressure for expulsion came from the Honduran agrarian elite. For the Honduran National Federation of Growers and Cattlemen (FENAGH), the Salvadorans represented a target of opportunity: expelling the Salvadorans could ease the shortage of land and weaken the social forces demanding land reform. By going along with the federation's suggestion, the Honduran government temporarily reduced popular clamor for land while avoiding a politically difficult showdown with the agrarian elite.

Under the expulsion order, Salvadorans were given 30 days to leave their lands. Those who remained were forcibly evicted by the Honduran army or police. In some areas, the expulsions proceeded in an orderly fashion, and the Salvadorans did not resist. In others, a semiofficial goon squad known as the Mancha Brava attacked Salvadorans violently, killing men, raping women, and mutilating the victims. Little evidence exists of generalized Honduran popular violence against Salvadorans; rather, the brutality appears to have been official policy, implemented by agents of the government and of major landowners.

The violence of some of the expulsions created a flow of refugees to El Salvador, whose stories fueled an intensely nationalistic response. Mob violence during soccer matches between the two countries, plus minor border incursions by both sides, further heightened tensions. In this climate, the Salvadoran president ordered a surprise air and land assault on Honduras with the intention of capturing the capital, Tegucigalpa. The military offensive is generally viewed in El Salvador as having been a great success, and Salvadoran military officers for a time described themselves as the Israelis of Central America. In reality, the initial Salvadoran air strikes were almost a complete fiasco, and Salvadoran ground forces, though they advanced onto Honduran territory along two roadways, quickly outran their supply lines and were forced to a halt by Honduran resistance. A cease-fire was arranged by the Organization of American States (OAS) after 100 hours of combat. Some two thousand people died (Anderson 1982, 111–26).

One cannot help suspecting that President Sánchez' decision to launch the war was affected by his domestic predicament. The Salvadoran military was quite confident of its superiority before the war, so Sánchez probably viewed the immediate risks as minimal. Salvadoran commanders expected the war to end quickly, and more decisively than it actually did.[5] In any case, the nationalist response produced by the war and Salvadoran "victories" brought Sánchez a political reprieve from both the left and the right. Even the illegal PCS rallied behind the government, as did the PDC, the PAR, and the PPS. The nationalist afterglow prevented major challenges from the civilian right for the remainder of Sánchez' term. The PCN benefited from the enhanced image of the military in the 1970 elections, in which it increased its strength in the Legislative Assembly and took back control of all but eight municipalities.

In the long run, however, the 1969 war was to prove disastrous for El Salvador, contributing in a number of ways to the conditions for civil war. In the aftermath of the war, the Salvadoran/Honduran border was closed and Honduras broke definitively from the CACM. This cut El Salvador off from overland trade with Honduras, Nicaragua, and Costa Rica, removing important markets for Salvadoran manufactured goods and contributing to an abrupt contraction in the industrial sector. This not only reduced employment, but substantially weakened precisely those sectors of the social elite who might have supported military-led agrarian reforms in the 1970s (Baloyra 1982, 30). Thus the expedient choice of war with Honduras undermined, in the long run, conditions for military autonomy from the agrarian elite.

The most immediate complication was the flow of Salvadoran repatriates, which increased during the "War of 100 Hours" and continued after the ceasefire. Salvadoran Planning Ministry sources estimate that 130,000 Salvadorans returned. The social impact of such a massive return migration was tremendous. Though many of the Salvadorans had been either tenant farmers or untitled squatters on Honduran national lands, they had invested heavily in the properties over the years, an investment that they lost when expelled. Many of the "refugees" returned to their departments of origin, particularly Chalatenango, Cabañas, and Morazan, along the Honduran border. Living conditions in these locations were extremely poor, and the arrival of tens of thousands of additional people exacerbated the already extreme scarcity of tillable land, employment, and informal sector commercial opportunities. The closure and militarization of the border further complicated this situation, since many Salvadorans in the border areas had engaged in trading and commerce with Honduras. The mass repatriation of Salvadorans after the 1969 war contributed to making the northern departments fertile ground for revolutionary political organizing, which focused in these areas from the mid-1970s onward.[6]

The war also catalyzed within the left a faction dedicated to armed struggle. Since 1963, the Communist labor leader Salvador Cayetano Carpio had become increasingly impatient with what he perceived as the excessive caution of the PCS. The party required its affiliated unions to operate within the legal constraints imposed by the Ministry of Labor, which made it essentially impossible to organize a strike. In 1967, PCS unions had begun violating labor laws, carrying out strikes without government permission, organizing solidarity strikes in other factories, and defending themselves with sticks against attacks by the National Guard. The 1968 teachers' strikes and the military repression had radicalized a group of young workers. Carpio, by this point the secretary general of the party, had begun pushing, without much success, toward armed struggle. The PCS decision to support the "fratricidal war" against Honduras crystallized his frustrations with the party's conservative drift, and in 1970 he withdrew from it to form the core group of a clandestine politicomilitary organization that within two years would begin isolated guerrilla attacks under the name of the Popular Forces of Liberation—Farabundo Martí (FPL). Shortly thereafter, other elements of PCS youth, along with radicalized members of the PDC, would form another armed group called the People's Revolutionary Army (ERP), which went into action in 1971.

The Crisis of 1972

The contradictions inherent in trying to secure electoral legitimacy for institutional military rule came home to roost in 1972. The PCN had swept the PDC in the 1970 elections, largely because of fear of renewed hostilities with Honduras and a resulting sense that the official party should be given the strongest possible mandate. Sánchez however, "chose to regard the vote as an endorsement of his reformist initiatives," increasing conservative hostility toward him (Webre 1981, 142). He was feeling international pressure to consider reforms in the wake of a report from the Human Rights Commission of the OAS, which criticized El Salvador for not providing sufficient employment for its people (Gordon 1989, 127). In 1970, Sánchez convoked a First Congress on Agrarian Reform. At the opening session of the new assembly, he announced plans to push forward reform legislation affecting underutilized lands. In his Independence Day address of 1970 he reiterated that further reforms must take place: "The Salvadoran people are noble; they have trusted and continue to trust their leaders. But they have now reached their limit. At this moment, the reforms under consideration are like a rock teetering on the edge of a precipice that no one and nothing can prevent from falling" (quoted in Webre 1981, 143). The first specific measure was the irrigation and drainage law, which provided the state with limited rights to claim private lands in the public interest. Angry members of the agrarian elite responded that the government was reckless and was serving "the communist cause." There were rumors of a coup d'état to block its implementation (Webre 1981, 143–44).

Several actions by the left in late 1970 and in 1971 reinforced agrarian elite perceptions that the military government was abandoning its anticommunist functions. The funeral march for PCS leader Raúl Castellanos Figueroa showed the extent of support for the organized left, despite the fact that the PCS was legally excluded from politics. In January 1971, a young industrialist named Ernesto Regalado Dueñas, offspring of two of the country's most powerful families, was kidnapped and killed. The kidnappers, members of a cell of what became the ERP, demanded a one-million-dollar ransom but were unable to collect it (Cienfuegos 1993, 16). Though the military immediately carried out a crackdown on suspected subversive organizations within the National University, forcing the kidnappers into hiding, the perpetrators were never caught.[7]

Right-wing frustrations and discontent increased when, in July 1971, the ANDES teachers' union went out on strike again, supported by massive street demonstrations including the middle classes, peasants, students, and especially the urban poor from "shanty towns" around San Salvador. Several of the demonstrations turned violent, vandalizing public buildings. ORDEN and the regular security forces responded with violence, but the impression had been made that the government was not fully in control (McClintock 1985a, 163–64). A steady stream of demonstrations occurred at the National University. Webre argues that Salvadoran conservatives

> saw the regime not only as a government that was irrationally hostile to the interests of the more substantial sectors of society, but also one that irresponsibly tolerated and even pampered those whose activities demonstrated contempt for the sacred traditions of Salvadoran society and posed an immediate threat of social disintegration. It must have particularly disturbed oligarchs that there was—in spite of periodic coup rumors that may have represented mere wishful thinking or attempts to offer self-fulfilling prophesies—little evidence of unrest within the military. (1979, 152)

International events increased the political fears of the oligarchy. In Peru, the military had seen fit to implement a major land reform program at the expense of the agrarian elite in 1968. The existence of reformist sentiments within the military made the civilian elite less confident that the military institution could be relied upon. Conservatives were further alarmed by the fact that the Christian Democrats were being allowed to compete so freely in elections. The election in Chile in 1970 of the Marxist Popular Unity candidate Salvador Allende as successor to Christian Democrat Eduardo Frei gave the oligarchy, and conservative elements of the military, proof that Christian Democracy would merely serve as a bridge for the left to take power.

The agrarian elite's discomfiture took electoral form in 1972 when the new United Independent Democratic Front (FUDI), ran General Medrano as its candidate. He had considerable appeal to conservative elements of the oligarchy:

> Medrano was the man who had pacified labor in 1966–68, a man who understood the operation of the political economy of export agriculture

in El Salvador, a man who understood why it was necessary to keep labor organizers out of the Salvadoran countryside, and a man who could
take initiative during times of crisis. Quite literally, he represented an opportunity to return to the golden past when Salvadoran presidents did not
have to talk about reformism, when junior officers were easily put in their
place, and when there was no need to appease so many professionals and
intellectuals who, the conservatives insisted[,] had never met a payroll in
their lives, did not know how to read a balance sheet, and did not understand how Salvadoran society "worked." (Baloyra 1982, 47)

In other words, Medrano was the candidate of the system of 1932, an officer
who understood, as Martínez had in the early years, the appropriate role for
the armed forces and the state. Medrano's electoral support went beyond
members of the oligarchy: whereas ORDEN had once been available to help
turn out the vote for the PCN, at least part of ORDEN supported Medrano
(who had resigned as head of ORDEN after his removal from the National
Guard). His campaign prefigured the civilian right's decision to form its own
political party in the 1980s in reaction to the military's willingness to govern
jointly with the PDC and implement land reform. Between them, FUDI and
the older conservative PPS received 100,000 votes, many of which came at the
expense of the official party.

Medrano's candidacy put security force and intelligence officers in a
quandary. While important elements of the economic elite supported
Medrano, it was still unlikely that he would succeed. As a result, officers who
were politically and personally close to Medrano nonetheless supported the
candidate of the PCN, Colonel Arturo Armando Molina. Captain Roberto
D'Aubuisson, a close affiliate of Medrano and an officer with a reputation as
a countersubversion specialist and interrogator, served as the coordinator for
the Molina campaign in the eastern zone of the country. Other officers who
later emerged as prominent, hardline guerrilla-fighters, such as Captain
Domingo Monterrosa, were also instrumental in the campaign (Mena Sandoval 1992, 84–93).

The other electoral opposition to the military came from the Christian
Democratic Party, which had joined with the social democratic National
Revolutionary Movement (MNR) and the Communist front National Democratic Union (UDN) in coalition called the National Opposition Union
(UNO). The coalition ran their most electable candidate, San Salvador
mayor José Napoleón Duarte, with MNR leader Guillermo Ungo as his running mate. They campaigned effectively, despite harassment and one attempt on Duarte's life in which his driver was killed (Gordon 1989, 133). Although serious, the pressures against the UNO campaigners were markedly
lower than the widespread killings and beatings that had been directed

against Democratic Action activists after 1944, even though the electoral challenge they posed was greater.

UNO probably won a plurality and possibly even a majority (Webre 1979, 170–74). Returns from rural areas showed the PCN leading, but as urban precincts came in, the trend turned strongly in the direction of UNO. The Central Elections Committee suspended public announcements of the vote count and declared PCN candidate Molina the victor the following day. Former army Captain Francisco Emilio Mena Sandoval reports that a meeting took place in the *cuartel* of the Third Brigade as soon as it became clear that the UNO coalition was winning at the national level. A specific plan was put forward to "fix" the completed ballots to ensure that the official candidate would win in a recount: a team of officers and soldiers equipped with erasers, official stamps, pens, and blank ballots was to go to the buildings in the zone where the ballots were kept to (1) nullify ballots that had been marked for UNO; (2) complete all blank ballots in favor of the PCN; and (3) as necessary substitute PCN ballots for UNO ballots to change the percentages without altering the total number of votes. Mena Sandoval indicates that similar actions took place across the country, and other officers interviewed corroborated the army's extensive involvement in doctoring the ballots (Mena Sandoval 1992, 90–91).[8] Molina's election was confirmed by the Legislative Assembly in a hastily and irregularly called session that the opposition boycotted.

The immediate postelection period was plagued by a series of guerrilla attacks, fires, and "incidents of terrorism." An assault by ERP guerrillas on 2 March killed one National Guardsman and wounded a second, after which the assailants fled in the direction of the university carrying the guardsmen's G-3 rifles (Harnecker 1993, 70). The security forces failed to catch the assailants despite a disruptive search of the university. This attack was accompanied by a number of less significant actions. As was the case with the Regalado Dueñas kidnapping and assassination, "Sánchez Hernández found it necessary to deny rumors that the government was behind the wave of disorders. It was not true, he insisted, that his regime was attempting to create the conditions for military intervention in the form of a 'self-coup' (*autogolpe*)" (Webre 1979, 174).

The military action begun by the left was, at this point, little more than an annoyance for the government. Though such actions might have played into Medrano's hands had they occurred before the election, in the wake of the blatant electoral fraud they had little impact on the factional balance within the military. The electoral fraud signified for many the bankruptcy of institutional military rule and the PCN. Even before the election, serious rumblings occurred within the officer corps over Sánchez' imposition of his candidate without consultation with them. Some of the officers present at the meeting where Molina's candidacy was announced had challenged the whole idea of holding elections in which the outcome was predetermined (Mena Sandoval 1992, 79–82).

On 25 March 1972, these rumblings took more concrete form as the Artillery Battalion at the Zapote barracks and the First Brigade, both in San Salvador, rebelled, seized control of strategic positions within the city, and took the president prisoner. The movement, led by Colonel Benjamín Mejía, apparently had co-conspirators in other important barracks in San Miguel, Santa Ana, and San Vicente, but the rebels in those barracks failed to secure full control of the units and were forced to surrender. A key cavalry officer failed to carry out his role in the coup, disrupting coordination among rebel units.[9] Another blow to the conspirators was the fact that the security forces—the National Guard, the National Police, and the Treasury Police—remained loyal to the government. Although the Artillery Battalion bombarded the air force base at Ilopango, a handful of aircraft got airborne and successfully bombed the Artillery and First Brigade barracks (Mena Sandoval 1992, 95–99). The combined efforts of the air force, the security forces, and loyal army units from outside the capital were sufficient to defeat the rebels, who surrendered between 4:15 and 5:00 p.m. Around a hundred people were killed, most of them soldiers, and another two hundred were wounded (McClintock 1985a, 168–70). A decisive factor was the failure of the rebels to capture the minister of defense and other senior officers, who were able to coordinate the very rapid counterattack.

Even if Mejía's forces had managed to hold through the first few days, the long-term prospects for the coup were dim. Under the auspices of the Central American Defense Council (CONDECA), Nicaraguan and Guatemalan planes began flying combat supplies into San Miguel, which would have made it possible for the Third Brigade and other "loyalist" units to fight a protracted campaign against the *golpistas*, had this been necessary (Cabarrús 1983, 44; Dunkerly 1985, 86).

The first indication of the political agenda of the *golpistas* was a radio announcement by Mejía that the movement was one of *juventud militar*—that is, made up of younger officers of reformist orientation who were not complicit in the corruption and fraud of the existing regime. Mejía himself, though a senior officer, was nonetheless widely recognized as a reformer. He had a reputation as a romantic and military eccentric whose scrupulous honesty called attention to him in the context of the Salvadoran military. Partly as a result of the low income his honesty brought him and partly out of solidarity with the poor, he lived in very humble quarters.[10] Several of the other officers involved had been participants in the 2 April 1944 revolt against Martínez (Castro Morán 1989, 235). Junior officers, among them Pedro Guardado and Adrián Ticas, were later involved in the 1979 coup (Mena Sandoval 1992, 97).

The movement's political alignment with the civilian UNO coalition emerged later in the day, when Duarte went on a San Salvador radio station and called upon people to obstruct the forces that were moving into the city to defeat the *golpistas*. Apparently Duarte was not involved in the plot in advance, but was called upon by the conspirators once it became clear that the movement was in trouble and would need popular support. His decision to comply led to arrest, torture, and exile, for him and other UNO leaders, many of whom attempted to take shelter in embassies after the coup collapsed. Mariano Castro Morán (1989, 235) argues that Duarte's radio call for popular support for the *juventud* "sealed the military fortunes" of the rebellion. While much of the officer corps was sympathetic to greater reformism and objected to the election fraud, the thought of an alliance between the military and a popular civilian "mob" turned additional officers and units against the rebellion.

The coup was, in addition, not sufficiently organized to take advantage of latent support within units outside the capital. The coup generated a great deal of confusion. Soldiers who had been awakened and ordered to take up defensive positions in the capital were unaware of which side they were on. Reporters who stopped a patrol and asked them whether they were loyalists or rebels were told, "They awakened us at eleven o'clock last night. We don't know what's happening" (Webre 1979, 177). Mena Sandoval's account is quite similar: "Along the Panamerican Highway we encountered very confused soldiers. Some said they supported the coup, others said they were with the forces of the east [who were marching against the rebels], others may have been in accord with the coup but in the confusion had joined forces loyal to the government" (1992, 96). This loss of potential support resulted from clandestine planning and the involvement of a relatively narrow base of officers. It also demonstrates the importance of personal loyalties and hierarchy. Soldiers fought on whatever side their commander chose or, if their commander was not present, found themselves taking orders from whatever officer happened to be on the scene, usually without explanation. As a result, the makeup of forces in the coup was extremely volatile from one hour to the next.[11]

From 25 March until 10 April 1972, the country was placed under martial law, and constitutional guarantees were formally suspended until 3 June 1972. During this period, intense repression was directed against UNO members and other civilian regime opponents, a well as unlucky curfew violators, many of whom were shot on sight (Gordon 1989, 137; McClintock 1985a, 170).

The Molina Administration: Repression and Reform

Having depended on overt fraud to be elected and on the protection of the security forces to take office, Molina was on shaky political ground from the outset and beholden to very conservative interests for his political survival. As Webre (1979, 185) puts it:

He needed an issue upon which he could base his right to govern and he found it in "law and order" and "anti-communism." Virtually Molina's first official act was to join the government to the conservative assault upon the National University. On July 19, explaining that the institution "had fallen into the hands of the Communists," Molina secured a decree from the Legislative Assembly abrogating the university's organic law and ordered troops to occupy the central campus in San Salvador as well as the outlying regional centers in Santa Ana and San Miguel.

Faculty and administrators were exiled and the university remained closed for over a year, reopening under tight government control. Meanwhile, Molina selected the hardliner Carlos Romero as defense minister and named officers from the *tanda* of 1955, led by a notoriously conservative colonel named Roberto Escobar García, to most of the key military commands in the country.

During Molina's administration, the inherent dilemmas in the model of 1948 became increasingly acute. By the end of his term in office, he would attempt a comprehensive land reform process and would be forced to reverse himself. Hardline elements in the military had developed increasing political and institutional autonomy and responded to leftist opposition in markedly more violent ways. A reformist junior officers' movement had begun to coalesce, and Molina was denied his choice of successors in favor of an officer with close ties to the agrarian elite. In the process, rapidly growing peasant organizations fell prey to increasingly violent treatment at the hands of the security forces and ORDEN, and were transformed from social movements seeking specific material benefits into political organizations advocating revolution. Nascent guerrilla organizations gained increasing influence over these mass popular organizations, moving them toward a more confrontational and militant stance. The repression and failure of reforms under Molina, therefore, contributed to heightened conflict that would take on revolutionary dimensions by the end of the decade.

As had Osorio and Rivera before him, Molina sought to match his stern anticommunist actions with expansion of the role of the state in the economy, with an emphasis on modernizing and stabilizing capitalism in El Salvador, promoting industrial development, and improving social conditions. Molina's "Economic and Social Development Plan 1973–1977" proposed to exert greater control over export markets and channel export earnings into industry, new export products, and small and medium businesses. The plan included expansion of "*zonas francas*" for assembly-for-export industries, international borrowing for productive investments, increased import substitution industrialization, restriction of imports from outside the CACM, promotion of tourism, and regulation of international investment to prevent its penetration of strategic sectors of the economy. Though the plan depended largely on increased employment and trickle-down to improve social conditions, some components directly addressed distributional problems: the government proposed to use fiscal policy, minimum wage laws, social services, and, in a major innovation, land reform, to increase lower-class incomes and welfare (Gordon 1989, 147–49).

Molina created a National Planning Council (CONAPLAN), as a direct dependency of the presidency, to implement these measures. CONAPLAN was later converted into the Ministry of Planning. The government increased its control over the economy by expanding state regulation of the coffee market and creating a new cabinet-level Monetary Board to regulate currency. The government borrowed heavily—international debt grew almost threefold under Molina—and invested it through a variety of new public sector agencies that targeted new sectors of agriculture, cooperatives, small and medium-sized businesses, and other enterprises. Overall, public investment increased at a rate of 22 percent annually (Gordon 1989, 150–60). These statist measures were accompanied by increased military control over state agencies that had previously been controlled by civilians, such as the Salvadoran Institute for Industry Promotion (INSAFI), the Central Reserve Bank, the Salvadoran Coffee Company, the Rio Lempa Hydroelectric Power Commission (CEL), and various others (Gordon 1989, 159–60).

All of these new agencies and job positions for military officers greatly expanded the spoils of government. Thanks to what one U.S. diplomat referred to as "blatant stealing," the directors of some of these agencies became millionaires in short order and began to acquire the conspicuous trappings of power, such as large lakeside mansions and luxury automobiles. Businessmen came to see officers as unwelcome competitors and social pretenders, intensifying the contempt with which the urban industrial and commercial bourgeoisie viewed the military.[12]

Despite increased military influence over the economy, Molina found it difficult to implement aspects of his plan that directly challenged core interests of the agrarian elite. In 1972, CONAPLAN produced an Agricultural Development Plan for 1973–77 that called for redistribution of lands to redress the "most important limiting factor in the low level of rural incomes." It proposed measures to stabilize the "precarious" access to land while providing sufficient technical extension services to support development of small-scale, entrepreneurial farms (Gordon 1989, 166). The government published a few statements in newspapers seeking to develop support for these plans and held a National Seminar on Agrarian Reform in 1973 for members of the armed forces, during which prominent international land reform experts made presentations. In July and August 1973, deputies from the Legislative Assembly traveled to Peru to evaluate that country's experience with land reform (Gordon 1989, 167).

The National Association of Private Enterprise (ANEP) responded nega-
tively to this proposal, publishing a counterproposal to improve and stabilize
the availability of production credits, which would in theory make it possible
to increase the use of underutilized lands. The ANEP proposal included no
redistribution of land (other than voluntary sales) and faulted the state for "instability of leadership" and for interfering in the market (ANEP 1972, cited in
Gordon 1989, 168). Molina quickly yielded to this and other objections from
the private sector and the armed forces. In late 1973, most of the officials responsible for planning the reform abruptly resigned their positions and were
replaced by individuals closely identified with the most conservative of agrarian interests.[13]

The land reform issue did not go away. Rural social conditions had been
gradually deteriorating in El Salvador since the 1960s as a direct result of the
continual expansion of export agriculture. As lands that had previously been
available to tenant farmers for food crops were turned over to cotton, cattle,
and sugar, peasants had to rent more marginal lands or lost access to land altogether, becoming entirely dependent on agricultural day labor. Since production of the new products was highly mechanized, relatively few found positions as permanent workers (Brockett 1990, 67–95; Williams 1994). Perhaps
one of the most concrete indicators of the resulting insecurity of access to food
was a 46 percent increase in the incidence of child malnutrition from 1965 to
1975 (Brockett 1990, 84). The repatriation of hundreds of thousands of peasants from Honduras in 1969 compounded the problem of land availability.

As landlessness increased from 12 percent in 1961 to 29 percent in 1971, and
swelled to 41 percent by 1975, competition for the few available jobs in rural
areas drove down agricultural wages (a 25 percent decline between 1973 and
1976) despite a period of favorable coffee prices (Brockett 1990, 149). Government policy did little to ameliorate these hardships. Initiatives such as the Program for Promotion of Communal Cooperation (FOCCO), which began
with local infrastructural projects in 1969 and shifted into promotion of agricultural coops, craft production, and small industries from 1974 onward, could
hardly compensate for shrinking access to land and falling wages. In fact, one
government industrial program, the construction of the Cerrón Grande hydroelectric dam, flooded 135 square kilometers of rich farmland in the center
of the country, leading to intense conflict between the government and peasants in the area (Gordon 1989, 164).

The government hoped that industrial development would provide enough
employment to compensate for the loss of jobs and land access in rural areas.
Though industry expanded in the early 1970s, however, it did so too slowly to
absorb the surplus labor pool, and the cost to the state per job created was quite
high.[14] Privately controlled banks tended to favor loans in agriculture, leaving
the state to finance industrial expansion with its more limited resources (Gordon

1989, 145). Moreover, real wages fell in the industrial sector from 1973 onward as rapid inflation was triggered by higher energy prices (Gordon 1989, 162).

Molina could not afford to ignore these worsening hardships for poor Salvadorans. There had been a gradual increase in rural organizing during the 1960s and early 1970s, some of it encouraged by the government as a kind of vaccination against communism. One such structure was the Salvadoran Communal Union (UCS), which was designed as an anticommunist cooperative movement, guided by advisors from the American Institute of Free Labor Development (AIFLD) (Brockett 1990, 151). By 1973, UCS was actively and vocally calling for land reform. Other organizations more independent of the government were already moving toward a more radical stance. The first and most important independent rural organization was the Christian Federation of Salvadoran Peasants (FECCAS), which had its origins in rural organizing work begun in 1964 by the National Union of Christian Workers (UNOC). FECCAS became a separate entity in 1969 and grew rapidly, building on the consciousness-raising work of the Catholic Church.

This work in rural areas followed the Second Conference of Latin American Bishops in Medellín, Colombia, which had reoriented the Church toward a "preferential option for the poor" (Cardenal 1987, 434). The work of post-Medellín priests and lay "delegates of the word" challenged peasants to overcome passivity and victimization and actively construct better lives for themselves and their community. This naturally led them into conflict with local landowners, who were unwilling to make concessions regarding wages, rents, or incursions by landless peasants. The landowners' intransigence is illustrated by an anecdote told by a landowner and former agrarian reform official, Leonel Gómez, who in the early 1970s accompanied a group of peasants to a meeting of local landowners in the western part of El Salvador. The peasants asked the landowners to help them purchase a cow, which would allow them to begin a herd to provide milk for their children and generate a bit of supplemental income. The landowners rejected the proposal and later explained their decision to Gómez by saying, "Think of the precedent."[15]

In fact, peasants who organized risked worsening their situation. Members of FECCAS risked being denounced by members of ORDEN, blacklisted, and fired by their employers (Cardenal 1987, 438–43). Since existing labor laws provided few protections for rural workers, blacklisted workers had no legal recourse. Faced with constant frustrations and a tightening system of control and repression, FECCAS members became increasingly political. By 1974, FECCAS was transforming itself from a social movement into a semi-clandestine revolutionary political party (Gordon 1989, 181).

Repression tended to further radicalize the popular opposition. Two priests were assassinated and 78 people were wounded in attacks by government forces or their paramilitary supporters during the Molina regime. In November 1972, the Treasury Police captured a peasant from a small hamlet in Santa Ana. His headless body was found three weeks later. In 1973, security forces attacked the headquarters of several urban unions (Cardenal 1987, 448). In May 1974, National Guard troops raided another village, killing several people and disappearing others. On 29 November 1974, the National Guard, along with ORDEN members, attacked the village of La Cayetana in San Vicente, killing 6 and disappearing 13. Most residents of the village were members of FECCAS. The violence occurred "in the context of a land dispute between villagers and a neighboring estate owner," indicating the security forces' responsiveness to pressures from the local oligarchy (McClintock 1985a, 170–72).

The killings at La Cayetana stimulated popular protests. In December 1974, a priest led ten thousand peasants in the first demonstration by rural popular organizations in San Salvador (McClintock 1985a, 173). When the National Guard and ORDEN murdered six peasants in the village of Tres Calles in Usulután, peasant organizations were convinced that the government had declared war on them (McClintock 1985a, 173).

On 30 July 1975, about two thousand university and secondary school students demonstrated against the amount of money the government was spending to host the Miss Universe contest and against the use of force to break up a similar demonstration a week earlier in Santa Ana. As the march passed near the main public hospital, National Guard forces opened fire with automatic weapons, killing at least 37 and taking away an undetermined number of the wounded who were never seen again.

These violent actions catalyzed a series of alliances among sectoral and regional organizations that reshaped them into national mass organizations. In June 1974, FECCAS, along with the smaller Union of Rural Workers (UTC), based in Usulután, joined with the teachers' union (ANDES) and two urban labor federations, FUSS and the National Trade Union Federation of Salvadoran Workers (FENASTRAS), to form a broad opposition organization named the United Popular Action Front (FAPU). FAPU's discourse and goals were explicitly political, calling the Molina government "fascistoid" and calling for revolution and democracy. In 1975, FECCAS, the UTC, and ANDES withdrew from FAPU to form a new and even more militant organization, the Popular Revolutionary Bloc (BPR), while FAPU continued as an umbrella for urban labor unions. By 1976, FAPU's 30,000 members and the BPR's 60,000 gave them the capacity to stage massive demonstrations and press demands at the local level (Montgomery 1982, 126).

While these developments were taking place, guerrilla organizations were gradually expanding and extending their operations. Serious ideological and strategic differences kept the ERP and FPL from unifying and the ERP itself split in 1974, creating a new group called the Armed Forces of National Resistance (FARN, usually referred to simply as the RN). These guerrilla groups did not yet present a serious military threat to the government: during all of Molina's term, there were a total of 31 attacks, in which 24 security personnel and 18 ORDEN or other paramilitary members were killed, 11 people were wounded, and 8 people were kidnapped (López Vallecillos 1979b, 871). Occurring over a five-year period, this level of violence was scarcely more than a nuisance, especially in a country with a nationwide nonpolitical annual homicide rate of 130 per 100,000, approximately five times the level of the average large U.S. city (Cohen 1984, 8, 10). Nonetheless, their intermittent raids on security force posts, and the difficulties the government encountered in capturing them, created an impression of weakness on the part of the government.

The more important work of the guerrilla organizations during this period was their involvement in the popular organizations. The FPL had carried much of the organizing work that led to the formation of the BPR, and its rather rigid ideological perspective regarding the appropriate class base for revolution (peasants and workers, no middle sectors) was reflected in the positions adopted by the BPR (Harnecker 1993). The RN worked extensively in urban labor unions, particularly in FENASTRAS, and its ideological outlook favoring a multiclass antifascist alliance was reflected in FAPU's discourse (Cienfuegos 1993). Since the government had infiltrated the popular organizations, it was fully aware of the connections between the mass movement and the guerrillas. This awareness made the popular organizations seem more threatening to the government, and served as a pretext for violent retaliation against unarmed members of the popular movement whenever the guerrillas carried out operations.[16]

The Absence of Reformist Allies in the Private Sector

After two years in office, Molina faced a watershed. If the militarized state had the autonomy to mediate conflicting interests in society, the mid-1970s was the time to prove it. Unfortunately for Molina, two factors militated against successful state intervention on behalf of the landless: the increased power of conservative factions within the military, and the failure of two decades of industrial policy to create an industrial and commercial elite strong and independent enough to counteract agrarian oligarchs. In theory, industrial and commercial elites should favor land reform, especially in a country with relatively high protective tariffs: land reform should increase the incomes of rural households and therefore augment demand for industrial products. Though El Salvador had, by the late 1960s, a number of wealthy families whose investments were primarily in industry and commerce (Aubey 1969), this "bourgeois" group lacked significant autonomy from the "oligarchic" families whose interests were primarily in agricultural production, processing, and exporting, and who controlled most of the country's banks.

There were several reasons for this subordination of industry and commerce to agriculture. First, though numerous industries were owned by families with no involvement in agriculture, most of the actual *capital* in the industrial sector (54.7 percent) was controlled by diversifying coffee growers, processors, and exporters. These same diversified oligarchs controlled 51 percent of capital in commerce, 49.9 percent in construction, and 43.7 percent in services (Gordon 1989, 57). Industrial production was heavily concentrated in a few large firms: the 99 largest industrial corporations (of a total of 810) produced 63 percent of all value added in the sector (Colindres 1977, 129). Moreover, oligarchic capital played a major role in the leading firms in the industrial sector: in 1973, 20 industrial corporations controlled 50 percent of all industrial capital and the 19 top coffee processors and exporters were owners or co-owners of 13 of these 20 top firms. Four of the remaining firms were foreign-owned, limiting their weight within upper-class factional politics (Pelupessy 1987, 73). Though some 50 foreign companies invested in El Salvador during the 1960s, most entered into joint ventures with Salvadoran capitalists, primarily coffee producers, processors, and exporters (Pelupessy 1987, 72). The dominant position held by agrarian interests was compounded by their almost complete control of the banking sector, which systematically favored the agricultural sector in its loaning practices.[17]

The economic dynamics of the 1970s tended to further weaken the position of the industrial and commercial sectors. Production of traditional export crops — coffee, sugar, and cotton — increased very rapidly in response to favorable prices, enhancing the earnings of the sector and the oligarchic families that controlled most production, processing, and exporting.

The balance of factional economic power within the upper classes meant that relatively few business leaders were willing to advocate land reform. Members of the agrarian or processing elites held most of the top offices in ANEP and other private sector peak associations (Colindres 1977, 149–57). For the agrarian elite, land reform was not only an attack on unrestricted property rights, but represented the first initial steps toward communism, even if implemented by the armed forces. This equation of reformism with communism originated, according to Jeffery Paige (1994), with the rebellion of 1931–32. It proved to be a powerful tool for maintaining antireformist discipline within the business elite as well as persuading military officers to oppose land reform initiatives.

Molina not only lacked reformist allies in the private sector; he also faced an increasingly powerful and autonomous hardline faction within the armed forces, reinforced by internal security assistance provided by the United States. ANSESAL, which coordinated domestic intelligence collection and analysis, became more of an operational agency during the 1972–75 period, when it began collecting more of its own intelligence through operatives who were ostensibly Customs agents.[18] The intelligence offices of ANSESAL remained in the presidential compound, but a second operational headquarters was set up elsewhere, presumably to increase independence from the presidency (Mc-Clintock 1985a, 219). In addition, the National Guard's Special Investigations Section (SIE) was expanded with help from the Office of Public Safety of the U.S. Agency for International Development (AID). With the growth of SIE, the National Guard, long the military agency most closely aligned with the oligarchy, played an increasingly autonomous role in the national intelligence network and provided much of ANSESAL's operational capacity. ANSESAL itself had extensive independent contacts with the private sector; in particular, it served as an employment agency for landlords and industrialists looking for so-called *supernumerarios*—National Guard and other security force personnel who would do security work for companies and farms (McClintock 1985a, 220).

A nascent movement of junior officers provided one of the few counterweights to these developments. In 1976 the Movimiento de la Juventud Militar (Military Youth Movement [MJM]) began to protest, from within the regular army, the corruption and domination by the security forces that characterized the Molina regime (Movimiento de la Juventud Militar 1976, 1–3). James Dunkerly describes the MJM as a "semi-clandestine" organization of officers who argued for "retaining faith in the original PCN project"—that is, the idea that limited reforms were necessary to preserve long-term stability (1985, 105). The MJM was, in part, the fruit of the RN's organizing efforts within the army. In an open letter "To the Army" written in February 1976, the MJM denounced the growing corruption within the army and in "key points" of state institutions. It condemned the Molina government as "unpopular, anti-democratic, and inefficient" and refers derogatorily to "la camarilla policíaco-terrorista de Molina" ("the police-terrorist clique of Molina"). The reference to "police" reveals that discontent about corruption and violence was overlaid with institutional objections to the increasing political dominance of the security forces over the army. Elsewhere in the document, the phrase "police-oligarchic cliques" refers to the close relations between the security forces and the agrarian elite. The letter speaks of a growing number of officers who, "by means of a process of sensitization and political education, realize that their place is with the people, and not in the service of a closed elitist minority that controls and appropriates the benefits of almost the entire wealth of the nation, or of powerful interests foreign to El Salvador" (MJM 1976, 2). The document concludes (4–5) with an agenda:

The Fatherland is First: We fight to eradicate all vices and privileges in El Salvador.

The Fatherland is First: We fight as soldiers to establish a *real* democracy.

The Fatherland is First: We fight so that major political decisions are not made within closed circles of police-oligarchic cliques, nor in the luxurious offices of large transnational corporations.

The Fatherland is First: We fight to establish, on the side of the popular sectors, a process of democratic transformations in which the people themselves would have an effective participation.

The Fatherland is First: We do not collaborate with the methods of repression over the people, nor the curtailment or restriction of popular liberties.

The Fatherland is First: We will not permit the sullying of the honor of the Army, tolerating corruption, or permitting the police cliques, who are in the service of the oligarchy, to continue using soldiers and the Army for their bastard goals.

The Fatherland is First: Let us pull together, comrades, and struggle to change governmental structures, shake the conscience of the nation, to eliminate forever worn-out, immoral, and antipopular methods of government.

The Fatherland is First: Let us struggle, as soldiers, on the side of popular, democratic forces, to achieve A DEMOCRATIC GOVERNMENT OF NATIONAL SALVATION. Tomorrow may be too late, comrades in arms.

The language of this statement clearly reflects the influence of the left and indicates that the reformist agenda of the military *juventud* was more radical than Molina's. The militant language notwithstanding, many of the issues that the MJM addressed reflected broad concern within the army officer corps. The distinction the letter draws between the agendas of the army and the security forces is particularly important. The army is described as pro-popular, democratic, in favor of social equity, honest, and honorable, while the security forces, high command, and oligarchy are depicted as violent, corrupt, and antidemocratic. In interviews, officers with a wide range of current opinions, including some who held hardline views by the late 1980s, described themselves as having subscribed to this general picture of the institutional issues in the late 1970s.[19]

A powerful unifying grievance among junior officers appears to have been electoral fraud and the professional indignity that this imposed upon the military as an institution. Many were personally offended by the extent of corruption at higher levels in the military, and angry at the damage it did to the prestige and integrity of the armed forces as an institution. Out of this concern about corruption and electoral fraud emerged a belief among many officers that a civilian president would be more convenient and safe for the military.

This movement was neither an immediate threat to Molina nor a meaningful source of support for his attempt at reform in 1976, because the junior officers were too skeptical of Molina and his government. The MJM remained a diffuse group until 1979, when serious organizing to oust Molina's successor began.

The "Agrarian Transformation" Crisis

Even without reformist allies, Molina recognized by the mid-1970s that the state had to act to prevent a social explosion. In 1973 he was shouted down when he floated the idea of land reform; in 1975, having learned from that experience, he attempted to push through a series of concrete measures with a minimum of public discussion. Decree 302, introduced in the Legislative Assembly in June, created the Salvadoran Institute for Agrarian Transformation (ISTA). PCN deputies attempted to insert amendments to the bill (suggested by the National Association of Private Enterprise) that would have exempted highly productive farms, regardless of their size, from expropriation by ISTA. Molina managed to suppress these amendments, and the bill was promptly passed (Gordon 1989, 190).

This initial success evoked some ominous responses from within the armed forces. In August a new death squad called the Armed Forces for Anti-Communist Liberation (FALANGE) announced its existence and sentenced a wide range of regime opponents to death, including members of ANDES, journalists, priests, and trade unionists. This new force was probably a creation of ANSESAL, reflecting the more conservative views within the security forces with encouragement from the more reactionary voices within the private sector (McClintock 1985a, 174–75). In a revealing protest against Molina's reform initiative, FALANGE called for a liquidation of regime opponents in the style of Martínez, including "communists who are in government through the stupidity of those who govern, and even those military men who contemporize with them" (quoted in McClintock 1985a, 175).

The conflict between Molina and the agrarian elite and its military allies came to a head after 29 June 1976, when the legislature passed Decree 31, creating the First Project of the Agrarian Transformation. The initial project targeted an impoverished lowland cotton-growing area in Usulután and San Miguel, where the government proposed to redistribute small holdings to 12,000 peasant families. The five major landowners in the area, each of whom had incomes equal to that of almost 7,000 local families, were to be compensated for the lands expropriated (Whitfield 1994, 108).

Decree 31 had been prepared by the Planning Ministry in close consultation with Jesuit social scientists at the University of Central America (UCA), which was generally viewed as a center of reformist and even radical academic thought and which had already suffered its first bombing in response to the publication of a journal on liberation theology. The UCA had been invited to participate in designing the reforms by Planning Minister Atilio Vieytez, who had been a professor at the UCA (Whitfield 1994, 108–11).

The decision to turn to the UCA for political support partly reflected the isolation of the government on the land reform issue. Only the U.S. embassy, the UDN (front for the PCS), and the UCS openly endorsed the initiative, while the more radicalized popular movements and other political parties opposed it as a sham. Lacking genuine broad support, the government arranged a show of enthusiasm for the reform plan by its rural clients, bringing between 70,000 and 100,000 peasant members of ORDEN to the capital city for a demonstration, the largest demonstration in El Salvador in 15 years (Baloyra 1982, 57–59).

The country's landed elites did not react well to the news: "In spite of the fact that the model adopted in the transformation was Taiwan's—and not Cuba's—that most of the land involved was government property, that the United States Agency for International Development (AID) would provide the money for compensation, and that the 'agrarian reformers' were wearing a uniform that had always defended their privileges, the traditional oligarchy and much of the Salvadoran private sector went on the warpath" (Baloyra 1982, 57). On 8 July the National Association of Private Enterprise (ANEP) endorsed the general idea of reforms to "achieve an integral development of the country" but objected to a "political economy inspired by the methodology and principles of central planning," and to the secrecy with which the transformation plan had been prepared. The statement protested that the lands involved in the first project of the Agrarian Transformation were among the best-utilized in the country.[20] The government replied that the reform plans had been announced long in advance, disputed the claims that the land was efficiently utilized, and emphasized, in response to the language of the ANEP statement, that "while it is no sin to have a high income, neither is it a sin to be born," implying that the government was prepared to side with the poor and disadvantaged in this case.[21]

ANEP's second attack made a series of points that were to be recycled by the agrarian elite through the remainder of the 1970s and well into the 1980s.[22] It disputed the accuracy of ISTA's figures, arguing that statistics compiled by "planning functionaries" could not convince those who, "in the affected zone or outside of it, know the reality of production and the high degree of utilization and efficiency of these lands." The population density was high in the affected zone, and it would be impossible to give land to every individual. The reform would reduce production, with disastrous effects nationwide. The statement ended with thinly veiled threats, asking whether "the citizenry would conform to a measure with such grave consequences, just because it has been announced. The Executive Power needs to consider, with great responsibility, the baneful consequences for the future of the country and for the next government that can derive from measures taken so precipitously and which so seriously compromise the future of the country."[23]

The government's response (14 July) reiterated and strengthened its commitment to reform, quoting UCA studies demonstrating that the lands in question were not producing to their capacity. The UCA had by this time suffered a number of bomb attacks in retaliation for its involvement in promoting the reform (Whitfield 1994, 110). "For any person even modestly versed in the problems of economic and social development in underdeveloped countries," the government declared, "it is clear that the problems deriving from the dramatic conditions of life of the population are not resolvable by means of a focus purely on aggregate productivity."[24] El Salvador could produce 20 times as much and still not solve its social problems, the statement observed, and industrialization would require the country to develop an internal market, which the agrarian reform would promote. The government accused ANEP of representing a "small sector" whose members were taking luxury vacations abroad while the reform plan was being prepared. Finally, the statement reaffirmed that the government, "faced with the impossibility of reconciling the interests of a minority that has everything and a majority that has nothing, reiterates its historic and irrefutable commitment to the latter."[25]

On 15 July ANEP charged the government with "verbal violence," "demagogic and classist language," and accused Molina's "planning group" of using language imprecisely, in the manner of demagogues of other latitudes, "especially those countries where liberties and citizens' rights are in danger," a reference to the East Bloc. The public war of words continued with "The Government Reaffirms Its Position with Respect to ANEP," an official statement making the following points: (1) the government alone was responsible for public policy in the country; (2) ANEP is a selfish and intransigent organization attempting to hide behind claims of social conscience; (3) ANEP was unable to deny the necessity of an agrarian transformation; (4) reforms would prevent violence in the short run and dictatorship in the future (an attempt once again to package reforms as anticommunist tactics); (5) the government would listen to ANEP or any group, but was not obligated to obey; (6) ANEP was the party responsible for verbal violence; and (7) the government had committed itself to carrying out the reforms and promised not to fail the country's majorities.[26]

At this point ANEP and its affiliates "saturated the media with a barrage of propaganda. The tone of this campaign was one of hysterical anti-Communism" (Baloyra 1982, 59). The private sector created a number of new "organizations" and federations that ran advertisements condemning the government's actions. The most important of these was the Agriculturalists' Front of the Eastern Region (FARO), which called upon landowners to resist the implementation of the reforms.

In retrospect, the main audience for this public exchange of views was the military. No other constituency in the country had the power to block Molina's reform plans, and ANEP statements condemned Molina and reformist elements of the military while scrupulously avoiding criticism of the military as a whole. As Baloyra puts it, "As astute an observer as Zamora could not detect a single instance of criticism against the military institution among the proclamations of the ANEP against the transformation. . . . [T]he behavior of the private sector vis-à-vis the government seemed an attempt to undermine support for Molina and his initiative, but not to question the legitimacy of the military's presence in power" (1982, 62). In September, a death squad announced itself as the White Warrior's Union (UGB) and raised the stakes by threatening to execute businessmen and legislators who supported the reformist initiative, several of whom the UGB named (Gordon 1989, 199). By October 1976, Molina had been forced to back down—not only a defeat for him and for the reformist program, but a loss of institutional political power for the military. The UCA, finding itself politically isolated, published a searing editorial entitled, "¡A Sus Ordenes, Mi Capital!" ("At your command, Capital!") and suffered further bombings of its facilities (Whitfield 1994, 111–12).

It is generally held that Defense Minister Carlos Romero prevented the reforms from going through, probably by threatening a coup (Montgomery 1982, 90).[27] We have already noted the military conservatives' strength and autonomy, which was reinforced by a generational conflict within the military over seniority, advancement, and the presidential succession. At the time of the agrarian reform crisis, President Molina had already decided that his successor would be either Carlos Eugenio Vides Casanova or José Guillermo García.[28] These two officers, from the *tandas* of 1957 and 1956, respectively, were well known within the officer corps. Both had held choice positions under the Molina government and were seen as among his heirs apparent. Yet the ascendance of either García or Vides to the presidency would virtually ensure the immediate retirement or marginalization of all officers senior to them, and most of the top commanders in the military at this time were from the *tanda* of 1955.

Although the defense minister of a given government was usually seen as next in line for the presidency, Defense Minister Carlos Romero was actually one year senior to Molina. Choosing him as president would block the advancement of the *tandas* of García and Vides, creating potentially intolerable pressures from below for a coup. Molina and his advisers doubted that Romero would be able to complete his term under such circumstances, and therefore decided in favor of the younger officers.[29]

Molina, however, reversed his decision. With political and financial support from conservative civilians, Defense Minister Carlos Humberto Romero and a group of officers of the *tanda* of 1955 led by Colonel Roberto Escobar García pressured Molina to back down on the land reform and alter his choice of successor. This group of officers was in a position to carry out a coup because Escobar García's *tanda* controlled most of the largest troop commands in the country and had the support of elements within the security forces and the intelligence network.[30] The generational issue therefore dovetailed with the land reform issue: Romero, and his backers from the class of 1955, had strong personal incentives to join the oligarchy's challenge of Molina and his policies.

Molina's acquiescence sealed the fate of the Agrarian Transformation and put a more mercenary leadership group in power. The decision weakened the institutional autonomy of the military and contributed directly to an expansion of state terrorism during the next government. Had Molina chosen to resist the threats, he might have succeeded. Colonels García and Vides, who had broad support within the officer corps, might well have been able to rally sufficient support from the middle ranks to resist a coup, since they would have had the twin advantages of supporting an incumbent president and being able to promise faster advancement for subordinates than could the more senior group around Romero. On the other hand, the security forces (despite their history of supporting incumbent presidents against coup attempts) would almost certainly have supported Romero. Molina would have been forced to depend on the generally less well-trained regular army, whose reliability in a crisis was difficult to gauge, as the relatively easy defeat of the *juventud* movement in the 1972 coup had made clear.

Post-Mortem

The failure of land reform and the imposition of an antireform presidential candidate supported primarily by the security forces marked the final decline of the Revolution of 1948. These events erased any pretense that the military was the institutional core of a corporate state. The 1972 elections had proven that the PCN could no longer reliably win elections on the basis of its legitimacy with the electorate, and henceforth all elections were tightly controlled affairs. At the same time, Molina had found that he lacked the independence from conservative elites to carry out an agrarian reform that was needed both to recover the legitimacy of the PCN and, on a more basic level, to appease the increasingly angry and mobilized peasantry. The military's industrialization policies had failed to create an autonomous industrial class willing to support the military on the agrarian issue. Within the military, the mercenary relationship of some elements of the armed forces to the economic elite, combined with the rigid *tanda* system and its self-declared anticommunist institutional mission, made it easier for social elites to steer the military toward an increasingly violent response to popular protests and away from efforts to help the poor. U.S. technical and material aid to the most repressive subagencies of the military further shifted the balance of power away from the regular army and its tradition of more moderate, reformist strategies. Finally, the rich spoils associated with controlling state agencies in the 1970s made officers more interested in prolonging their time in office than in developing a viable long-term strategy for governing the country.

Perhaps the most damaging precedent of the Molina years was that the most conservative elements of the upper classes came out of the land reform crisis of 1976 better organized than before, focusing their approach to political mobilization on working *through* the military. This not only reinforced the most violent sectors of the military; it also established a pattern that would continue, with extremely violent consequences, into the next several years. Private sector interests, in lieu of seeking political legitimacy of their own, expressed themselves politically by conspiring with elements of the armed forces to impede the state's reformist projects. As polarization increased in the late 1970s and early 1980s, this approach to politics would give rise to death squads and mass murder by security and intelligence forces, encouraged by civilian rightists seeking to block state reforms.

FOUR

EXPERIMENTS IN STATE TERRORISM: REPRESSION AND POLARIZATION UNDER CARLOS ROMERO

They closed the escape valves until the whole country blew up.
—Lieutenant Colonel Mariano Castro Morán

The protection racket seemed alive and well when Carlos Romero was elected to the Salvadoran presidency. Conservative civilians expected him to make quick work of the leftist opposition and put a permanent halt to reformist challenges. Carlos Romero's campaign had received "massive financial support" from conservative business organizations, including the National Association of Private Enterprise and the Agriculturalists' Front of the Eastern Region, which had led the fight against land reform (NSA 1989a, 12). The private sector had literally paid for Romero's presidency and expected him to act in accordance with their wishes. Most historical accounts claim that Romero fulfilled these expectations and delivered an uncompromising repression. Horrific state violence did indeed take place under Romero (and in the months prior to his taking office), yet despite the intensity of violence in comparison with Molina's administration, a closer examination of Romero's brief presidency reveals periods of unexpected restraint.[1] Romero allowed significant political openings to take place in August through November of 1977, just after his inauguration, and again from January until March of 1979 during a period of particularly intense international scrutiny. Moreover, despite pressures from the conservative social elite to permit an all-out dirty war against the left, Romero failed to give *carte blanche* to the security forces. Ironically, the security forces had to wait until Romero was overthrown in a reformist junior officers' coup to implement the kind of bloodbath that conservative civilians and officers alike believed necessary.

Like previous Salvadoran military governments, Romero's turned out to be a balancing act. Romero's ability to respond coherently to the political and social crisis was restricted by the weaknesses of the military as an institution and by the influence of both domestic civilian elites and the United States. The basic dilemma of his regime had to do with repression: conservative civilian and military factions advocated greater repression, while the United States (sometimes) and the OAS, popular organizations, and junior officers urged restraint. In contrast to previous military regimes, Romero's largely abandoned the goal of earning popular legitimacy (only in the final month of his government did Romero seriously court popular support), making him dependent largely on the armed forces, civilian elites, and international recognition. In such a context, the factional and generational politics of the military took on even greater importance, and Romero was in trouble on both counts. The choice of Romero as president blocked the advancement of capable and ambitious officers from the *tandas* of 1956 and 1957, the so-called *Equipo Molina*, who had expected to gain top posts, including the presidency, after Molina's term and therefore posed a constant threat of coup d'état. As the security forces used more repression and the country became more polarized, junior officers became increasingly restive, concerned about the viability of repression and about their own long-term futures.

Romero's generational problems were compounded by the fact that he was not particularly well respected within the military. Despite his hardline image and affiliations, Romero was not an outstanding soldier. As a U.S. diplomat remarked, "He talked a tough line, but smart he wasn't."[2] His political affiliation with the oligarchy stemmed in large part from his background as one of the country's premier jockeys, a skill that gave him "special entrée in the circles of the elite" (Dunkerly 1985, 105).[3] Romero had spent six years in Mexico taking courses in horsemanship; this prolonged absence, combined with his abysmal performance as the army's logistics chief during the Honduran war, diminished his prestige within the officer corps. His performance in the 1969 war contrasted markedly with that of Colonel Ernesto Claramount, who ran against him in the 1977 elections as the candidate of the National Opposition Union. Claramount had led one of the most successful advances into Honduras as part of the difficult "Northern Front" assault. In contrast, Romero's failure to mount an effective resupply operation for the fast-moving Eastern Front forces caused this offensive to grind to a halt (Anderson 1981, 117–22; Dunkerly 1985, 105; McClintock 1985a, 235n.).[4]

It was Romero's bad fortune to depend more heavily than previous governments on U.S. support and recognition precisely when a new U.S. president, Jimmy Carter, was making human rights into a high-profile foreign policy issue. The Ford administration's ambassador to El Salvador, Ignacio Lozano, Jr., had pushed hard on one human rights case involving a U.S. citizen who had disappeared at the hands of Salvadoran security forces, but Lozano had been operating without significant support from Washington (SS 2056, 3 May 1977).[5] Carter appointed such highly motivated and bureaucratically skilled human rights advocates as Patricia Derian and Mark Schneider (respectively assistant and deputy assistant secretary of human rights and humanitarian affairs).[6] With the new Carter team in place, Washington finally began to respond to Lozano's pressures and recalled him in March 1977 for "consultations" to rebuke the Salvadoran government for its lack of cooperation on human rights questions. In the same month, the State Department published an unfavorable human rights report on El Salvador and announced that aid levels would be cut to countries that manifested gross and consistent patterns of human rights abuse (Gordon 1989, 220). The Salvadoran government responded by preemptively renouncing all U.S. military assistance, which amounted to only $2.5 million in low-interest credits and $600,000 in grants.

In May, the United States raised the stakes by threatening to postpone an Inter-American Development Bank loan for a hydroelectric facility (ST 105097, 9 May 1977; ST 106224, 10 May 1977). Lozano cabled Washington that he believed pressure on the IDB loan might change the new Salvadoran government's attitude toward human rights (SS 2297, 17 May 1977). Two days later, the Salvadoran government contradicted him by invading the town of Aguilares and killing dozens. A month later, before Romero's inauguration, Lozano was removed from his post with no immediate replacement named (NSA 1989a, 11).

Although the initial U.S. efforts on behalf of human rights were not very effective, Romero took office in a climate of international scrutiny and overt linkage of aid to human rights performance—hindrances that previous Salvadoran presidents had not had to face and that led this hardliner president intermittently to rein in the forces of repression.

The Regency

The period between Romero's election and inauguration proved to be an extremely dangerous one for his opponents. Eight days after the fraudulent election of 20 February 1977, government forces fired on a protest vigil being held in downtown San Salvador. The demonstration had begun on 21 February with a march led by Colonel Claramount, the candidate of the National Opposition Union. Between 40,000 and 60,000 people attended the initial demonstration, and a vigil was maintained in the Plaza Libertad afterward. At around 12:30 am on 28 February, National Guard, army, Treasury, Immigration, and Customs Police units surrounded the plaza, leaving only one street unblocked, and ordered the crowd of about 6,000 to disperse. Many left. Claramount asked the 1,500 to 2,000 people remaining to gather closely around El Rosario Church and sing the national anthem. The government forces, unmoved, opened fire. Accounts of what happened subsequently are somewhat confused, as might be expected. Hundreds of those who attempted to escape through the one "open" street were captured, and apparently some of these were killed. Witnesses saw about 160 bodies being loaded onto trucks and removed from the plaza; at least 15 people attempting to escape were killed, and second-hand accounts refer to over 100 corpses seen at a public hospital in the city. Some reports say that the security forces fired for more than four hours (Americas Watch and ACLU 1982a, 39–40; Gordon 1989, 216; McClintock 1985a, 183–84).

This action was a clear and bloody signal to the opposition political parties that the era of electoral competition and political opening was over. The high command may have seen Claramount as trying to divide the military through his calls to opposition and unity on the part of "all democrats, both civilian and military" (Gordon 1989, 216). The immediate reaction of the popular movement to the massacre at the plaza was spontaneous demonstration and rioting in San Salvador and Santa Ana. Leaders of the Popular Forces of Liberation have since criticized their own failure to better coordinate the popular response: since they themselves did not take elections seriously, they failed to recognize the potentially insurrectionary situation created by the fraud and subsequent repression (Harnecker 1993, 189–90). Nonetheless, the guerrilla organizations and their associated popular organizations benefited from the crackdown as large numbers of people abandoned the conventional political parties and joined the popular movement in the following months (Dunkerly 1985, 107–9).

Between the massacre and Romero's inauguration, an unusually high level of repression and violence continued. A Jesuit priest from Aguilares in Chalatenango, Rutilio Grande García, was ambushed and killed along with an elderly man and a young boy (NSA 1989a, 6). Between 20 February and the beginning of April, roughly 300 people were arrested and 130 disappeared in what appeared to be a purge of key opposition figures, most of them associated with the National Opposition Union (NSA 1989a, 7). On 1 May a National Guard unit attacked a May Day rally in a San Salvador park (held in violation of a ban on public demonstrations), killing 8 and wounding 16. Official sources claimed that the Guard was engaged by 50 armed men, but Church sources strongly contested this version (NSA 1989a, 13). On 11 May another priest, Alfonso Navarro Oviedo, along with a 15-year-old boy, was machine-gunned at a parish hall near San Salvador. The official account claimed that the location was a training center for guerrillas, a charge the Roman Catholic Church vehemently denied. The White Warriors' Union (UGB), which was a death squad name used by the National Guard and ANSESAL, claimed responsibility (McClintock 1985a, 178–81; NSA 1989a, 10).

The San Salvador killings were followed by the military occupation of the town of Aguilares in Chalatenango, in which at least 50 people were killed and 3 priests were arrested and deported (McClintock 1985a, 185; NSA 1989a, 10).

Since the beginning of 1977, 12 priests had been deported in addition to the 2 killed. On 20 June, with Carlos Romero still not yet sworn into office, the White Warriors' Union ordered the 50 Jesuit priests in the country to leave or face "immediate and systematic" execution (NSA 1989a, 10–11). Conservative civilians hated the Jesuits for having "betrayed" the upper classes. The Jesuit-run University of Central America and the San José high school, both of which educated the children of elite families, had played a prominent role in promoting liberation theology, popular education, and land reform. Their religious and organizational work in the Aguilares area had helped make it one of the strongholds of the Christian Federation of Salvadoran Peasants (FECCAS) and later the Popular Revolutionary Bloc (Cardenal 1987). The UCA had suffered bombings in 1976, but the death threats represented a considerable escalation.

The increased repression brought countermeasures by the left. Before the February elections, the People's Revolutionary Army (ERP) had kidnapped the director of the Tourism Institute, Roberto Poma, and demanded the release of two key political prisoners and a ransom of 6 million colones (about $3 million), conditions that the government met (Gordon 1989, 207). In April, the Popular Forces of Liberation (FPL) followed the ERP's lead by kidnapping the minister of foreign relations, Mauricio Borgonovo Pohl and demanding the release of 37 activists (7 of them FPL members) who had been captured by the military. The government denied it had the individuals named in custody and refused to negotiate with the "terrorists" of the FPL. The Borgonovo family, one of the wealthiest in the country, negotiated with the kidnappers, pooled its liquid assets with those of other families, and offered the FPL a ransom that, according to one former combatant, "could have financed the war for three more years." In the end, the FPL turned down the ransom and stuck to its original demand for the release of political prisoners. When the government refused, they executed Borgonovo (Harnecker 1993, 180–84). Both Poma and Borgonovo represented the kind of modernizing capitalists who might have been open to reformist measures. Their killings helped foreclose the possibility that a strong moderate faction would emerge within the business community.

Once Romero was inaugurated on 1 July 1977, the intensity and kind of violence changed abruptly. The most blatant forms of state violence in urban areas diminished and remained at lower levels for about four months, despite an increase in guerrilla assassinations, kidnappings, attacks on government posts, and propaganda activity in September.[7] Shortly after taking office, and just three days before the White Warriors' deadline for the Jesuits' departure, Romero announced his opposition to terrorism of the right and the left, denounced the threats against the Jesuits, made "ostentatious visits to them," and provided armed guards for their homes (Dunkerly 1985, 109).

No one seriously claims that this reduction in violence reflected a commitment on Romero's part to less repressive state conduct. On the contrary, it appears to have been imposed by international pressures, and the types of violence that were suppressed—high-profile urban assassinations, disappearances, and attacks on demonstrations—were precisely the kind that could be expected to attract international attention.

McClintock claims that in rural areas government violence continued as before: military attacks similar to the one in Aguilares took place in several areas of the Chalatenango, Morazán, San Vicente, and Cabañas departments, with reports of detentions, "disappearances," and killings following these operations (1985a, 187). Dunkerly records that "in Chalatenango alone, the 'low profile' of mid-1977 led to 28 political arrests, seven municipality-wide joint searches with ORDEN, one three-day military occupation, several cases of smallowners' crops being fired, seven killings and three rapes by National Guardsmen in a period of six weeks" (1985, 115).

The dynamics of violence before and after Romero's inauguration reveal a characteristic of international human rights pressures that was to become extremely important in subsequent years. International pressures are directed toward the top levels of government, primarily the head of state. When the actual forces of repression have little loyalty to the current head of state, they are relatively free to act, since anything they do will merely taint an administration that they themselves do not especially support. Between Romero's election and inauguration, it was convenient for the security forces to carry out more extreme actions, since any international criticism would be directed against the lame duck Molina. Once Romero took office, he became personally accountable for the killings and death threats. Since the security forces had an interest in protecting the stability of his presidency, Romero could count on their cooperation in constraining some of the most overt urban violence.

Conciliation and Criticism

Besides renouncing the threats against the Jesuits, Romero received two U.S. State Department officials, Richard Arellano and Patricia Derian, to discuss human rights matters, and invited the Inter-American Commission on Human Rights to send a delegation to investigate conditions in El Salvador. These measures, plus the reduction in some of the most egregious abuses, caused U.S. officials gradually to slacken the pressure. As of September, the Inter-American Development Bank had still not approved the suspended loan for the San Lorenzo hydroelectric dam, but the United States had announced the appointment of a conservative new ambassador. Frank Devine, drawn from the professional diplomatic corps, had close ties to the U.S. Chambers of Commerce in Latin America and was personally hostile to the human rights policy.[8]

In late August, the United States granted a $12.7 million urban development project loan. On 3 November, the IDB lifted the suspension of the $90 million hydroelectric loan. State Department official Richard Arellano testified in Congress that the extreme "abridgement" of human rights that had occurred during Romero's period as president-elect had been "anomalous" (Latin America Bureau 1979, 47–51).

A few months of reduced repression allowed the popular left to step up their protest activities. The Popular Revolutionary Bloc (BPR) staged a march on 30 July to commemorate the massacre of students in 1975. From then to the middle of November, the BPR and the United Popular Action Front (FAPU) held at least 13 major demonstrations and 11 major labor strikes in various parts of the country (Gordon 1989, 225–26). The strikes shut down the Rio Lempa electrical generating system, as well as textile mills, clothing factories, bottlers and confectioners, mines, and the construction of the new airport. These actions focused on the demands of workers and on repression: political prisoners, the disappeared, and the commemoration of those who had died in earlier crackdowns. They were complemented by two major land occupations by the BPR, and urban strikers learned to adapt the rural tactic of mass occupations to the factory setting, greatly increasing the impact of their strikes and the difficulty of removing them (Gordon 1989, 227).

The private sector was most alarmed by a demand for a minimum wage increase submitted to the Ministry of Labor by rural workers just prior to the harvest season. Increased landlessness translated into falling rural wages during the late 1970s, at the same time that earnings from coffee and other export crops were setting new records. Workers organized under ATACES (which was affiliated with the Salvadoran Communist Party) and by the Federation of Rural Workers (FTC), which comprised members of FECCAS and the Union of Rural Workers (UTC), presented relatively modest wage claims based on the Ministry of Planning's estimates of coffee, cotton, and sugar profits. When the government rejected these demands, the two labor federations occupied the Ministry of Labor building and held between 150 and 200 hostages. The choice of this action rather than a major rural strike probably reflects the security forces' restraint in urban areas, and the ongoing repression to which organized campesinos in the countryside were subject. Security forces came to the Ministry but held off action, allowing negotiations to take place. The government accepted the mediation of the archdiocese, represented by Monsignor Ricardo Urioste. The settlement reached provided for a fresh round of negotiations but no immediate concessions (SS 5234, 1977; Latin America Bureau 1979, 36–42).

These modest compromises enraged the oligarchy. The Association of Private Enterprise (ANEP) launched a media campaign reminiscent of the attack against Molina. Its "Statement to the Government of the Republic" charged Romero with having been affected by the "psychological warfare" of the "red conspiracy," by which ANEP presumably meant the human rights pressures being brought to bear on the regime. The association accused the Romero government of an "indifference," "tolerance," "fear," and "incapacity" that would ultimately lead to "an utter disrespect for those human rights they say they are defending." It closed with the words, "Enough of the fears and hesitation."[9] The coffee growers' association, ABECAFE, which was particularly worried about rural demonstrations calling for higher wages during the coffee harvest, issued a clear public warning that if Romero intended to stay in office, he needed to uphold his protective function in the tradition of Martínez: "It is time we realized that internal security against whatever may eventually prejudice the integrity of our homeland is the first priority. . . . Many years ago one of our rulers understood this very well when he made the Republic's internal security, peace and order a primary and indispensable condition for the development and prosperity of our country."[10]

This was not the civilian and military hardliners' only response to Romero's unexpected caution and moderation. A group that Former Ambassador Frank Devine identifies as "ultra-conservatives" and "free-wheeling elements of the security forces" plotted to assassinate him and make it appear the work of the Communists. Devine believed at the time that they hoped to persuade the Carter administration to abandon its human rights pressures on the Salvadoran government (Devine 1981, 18). More likely the goal was to discourage Devine himself from being an effective exponent of human rights. As his own account of the period reveals, they were entirely successful.

The Public Order Law

Faced with harsh criticism from the right and muted commentary from Washington, Romero shifted to the right, announcing the Law of the Defense and Guarantee of Public Order on 25 November 1977. The new measure suspended constitutional protections and provided the security forces with arbitrary arrest and detention powers against demonstrators, labor activists, and others suspected of "subversive" speech. The law remained in effect a little over a year, providing legal cover under which the security forces could be increasingly arbitrary. Rather than focusing on the guerrilla organizations, the security forces arrested and in many cases disappeared an increasingly broad range of labor, student, neighborhood, Church, and Christian Democratic activists, without regard to whether they could reasonably be considered a threat to the state (Gordon 1989, 248–49; McClintock 1985a, 194). Of 715 politically motivated arrests reported by the archdiocese of San Salvador before the law was suspended in March 1979, the government had evidence of violent or illegal activity for only 83 persons. The balance were held on the basis of extrajudicial confessions (Gordon 1989, 248).

Increased political imprisonment was accompanied by widespread murder of suspected subversives. During 1978, killings by government forces and death squads averaged 57 per month (Socorro Jurídico Cristiano 1984). Virtually all of the violence at this stage was carried out by the security forces. Documentation by Socorro Jurídico Cristiano of forced disappearances and executions shows the National Guard, special agents of the National Police, the Treasury Police, and *agentes vestido de civil* (plainclothesmen) as the perpetrators, with National Guard actions sometimes supported by ORDEN members. Numerous informants from human rights monitoring groups and from the military indicated that during this period plainclothes agents were almost invariably from one of the security forces.

U.S. reaction to the Public Order Law was mild. Ambassador Devine told the American Chamber of Commerce that "any government has the full right and obligation to use all legal means at its disposal to combat terrorism" (NSA 1989a, 15). Although much of the opposition confronting Romero was in the form of demonstrations and strikes, this remark shows that Devine saw the kidnappings, bombings, and assaults on security forces posts going on at the time as justifying draconian legal measures. It seems likely that Romero read the comment as a signal that the United States would now tolerate repressive measures, whether legal or not.

The Militarization of the Left and the Tightening of the Protection Racket

The crackdown was in a sense a boon to the guerrilla organizations of the left. The Popular Forces of Liberation (FPL) and the National Resistance (RN) had been working since the early 1970s to radicalize organizations of workers, peasants, urban slum dwellers, and students. As peasants' and workers' wages fell while capitalists earned more than ever, the FPL and RN redoubled their efforts to steer existing groups toward a more militant, revolutionary posture or even to form their own unilaterally controlled organizations, like the Union of Rural Workers. The FPL and RN focused initially on the material demands of the group they were trying to organize. As government violence increased, however, they found that repression became the most effective rallying cry. By 1977, organizations focused their demands on the release of captured members, although sometimes they could only denounce their murder at the hands of the security forces. The Popular Revolutionary Bloc and the United Popular Action Front continued to grow, and the People's Revolutionary Army, which had previously focused on military preparations, established its own popular organization, the Popular Leagues of February 28 (LP-28), named to commemorate the massacre at the Plaza Libertad vigil (Harnecker 1993, 115–90).

Repression also moved organization members toward armed struggle, precisely the political transformation desired by the core guerrilla groups. Popular organizations began to retaliate against state repression through vandalism and sabotage of economic targets. Members increasingly obtained and carried sidearms, a process known as *pistolización*. It was a relatively small step from this to the formation of militias, which were initially dedicated to self-defense of demonstrators and organizations but soon became the guerrillas' auxilliary. During 1978, the security forces found it increasingly dangerous to attack large demonstrations, since armed militias would open fire (Cienfuegos 1993, 23–25; Harnecker 1993, 163–75).

The militias also allowed the popular organizations to fight back against ORDEN, with considerable effect.

> In an action typical of this period, ORDEN seized a number of FECCAS–UTC leaders in La Esperanza, near San Pedro Perulapán, on 22 March. The next day one was found decapitated. This led to a gun battle between ORDEN and peasant militants resulting in nine more deaths and a score of wounded. Four days later five ORDEN members were executed by the FPL, the vigilantes responding by driving villagers out of four nearby *pueblos*, 2,000 of them taking refuge in San Pedro. Further clashes resulted in another 15 dead and 50 wounded. Five members of FECCAS were shot in a subsequent demonstration in the capital in which four embassies and the cathedral were occupied by union militants in protest at the repression. (Dunkerly 1985, 116)

In Tenancingo 15 were killed, and in the department of Cuscatlán 29 died in a series of incidents apparently initiated by ORDEN (NSA 1989a, 17). In late April the government announced a campaign against the Popular Revolutionary Bloc and accused the Catholic Church of supporting it. During a two-month period, 15 BPR members were killed, 56 wounded, and around 100 imprisoned. Though the popular organizations took heavy casualties, their willingness and ability to fight back gradually curbed the participation of publicly known members of ORDEN in repressive actions, as they themselves became vulnerable to reprisals. Although a polarized climate of what the journalist Frank Smyth calls "house-to-house espionage and counter-espionage" persisted and deepened in many communities, ORDEN members themselves gradually became more cautious about direct actions against the popular organizations, and many withdrew (Harnecker 1993, 174–75; SS 4843, 24 August 1979). The decline of ORDEN in no way reduced rural repression, which increased during this period, mainly at hands of the National Guard (SS 4843, 24 August 1979).[11]

The government had even less success in suppressing the guerrilla forces, which were more formally and clandestinely organized. The 13 months of the Public Order Law saw a marked increase in kidnappings of prominent businessmen, both Salvadoran and foreign, by the three main guerrilla groups. On 14 May, two wealthy Salvadorans, Ernesto Sol Meza and Luis Méndez Novoa, were kidnapped by the Popular Forces of Liberation. Sol Meza was ransomed for $4 million, Méndez Novoa for $100,000. On 17 May the National Resistance kidnapped the Japanese industrialist Fugio Matsumoto and demanded the release of political prisoners. He was found shot to death in October. Two more prominent kidnappings took place in June, with the People's Revolutionary Army claiming responsibility for one of the abductions. In August, the National Resistance kidnapped a Swedish executive named Schel Bjork, demanding, among other things, the publication of a manifesto in newspapers in Sweden, Japan, Panama, and Costa Rica (NSA 1989a, 17–20). In November and December, it kidnapped an executive for the Phillips corporation, two British bankers, and a Japanese businessman, once again demanding ransoms, publication of political manifestos, and the release of political prisoners. In January 1979, it kidnapped Ernesto Liebes, president of the country's largest coffee export firm. His family and company failed to ransom him before the deadline, and he was found dead in March. In February, a coffee grower, Jorge Alvarez, was kidnapped, the twenty-second victim in less than 20 months (NSA 1989a, 22–26).

The strategy of kidnappings was enormously remunerative for the guerrillas: the National Resistance alone had reportedly amassed some $36 million in ransoms by early 1979 (NSA 1989a, 26). It had a devastating effect on the country's economic elite and the international business community. Many prominent capitalists and executives left the country, and several foreign embassies withdrew their personnel. Needless to say, the persistent vulnerability of elite Salvadorans to kidnappings and killings (several were killed attempting to defend themselves against kidnapping) increased the vehemence with which the upper classes demanded that the military control the situation. The military was failing to uphold its part of the protection racket.

The description of the military's role as a protection racket went beyond analogy during this period. A significant portion of the kidnappings in the late 1970s were perpetrated by members of the armed forces in the guise of guerrillas. A former U.S. diplomat described the military as "essentially a mafia-like organization. Military officers were kidnapping people, and there was extensive informal transference of money from the oligarchy. The kidnapping was partly to put the fear of God into the oligarchs." Colonel José Ramón González Suvillaga (*tanda* of 1956) and Major Guillermo Antonio Roeder (*tanda* of 1961) were operating substantial kidnapping rings.[12] Sometimes these operations were combined with security services in literal protection rackets. Military officers rented the services of troops to provide security for wealthy families and businesses, or operated private security businesses themselves. Major Roeder, who built an opulent lakeside mansion on the proceeds of corruption and kidnapping, is widely reputed to have kidnapped his own security clients. As the same U.S. diplomat put it, "Many in the military viewed kidnapping as a legitimate transfer of wealth. It also brought with it a transfer of political power."[13]

Former Captain Mena Sandoval was part of a special military investigations team funded by the owners of Banco Cuscatlán. He insists that some kidnappings were carried out by intelligence sections of security force units, principally units of the National Guard, the same subagencies that were carrying out death squad activities (1992, 131–32).[14] Thus, the security forces significantly augmented the genuine leftist threat, especially for the wealthiest citizens, in order to extract resources from the private sector. Ironically, the agencies most dedicated to the political protection racket were those most involved in the literal protection racket of kidnapping wealthy civilians, then offering their families security services. This pattern was to continue through the 1980s.

The left did not confine its activities to kidnappings during this period. Though useful for obtaining funds and pressuring for the release of political prisoners, kidnappings required extensive planning and entailed considerable risk for the combatants involved. The guerrilla organizations carried out increasing numbers of lower-risk bombings (including propaganda bombs that distributed leaflets), machine-gunnings of buildings, and assassinations. They also carried out armed propaganda, occupying commercial radio stations and broadcasting political statements. By late 1978, guerrilla attacks of one kind or another were occurring at the rate of one per week (Dunkerly 1985, 117).

Guerrilla activities were supplemented by the increasing militancy of the popular organizations. The strategy of occupying churches, cathedrals, and foreign embassies drew international press attention while requiring the security forces either to make concessions or use extreme force to remove them. By 1978, the connections between the guerrillas and the popular organizations had become increasingly obvious, as they coordinated timing, target selection, demands, and political statements (Gordon 1989, 250–51).

Most of the guerrillas' attacks were directed against the security forces, rather than the regular army. This was intentional: the security forces were known to be the most involved in death squad activity and in capturing, torturing, and disappearing militants from popular organizations. Moreover, members of the People's Revolutionary Army and the National Resistance hoped that the regular army might yet emerge as a progressive force (Villalobos 1991). Since 1975, the RN, elaborating on the strategy of Farabundo Martí and the Communist Party in 1932, had been working with some success to develop sympathy among junior army officers (Cienfuegos 1993, 24). The selective attacks by the left did help polarize the armed forces, provoking differences of opinion regarding repressive violence and setting the stage for the open conflict within the military that emerged in 1979 (Majano 1989, 75). While the security forces had both a pretext to use greater violence (Majano 1989, 75) and personal scores to settle,[15] members of the army were less personally involved and could step back and look at the violence as the product of structural problems.

Pressure from the left and the evident failure of the Public Order Law began to split the business community. Debate began with the assassination of Father Rutilio Grande in 1977. By the end of 1978, some industrial and commercial leaders began to harbor doubts about the efficacy of the repressive campaign, combined with concern about the costs in terms of international support and investment and resentment of the privileged position enjoyed by representatives of agrarian interests within the state. From 1978 until the overthrow of Romero, a number of businessmen, mainly from the Salvadoran Industrial Association (ASI), began holding secret meetings with clergy, including Jesuits from the University of Central America, Archbishop Oscar Romero, and parish priests; politicians from the Christian Democratic Party and the social democratic National Revolutionary Movement; and military officers ranging from reformist captains to Colonel Carlos Eugenio Vides Casanova. Proposals for economic and political reforms to defuse the growing crisis were discussed at a private home or in a downtown office with an underground parking lot, so that participants could come and go discreetly. Despite the precautions, several participants experienced death threats, attempts on their lives, and vandalism against their property. After several months of meetings, this informal group produced a proposal for national dialogue on political and economic reform, which a number of business people dared to sign. Mysteriously, all signed copies of this document disappeared a few days later from a supposedly secure office. The office building in which the group met was bombed. No public proposal for dialogue was ever issued.[16]

At no point did this moderate faction of the elite gain a serious voice within the major private sector associations. Not even the leadership of the Salvadoran Industrial Association or the Chamber of Commerce would call publicly for major reforms or political opening, even though a significant number of industrial and commercial leaders favored reforms. Looking back, business leaders now attribute the scarcity of moderate voices to several factors. Most of the top leaders in business associations had lived through the 1932 revolt and its aftermath, believed in the efficacy of repression and linked reform to advances by communism (see Paige 1994).[17] Entrepreneurs who had come of age during the 1960s and early 1970s were generally much more skeptical about the efficacy of repression, though some of them took a hardline view. Those educated in the Jesuit high school (the Externado San José) and the University of Central America in the 1970s had had greater exposure to the social problems underlying the conflict.[18] But these younger members of the elite were only beginning to play a prominent role in their families' businesses and had little clout within business associations. Finally, many industrialists and merchants also had investments in agriculture or were involved in joint ventures with oligarchic families, and the agrarian elite controlled the executive council of the National Association of Private Enterprise, giving them the power to discourage reformist initiatives.

Moreover, the left was making considerable advances in urban labor organizing and was focusing its guerrilla activities in the cities as well. In contrast to its conscious strategy of avoiding attacks against the regular army, the left made no such distinctions among members of the private sector elite. Many of the victims of kidnappings were industrialists or merchants, rather than growers, and urban industrial plants were hit particularly hard by strikes, worker occupations (in which the workers were frequently armed and took hostages), and sabotage. The shared vulnerability tended to undermine whatever policy differences might have existed between different sectors, reinforcing the ideological hegemony of the fiercely anticommunist agrarian elite, whose attention and political activism focused increasingly on the government's inefficacy in suppressing the left.

Most of the agrarian elite took a very hard line on the activities of the left and the government's response. While moderate business leaders were holding furtive meetings in San Salvador to discuss reform proposals, agrarian families—including some with relatively modest holdings—were taking direct measures to ensure a higher level of repression.[19] Members of the agrarian elite were funding and organizing death squad activities in their local areas, with personnel drawn from the security forces, supplemented by private mercenaries.[20] A squad in Berlin, the Red Car Band, was operated by a civilian named Freddy Portillo; a squad around the town of Usulután was operated by the head of the Sixth Brigade, Colonel Elmer Gonzalez Araujo; another in Santiago de María (also in Usulután), was operated by Héctor Regalado, a dentist (Gibb and Farah 1989).[21] Similar activities went on in San Miguel and Santa Ana, though their coordinators are unknown. Close cooperation developed between civilian sponsors and the military commanders who acted as *padrinos* or godfathers to the death squads.[22]

The Santiago death squad, known as Regalado's Armed Forces (FAR), grew out of a Boy Scout troop that had been established earlier by a U.S. Peace Corps volunteer.[23] In its later incarnation as a death squad, the FAR was literally a protection racket: Regalado once had his "guards" blow up a pharmacy to convince the owner of the need for his protective services. When Regalado founded his Armed Forces, there was very little guerrilla activity anywhere in Usulután.[24] At the outset (1976–77), he ran the Boy Scout squad independently of the military and with private funds, though it coordinated its actions with ORDEN. Regalado charged local landowners by the man-hour for services, mainly killing activists. Later the military began providing clothes, shoes, guns, and transportation for his operatives. By 1978–79, Regalado worked in close consultation with both ANSESAL (the national intelligence agency) and the National Guard intelligence section in San Salvador, with messengers shuttling back and forth to prevent interception of radio or telephone communications. The FAR conducted joint operations with the National Guard and other units, "and were even ferried around in Army helicopters."[25]

In 1978, representatives of several of the more conservative agrarian families approached an aide to President Romero with a proposal to organize and fund a secret network operating on a national level, which would adopt the cellular structure of the left and carry out a full-scale dirty war against them, as in Argentina. The civilians specifically requested that ANSESAL intelligence officer Major Roberto D'Aubuisson be named to command the operation. D'Aubuisson was widely known as a protege of José Alberto Medrano, the former strongman of the National Guard who had formed ORDEN and suppressed organized labor in the late 1960s. President Romero declined the proposal at the time, though from 1980 onward significant elements of this proposal would eventually be put into place.[26]

Conservative civilians also began during this period to cultivate support among junior officers. Whereas powerful families in the past had depended upon their ties to the top echelons of the military, during 1977 and 1978 they began holding meetings with junior officers and offering them lucrative "moonlighting" opportunities. Junior officers were vulnerable to this temptation because, despite their professional rank and improved social status, most were from modest backgrounds and drew extremely low salaries. The availability of loans from the armed forces cooperative meant that most were chronically in debt.[27] The wealthy families' stated goal in reaching out to the junior officers was to circumvent the corruption of the high command, but Mena Sandoval argues that it was also a way of preparing stronger links to those officers who actually controlled troops, in anticipation of the political crisis that elites saw as imminent (Mena Sandoval 1992, 132). This strategy was only partially successful: it proved more difficult to establish links to numerous junior officers than it had been to buy off the colonels. Though the private sector succeeded in influencing many junior officers, they were not able to penetrate the lower ranks sufficiently to preempt the junior officers' movement that would briefly take power in October 1979.

The Opening of 1979

In January 1979, the Inter-American Commission on Human Rights of the OAS visited El Salvador to investigate charges of torture, disappearance, and extrajudicial executions. The rate of killing, which had averaged 57 per month during 1978, fell abruptly during January (to 10), and remained low in February (18) and in March (32). Romero's relative moderation during the commission's visit could not erase the evidence of mayhem during the previous 12 months, however, and the commission duly reported that the Romero government tortured and murdered its political opponents and systematically persecuted the Catholic Church. Romero traveled to Mexico on 19 January in an effort to "polish up his tarnished international image, break the increasing isolation of his government, and seek guaranteed delivery of twenty thousand barrels per day of Mexican crude" (NSA 1989a, 22). He got a tentative agreement on the delivery of oil, but was roasted in the Mexican press, which had access to advance copies of the IACHR report. During his visit, Archbishop Oscar Romero, who had just been nominated for a Nobel Peace Prize, was also in Mexico, attending a conference and drawing attention to the human rights crisis at home.

The United Popular Action Front increased the pressure and international attention by occupying the Mexican embassy and OAS office in San Salvador during Romero's trip (Baloyra 1982, 83). Shortly thereafter, it occupied the United Nations and Red Cross offices there. On 17 January the National Resistance kidnapped Ernesto Liebes, a businessman. The security forces retaliated by killing a priest, Father Octavio Ortiz Luna, and four of his parishioners, accusing them of being FAPU members (NSA 1989a, 22–27).

The violence continued in February. The People's Revolutionary Army bombed police stations and National Guard posts in the capital and in San Miguel, announcing that the actions were in retaliation for the killing of Father Ortiz. Following the established pattern of responding to guerrilla actions by repressing open civilian activists, the Romero government deported a Spanish priest and a Mexican nun, and arrested five labor leaders. The Popular Forces of Liberation proceeded to murder two prominent businessmen, and an unidentified group attempted to assassinate Vice Minister of Defense Eduardo Iraheta (NSA 1989a, 25–26).

Despite all of this leftist activity, Romero felt compelled to repeal the Public Order Law. The damage to his international image endangered delivery of a major loan from the Inter-American Development Bank. International financing had gained importance as a result of capital flight estimated at more than $300 million during the second half of 1978 (Gordon 1989, 255). On 26 February 1979, Romero announced the imminent release of all political prisoners and repeal of the Public Order Law.

Along with the repeal, Romero dismissed the head of the National Guard, General Ramón Alvarenga, who was reputed to have been instrumental in the killings and disappearances of 1977–78. Alvarenga was a convenient officer to sacrifice: an internal investigation in which Captain Mena Sandoval took part had uncovered extensive evidence of Alvarenga's corruption and involvement in kidnappings of businessmen. By dismissing him, Romero quieted the complaints of those elements of the private sector who were concerned about corruption and official kidnapping, while at the same time appeasing international opinion (Mena Sandoval 1992, 136).

The Carter administration saw the repeal as a "healthy sign of flexibility," and the Inter-American Development Bank promptly released a $16.3 million loan for livestock and animal health projects (Dunkerly 1985, 118; NSA 1989a, 26). Romero, however, was now in a hazardous situation. As had happened in 1977, the March "opening" led to greatly increased activity by the left, while the dismissal of Alvarenga generated hostility within the security forces.

The most important development was a series of strikes at two bottling plants beginning on 10 March. At one of them, the security forces stormed the plant, killing between 3 and 10 workers and wounding some 20 others. Although a bottling plant strike may not sound like a major political event, two aspects of these strikes made them significant. First, the plants were located astride the main east–west road leading out of San Salvador, which was the Pan American Highway as well as the route to the light industrial zone around San Bartolo and the international airport at Ilopango. Pickets, crowds of onlookers, and the heavy police presence effectively blocked commercial traffic to the eastern part of the country and led to a travel advisory by the U.S. embassy.[28] Second, the degree of cooperation that emerged between different popular organizations made the strikes particularly threatening to the elite. The bottling plant workers were affiliated with the Popular Revolutionary Bloc, but the United Popular Action Front (FAPU) called out the electrical workers of STECEL on their behalf, shutting down electrical power in most of the country. When the STECEL workers barricaded themselves in the Rio Lempa hydroelectric station and wired explosives to destroy the station should the security forces attack, President Romero was forced to back down (Dunkerly 1985, 126).

All told, 150,000 workers took part in sympathy strikes throughout the nation (Dunkerly 1985, 126). The popular organizations enhanced the impact of the strikes by setting up barricades in various parts of San Salvador. The guerrilla groups attacked police posts and cars. President Romero showed considerable restraint, the police attack at the bottling plant notwithstanding. Security forces were placed on alert but confined to their barracks to avoid confrontations and possible international repercussions. On 13 March Romero addressed the nation by radio, characterizing the events as the actions of "seditious groups" against "public order and the right to work." According to an embassy cable, "Romero warned that the tolerance shown by the security forces in this situation should not be mistaken for indifference" (SS 1333, 13 March 1979).

U.S. Policy Shifts Emphasis

The strikes of March caused consternation at the U.S. embassy, where officials were shocked by the extent of "communist" control of the labor unions.[29] Ambassador Frank Devine began issuing "situation reports" (sitreps) on the "Labor/Security Situation in El Salvador" as often as twice a day. These reports, alarmist in tone, related events ranging in importance from a 23-hour nation-wide electrical blackout to the spray-painting of slogans on walls.[30] In his first sitrep cable, Devine's commentary on Romero's address shows growing concern that the president was too soft on the left. Presumably on the basis of conversa-tions with members of the Salvadoran business elite, Devine remarked that

> President's nationwide radio broadcast fell short of most listener's [*sic*] ex-pectations. Although probably designed to reassure the public, many in-formal observers expected him to announce a state of siege and/or a cur-few. Security forces are unlikely to be pleased by his emphasis on moderation and patience. President himself probably finds this a less than easy or satisfying posture but may well have adopted it in one last effort to identify himself, in the face of [illegible] provocation, with the cause of moderation and respect for human rights. (SS 1333, 13 March 1979)

It is striking that Ambassador Devine assumed that "most listeners" would pre-fer stronger measures. In fact, many in the Salvadoran business community thought that Devine himself was overreacting, and that his fears could lead the United States either to abandon Romero's regime or to intervene against it.[31]

An airgram from the embassy summarizing the activities of El Salvador's la-bor movement since August 1977 notes the "unprecedented display of labor union power," particularly the unexpectedly high degree of cooperation among different federations. Ironically it singles out the minister of labor, Colonel Roberto Escobar García, a notorious rightist, as "overly passive and cautious" (SS A-32, 11 May 1979). Labor unrest and kidnapping had dramati-cally reduced foreign investment in the country: in 1979 private investment reached barely $5 million, compared with $32 million in 1978, "which was it-self considered a bad year." The Japanese business community had shrunk from 2,400 in 1977 to 200 in 1979 (Dunkerly 1985, 127).

Only in sitrep number 3 (SS 1373, 15 March 1979) did Devine reveal insight into the possible counterproductivity of violence. He wrote that the assassina-tion of the labor leader Oscar Armando Interiano "might well cause CUTS [the United Confederation of Salvadoran Workers] and its constituent unions to take an even harder line against the government." The cable traffic from this period that is now public does not indicate what, if any, message the em-bassy delivered to Romero regarding the security situation. Probably it pres-sured him to act with greater firmness.

Plotting against Romero

Romero was already feeling considerable heat from the Salvadoran private sector and its rightist allies in the military. On 21 March he issued a rather de-fensive statement that the government had acted with "deliberation and prudence" in recent labor unrest. The Salvadoran Industrial Association and other private sector groups held "emergency meetings" on 22 March, prompting the president to call an "emergency meeting of his cabinet" (SS 1514, 22 March 1979). Markedly diminished opposition activity in April provided Romero with a welcome breather, but the March crisis had crystallized fear and doubts about him, helping to set in motion two coup plots that began to develop into serious threats during April and May.

One plot involved ultra-rightists responding to the widespread view within the private sector and the security forces that Romero was too soft and in danger of losing control of the situation.[32] This plot included former National Guard commander Ramón Alvarenga, Vice Minister of Defense Eduardo Iraheta, and a group of civilian rightists. The Hill and Regalado families were involved (Dunkerly 1985, 127), as were a group of younger businessmen who had organized a far-right group called the Salvadoran Nationalist Movement (MNS). According to a founding organizer, "we began by pressuring Romero, then planned a coup against him. We met with some officers in May 1979, trying to get something going before it was too late."[33]

The other plot involved colonels from the *tandas* of 1956, 1957, and 1958, led by Carlos Eugenio Vides Casanova and Guillermo García. This plot was motivated by generational interests reinforced by concerns about Romero's ability to maintain order. The conspirators had been associated with the Molina regime, though they had all distanced themselves from his land reform proposals. Their agenda was not clear at this point, aside from installing themselves in positions of power.[34]

Neither movement was successful. The hardline group was unable to assemble enough support, and the Vides/García plot met with resistance among junior officers—the first indication to higher-ups in the military of the developing groundswell of discontent in the lower ranks.[35] From late 1978 onward, the junior officers' movement, which had remained relatively quiescent since its public statements in early 1976, developed a momentum of its own. Captains and other lower-ranking officers were feeling each other out and discussing why the country seemed to be headed toward greater and greater violence, and what should be done about it. Some of the officers involved in these discussions had participated in "study groups" organized by the National Resistance, in which officers and civilians had met to examine socioeconomic and political issues.[36] Others had studied political science at the University of Central America and been influenced by the political and social analysis of the Jesuits.[37] The largest number were simply uncomfortable with the roles that they had been required to play in corruption and fraud and alarmed by the increasing violence and the obvious failure of repression to eliminate the challenge from the left. Lieutenant Colonel René Guerra y Guerra began recruiting reformist officers in November 1978. In the same month, Captain

Francisco Emilio Mena Sandoval was transferred to a staff position in the high command (Estado Mayor) that required him to travel to barracks throughout the country and evaluate their weapons inventories and preparedness. Mena, who was by this point evolving into a dissident against Romero, used this position to meet with junior officers and discuss the crisis (Mena Sandoval 1992, 157–65).

Junior army officers found considerable consensus regarding the need to act. By March or April 1979, they had decided to form a core group to plan a coup. As their agenda developed, they agreed that the security forces would have to be disbanded after the coup, or, at a minimum, separated from the military in order to break the spiral of repression and popular reaction, and that officers involved in corruption and assassinations must be tried and punished (Mena Sandoval 1992, 164–65). Not surprisingly, junior officers were unresponsive when Vides and García approached them. There was little reason to think that merely bringing ambitious colonels from two slightly more junior *tandas* into power would change the corruption and violence that were contributing to the crisis.

The plots against Romero, of which he was aware, exerted contradictory pressures on him.[38] The existence of both the far right plot and the generational plot implied a need to demonstrate greater control, while the junior officers' movement created internal pressure for greater government legitimacy and responsiveness to popular demands. Initially, Romero bowed to the pressures from the right (and from the United States). At the beginning of May, faced by a new series of "extraparliamentary" actions by the popular organizations, he responded with great violence (SS 4806, 25 May 1979). On 4 May the Popular Revolutionary Bloc occupied the French and Costa Rican embassies, demanding the release of five of its leaders arrested in late April. On 5 May BPR members occupied the Metropolitan Cathedral of San Salvador, eight churches, and five schools. On 10 May, National Police fired upon demonstrators at the cathedral, killing 23 and wounding 70. The shooting was filmed by a CBS news crew and televised around the world. This was one of the first times the violence in El Salvador was effectively "witnessed" abroad. Undeterred, the BPR occupied the Venezuelan embassy on 11 May, holding the ambassador and seven others hostage. On 22 May, after the Venezuelan ambassador managed to escape, police fired on a group of protesters who were delivering food to the BPR members occupying the embassy. Fourteen were killed, and the Venezuelans announced their intention to break diplomatic relations with El Salvador over the incident (NSA 1989a, 29).

Following the assassination of Education Minister Carlos A. Herrera Rebollo by the guerrillas of the Popular Forces of Liberation, the government declared a state of siege[39] An embassy cable quotes an unconfirmed report of "a recent meeting at which member of security forces had told group of

Salvadoran businessmen that state of siege would be used as means of getting rid of 'troublesome' labor and other leaders" (SS 3093, 6 June 1979). Confirmation of an intent to settle some scores is provided by the civilian death toll: according to the Archdiocesan Secretariat for Social Communication, 160 civilians were killed by government forces in May, compared with 58 in April, 38 in March, and 18 in February (Universidad Centroamericana 1981, 12). (See Table 1.)

Table 1

State Violence in El Salvador, 1979

	Jan	Feb	Mar	Apr	May	Jun	Jul	Aug	Sep
Civilians killed	15	18	38	58	160	141	53	45	52

Source: Archdiocesan Secretariat for Social Communication (Universidad Centroamericana 1981).

Legitimacy as an Afterthought

Romero's problem was that his regime had virtually no political legitimacy. He could not claim to have been legitimately elected, and he was clearly not even the pre-eminent leader in the armed forces. More importantly for most Salvadorans, he had shown no capacity or will to mediate among conflicting interests in Salvadoran society. Nor did he have an organized base of political support: the official party, the National Conciliation Party, was in almost complete disarray, especially in rural areas, where it had been largely supplanted by the paramilitary elements of ORDEN and the "territorial" militias (Majano 1989, 13–15).[40] The best Romero could do was to postpone his overthrow by satisfying whatever set of critics he thought posed the most immediate threat. This ad hoc strategy dug him ever deeper into an impossible situation. The experiment in repression during 1978 had not only failed to suppress the left but had in fact radicalized it and hastened its progress toward taking arms *en masse*. Yet Romero seemed unable or unwilling to authorize more draconian measures, presumably because he could not afford to lose international recognition and aid. Meanwhile the political openings forced upon him in late 1977 and early 1979, in the absence of other measures to bolster his political legitimacy, had merely opened the door to massive strike actions by the left and increased guerrilla attacks against wealthy civilians and the security forces.

On 18 May 1979, in a last-ditch effort to build political support by posing as a corporatist mediator, Romero called upon political, student, Church, labor, professional, and other "legally recognized" groups to join the government in a National Forum to discuss social and political issues. The proposal fell flat when most legal opposition organizations refused to participate, forming instead a Popular Forum (Foro Popular) that included the Christian Democrats, the National Revolutionary Movement, the National Democratic Union, and the United Confederation of Salvadoran Workers (CUTS).

In July 1979, the Somoza dynasty in Nicaragua collapsed, sharpening everyone's awareness that Romero's government could likewise fall to a popular revolution. The political failure of the National Forum idea, plus his increasing international isolation, created obvious parallels to Somoza's decline. Romero began to reconsider his opposition to socioeconomic reforms. In August 1979, he and Defense Minister Federico Castillo Yanes met with a group of four majors and five lieutenant colonels who had just returned from a two-month political warfare course in Taiwan. Citing the forthcoming October OAS meeting, Romero ordered the officers to form a task force to propose "social changes," based on their training in Taiwan, that would undercut popular opposition. He feared that the OAS condemnation would further isolate him internationally and trigger unrest in El Salvador, and he hoped to preempt this by instituting some significant measures. According to an officer who was part of the group, "He asked us to speak out frankly, which officers were not at that time accustomed to doing. This was unusual. There used to be repression of officers who spoke critically." In the end, however, Romero found the recommendations of the working group to be too radical and chose not to put them into effect.[41]

In early September, Romero tried another tack by announcing that his successor as president would be a civilian. This idea, though welcomed by the U.S. embassy, predictably met with resistance in military circles. The upper levels of the officer corps were still firmly committed to military rule, if only because the *tandas* that were reaching the upper ranks expected to have their opportunity to govern. Officers also worried that a civilian president might appoint a civilian minister of defense. In response to their concern, Romero prepared a new law that provided for a position "akin to our chairman of the joint chiefs of staff—to which the military commanders would elect one of their number to serve as top-ranking military figure in the government at such times as a civilian might be minister of defense" (SS 5202, 11 September 1979). Even if a genuinely open election had been held at this point, it is unclear whether it would have quieted the left. None of the major guerrilla or popular organizations at this point saw elections as a viable path to political power, in part because they doubted that any government, civilian or otherwise, could gain control over the security forces.

U.S. Policy Drifts

Despite the alarmist cables sent by Ambassador Devine during the strikes of March 1979, U.S. policy toward El Salvador appears to have received little high-level attention until the Somoza government in Nicaragua fell in July.

At a regional meeting in Costa Rica, ambassadors and embassy officials agreed that neither a coup from the right nor a young officers' coup would reliably serve U.S interests, and "the more politically sensitive ambassadors at the meeting . . . stressed the need to broaden the range of American political contacts in the country" (Keogh 1983, 155).

In July, following Somoza's collapse, Assistant Secretary of State for Inter-American Relations Viron Vaky traveled to San Salvador to meet with President Romero and his senior cabinet. Vaky came away alarmed by what he saw. He wrote to Washington, "I do not sense that Romero and his government really comprehend the nature of the issues they face, of the polarization process and the pressure building against them, and of what it is really going to take to cope with them. They seem not to understand the difference between critics and enemies or how to distinguish between subversion and dissent" (Tegucigalpa 4063, 26 July 1979). Vaky found that the Salvadorans were expecting the United States to tell them to "circle the wagons against communism." Instead he advised them to make some kind of significant concession to calm popular discontent.[42]

While Washington was pushing Romero to allow a political opening, Ambassador Devine was trying to persuade Washington to commit itself to Romero and jettison the human rights policy. In a secret cable, Devine warned Washington not to repeat its failure to support Somoza. After claiming that the Salvadoran military was so unreliable and ill-equipped that it could survive at most four to six weeks in a civil conflict, Devine wrote, "The Romero government is not an attractive one with which to associate ourselves but perhaps we are at the point now where it may be better than any of the conceivable alternatives which we are likely to get as the result of an armed insurrection, assisted from abroad, and which could easily turn into a mass uprising led by the radical, revolutionary, extremist left. To put it very starkly, have events in Nicaragua so threatened our strategic interests in Central America that we should now give the latter at least momentary preference and precedence over our other objectives?" Arguing that Romero was incapable of understanding, much less implementing, the human rights improvements that Washington was demanding, Devine suggested that Washington ease its human rights pressures and provide Romero with security assistance (SS 4175, 26 July 1979). He supplemented this cable with a personal letter to Vaky, inquiring whether rumored Pentagon and CIA support for military aid reflected a "sea-change" in Washington in favor of a more lenient and helpful posture toward Romero.[43]

Devine's suggestions elicited a diplomatic but clear warning from Vaky, who played down the internal divisions in Washington and added: "You should perhaps know for your own information, however, that there are those who take the position that if our admitted objectives of advancing human rights and containing Castroism were to conflict with each other, the contradictions should be resolved in favor of the latter. I do not think the President would agree with that. In any case, there is an element of obsession with the Cuban/Soviet 'menace.' "[44]

In September, the new Assistant Secretary, William Bowdler, toured the region to explain U.S. Nicaragua policy to members of the "private sector" in the other countries. In a cable sent on 7 September (SS 5113), Devine advised against a visit to El Salvador on the grounds that Salvadorans would probably not be in a mood to focus on the problems of a neighboring country, especially after the assassination of President Romero's brother on the night of 6 September. It seems remarkable that Washington would need to be told this, but El Salvador was at this point still receiving little attention. One of the unintended results of Bowdler's visit was a hardening of President Romero's position: Bowdler's wish to discuss Nicaragua in the midst of a major crisis in El Salvador inadvertently sent the message that the United States was not seriously concerned about the Romero regime (SS 5490, 25 September 1979).

In his 7 September cable, Devine also advised Bowdler not to meet openly with Archbishop Romero, who was by then deeply involved in a junior officers' conspiracy to oust Romero. Devine probably feared that such a meeting would be interpreted as U.S. support for the plot. In fact, as we will see in the next chapter, the United States had little if any role in the coup that ousted Romero. Washington was reluctant to support the junior officers because of the possibility risk that their coup could destabilize the armed forces. The administration was still weighing its options when Romero fell.

Reflections on Violence under Romero

The response of the Romero government to the growing challenge from the left was shaped by conflicting elite-level political pressures both inside and outside the state. Some elements of the private sector elite were calling for greater protection, while others were expressing concern about the damage repression was causing to El Salvador's international image. The United States and the OAS condemned government abuses, yet the panicky U.S. embassy also pressured the government to restore order. Different factions of the military were calling for opposite measures, and each threatened to overthrow Romero. The result of these contradictory pressures was an inconsistent policy that intermittently provoked greater militancy on the part of regime opponents, then provided them with the political space in which to act.

Yet intermittency alone does not explain the failure of repression to contain the opposition. The experiment with increased violence during 1978 had, after all, failed in its own terms. The greater arbitrariness of state violence under the Public Order Law had given an ever-broader cross-section of Salvadorans the incentive to take arms in self-defense. The increasing numbers of militants willing to support the organizations of the left were motivated less by ideological conviction than by personal hatred of the security forces based on experience.[45] Peasant and worker organizations that had avoided violent actions found their members captured, tortured, and killed as if they were guerrillas. The intensity and arbitrariness of violence made it rational to arm oneself in self-defense, which often proved to be the first step toward joining the guerrillas (Mason and Krane 1989, 176–77). Thus, although the opening of early 1979 no doubt facilitated leftist militancy in March 1979, the new opposition configurations established during 1978—particularly armed protesters and popular militias—would inevitably have posed a serious challenge to the state. When the state turned to wholesale slaughter against the popular movement in 1980, these armed and radicalized militants quickly became a guerrilla army, and civil war began.

If the arbitrariness of state violence was the main reason for its counterproductivity, what accounts for such arbitrariness? First, the security forces had only a limited ability to target the guerrillas through infiltration and intelligence gathering.[46] Any general increase in state violence brought with it increased arbitrariness, as state forces outran their intelligence (SS 3905, 16 July 1979; this issue is discussed in greater detail in Chapters Five and Six). Second, the Salvadoran state security apparatus found it difficult, for ideological reasons, to differentiate between protesters with valid grievances and guerrillas intent on the violent overthrow of the government. The failure to make this distinction was partly a legacy of 1932 and partly the result of ongoing incentives for the security forces to adopt the intransigent antireformism of the most conservative sectors of the civilian elite. Anticommunist ideology was intrinsic to the Salvadoran military and its conception of its mission, but anticommunism can encompass reformism, as illustrated by the reformist, "good government" imperative in U.S. counterinsurgency doctrine, or the reformism of Taiwanese political warfare doctrine (Shafer 1988).[47] The Salvadoran agrarian elite, in contrast, viewed any reformism or concession to labor as equivalent to communism. At some level, this is simply a matter of interests: landed elites demand unconditional control over their property and do not want to bargain collectively with their workers. Their belief that they could continue to enjoy these core interests stemmed from the experience of 1932, when repression worked and provided decades of relative quiescence on the part of peasants. Paige (1994) adds the observation that in 1932 reforms opened the door to an attempt at armed revolution: Salvadoran elites thus had a historical precedent —or at least a historical rationale—for rejecting reformism as the thin edge of communism.

This kind of thinking, which seems most understandable among the agrarian upper classes, held sway within the security apparatus. Its officers had not only inherited the tradition and supposed lessons of the *matanza*, but had ongoing incentives to accept this antireformist point of view. Suppressing reform and reformists meant an expanded role for agents of repression; political closure and the polarization it created allowed the security forces literally to extort more resources from the private sector.

Romero's interests and those of the security forces in charge of repression were distinct. While the security forces were committed as institutions to a purely repressive strategy, Romero as president had to consider the broader political viability of his regime, which required him to retain some degree of legitimacy in the eyes of both his population and his foreign benefactors. Romero's downfall can be traced to his dependence on security forces that were essentially mercenaries for conservative civilian interests. He needed the security forces to defend him against popular unrest and against challengers from the generation of Vides and García. In practice, the security forces sided with hardline civilians against the president when he proposed reforms or attempted political openings. Without the backing of the security forces, he could not adopt the policies that might have calmed the mass opposition.

Ironically, after two years of reacting to conflicting demands of the internal right and the international community, Romero was unseated by the threat that he had seen as least important: junior army officers who were hoping to break the cycle of violence by giving the opposition the radical change it wanted. Though Romero had been aware of the junior officers' discontent, few observers had predicted the strength of the movement or the radicalism of its agenda. The next two chapters examine the reformist coup, its eventual failure, and the bloodbath that resulted.

FIVE

THE REFORMIST COUP AND THE FIRST
REVOLUTIONARY GOVERNING JUNTA

Some of the greatest tragedies begin with good faith. You don't have to look for
bad faith to find the seeds of disasters.
— Héctor Dada, former cabinet member, in the First Revolutionary Governing Junta

The rich weren't seriously afraid of the left, or at least were equally if not more
afraid of us. They thought we were as great a threat as the left, which is ridiculous.
— Former cabinet member, in the First Revolutionary Governing Junta

Elements of the military used violence to unseat the first junta. The junta was
vulnerable to this because of its immaturity.
— Colonel Adolfo Majano, Former junta member

On 15 October 1979, President Carlos Romero was overthrown in an almost
bloodless coup carried out by a movement of junior officers. It was, as one of
the participants said, "the most widely advertised coup in Latin American history."[1] Indeed, by September 1979 it was a foregone conclusion among informed people in San Salvador that Romero would be ousted: the only questions were when and by whom. It was in fact who did it, and their intention,
that caught most people by surprise. Hardliners from Romero's clique, the
generational movement of the Equipo Molina, and reformist junior officers
closely advised by Jesuit professors from the University of Central America and
Archbishop Oscar Romero had had coup plots under way since April. It
turned out to be the junior officers' movement, "the surprise one," that mobilized thousands of troops, threw Romero out, and set the initial agenda of a
new joint civil–military government.[2]

Unlike previous coups that had only captured capital city barracks, this
movement included almost all of the military installations in the country. Even
the National Guard, usually the loyalist coup-breaker in the past, rode this one
out. Only the National Police and one company of air force airborne troops
sided, briefly, with President Romero. Like the coup of 1960, the movement of
1979 was a response to the failure of repression to deliver political stability. It
sought to establish a legitimate government by including opposition civilians
and announcing radical reforms that would fundamentally change the economic structure of society and end the protection racket. The night of the

coup, the conspirators released a proclamation that denounced the "ancestral privileges" of the "dominant classes" and promised "an equitable distribution of national wealth" by reforming agriculture, the tax system, social services, and labor laws. An end to repression would be achieved by dismantling ORDEN, combating "extremist organizations that violate Human Rights," restructuring the security forces, prosecuting human rights violators, and reforming the judiciary. The armed forces would create "a propitious climate for the holding of genuinely free elections within a reasonable time frame" (see Appendix A). The junior officers' emphasis on broader political participation and ending military impunity anticipated key elements of the peace settlement signed by the government and the guerrillas more than a dozen years later.

The private sector was initially relieved by Romero's overthrow, but once the business elite saw the makeup of the new government, relief turned to horror and shock. As one businessman put it, "We thought all was lost."[3] Within a few days of the coup, a new Revolutionary Governing Junta (JRG) had been formed. It included Guillermo Ungo, who represented the Social Democrats of the National Revolutionary Movement (MNR) as well as the Foro Popular, in which the Communists were represented; Román Mayorga Quiros, the rector of the University of Central America (UCA); Mario Andino, an engineer for a multinational firm and a representative of the openly reformist faction of private industry; Colonel Adolfo Majano, who represented the reformist current within the military; and Colonel Jaime Abdul Gutiérrez, a relatively unknown military engineer and member of the Equipo Molina. The junta assembled a cabinet in which all but three ministries were headed by Christian Democrats, Communists from the National Democratic Union, Social Democrats, or reformist technocrats with ties to the UCA. The remaining three were headed by moderate members of the business community. The most unusual feature of the government was the prominent role of UCA faculty: Mayorga and Ungo, plus seven cabinet ministers, had taught there (Castro Morán 1989, 275–77).

The presence of Gutiérrez on the junta should have been a warning sign to supporters of reforms. He promptly named a conservative officer from the Equipo Molina, Colonel Guillermo García, as defense minister. García, in turn, tapped senior colleagues from his own and adjacent *tandas* for most of the important command positions in the military. Gutiérrez had infiltrated the junior officers' movement, allowing the Equipo Molina to piggy-back on the reformists' broad organization of troop commanders. Naming García as defense minister was the first move in an intense power struggle between reformists and hardliners within the military. In the immediate aftermath of the coup, however, most observers believed that the reformists had the upper hand.

A series of early steps suggested a serious reformist intent to move from coercion to popular legitimacy as a basis for governance. The military members of the junta released all surviving political prisoners and announced an investigation of human rights violations from the previous administration, with punishment for violators and a purge and reorganization of the security forces, again foreshadowing a key element of the peace accords 12 years later. Sixty-six senior officers were summarily dismissed from the service (two-thirds as many as were purged in 1992 by the controversial Ad Hoc Commission). Sixty National Guardsmen soon followed. The junior officers' movement established a Permanent Council of the Armed Forces (COPEFA), made up of the *enlaces* (liaisons) to the coup plot from each of the barracks in the military. COPEFA would evaluate all measures carried out by the junta to ensure compliance with the intent of the Proclama.

Yet repression *increased* after the coup. State violence in October occurred at triple the level of September, and after a brief pause in November, violence escalated to five times the levels seen during the last, bloody months of Romero's administration (Universidad Centroamericana 1981). By December, the investigative process had ground to a halt, and neither the junta nor reformists in the military proved able to halt killings by the security forces and death squads. After the JRG passed a law that froze land holdings—a crucial step toward major land reform—members of the military high command bluntly informed the civilians in the government that reforms would go no further. At the end of December, the civilian cabinet issued an ultimatum to COPEFA to save the reform process. The junior officers' council responded that it could not comply with the government's demands, prompting all civilian members of the government to resign.

The period from the October coup until the end of 1979 presents a number of paradoxes. The coup took place in a context of rising polarization and mass opposition, and itself catalyzed protests and military actions by the left; yet opposition activities in and of themselves are not an adequate explanation of the dramatic fluctuations, or the far greater intensity, of state violence during this period. Opposition activities after the coup were a little more intense than they had been under Romero; they certainly did not increase by factors of three or five, as did state violence. Although the People's Revolutionary Army engaged in some minor military adventures the day after the coup and the Popular Revolutionary Bloc organized large demonstrations and building takeovers, the Communists in the National Democratic Union joined the government, and the National Resistance and United Popular Action Front chose to wait and see.

The mixture of reform and repression presents another set of puzzles. Many observers have attributed it to an intentional, U.S.-sponsored policy of combining reforms and coercion to block the left. If this was a deliberate policy, on the part of either the armed forces or the U.S. government, it was an unsound and irrational one. As this chapter will show, any contributions that the reforms made to political stability were more than outweighed by the destabilizing and provocative effect of state violence.

The final puzzle of the post-October period is that despite its unprecedented strength, the coalition built around the junior officers failed in its challenge to upper-class and military privileges. We must not minimize the challenges they faced—the organizational strength and institutionalized impunity of the security forces and intelligence services, the security forces' access to the financial power of the conservative upper classes, and the organizational weaknesses of the reformist movement itself, but neither should we treat their defeat as a foregone conclusion. The reformist movement in the military in 1979 was far stronger than any of its predecessors, enjoying the support of more than half of the officers in the military. Technically skilled members of the reformist elite controlled strategic positions within the state apparatus, while the reformist junior officers continued to control the majority of troops and took steps to institutionalize their influence within the state through COPEFA. Moreover, many of the members of the mass organizations of the left had high hopes for the junta, forcing their more skeptical leaders to give it, for a time, the benefit of the doubt. With respect to socioeconomic reform, the 1979 reform agenda went considerably farther than the 1992 peace accords it foreshadowed. Moreover, resistance to the reformist project was initially weak. Private sector elites, unprepared for the strength and coherence of the reformist challenge, found themselves cut off from their accustomed channels of influence in the military when the junta dismissed most of the senior officers they had been working with. Yet within two and a half months, the civilian supporters of the reform movement resigned from office, setting the stage for the escalation of state violence in 1980.

This chapter attempts to explain these outcomes by focusing on the intra-institutional politics of the military; on intra-state conflicts between civilian reformists and repressive factions of the military; and on patterns of interaction between competing state factions, the conservative civilian elite, and the revolutionary left. I argue that the dynamics of state violence during this period and the mixture of reform initiatives and coercion reflect internal conflicts between reformist and repressive factions within the armed forces. The increased violence in the wake of the coup stemmed indirectly from the very strength of the reform movement: the reformists' agenda constituted a challenge to the interests of ambitious senior officers and to the privileges and impunity of the state security apparatus. This challenge led to the formation of a defensive alliance between senior commanders of the armed forces and members of the most repressive agencies. This renewed hardline alliance was reinforced by conservative civilians, who, after a brief period of bewilderment, rallied and provided financial and political encouragement for repressive terrorism by state forces.

I argue that the reformist movement's organizational weaknesses made it vulnerable to the Machiavellian tactics of the new military high command. The core of the reform movement was made up of young, politically inexperienced officers who were easily subordinated, intimidated, outmaneuvered, and conned by their superiors. Those few senior officers on the reformist side were either relatively unknown (a liability in a service based on personal loyalty) or so dedicated to preserving military unity that they were unwilling to act decisively against the hardliners. The reformists' links to the civilians who made up the new government were few, personal in nature, and easily disrupted, and their ties to any sort of mass popular base were even more tenuous. The reformist formula depended upon the cooperation of the left, yet the revolutionary organizations remained deeply suspicious of the military.

Hardline elements exploited these weaknesses and undermined the viability of the reformist project by carrying out violent attacks against precisely those social and political groups whom the reformists hoped to appease. Hardliners in the military used violence with the specific intent of destabilizing the junta and driving it from office. Thus the dynamics of state violence during this crucial conjuncture were not only a consequence of intra-state political competition but also a tool that hardliners used to shape the political arena and create contradictions for reformist leaders—in the form of thousands of state murders committed against potential supporters—sufficient to drive them from office.

Finally, I argue that U.S. actions, like those of the Salvadoran state, reflected conflicting policy currents rather than a single, coherent policy. Although senior Carter administration officials reluctantly conceded that a reformist coup was the best available outcome, in practice the United States did little to support the reformist agenda. In part, this reflected a lack of information regarding the political potential of the reformist movement. Colonel Gutiérrez—hardly a disinterested party—was one of the main informants for the U.S. Central Intelligence Agency (CIA) regarding the coup.[4] His reports tended to downplay the importance of the reformist movement and made it sound as if he and his fellow senior officers were fully in control. This distortion was reinforced by Ambassador Devine, who described the reformist movement as a threat to the military chain of command. Devine repeatedly asked Washington to consider restoring military aid for El Salvador. The administration, operating on the assumption that the left posed the most imminent threat, instructed Devine to continue pressuring the junta to maintain order, a stance that played directly into the hands of hardliners in the military.[5] Meanwhile, U.S. defense attachés and CIA agents were maintaining close contacts with the most right-wing elements of the armed forces, in the process sending signals of support that contradicted official Washington support for the junta (SS 1886, 13 March 1980).

The Military Youth Movement

Jovenes son todos ellos que no tienen complicidad con el pasado. (The young are those who have no complicity with the past.)
—José Ingenieros
   From an interview with Lieutenant Colonel Mariano Castro Morán, August 1989

The Juventud Militar was only a movement. An army needs structure.
—Former member of the Revolutionary Governing Junta

By the late 1970s, decades of protection racket politics had created conditions in which junior officers in the Salvadoran army had serious grievances against their superiors and with the hardline security apparatus as a whole. Most of the officers in the Salvadoran military had been recruited from the lower and lower-middle classes. Despite efforts during academy training to distance them from the civilian population, most officers retained, at least for a time, a sense of their own humble origins. They were typically posted in provincial barracks during their first years out of the academy, and therefore most married women from modest provincial families. While high-ranking officers in the 1970s gained access to considerable wealth through corruption and achieved somewhat greater social status, most middle-ranking and junior officers continued to identify themselves more with the lower classes. Most, in fact, could not afford even a very modest house on their official salaries and were deeply in debt. The need to moonlight for wealthy patrons, usually in some protective capacity, rubbed many junior officers the wrong way while making them vividly aware of class relations within Salvadoran society.[6]

Junior officers tended to have a longer-term vision than their superiors, who were enjoying their moment at the top and who generally hoped to keep the racket going just a little while longer. The future prospects for junior officers depended on the ability of the military to find a sustainable institutional role. As we have seen, military presidents consistently followed policies of expediency tailored to keep themselves in positions of power from which they could profit, while allowing the overall political legitimacy of the military-led state to decline precipitously. Their insistence on keeping the military in control of government without any effective inclusionary corporatist mechanisms meant growing alienation between "the noble armed institution" and the people it supposedly served. The increasingly violent governments of Molina and Romero had created conditions for a social explosion, and junior officers began to doubt that the military institution would survive in the long run.

These general concerns were exacerbated by three issues of military honor: electoral fraud, persecution of the Church, and state violence. Many junior officers were particularly offended when they were ordered to stuff ballot boxes and alter ballots, which became necessary when the military's half-hearted efforts at legitimation gave way to more overt protection racket policies. They were concerned not only about their personal honor but also about the impact of these practices on the institution.[7] Attacks on the Church led many officers "to seriously question whether they were being well led" (Majano 1989, 12). The prevalence of torture, disappearances, and death-squad-style murders under Romero disturbed many officers. Some objected on principle, and many felt that such actions brought disgrace upon the military, both at home and, perhaps more importantly, in the eyes of the international community.

Beginning in late 1978, junior officers began talking seriously among themselves about taking some kind of action to break out of the downward spiral into which Romero, and the protection racket system in general, had led the country. As noted earlier, some of those involved had taken part in the study groups organized by the National Resistance in the mid-1970s, some had been members of the military youth movement that challenged the Molina government on land reform, and others had studied at the University of Central America or the National University and been influenced by the relatively left-wing intellectual ambiance of both institutions.

One of the first organizers was Captain Francisco Mena Sandoval, who, though a proficient airborne infantry officer, had always been uneasy about military corruption and brutality. Mena was also something of a maverick: he had been thrown out of the military academy for protesting against his superiors' abuse of authority but had regained his place by staging a hunger strike in front of the Presidential Palace, an unusual strategy for an aspiring military officer. Though impulsive, volatile, and prone to errors in political judgment (see below), Mena was to prove one of the mainstays of the reformist movement and was one of the few officers willing to abandon the military and join the guerrillas when the reformist project finally collapsed in late 1980.

Another of the early organizers was Lieutenant Colonel René Guerra y Guerra, who had spent much of his military career outside the country obtaining advanced degrees in electrical engineering. His international experience gave him a more cosmopolitan political outlook than most of his colleagues but also meant that he was relatively unknown within the officer corps. Nonetheless, his reformist vision, his technical skills in arranging secure telecommunications, and his contacts at the University of Central America proved vital to the movement.

Captain Román Barrera, another early leader, felt that a government based on electoral fraud was "unsustainable" and doubted that his superiors understood the economic or the political roots of the growing insurgency. "The country was a banquet for the subversives, with so many frustrations and injustices," he told me.[8] As an artillery officer, Barrera was technically sophisticated, respected by his peers, and able to provide heavy weapons support for the coup should that prove necessary. Both Guerra and Barrera had cousins who were priests. Barrera's had been a clandestine member of the Popular Forces of Liberation and was killed by the government (Whitfield 1994, 188).

By March or April 1979, army and air force captains had reached a rough consensus that Romero needed to be removed and the drift toward greater violence stopped. They agreed on the following points:

(1) They needed to find a core group of officers who could actually organize a movement.

(2) After the coup, the security forces—the National Guard, the Treasury Police, and the National Police—would have to be broken up, or, at a minimum, separated from the military.

(3) Officers involved in corruption and assassinations would have to be tried and punished, or else the movement would have no credibility.

(4) The movement would have to remain "out of the hands of the United States," but any government created by the coup would need U.S. support. Though conspirators differed in their thinking on how corrupt and violent senior officers should be punished, a significant number, including Mena Sandoval, favored executing them by firing squad, in effect treating their crimes as treason (Mena Sandoval 1992, 15, 164–65, 175, 188).[9]

The first step was to identify supportive officers in every barracks in the country. This strategy eventually made possible a well-coordinated nationwide movement that avoided the isolation that led to the military defeat of the *golpistas* in 1972. Mena Sandoval, traveling around the country to inspect equipment and weapons storehouses, helped build the movement. His next assignment, to the logistics and repair center known as Maestranza, allowed him to talk with officers from various military units who came in with equipment needing repair (Mena Sandoval 1992, 167–68).

Captains were also able to use the armed forces' own telecommunications system to organize. During the night, captains were in charge of barracks around the country while their superiors slept, so conspirators could pick up the telephone and be assured of reaching a fellow captain.[10] A core group of captains from the *tandas* of 1967 and 1968 were in the midst of their second year at the High Command and General Staff School, which they attended while still holding troop command positions. Meeting regularly in the course of their studies allowed them to proceed with planning (Majano 1989, 32–33). Even so, it is remarkable that the conspirators were able to assemble such a strong movement, given the history of internal surveillance and repression of dissident officers. As Romero became concerned about the plotting against him, he shifted more funds into the National Special Services Agency (ANSESAL) and ordered it to increase internal investigations within the military.[11] What made the movement grow, above all, was the nearly unanimous sense, even among officers with conservative instincts, that some sort of change was necessary, lest the Salvadoran military go the way of the Nicaraguan National Guard. By August

1979, the movement was so broad and secret that officers who had recently joined the conspiracy were attempting to recruit officers like Mena and Barrera, who had begun it (Mena Sandoval 1992, 168).

Core conspirators, including Mena Sandoval, Guerra y Guerra, and air force Major Alvaro Salazar Brenes (who had recently resigned his commission), had close ties with the University of Central America and frequently sought guidance from the Jesuits. Guerra and Salazar had studied there, and Mena had become friendly with them through a relative who belonged to the order. The Jesuits, for their part, recognized the potential importance of the junior officers' movement, although they were not informed of the specific details of the coup plot until August. Whenever Mena visited, several of the Jesuits would clear their busy schedules and "gather the high command" to talk with him (Mena Sandoval 1992, 173). In September the University provided the conspirators with a copy of a document that had been prepared for the proposed National Forum. Entitled "A Democratic Solution to the Salvadoran Crisis," but usually referred to as "The Yellow Book," it laid out a set of guidelines for structural and political reforms. It circulated among the officers, who studied and discussed it, "little by little getting a grip on its contents, at least in its most general aspects" (Mena Sandoval 1992, 173–74). From August onward, the officers consulted regularly with the Jesuits, as well as with Archbishop Romero, who saw in Mena and the others the potential for reforming the armed forces from within and avoiding civil war (Mena Sandoval 1992, 173–74).

In August 1979 the conspirators formalized their Military Coordinating Committee, made up of Lieutenant Colonel René Guerra y Guerra, former air force Major Alvaro Salazar Brenes, Colonel Jaime Abdul Gutiérrez, Captain Román Barrera, and Captain Francisco Mena Sandoval. Gutiérrez' presence was controversial from the start. He had learned about the movement from Mena Sandoval, who worked under him in the Maestranza. Perhaps because Gutiérrez had been involved in the coup of 1961 along with other moderate and respected officers such as Mariano Castro Morán, Mena felt free to discuss his concerns about the current situation with him. It is indicative of Mena's lack of political sophistication (a quality he shared with many of the junior officers involved) that he was not aware of how different the goals of the Gutiérrez/García/Vides cabal were from his own. Once aware of the junior officers' activities, Gutiérrez informed Mena and Guerra that the coup plot of the Equipo Molina was well under way and suggested joining the two conspiracies. Faced with discovery by an untrustworthy superior, the original conspirators did not know what to do. Guerra consulted with Archbishop Romero, who agreed that Gutiérrez should be kept out of any leadership position, but that he would be easier to control inside the movement than outside. It was decided to include him in the coordinating committee (Keogh 1983, 166).

The Competition for Control of the Movement

Incorporating Gutiérrez into the movement appears, in retrospect, to have been a serious error. He immediately began contesting the junior officers for control, attempting to discredit Guerra as a leftist, and seeking to include his colleagues García and Vides in the plot. He scheduled special meetings at which García and Vides addressed the conspirators, and he made a point of not inviting Guerra (Keogh 1983, 166). As we have seen, García and his colleagues had tried to organize their own movement as early as April 1979 but found little support among junior officers, who were already developing their own plans.[12] Frustrated, García had sought a role in a rightist autogolpe being planned by Deputy Defense Minister Eduardo Iraheta.[13]

The inclusion of Gutiérrez in the reformist movement was a windfall for García. Though he never formally joined the conspiracy, he built support for himself, even among junior officers, by tailoring his views to his young and idealistic audience. According to Mena Sandoval, García and Vides declared themselves in full support of the young officers' "just struggle." Mena writes, "I personally, when I listened to García talk about institutionality, love of profession, commitment to the fatherland . . . I truly believed what he was saying" (Mena Sandoval 1983, 448).

One officer claimed that only a handful of the most rightist junior officers within the movement supported García, naming José Ricardo Pozo (*tanda* of 1969) and René Arnoldo Majano (*tanda* of 1968).[14] It seems clear, however, that support for García and the others was not confined to these two individuals. On 6 October 1979, delegates to the Military Coordinating Committee met to elect members of the post-coup junta. With 30 of the 37 delegates present, Colonel Adolfo Majano was elected unanimously to represent the military on the junta. In choosing the second military member of the junta, a majority of 17 voted for Guerra, but 7 voted for García, 2 for Vides Casanova, and 1 for Gutiérrez.[15]

The following day, all 37 delegates were present in the capital, and a second meeting was convened. Gutiérrez persuaded them to hold a second vote. Guerra was meeting with Archbishop Romero to brief him on the status of the conspiracy, and Gutiérrez took advantage of Guerra's absence to claim that he was too left-wing to be trusted, insinuating that he had connections to the radical left. Gutiérrez urged the young officers to vote for his colleague García. In the repeated votes that followed, a persistent deadlock developed in which neither Guerra nor García earned a majority: 14 of those present voted for García versus 17 for Guerra. This stalemate was resolved, in the early hours of the morning, when Captain Mena Sandoval proposed Gutiérrez, the least powerful of the Equipo Molina officers, as a compromise candidate. Mena's intention seems to have been to prevent the movement from breaking down or losing its momentum just a week prior to the planned date for the coup. Exhausted, a majority of officers backed Gutiérrez.[16]

The Role of the United States

As happens whenever a coup occurs in a country in which the U.S. embassy has played a prominent role in the past, there was considerable speculation about the possible U.S. contribution to the October coup. The available evidence suggests that although the embassy was aware of the coup, it did not play a major role in making it happen or determining its outcome. By early October, the embassy had a fairly accurate idea of what was in the offing. Participants in the coup contacted embassy officials, describing the movement's plans and asking that the embassy keep its distance but offer prompt recognition, technical assistance, and money once the new government was installed (ST 269875, 6 October 1979). The embassy learned through other sources that the movement had support from the Church, and that even the Christian Democratic Party and important sectors of the business community were beginning to see a reformist coup as the only option (SS 5772, 10 October 1979).[17] With this information in hand, the State Department prepared a lengthy policy paper that examined a wide range of possible outcomes and weighed whether the United States should actively support the reformist coup, keep its distance, or continue to support Romero. The paper concluded that the costs of continued support for Romero were high and that the most likely outcome was a successful reformist coup. A failed coup, it warned, could lead the Romero government to impose even harsher policies and might cause a dangerous split in the military.[18]

Washington moved cautiously, even though an internal memorandum judged that "a successful coup carried out by the moderates, leading to a joint civilian/military *junta*, offers the cleanest solution to our policy dilemmas and does not threaten the safety of American citizens."[19] The primary concern was "whether a coup scenario provides any viable alternative to insurrectional violence, or whether a coup would not split the military, create vacuums and bring further violence effectively opening the way to the extremists" (ST 264095, 9 October 1979). Assistant Secretary of State Vaky instructed Devine to meet with Archbishop Romero and leading Christian Democrats to test whether the existing policy of encouraging the Romero government to hold elections had any remaining value before the administration moved on to something new. Devine was uneasy and asked for reconfirmation of his instructions, fearing that a meeting with the archbishop could be misinterpreted as U.S. support for the reformist coup. Evidently he preferred not to send such a message. The meeting with Archbishop Romero and Román Mayorga confirmed that they saw the country as too polarized for elections and thought that the coup presented the most promising outcome and the fewest risks. They rejected Devine's pleas to consider waiting for elections (Devine 1981, 136–67; SS 5835, 11 October 1979).

Despite foreknowledge, declassified State Department documents and interviews with State Department officials suggest that the United States was not involved in planning the coup. Dermot Keogh (1983, 155–57) argues that the view from the State Department is not the whole picture. Basing his arguments on anonymous interviews, Keogh claims that a coalition of officials whom he calls the "security lobby" organized through the National Security Council to use the resources of U.S. intelligence agencies to develop "a predictably 'safe' military solution" while keeping the State Department in the dark. Particular attention has focused on the possibility that the United States influenced the outcome of the two votes in which Guerra was initially elected to the junta and subsequently replaced by Gutiérrez. A young officer told Carolyn Forché (1980): "The United States opposed the naming of Guerra y Guerra and instead proposed two names: Colonel José García and Colonel Jaime Abdul Gutiérrez. We needed American support, and we agreed to this." Asked why the United States favored Gutiérrez and García, the officer answered "There are other ways for you to find that out." According to Keogh, "Gutiérrez was a leader of the group chosen to defend American security interests in post-Romero El Salvador" (1983, 157).

There is every reason to think that some U.S. officials preferred conservative senior officers and distrusted the junior reformists. It is almost universally believed among Salvadoran military and political elites that Gutiérrez and Colonel Nicolás Carranza (who became vice minister of defense after the coup) were on the CIA payroll. The CIA routinely establishes contacts with national telephone systems, so officials like Gutiérrez, Carranza, and García who had held top positions in ANTEL in the 1970s were likely to have had such connections.[20] The fact that Gutiérrez' name appears as a source in CIA documents regarding the October coup confirms some connection between him and the Agency. Yet Keogh goes beyond his evidence in concluding that the United States acted decisively to ensure the success of the favored group. To make such an argument, he would have to demonstrate that U.S. operatives altered the outcome of the crucial votes that brought Gutiérrez onto the junta. According to Tommie Sue Montgomery (1982, 196), the United States at most encouraged Gutiérrez and García to call the second meeting that deposed Guerra and installed Gutiérrez in his place. I was unable to uncover any evidence that the United States did even this much, although several of my informants made it clear that Gutiérrez and García, in their efforts to persuade the young officers to support them, played up "on more than one occasion" their connections to the embassy and claimed that Guerra's presence on the junta would jeopardize U.S. support (Majano 1989, 54).

In general, whatever the United States may have done, there are good reasons to think that Gutiérrez and his colleagues possessed, by themselves, the political skills and influence to shift the course of events in their favor. There is no particular reason, for example, to think that they required U.S. coaching to call for a second meeting to obtain a more favorable outcome. The fact that all of the additional delegates who attended on 7 October voted for García does suggest that perhaps U.S. agents had gotten to them, but the key point is that these votes, by themselves, were not sufficient, and García was not elected. In fact, many of the circumstances that eventually put Gutiérrez and García in positions of power involved extraordinarily good luck which the United States was unable to supply. Gutiérrez discovered the Juventud plot through being the commanding officer of the politically naive Captain Mena Sandoval. It also seems to have been an incredible stroke of bad luck for Guerra that he was absent from the 7 October meeting. Guerra had in the past articulately defended himself against red-baiting, and he knew how to exploit the corrupt reputation of Gutiérrez and the others to undercut support for them among idealistic junior officers. In Guerra's absence, however, Gutiérrez was able to sway the officers. Finally, it was remarkably lucky for Gutiérrez that Mena Sandoval, with his strong reformist credentials, chose to back him as a substitute for the unelectable García. This decision, made in exhaustion and without sufficient understanding on Mena's part of its consequences, could not have been controlled or in any way predicted by the United States. Gutiérrez himself was extremely surprised by the outcome. When Mena informed him of the night's events, Gutiérrez' "smile reached from ear to ear" (Mena Sandoval 1992, 180).

In sum, it is likely that the main impact of the United States in this sequence of events came through the junior officers' well-founded perception that Gutiérrez and García would have the backing of the U.S. embassy. In the wake of the collapse of the Somoza regime, the young officers were reluctant to be without U.S. support. No one can say how the votes might have come out had Gutiérrez and García not been able to make credible claims of U.S. backing in their lobbying efforts from September onward. This may be one of many cases in Central America history in which the preferences of the United States, even in the absence of a deliberate effort to control events, carried great weight because of the internalization of U.S. concerns by key actors.

The Coup

The plan developed by the Coordinating Committee was a militarily robust one that, unlike those of 1960 and 1972, did not depend upon capturing the president or the minister of defense. Instead, the junior officers were prepared to take control, or at least neutralize, all of the army garrisons in the country, thereby leaving the Romero government with virtually no forces to command. The planning had been highly decentralized: the liaisons between the Coordinating Committee and each military unit were responsible for finding sympathetic officers and developing a plan for taking control of the troops on the day of the coup. The committee was responsible for deciding on a date for the action.

On 12 October word of the Juventud coup was leaked to the head of the air force. President Romero, who was in the United States for a medical checkup, was promptly recalled.[21] Air force Captain Felipe Mejía Peña was arrested, and a warrant was put out for Mena Sandoval. Gutiérrez confronted Mena at the Maestranza shop and tried to place him under arrest, saying, "The government knows everything, they've already screwed us, and now I have to comply with the order to detain you and send you to the Treasury Police." Unless he was willing to expose his own involvement, Gutiérrez had little choice but to follow the arrest orders, and Mena's detention would not have harmed his own interests in the coup. Mena drew a sidearm, warned Gutiérrez not to attempt to arrest him, and fled (Mena 1992, 182).

Mena quickly met with Barrera and other conspirators, and they agreed that although they had lost the element of surprise and would need to postpone the coup for a day or so, they would not scrub their plans. Mena and two security officers hid out in brothels for two days, receiving periodic updates from other conspirators who were not being sought. Apparently the government lacked full information on the membership of the conspiracy and was seeking only the handful of officers known to one informant (Mena Sandoval 1992, 182–85; Montgomery 1982, 10–13).

The coup took place on the morning of 15 October. It was timed so that the captains would be on duty and armed, while their superiors were unarmed, eating breakfast. At the Artillery Brigade, Captain Barrera approached his commander, Colonel Eliseo López Abarca, and instructed him to relinquish command. López complied without resistance. At the Third Brigade in San Miguel, where relations between the junior officers and their commander were particularly bitter, a bodyguard was killed in the process of arresting the commanding officer, and the colonel was subjected to some abuse at the hands of his former subordinates.[22] Even though the conspirators in Santa Ana started too early, thus jeopardizing the movement elsewhere, all of the major barracks in the country were under control shortly before eight o'clock in the morning (Keogh 1983, 171–73; Mena Sandoval 1992, 183; Montgomery 1982, 7).

In contrast to the 1972 coup attempt, neither the air force nor the National Guard moved to support the beleaguered president. Ironically, the commander of the air force had disabled his own aircraft on 11 October after he was notified of the impending coup by a mechanic. This prevented air power from being used against rebellious garrisons, as it was in 1972. In the National Guard headquarters in San Salvador, the movement did not have enough support to arrest senior officers and take control. The seven or eight officers, mostly lieutenants, who supported the movement could do little more than step forward and attempt to persuade their colleagues to support the coup. They were overruled and arrested (Majano 1989, 48). Nonetheless, Guard commanders accurately sized up their military situation, and realized that without support from the air force, and with all of the barracks in the country siding with the *golpistas*, their situation was hopeless. Only the National Police attempted to resist the coup, and not for long, since they lacked heavy armament.[23]

Things went much less smoothly at the level of leadership. Both Gutiérrez and Majano showed up late for their own coup. Gutiérrez arrived 45 minutes late for his rendezvous with Guerra and Salazar Brenes. When he did get there, he was in civilian clothes and carrying a machine gun in his briefcase. He told Guerra that they should not proceed with the coup in Majano's absence (Keogh 1983, 171). Majano, who was to have met with Guerra, Gutiérrez, and Salazar, went instead to the military academy. Majano claims that he went there to prepare it as an alternative headquarters should something go wrong at San Carlos, where the junior officers had set up their command post (Majano 1989, 50), but his delayed arrival was widely perceived among *golpistas* as excessive caution.[24]

Guerra, suspicious of Gutiérrez, telephoned the First Brigade headquarters (San Carlos barracks) and learned that the coup was going according to plan. When Guerra, Gutiérrez, and Salazar arrived at San Carlos, Gutiérrez promptly changed into his military uniform and started giving orders. Guerra sent an armored car abandoned by Defense Minister Iraheta, with two trusted officers, to fetch Majano, who arrived at 10:30 (Keogh 1983, 172).

The balance of the day was spent persuading Romero and his staff to leave the country. Romero, Iraheta, Defense Minister Federico Castillo Yanes, and four other colonels had gone to the National Guard, only to discover that the National Guard, "was sitting it out" (Montgomery 1982, 13). While Romero went into hiding again, Iraheta proceeded to the air force base at Ilopango, where the Airborne Company, under the command of Major Domingo Monterrosa, was still willing to support the president.[25] The coup leaders issued an ultimatum to Romero to leave the country by 3:00 p.m. (SS 5859, 15 October 1979). The military situation spoke for itself: he left the country at 5:00 p.m. on a Guatemalan air force plane.

The Balance of Power after the Coup

In the immediate aftermath of the coup, it was unclear which of the two main factions in the conspiracy would dominate. Each had different advantages. Gutiérrez used his position on the junta to unilaterally name his colleague

Guillermo García as minister of defense before the junta was fully formed. García proceeded during the next several days to name allies from the *tandas* of 1956, 1957, and 1958 to all major troop commands in the country. He also named the highly competent but extremely hardline Colonel Nicolás Carranza to be deputy minister of defense, a position from which he controlled the day to day operations of the military.[26] Junior officers disputed Carranza's appointment, but García and Gutiérrez pulled rank. The younger officers, who were not in a position to contact their colleagues, were forced to back down.[27]

The more reformist military member of the junta, Colonel Majano, did not challenge the appointment. This single failure illustrates the central weaknesses of the reformist movement. Within the reformist camp, the junior officers were the most determined and the most radical, but had the least authority unless they could organize themselves to act collectively. More senior officers, like Majano and Salazar Brenes, tended to have stronger commitments to "institutionality" and were reluctant to foment division and conflict.

The more radical captains were less concerned about military unity and were in a combative mood in the immediate aftermath of the coup. They were in control of barracks—and most of the combat troops—all over the country. Having risked their lives to take control and arrest their superiors, they expected to hear a public proclamation consistent with their thinking. Most had expected more resistance by conservative elements than actually took place and had prepared themselves emotionally and militarily to fight. They were, as Majano puts it, "ready for anything." The coup had brought to the surface some junior officers' deep hostility toward superiors. At the Third Brigade in San Miguel, the captains briefly rebelled against the coup leadership when they learned that certain full colonels would remain on active duty (Majano 1989, 49, 65–71; Mena Sandoval 1992, 185).[28]

The threat of further rebellion by the junior officers was sufficiently compelling to ensure that the makeup of most of the new government, and its first public pronouncements, were in line with their reformist agenda. Aside from Majano and Gutiérrez, the membership of the junta was not determined until after the coup. The majority of military conspirators elected the rector of the University of Central America, Román Mayorga Quiros, to the junta. He held out for commitments from the *golpistas* that at least one of the junta members would represent the Foro Popular, that the military would be purged of "murderers and torturers," and that a serious program of reforms would "de-oligarchize" Salvadoran society.[29] Gutiérrez attempted to put through a more conservative proclamation and to block the selection of a junta member from the Foro Popular. He was overruled on both points: the proclamation issued was one drafted primarily by Guerra in consultation with scholars at the UCA (see Appendix A), and the Foro Popular was allowed to name the social democrat Guillermo Ungo to the junta (Majano 1989, 62; Mena Sandoval 1992, 183–85).[30] The fifth member, Mario Andino, an engineer, was selected at the last minute to represent the private sector.

A new cabinet drew primarily upon the political parties included in the Foro Popular and upon a network of reform-minded technocrats known to Mayorga. The resulting government included many highly educated, talented, and socially concerned individuals. It was also, from the point of view of many conservative and centrist officers, frighteningly left-wing.[31] Five cabinet-level posts went to the Christian Democrats, five to the National Democratic Union (a legal front for the Communist Party), and four to the social democratic National Revolutionary Movement. The minister of planning, Alberto Hart Déneke, and his subsecretary, Mauricio Silva Argüello, were technocrats affiliated with the UCA. The minister of agriculture, Enrique Alvarez Córdova, was loosely affiliated with the National Conciliation Party, had been the director of the National Institute of Agrarian Transformation under the Molina government, and may have been a member of the Communist Party.[32] Progressive technocrats affiliated with the university occupied many subcabinet positions and played a key role in drafting reform legislation (Castro Morán 1989, 278). The power of the leftist party members and reformist technocrats was offset by the control of three important ministries—Justice, Economy, and Treasury—by figures associated with the private sector.

Initially, the high command and Gutiérrez were forced to accept a policy agenda shaped by the junior officers and oriented toward a break with the past. On 17 October, Colonel Majano ordered the release of 73 striking workers who had been arrested the day after the coup. On 18 October, the Revolutionary Governing Junta jointly ordered the release of all political prisoners detained before the coup. It also announced that it would be a temporary government with elections scheduled for no later than February 1982—a promise that cannot have warmed the hearts of Gutiérrez and García.

One of the junta's first actions, prior to the withdrawal of the junior officers from the scene, was to dismantle ANSESAL and the intelligence units within the security forces. The Salvadoran political scientist Rafael Guido Véjar asserts that Majano was instrumental in this decision, and was "smart to do it. He recognized that these institutions were the power base of the right within the armed forces. He chopped out the right's apparatus within the armed forces."[33] On 26 October, Majano announced that the National Police, the Treasury Police, and the National Guard (which made up the main institutional base of the hardline faction) would be reorganized, pending a process in which officials would be "judged and their real involvement in torture and corruption investigated." This phrasing implied that investigation would not be confined to officials of the Romero administration. On the same date, the junta jointly issued Decree 9, which established a special investigative commission to look into the thorny question of political prisoners and the "disappeared." The decree was presented at the press conferences by Colonel Gutiérrez, a fact that probably lent it greater weight with the security forces, as a signal that they could no longer act with impunity. On 6 November Decree 12 disbanded ORDEN and made any action done in its name illegal (Baloyra 1982, 90–91).

Pressures from the junta on human rights grounds continued into November, and Gutiérrez and his allies appear to have felt compelled to play along, although in practice the military high command threw as many roadblocks in the way of investigations as they could.[34] On 10 November, a civilian court convicted an ORDEN leader for killing a teacher. On 14 November, 60 National Guardsmen (not officers) were dismissed from the service for "various violations" (Foreign Broadcast Information Service [FBIS], 14 November 1979). On 19 November, the junta appointed an additional commission to investigate secret burial sites (FBIS, 21 November 1979). On 28 November, the special investigative commission called for the trial of ex-presidents Molina and Romero and the former directors of the National Police, the National Guard, and the Treasury Police under the past two administrations. The commission claimed to have concrete evidence linking these commanders to 50 deaths (FBIS, 28 November 1979). This was followed by orders from the junta for a pretrial hearing and to the attorney general to gather additional evidence on the former chiefs (FBIS, 5 December 1979).

The hardline faction felt extremely threatened by all of these measures. Shortly after the coup, Héctor Regalado, who had been running the Boy Scout death squad in Usulután, went into hiding, expecting the reformist military to come for him.[35] Colonel Roberto Santibañez, who headed ANSESAL under Romero, spent the two days before the coup destroying files that could implicate him or his associates in human rights violations. After the coup, Major Roberto D'Aubuisson, who had worked for a time in ANSESAL, was sent by either García or Carranza to salvage its files. He spent three to four days at ANSESAL headquarters after the coup, then went into hiding, taking many of the files with him. He later told a U.S. official that after his review he was confident there was nothing in those files to link him to any violence, though perhaps to "one or two stolen cars."[36] Wearing dirty coveralls, a Caterpillar hat, and five days growth of beard, he slipped into Guatemala under an assumed identity "so that if anything came up about human rights violations, he would be out of the country and they wouldn't try to pursue anything legal with him." He resigned from the military and returned secretly to El Salvador, where he worked on intelligence files, "on assignment" from someone in the Ministry of Defense, most likely Carranza.[37] The fact that D'Aubuisson's return was sponsored by someone in the high command but had to be clandestine illustrates the tension between the high command and reformist currents. It is also an early sign of the alliance of convenience between high command officials and hardliners against the reformist junior officers and their civilian allies in government.

The New High Command

It's hard to think of García as a soldier, really. He was more of a 'military politician.' He was practiced in how to deal with civilians, civilian politicians.
— Former ambassador Robert White

I don't remember any attractive alternatives.
— Former U.S. embassy official, El Salvador

García was for García.
— Salvadoran businessman

The Equipo Molina that formed the high command after the coup was made up of colonels from the *tandas* of 1956, 1957, and 1958. Their primary grievances with respect to Romero were generational. Three of these officers— Gutiérrez, García, and Carranza—had held prime positions under the Molina administration. They had jointly controlled the national telephone company, ANTEL, and had engaged in false invoicing and misallocation of funds on the order of $16 to $18 million. Raymond Bonner (1984, 152) quotes a U.S. diplomat as commenting, "You're entitled to your piece of the plunder, but not to that magnitude." The gravy train came to a halt with Romero's election, which not only cost García the presidency, but removed García and his associates from their ANTEL positions and sent them to low-status troop commands or, in Gutiérrez' case, to a repair shop.[38]

Aside from their desire to oust Romero, the political agenda of the Molina team was ambiguous from the start. Although closely associated with Molina, they had all avoided making any public commitment to his reformist program.[39] The top few officers espoused a wide range of policy orientations. Gutiérrez came to be associated with military-led reformism, while Carranza was instrumental in organizing death squads and facilitating the far right's campaign of terror and propaganda against reformism. Colonel Carlos Eugenio Vides Casanova headed the National Guard during the violent period from October 1979 through mid-1983 and took extremely hardline positions on a number of occasions, yet as defense minister during the mid- to late 1980s he came to be seen as a moderating influence. During 1980 and later, the Equipo proved as a group to be open to both major economic reforms and massive use of state violence.

A strong consensus emerged in my interviews that the officers within this group were committed to their own power and the power of the military as an institution. Informants ranging from former U.S. intelligence officials to members of the Salvadoran left labeled them "institutionalists," by which they meant that these officers sought to maximize the institutional integrity and power of the military. Rubén Zamora summarized this institutional orientation during an interview:

> The civilians [in the government] in general didn't understand the problem of the military: rather than reformism versus conservativism, reaction versus progressiveness, the military worried mainly about its institutional survival. García represented institutionality. If institutional survival required reforms, he would do them. To maintain institutionality, were it necessary to lead reforms to shake off all these leftists that were seen to be a serious threat to the institution, they would do it. I don't tend to judge these people on a continuum of progressive to reactionary. Take a person like Vides Casanova: what is Vides? A reactionary, a progressive? He is a soldier who has to preserve his institution. He'll do what he has to. So you can't classify him politically very well. For this reason, civilian–military relations aren't well understood, because we don't speak the same language. The fundamental point of their agenda is to preserve the institution.[40]

Likewise, senior officers were willing to include civilians in government if necessary to ensure U.S. backing and international legitimacy, but they wanted only civilians who effectively subordinated themselves to military authority. As we will see in the next chapter, they also tolerated coup plotting and paramilitary activities by the extreme right as long as these did not directly threaten the high command's position.

The U.S. embassy in San Salvador during this period viewed the post-coup high command officers as more moderate than Romero.[41] This perception is based upon the high command's proclaimed openness to reforms, yet these officers subsequently proved themselves willing to use far greater violence than did Romero. During a confrontation with civilian junta members in late December 1979, for example, Vides Casanova reportedly declared that the military was prepared to kill two hundred thousand people if necessary to defeat the opposition (Keogh 1983, 183).

In fact, there is no particular reason to believe that the Equipo Molina differed significantly from Romero in intrinsic policy preferences. More likely, the main differences lay in their political circumstances within the military and in the international community. Unlike Romero, they faced a fully articulated, mobilized pro-reform movement within the junior officer corps that was challenging them on grounds of corruption and brutality. Also unlike Romero, they were screened from international accountability for human rights abuses by the fact that the civil–military junta, rather than a military president, was the head of state. Whereas violence rose and fell during the

Romero administration according to the balance between international and domestic pressures, the timing and intensity of violence under the post-coup high command primarily reflected the political fortunes of the Equipo Molina and of the hardline faction *within the military*. When the junior officers were strongest and most rebellious, violence was reduced. As the new high command suppressed its junior opponents, and as right-wing civilian support bolstered the security and domestic intelligence forces, unprecedented violence was unleashed against the Salvadoran populace. As we will see below, organizing and ordering new waves of violence proved to be one of the high command's most important tools for suppressing the reformist movement. Thus violence against civilians was both instrument and consequence of the suppression of radical reformism within the armed forces.

Most observers agree that the Equipo Molina were a powerful leadership group. During their years as administrators at the military academy, García and Vides had cultivated recognition and support among several cohorts, partially offsetting the distaste with which they were viewed by the most reformist of the junior officers.[42] They had taken special care of members of the *tanda* of 1966, the so-called *tandona* (the large class), most of whom were either captains or majors at the time of the coup. García and Vides had intervened repeatedly on behalf of individual cadets and officers from this group who had failed to perform or had been involved in malfeasance. The large number of successful graduates in this class was partly attributable to this protection.[43] Its size, in turn, gave the *tandona* disproportionate clout, since its members simultaneously controlled an unusually large number of commands. They provided political backing for the Equipo Molina officers, though they also appear to have had close ties with the civilian far right.

The Permanent Council of the Armed Forces

One of the key struggles between the high command and the Juventud movement was over the Permanent Council of the Armed Forces (COPEFA), which was established on 4 November 1979 to guarantee implementation of the Proclama (NSA 1989a, 46). The idea for COPEFA had been developed prior to the coup, in part on the advice of Román Mayorga (Mena Sandoval 1992, 171). By convening COPEFA, the junior officers hoped to regain an ability to push through reforms, over the opposition of the high command. The junior officers intended that COPEFA, which included representatives from every military unit in the country, would function as a review board that could veto actions by the high command that were inconsistent with the Proclama of 15 October, and apply pressure to implement the major reforms it called for (see Appendix A; Castro Morán 1989, 273). There were 26 representatives, one from each of the 13 barracks and one from each of the 13 other subagencies within the military, and each representative had an alternate.[44] This representational scheme gave the regular army disproportionate power within COPEFA. At this point the security forces, between them, numbered around 4,000, as compared with 8,000 regular army, navy, and air force troops; yet within COPEFA they had only 4 representatives versus 22 for the army and other services.

The idea of a representative counterweight to the high command and the security forces was never fully successful: COPEFA's power ultimately rested on the implicit threat of rebellion if the high command acted against the junior officers' wishes, and the council appears to have intervened successfully only once. Yet COPEFA was extremely threatening to many senior officers, who conducted an energetic campaign to neutralize it. Their principal concern was that COPEFA might become a prosecuting agency allowing junior officers to try and punish their superiors.[45] Given the announced intentions of many of the captains to shoot or imprison officers guilty of corruption or abuses, this was not an unrealistic concern. The high command used their prerogatives to keep the more radical junior officers who were COPEFA members out in the field on operations at times when COPEFA was to meet.[46] This meant that the more troublesome COPEFA representatives were replaced by their more moderate alternates; it also interfered with the ability of COPEFA to meet on short notice.[47] On 18 December the high command met with COPEFA members at the military academy. In the absence of many of the more reformist officers, the senior officers ordered the restructuring of COPEFA and replacement of elected representatives with members loyal to the high command. The COPEFA members present complied, swayed by arguments from senior officers that their organization, as originally formulated, posed a threat to the hierarchical integrity of the armed forces (Estudios Centroamericanos 1979, 34; no. 374:1088–89).[48] After this meeting, Colonel García told a foreign diplomat; "We have managed to control COPEFA and convert it into a consultative, administrative organ, so that it will no longer be attacking my orders as minister of defense. In doing this, I have guaranteed protection for officers of the National Police, the Treasury Police, and the National Guard—no one is going to judge them. We did this by having an assembly to which Colonel Majano was intentionally not invited. It is we who need to determine this situation, not the government" (Castro Morán 1989, 290).

Civil–Military Relations

The high command also clashed with civilians in the post-coup government over socioeconomic reforms and human rights. Implementing major reforms and ending repression were the keys to the junta's political survival. Without these, there was no reason to expect that the intense political crisis that had triggered the coup in the first place would be resolved, and the military would inevitably fall back into the protection racket that the reformist current viewed as untenable. The high command, for its part, having closed ranks with the most hardline sectors of the military in exchange for their political support,[49] had to oppose any reforms that might offend the civilian interests who had so much influence within the security forces. (They would reverse this position in 1980, when U.S. pressures for reform began to outweigh objections from the civilian elite.) The high command also had no incentives to restrict the repressive violence that both the private sector right and the hardliners in the security forces saw as necessary. On the contrary, this violence had the advantage of destabilizing the reformists.

From their first meetings with the new high command, the civilian members of the junta were uneasy. Mayorga met with some of the new military commanders, including García, National Police chief Carlos Reynaldo López Nuila, and National Guard chief Vides Casanova on 16 October. With Mayorga was Italo López Vallecillos, a scholar at the University of Central America known for his good contacts in the military. López knew of the connections among the Equipo Molina officers and was immediately disturbed by the cast of characters who had emerged from the coup. "This isn't what it appears," he remarked to Mayorga. Mayorga considered withdrawing from the junta at this point, but was persuaded by Archbishop Romero to stay with it. "As a Christian, you must accept," Romero told him, "Even if there is only a 1, 2, or 5 percent chance, you must take the risk, because the alternative is war." Once committed to serving, Mayorga paid relatively little attention to the problem of the military, focusing his efforts on developing the reform policies of the government and trusting the junior officers to prevent significant obstructionism by the high command. Junta member Guillermo Ungo, however, kept closer watch on the "power problem" from the outset. According to Mayorga, "He didn't like the lack of consultation and the repressive attitudes that were exhibited. Memo [Ungo's nickname] was personally ill-at-ease about being guarded by the security forces. He thought something could happen to our families."[50]

It took most of November for the new government to formulate its plans. It confronted the senior military officers in December. Several active-duty officers charged that the junta intentionally dragged its feet in the implementation of reforms in order to create a revolutionary situation. Implicit in this view is the accusation that the politicians from the National Democratic Union, the National Revolutionary Movement, and the Christian Democratic Party were in league with the radical left or were in fact controlled by them. Other officers suggested more charitably that the junta was simply too diverse in its membership to function effectively as a group. Former civilian members of the government vehemently deny any deliberate foot-dragging. They agree, however, that their disunity slowed the preparation of reform legislation, and that they were too willing to believe the high command. The high command repeatedly hoodwinked the civilian members of the government, as happened when the cabinet presented a draft of the decree to freeze land holdings to the junta. Andino and Gutiérrez were opposed to it, and Majano was unsure whether there was enough political support to move ahead quickly. Saying that they had to clear the proposal with the military, he and Gutiérrez gave it to García, who said he would distribute the draft to the barracks and then promptly "stuffed it in his desk."[51] Waiting for a response from García delayed the law for weeks and angered the popular organizations.

Several officers, and a former U.S. embassy official, also accused the junta of seeking to "decapitate" the military by combining popular pressure and manipulation of the junior officers. The obvious and admitted naiveté of most members of the cabinet regarding the military makes such charges implausible, and one former cabinet minister explicitly denies any such intent.

> Many people said that *the* mistakes were putting García and Gutiérrez in powerful positions. Yet during our time in office, we didn't seriously contemplate taking any measures to reverse that decision. We never got into the issue of internal affairs of the military. It was very clear to us what the problem was, but I doubt any of us were thinking of making structural changes in the armed forces. It was never discussed to my knowledge. What we were calling for were fundamental economic changes and a stop to the repression. To the extent that the armed forces were preventing these things from happening, I suppose we were indirectly challenging the power structure and authority of the army. But not directly.[52]

Another former member of the "left wing of the cabinet" claimed that he knew of no such intent, and that if there had been such discussions, "I would have known about it."[53]

In fact, the *failure* to intervene in the internal authority structure of the military appears to have been the junta's crucial error. Although the junior officers had ensured that reformist civilians took office, this government, once in place, found itself interacting almost exclusively with senior officers. The junior officers went back to their regular posts, leaving the civilians to deal with a high command that was committed to dismantling both the reformist movement in the military and the civilian government it had brought to power.

Zamora, as minister of the presidency, was the key point of contact between the civilian government and the high command. He describes civil–military relations during this period as "very stormy." Another cabinet official described several meetings held in December 1979 at which Agriculture and Planning Ministry officials presented plans for land, banking, and commercial reforms to the junta and cabinet. Defense Minister García sat silently through the meetings, then asked for time, near the end, to deliver the following message: "All of the shit that you have been discussing is not going to happen. We are not going to permit it."[54]

In fact, part of the reform was carried out. Decree 43, issued on 7 December, froze all major land transactions retroactively to 15 October, thereby preventing large landowners from breaking up their holdings and distributing them among relatives and friends. This was, of course, a preliminary step in the implementation of a major land reform, a fact not lost on the country's private sector. Minister of Agriculture Enrique Alvarez went on national television on 11 December to outline the sort of land reform planned (*Estudios Centroamericanos* 1979, 34: 1116–18). Seven days later, the junta approved Decree 75 and nationalized control of coffee and sugar exports (Baloyra 1982, 91; *Estudios Centroamericanos* 1979, 34: 1090).

Román Mayorga credited COPEFA with a crucial role in gaining high command approval of Decree 43. When it became clear that García was stalling, civilian junta and cabinet members contacted representatives of COPEFA and insisted that they act. Mayorga did not know exactly what action COPEFA took, but he believed, on the basis of the timing, that the junior officers were decisive in winning a favorable response from the high command.[55] This was the first and last time COPEFA successfully played its intended role.

The November Truce: The Junta Gets Its Chance

The successful COPEFA intervention was welcomed by the reformists of the junta and cabinet, who by early December were desperate to carry out some kind of significant reform legislation. At the beginning of November, the junta had negotiated a 30-day truce with the Popular Revolutionary Bloc (BPR) in which the popular organization agreed to halt all street actions and provide the government with a chance to prove itself. If it failed to do so, it would be confronted by massive protests.

The left was initially mistrustful of the coup and the junta. While the BPR/Popular Forces of Liberation (FPL) and the United Popular Action Front/National Resistance held off action for a few days to assess the situation, the People's Revolutionary Army (ERP) and its popular wing, the Popular Leagues of February 28, attempted to trigger insurrections in Mejicanos, Cuscatancingo, and in San Marcos (Estudios Centroamericanos 1979, 34: 1006). Security forces, ordered into action by Defense Minister García over the objections of Colonels Majano and Guerra, crushed these rebellions, killing at least a hundred persons. After this defeat, ERP leader Joaquín Villalobos granted the new government a partial truce but warned that Salvadoran history "is full of military coups led by people who at first adopt the platform of the people before allowing things to go back to the way they have always been" (NSA 1989a, 42).

On 25 October, the BPR took over the Labor and Economy ministries, taking some 300 people hostage, including the ministers of labor, economy, and planning. Among their 100 demands were the release of political prisoners and a series of socioeconomic conditions that would have been impossible for any government to meet, such as the provision, within 15 days, of a potable water supply to all the *colonias* of San Salvador. According to Rubén Zamora, who carried out the negotiations, the BPR leaders were aware that their specific demands were unrealistic: their real goal was to make clear to the new government that they expected prompt, dramatic action. Zamora provided the following account of the negotiations in an interview:

> Juan Chacón [who represented the BPR] said, "I don't care what you do, we'll give you 30 days to do this." I insisted that we couldn't do this in 30 days. I said I couldn't negotiate these terms. Chacón said, "That doesn't matter to me. We are going to leave the ministries, but be aware that we are giving you 30 days." I understood the message. . . . We signed the agreement for the departure of protesters from the ministries, and I went directly to the Casa Presidencial and talked with the junta. I recall that I told them, "Gentlemen, we have 30 days. If in 30 days we haven't taken the measures necessary to demonstrate to these people that we seriously want socioeconomic changes and democracy, we're not going to be able to go ahead."[56]

The BPR kept its word and suspended demonstrations for one month. The junta also communicated, through indirect means, with members of the other popular organizations and guerrilla groups, and all reduced their activities during November to give the government time to act.[57] There were a few minor incidents during the month, but diverse sources agree that the level of confrontation was dramatically lower than it had been in August through October. The Popular Forces of Liberation (the guerrilla group closely tied to the BPR) broke the truce somewhat early, with the kidnapping, on 28 November, of South Africa's ambassador to El Salvador, Archibald Gardner Dunn (NSA 1989a, 48).

The truce was a tenuous thing. Although the civilian right and hardline elements of the military assumed that the civilians in the government were politically indistinguishable from the popular organizations, in fact the ties between the two were very weak. The ERP initially viewed the coup as an opportunity to exploit instability of military command in order to spark insurrections. In its statements against the junta, the ERP-affiliated LP-28 cited the undistinguished history of past reformist coups and declared, "The people have the right not to believe in it."[58] According to a former senior civilian member of the first post-coup government, the ERP (and LP-28) refused to communicate with the junta.[59] LP-28 withdrew from the Foro Popular on 24 October, citing its participation in the junta.

Relations were somewhat better with the FPL/BPR, which held the Jesuits in high regard because of the dedicated work of Rutilio Grande and others in rural areas of the San Salvador, Cuscatlán, and Chalatenango departments, where the BPR had its strongest base. Yet both organizations were hostile to reformism, fearing that reforms at that point might reverse the momentum toward revolution that had built during the latter part of the decade. In their view, anything short of a peasant/worker revolution and the elimination of the existing military and state would ultimately serve only "the global interests of the dominant classes." In retrospect, FPL leaders acknowledge that they may have underestimated the importance of smaller gains "in a country where the oligarchy has resisted even the most minimal reforms" as a step along the way to more profound changes (Ellacuría 1979, 943–46; Harnecker 1993, 207–211). The risks of misunderstanding were increased by the lack of channels of communication. The minister of education, Salvador Samayoa, was a clandestine FPL member. Other members of government had to communicate indirectly through friends and relatives who happened to have FPL contacts.[60]

Junta members Ungo and Mayorga, as well as a number of the junior officers, maintained ongoing discussions with the United Popular Action Front/National Resistance. The RN was willing to remain neutral as long as the junta acted upon all of the reforms the Proclama called for. The RN's principal goal was the removal of the existing repressive military regime, and leaders were open to the possibility of a Torrijos-style populist military regime that the left could influence through popular mobilization and pressure. Toward this end, RN seriously discussed joining forces with progressive sectors of the military to overthrow the conservative high command. During November, its leaders developed a plan to mobilize as many as ten thousand militia members to support a second coup to be led by junior officers before the end of the year. The plan never materialized, in large part because of the caution of the reformist officers.[61]

There was a gap between what the RN was willing to discuss privately and the group's public posture. As one member of the junta cabinet put it, "They were unwilling to expose themselves and participate openly at that point."[62] The discourse of the left during this period was extremely radical, so the RN felt obligated to maintain a public posture that was more radical than its actual political goals. Moreover, like the other groups, members were not confident of the outcome of the junta's reform efforts and were reluctant to lose the momentum of popular mobilization.

The junta found itself very isolated. Members had only tenuous and secretive ties to the popular sectors, the high command was recalcitrant, and the junior officers had disappeared from view after 17 October.[63] The political parties that made up the government—the National Democratic Union, the Christian Democrats, and the National Revolutionary Movement—had organized supporters, but they were few in number compared with the popular organizations of the left. Although the Foro Popular included many of the unions that made up FAPU, FAPU itself, as already noted, was unwilling to support the government openly. The long-term acceptance of the government by the popular left, and therefore its ability to restore some general sense of governability to the country, depended upon its ability to deliver reforms and stop repression. It was obviously vulnerable to the autonomous ability of the military high command and the security forces to unleash violence against the popular movement.

Looking back on this conjuncture, it seems that the popular organizations may have missed an important opportunity by adopting such an adversarial posture. The left's initial confrontations with the government in late October made it more difficult for the junta to retain the active support of junior military officers. A core group of officers who maintained ongoing talks with all of the groups on the left understood that the left had internal reasons for maintaining a high level of popular mobilization and militancy.[64] Yet most of the junior officer corps were not party to these talks, and the demonstrations shook their confidence in the reformist path. Rightists inside and outside the military took political advantage of the left's mobilization, charging that by negotiating the truce the civilian reformists were merely buying time for the revolutionary left to strengthen itself and take power.

Thus, although the revolutionary left was correct in observing that the conservative factions of the military were still entrenched, their own posture and radical discourse helped accelerate the reconsolidation of the right. It may also have impeded the creation of a stronger alliance with the reformist current of the military: as former army captain and current ERP member Marcelo Cruz puts it, "The officers were interested in an alliance, but not willing to substitute one kind of dictatorship for another."[65] Moreover, the return of the politico-military organizations to kidnapping and guerrilla actions in late November helped conservatives within the military frighten reformist junior officers into obedience to the high command.

Leaders of the Farabundo Martí National Liberation Front (FMLN) have since expressed regrets about their own rigidity toward the junta. As already noted, groups had different reasons for opposing the junta, and different levels of hostility. All the popular organizations felt they had made tremendous sacrifices in confronting the Molina and Romero governments, while the political parties were reaping most of the benefits of participation in the new government. These resentments were partially balanced by a recognition that much of the popular base was hoping that the new junta might actually improve conditions.[66] The Sandinista victory in Nicaragua also had an effect. So long as popular organizations sensed an opportunity for outright victory, the half-measures offered by the junta seemed less appealing than they now do in retrospect.

The Private Sector Fights Back

The coup brought about a parallel shakeup within private sector associations. Many of the leaders of the National Association of Private Enterprise (ANEP) were deposed immediately following the October coup, replaced by more moderate businessmen. To the surprise of many, ANEP maintained virtual silence regarding the junta, in stark contrast to its vitriolic antireform pronouncements during most of the 1970s. Other business associations were cautiously cooperative: the Chamber of Commerce and Industry formed a committee to advise junta member Andino on private sector concerns (ST 291354, 8 November 1979).[67] Notwithstanding these public courtesies, resistance quickly developed behind the scenes. While the cabinet worked to draft and build support for major reforms, conservative forces within the private sector rallied to recover lost ground. They were aided by the fact that most members of the business elite viewed the junta with, at best, distrust; the more conservative elements reacted in "terror."[68]

Rightist civilians at this time viewed Mayorga and the technocrats from the Jesuit/University network, the National Democratic Union, and social democrats like Ungo as a polite front for the guerrilla left. Many business leaders suspected that the strategy of the "leftists" in the government was to encourage the popular organizations to put pressure on the government, so that they could go to the military and say, "Look, our constituency demands these things." As one businessman put it, "Ungo and Mayorga wanted them to keep the pressure up so that they could confront the military."[69]

Paige's extensive interviews with members of the private sector elite revealed this perspective to be common among the Salvadoran upper classes and traceable to the events of 1932. The social elite of the 1930s felt that the political opening and mild reformism of the 1920s had directly strengthened the Communist Party. For them, reformism was tantamount to communism. For a privileged class interested in resisting any and all concessions to subordinate classes, this was, as Paige points out, a self-serving view (Paige 1994). Rubén Zamora, who has no reason to give the civilian right the benefit of the doubt, claimed that the private sector elite "didn't distinguish that clearly between the government and the popular movement. They saw all of it as a great conspiracy."[70] Another cabinet member said, "The rich weren't seriously afraid of the [revolutionary] left or, at least, were equally if not more afraid of us. They thought we were as great a threat as the left, which is ridiculous."[71]

The junta was threatening in part because it was composed of people at least as educated and sophisticated as members of the upper classes themselves. One businessman and former government official commented that it was difficult for the private sector to see the mass organizations as a threat, partly because they assumed that the military would take care of the problem as they had in the past, and partly because they held the common Salvadoran in such contempt.[72] The post-coup government, however, was not a bunch of peasants, but a collection of professionals and educators, who, as a group, had historically supported the private sector.

Craig Pyes (1983i) recounts the details of an assassination attempt against a former Salvadoran ambassador to the United States, Ernesto Rivas Gallont. Pyes' informant, a death squad operative named "Gordo," acted "not because he thought the Salvadoran ambassador was a guerrilla, but because he believed he was an intellectual and posed more of a threat than the person carrying the gun." Rivas had been among the businessmen who joined Church leaders, academics, and opposition politicians in drafting a reform proposal in 1979.[73] The same general thinking applied to reformist technocrats and left-leaning priests. The implications of this view, which was shared by hardline sectors of the military, cannot be understated. First of all, the conflation of elite reformism and popular mobilization meant that the installation of Mayorga, Ungo, and their reformist colleagues in government greatly intensified the propertied classes' perception of threat. After the October coup, few business people spoke out in favor of reforms, in part because of direct intimidation, in part because fear caused the propertied classes to pull together under hardline leadership.[74] The second corollary of the equation was that violence against the popular organizations equaled violence against the junta. Killing junta or cabinet members would have brought international condemnation and might trigger a second rebellion by junior officers. For the civilian right, therefore, the most politically expedient way to block elite-led reformism was to attack its popular constituency. The result was the very *matanza* strategy that President Romero had been unwilling or unable to deliver.

Such a strategy required a base of support within the military for a *Martinista* solution, yet the October coup had, at least temporarily, disrupted the hardline network within the military. Virtually all of the senior officers with whom the far right had been conspiring since May 1979 had been dismissed, leaving the civilian right with few high-level contacts. As Pyes (1983a) puts it, the oligarchy "felt dangerously exposed." It did not trust officers like Gutiérrez and García, even though they were known to be conservative,[75] because the elite suspected that they were under U.S. control, and the United States might let the left win in El Salvador as it had in Nicaragua. Landowners were worried that ideas from Ecuador and Peru, where the militaries expropriated private lands, might have infected the Salvadoran military.[76] The civilian far right was aware of the divisions within the military, but feared that García and Gutiérrez would sell out the interests of the private sector if necessary to keep themselves in power.

Aware of their vulnerability to the new high command, the private sector elite made it a priority to reconstruct their ties to middle-ranking officers. According to one informant, this contact-building was the first step in coup-plotting: "When Romero fell, I immediately started going against the junta. I started organizing to overthrow it. Given the illegitimate way the government had taken power, I didn't see another coup as illegitimate."[77] These organizational efforts, and the pressures that they imposed on the high command, began to have an effect in December, shortly after the junta pushed through the first significant reform legislation. The U.S. embassy acknowledged the growing pressure from the right in a cable: "Danger of rightist coup continues to be raised in some quarters, but evidence available to embassy indicates little immediate threat. However political and economic right is becoming increasingly vocal . . . [calling for] a halt to 'anarchy and corruption'" (SS 06976, 4 December 1979). During the second half of November, the civilian right began a publicity campaign, talking about the threat of communism posed by the junta (Estudios Centroamericanos 1979, 34:1093). On 10 December several thousand rightist women marched to protest against its failure to maintain "law and order." At the Casa Presidencial they were addressed by junta members. Majano's remarks were drowned out by chants of "Down with the junta" (Estudios Centroamericanos 1979, 34: 1093; FBIS, 11 December 1979).

The women's march was followed on 27 December by an even larger demonstration of roughly fifteen thousand rightists. It was a show of force by the oligarchy, a parade of personal armored vehicles, bodyguards and businessmen themselves carrying military-style weapons, while private airplanes and helicopters flew overhead. The march proceeded directly to the headquarters of the military high command, where the demonstrators demanded to see Minister of Defense García. Instead, they were addressed by Vice Minister of Defense Carranza, who expressed sympathy for their concerns about law and order (Estudios Centroamericanos 1979, 34:1093; NSA 1989a, 51.)

This second march was organized by a new rightist umbrella group known as the Broad National Front (FAN), which was an expansion of the Salvadoran Nationalist Movement (MNS). The MNS was formed by young civilian rightists in May 1979 as the basis for a coup against the weakening Carlos Romero (see Chapter Four).[78] The FAN combined different roles in a way that was to characterize the Salvadoran civilian right for the next decade: it was designed to serve as a "civic organization" to pressure the government, an intelligence organization to support loyal sectors of the military, and a paramilitary network to supplement the besieged hardline elements of the military.[79] It funneled money—as much as $10 million—to the security forces to support repressive operations. Roberto D'Aubuisson, who was organizing death squads during this period, helped to form FAN (Pyes 1983a). He too was playing multiple roles: coordinating intelligence for high command, helping to remobilize the death squads, and serving as "front man for the 14 [families], trying to prevent reforms from taking place."[80]

The mobilization of the civilian right combined with the high command's recapture of COPEFA to transform the political climate by the second half of December. Early in the month, it became clear that the "Honor Commission" appointed by the high command to facilitate the investigation of human rights was in fact doing everything it could to obstruct that process.[81] Vice Minister of Defense Carranza was working closely with the hardline network, including the security and domestic intelligence forces and civilian mercenaries, who were gradually reconstructing their organization and intelligence capacity (Pyes 1983c). With high command sponsorship, powerful civilian support, and a decreasing threat from the reformist military, the hardline faction was freer to operate, and the number of civilians taken out of their homes at night and shot to death began to climb.

Violence as Product and Tool

As we have noted, state repression more than tripled in the two weeks following the coup, paused briefly in November, then accelerated again to a level several times as high as the worst period of the Romero regime (Universidad Centroamericana 1981). The overall increase in intensity, as well as the fluctuations, appear to be related to intra-state political conflicts. Hardline elements reacted to the instability created by the coup by increasing repression. Then, as the reformist project disrupted the hardline institutions and seemed to threaten their personnel with prosecution for acts of violence (during November), state violence ebbed.

The constraining effect of the reformist movement did not last long. By threatening the interests of the security forces and the new high command, it inspired a stronger partnership between the two than had existed under Romero.

Various Salvadoran and U.S. observers have argued correctly that much of the violence carried out by the military was not centrally controlled. Looseness of command hierarchy pervaded the Salvadoran military. In the words of the journalist Shirley Christian, the Defense Minister "presided" rather than "directing." His authority depended upon the willingness of the 14 departmental and 3 security force commanders to obey. According to the 1981 report of the El Salvador Military Strategy Assistance Team (the Woerner Commission):

> In the Army, and in particular, the Public Security Forces, the traditional dichotomy between operational autonomy and highly centralized deci-

sion making process, [*sic*] has produced a command control system built upon leadership by exception and not a functioning chain-of-command. As a consequence, professional norms of behavior, standards of personal conduct, and the concept of accountability are not encouraged and enforced at each organizational level. The absence of a functioning chain-of-command is compounded by the predisposition toward violence by some security force personnel, as well as their demonstrated susceptibility to being co-opted by the right.[82] (Woerner et al. 1981, 47)

No integrated communications network existed to link army and security force units, so the departmental and zone commanders (usually the ranking army officer in the zone) were unable to control the security forces (Woerner et al. 1981, 39). Local security force units were effectively answerable only to their own directors, who were in San Salvador and unable to exercise direct supervision. The composition of the security force officer corps made this local independence all the more problematic. Half or more of the lower-ranking officers had been promoted through the ranks. They were poorly educated and deeply steeped in repressive and brutal practices. Many had long-established mercenary relationships with local property owners,[83] and were subject to peer pressure to prove themselves willing to act forcefully against popular opposition.[84] They were, as a group, more concerned about being too soft with the left than about the risk of killing the wrong person. A political officer in the U.S. embassy related the following conversation with a National Guard officer whom he described as a "savage individual": "He had also, he said, killed several other people who had been found near one of the houses he uses to hide out (he is on a FARN death list) simply because he suspected them of presenting a threat to him. Asked how he knew that they presented a threat, he said that he could not be sure; if not, he 'would have made a mistake'" (SS 8084, 19 November 1980). Since the top posts in the security forces were generally filled by hardliners (before and after the coup), a moderate army officer assigned to the security forces would find himself among superiors, colleagues, and subordinates who favored killing, virtually at random, suspected members of the left.

Local autonomy does not mean that the security forces were unaffected by factional politics at the top levels of the state. On the contrary, the balance of factional power between reformists and conservatives could change their incentives and willingness to commit violence. Officers in the security forces could be pressured to suspend their nightly missions to murder "subversives" if such actions might harm the armed forces as an institution. They reduced their violence in mid-1977 and early 1979 when international pressures made violence potentially harmful to President Romero, for instance.

They also had to consider the personal risks to themselves. Though they had enjoyed effective impunity before the October coup, they must have known that junior army officers had installed a new, largely civilian government and were talking about executing or imprisoning abusers of human rights. Although many people in the security forces knew and trusted most of the new high command, they had serious doubts about Majano, and Gutiérrez was virtually unknown. The formation of COPEFA, the possibility that it would play a prosecutorial role, the investigations into disappearances and clandestine cemeteries, the outlawing of ORDEN, and the conviction of an ORDEN leader for murder all helped increase the perceived risks. Even well-connected officers like Roberto D'Aubuisson feared capture and prosecution.

The result was a dramatic reduction in state violence during November, at least in urban areas where killings could be promptly documented and acted upon. Various informants noted the reduction; the "Chronicle of the Month" in *Estudios Centroamericanos* likewise indicates that the first week of November "began a period of greater tranquility, during which violent repression practically disappeared" (1979, 34: 1088)—that is, government forces did not fire upon demonstrators as they had in previous months. Statistics from the Secretariat for Social Communication of the Archdiocese of San Salvador indicate that killings fell from 159 in October to 10 in November (see Table 2). Though the figure of 10 is probably too low for the country as a whole, there was clearly much less violence in November than in the preceding and following months, at least in the vicinity of the capital.[85]

Table 2

Killings by State Forces before and after the October Coup

	July	Aug	Sept	Oct	Nov	Dec
Civilians killed	52	45	53	159	10	281

Source: Archdiocesan Secretariat for Social Communication (Universidad Centroamericana 1981).

Besides influencing hardliners' fear of prosecution, factional politics had a more direct impact on human rights as the high command, military hardliners, and reformists struggled over the authority to regulate state violence. As early as the morning after the coup, conflict developed between Guerra and Majano, on one side, and Gutiérrez and García on the other, regarding how the military should respond to attempted uprisings by the People's Revolutionary Army in Mejicanos and Cuscatancingo. García wanted to send troops; Guerra and Majano opposed this as too provocative. Majano and Guerra managed to prevent García from using army troops from the First Brigade, but García proceeded to send security force units to suppress the rebellions (Keogh

1983, 173).[86] Hardline majors, including Natividad Jesús Cáceres, Sigifredo Ochoa, and Roberto D'Aubuisson, led the assaults.[87] At least a hundred people were killed, many of them civilians (NSA 1989a, 42).

The suppression of the rebellions was part of a general surge in violence in October, most of which, according to verbal and written accounts of the period, followed the coup on the fifteenth (see Table 2). It included bloody attacks by security forces on demonstrators, as well as a rise in death-squad-type activity throughout the country—targeted assassinations, at night, during the state of siege. In repeated press conferences, the junta members were questioned about the seeming inconsistency of their claims to be making a fresh start and the high levels of violence, particularly against unarmed demonstrators. Majano, who was hoping to remain in power long enough to restructure and professionalize the military, could only respond that "some of the forces still need to adjust to the new spirit" (FBIS, 26 October, 1979).

By November, the reformists achieved a tenuous control. Majano traveled about the country, ordering the release of prisoners and pressuring security force units to cease and desist.[88] Various individuals told me stories of junior army officers successfully intervening to prevent violence by other army or security force units during this period. Nonetheless, on 13 November an ORDEN spokesman boasted that ORDEN would go underground to continue the fight against communism (FBIS, 14 November 1979).

By early December, it was increasingly clear that the high command and hardline sectors of the military were bent on resisting the reformists' efforts. As popular demonstrations resumed after the November truce, Mayorga, Ungo, and Zamora repeatedly called on the high command to instruct that the security forces and tanks be withdrawn from the vicinity of demonstrations. García's standard response was to claim that the civilians had been misinformed, but that if there were forces in the area they would be promptly removed. Then he would do nothing, and in several cases the security forces opened fire (Montgomery 1982, 162–63).[89] By repeatedly lying to civilian junta members about the location and actions of military units, García prevented them from interfering with repressive actions.

Meanwhile, someone in the high command, most likely Carranza, was sponsoring D'Aubuisson's intelligence and organizing activities.[90] D'Aubuisson assisted the high command in transferring the political spying functions that had been carried out by ANSESAL over to the C-II (intelligence) section of the joint staff (Estado Mayor Conjunto).[91] He also helped revive the operational aspects of ANSESAL (the actual killing) through a special "investigations" section of the National Police, commanded by Lieutenant Colonel Aristides Márquez, which began death squad operations in December 1979.[92] The section went on to become the most notorious, and most effective, death squad organization in El Salvador.[93]

There is evidence that high command and hardline efforts to reactivate the repressive apparatus were part of a deliberate strategy to destabilize the junta. One former junta member blamed "a conspiracy of the security forces with capital to impede the process of the reforms. They committed outrageous actions. It was never clear exactly who was committing them. . . . I'm not talking about all the security forces, but people within them who wanted to maintain the hard line, terrorism of the state."[94] This official points to "a stratum of majors and some lieutenant colonels who were opposed to changes." Archbishop Romero asked in a late December homily whether "internal forces within the institution [were] intentionally resorting to violence for their own purposes" (SS 7411, 27 December 1979).

The impulse to destabilize the junta resulted in part from the more conservative mid-ranking officers' sense that the armed forces had made a mistake in inviting left-wing civilians into the government. Many officers who were not particularly enthusiastic about reforms had initially accepted the idea of bringing in Mayorga, Ungo, and other social democrats as a way of demobilizing the opposition. As an officer who was a major at the time put it, "The armed forces accepted this as a cost of surviving." By December, however, many officers began to be uncomfortable with the presence in the government of leftists who were "taking advantage of the Proclama of the armed forces." Under the ideological onslaught of the civilian right, and aware of the increasing vitriol between the junta and the high command, those officers who were less committed to reformism began to see the junta as a threat to the "integrity of the armed forces."[95] In that situation, the only tool at the disposal of disgruntled military officers was to carry out acts of repression that would frustrate the junta, weaken its potential popular base, and force the civilians in the government to resign. Those who adopted this strategy were not under orders to do this, according to the officer I interviewed, but were acting on their own.[96]

Reflecting on the violence of December, former U.S. Assistant Secretary of State Viron Vaky remarked that "the increase in violence in late 1979 should have tipped us to how split things were. The divisions within the armed forces and the presence in the government of reformists made the right even more fearful . . . and brought to the fore the *matanza* approach of just liquidating the problem." Vaky sees a connection between this behavior in late 1979 and the murder of the Jesuits in October 1989. "This is the pathology: the automatic resort to violence to deal with threats of quite another kind."[97]

Although there may have been an organic backlash against reformism within the military, much of the blame for escalating violence must be laid at the feet of the high command. Officials at the highest level—the minister and vice-minister of defense—ordered repressive actions and were active in reconstructing the coercive apparatus. Former Captain Alejandro Fiallos argues that the high command turned to violence when its members found that guile and bluster were not enough to block major reforms.[98]

Increased violence against civilians had a self-reinforcing quality. It became the principal topic of communications between the civilian government and the military, and every time the junta proved unable to enforce its prohibitions on violence, it lost authority in the eyes of both civilians and soldiers. Every time the security forces acted with impunity, they became more confident that they could operate freely in the future. Violence helped expand the political space for the hardline sectors of the military to implement their preferred policy.

Moreover, by increasing violence the high command drove a wedge between the civilians in the government and their potential base of popular support. State terrorism directly undercut popular tolerance for the government, which in turn made for greater opposition militancy. Civilian officials realized that increased popular militancy would only strengthen the hand of the high command and the security forces. In an effort to curb the violence before it was too late, they pressed Majano to act more forcefully against the hardliners and the high command. Like the civilians on the junta, Majano found that his orders to stop the violence had no effect if given through the normal chain of command. By mid-December, he was traveling from barracks to barracks, directly ordering officers to stop the repression and trying to keep the reformists together despite the neutralization of COPEFA.[99] Junior officers were talking about carrying out another coup, perhaps with the help of elements of the left. Majano, committed to institutional unity, was unwilling to take such steps.[100] He asked the civilians to be patient, telling them that he was doing all he could and that building up the reformist movement would take time. As former junta member Román Mayorga puts it, "While he took time, they won."[101]

U.S. Policy Toward the First Junta

The United States greeted the new government with optimism. In a confidential cable sent 16 October Assistant Secretary of State Vaky wrote, "We urgently need full information on coup, what final junta make-up is, where real power lies, and how wide is A) support and B) participation by non-military sectors, i.e. Church, Christian Democrats, Private Sectors, etc. First indications look encouraging, and if this assessment is confirmed we will want to be responsive and supportive very quickly" (ST 269884, 16 October 1979). Once the makeup of the new government was clear, however, the United States was neither responsive nor supportive. Cabinet members met with AID officials in early November to request that the funds still in the AID pipeline— a few million dollars—be disbursed without a new formal agreement. U.S. officials claimed that they had to consult with Washington, and the matter was still unresolved when the cabinet resigned in January.[102] Washington did promise to increase its aid program to a level of $20 to $30 million, but did not reach this conclusion until early December. Major funds were never released (ST 310366, 1 December 1979). The State Department claimed that it was unable to obtain quickly disbursable Economic Support Funds because most of these were earmarked by Congress, and Development Assistance money required a formal plan (ST 310366, 1 December 1979). Curiously, after the fall of the junta, $9.1 million in ESF funds was found, and under the Reagan administration ESF funding climbed: to $44.9 million in fiscal 1981, $115 million by fiscal 1982, and $140 million by fiscal 1983 (Fagen 1987, 148).

It appears that this slow response really indicates not a lack of means, but rather a lack of enthusiasm. Ambassador Devine met with the full junta exactly twice, once to present his credentials, a second time to express concern about the government's ability to maintain order. He met separately with military leaders Gutiérrez, and Majano, García, and Salazar Brenes on several occasions to discuss military assistance and security concerns. Civilian members of the junta were disturbed that Devine had not even consulted them.[103] Meanwhile, the embassy consulted with Christian Democratic leaders, soliciting their political analysis and feeling out their reactions to proposed strategies (SS 6337, 1 November 1979).

A former senior embassy official stated that he and others in the embassy had grave concerns about the presence of the Communist National Democratic Union.[104] They also distrusted a number of officials who had been invited to join the government on the basis of their contacts with the University of Central America, suspecting that they were closet allies of the guerrilla left, and he expressed a sense of betrayal that they did not cooperate more fully with U.S. policy with respect to the military.[105] In retrospect, this seems a distorted view reflecting the strategic preoccupations of the day.[106] Other than Minister of Education Salvador Samayoa, who acknowledged in December 1979 that he was a member of the Popular Forces of Liberation, and Agriculture Minister Enrique Alvarez, whom the CIA identifies as a "long-term member" of the Communist Party, members of the government appear to have been exactly what they said they were.[107] The large number of them who fled the country to work as technocrats in international organizations, rather than allying with the guerrillas, would seem to vouch for their moderation. Moreover, the intense conflict between the junta and the popular movements demonstrates the considerable political distance between the two.

The embassy's other main concern was that the junior officers' movement, combined with the departure of senior officers, threatened the stability of the military. One cable from November 1979 reported that members of the reformist faction of the military claim—"perhaps with some exaggeration—that they have toppled one corrupt government and could replace the entire junta or any member who is either ineffective or strays from the established short-term goals." The cable goes on to claim that "the greatest danger to the military is the loss of discipline through the rupture in a functioning chain of command brought about by the discarding of some fifty senior officers and massive personnel shifts. A major concern of senior military officers is the reestablishment of that chain of command to control the junior officers" (ST 291354, 8 November 1979, quoting SS 6373).

These concerns, combined with an overly alarmist view of the activities of the left, resulted in a policy that sided decisively with hardline senior military officers and discarded any semblance of a human rights policy. The U.S. embassy under Devine ignored the massive increases in state violence, providing misleading (not to say patently absurd) reports to Washington, such as the following: "There is confusion as to who is shooting at whom and why. Early rumors were that terrorist groups and members of Christian Democratic Party were having another confrontation. Daily newspaper *La Prensa Grafica* claimed to embassy it was under attack by estimated 100 armed, masked men" (SS 6283, 31 October 1979). Such reports emphasized actions by the guerrillas, concerns about the security of the embassy itself, and the threat, which did not materialize until almost a year later, of arms flows from abroad (SS 6336, 1 November; 6593, 15 November, 6664, 20 November 1979).

In a lengthy background cable on human rights in El Salvador, Ambassador Devine wrote that "the [Romero] government, having to contend with a radicalized opposition using violent rather than legal methods, felt itself less restrained in resorting to violent tactics such as having persons 'disappear' as a means of silencing opposition." Devine then extended this justification of violent repression to the post-coup situation, blaming state violence squarely on the opposition:

> To maintain political momentum they must continue to provoke the government into human rights violations or failing this they will seek to use the JRG's response to the violations of past governments as political issue to discredit the new government and maintain popular support. Whatever steps the new government takes to try and rectify or correct human rights abuses, therefore, the radical left using its participation in human rights organizations such as committees of mothers and relatives of political prisoners and disappeared persons or the now radicalized Salvadoran human rights commission (CDHES) can be expected to heavily publicize continued anomalies in the human rights area [sic] in turn will lead to continued charges of human rights violations under the new junta. (SS 6785, 27 November 1979)

Thus not only were the state's violent actions the fault of the opposition (for having provoked them), but the opposition's objections to state violence were a political ploy. The violations themselves, rather than being a systematic policy of a significant portion of the state apparatus (and of the high command) are "anomalies." In such a framework of analysis, anything that the junta did to prosecute human rights violations would be an unwarranted concession to the "extreme left." The embassy was concerned only that state violence not be so excessive as to provoke an insurrection, as in Nicaragua. "If one is looking for parallels," it concluded, "situation in El Salvador may be more akin— although at hopefully lower level of violence—to situation prevailing in Guatemala rather than to one in Nicaragua" (SS 6785, 27 November 1979). Having reached that judgment, Devine cabled Washington to report the good news that "today, with human rights differences behind us," the embassy now enjoyed improved contacts with the Salvadoran military (SS 7097, 11 December 1979).

Consistent with this emphasis on security, the one type of aid that the United States delivered promptly was a small shipment of riot control equipment (protective vests, helmets, tear gas), accompanied by a six-member Mobile Training Team (MTT) (SS 6664, 20 November, 1979; NSA 1989a, 47). In a secret meeting with embassy political officers, leaders of the United Popular Action Front (FAPU) remarked that the embassy should give *them* the bulletproof vests: "We're the ones who are being shot at."[108] The same MTT, along with a group of "visitors" from U.S. intelligence agencies, assessed the government's military and intelligence capabilities. According to an embassy cable, "In both cases, visitors have been appalled at inadequacies of human, organizational, and other resources which they have unearthed." The cable goes on to record the embassy's disappointment that this information has failed to spark a sense of urgency in Washington (SS 7283, 19 December 1979).

The modest constraining effect that U.S. human rights concerns had had under Romero was lost. In those days the United States had sent a mixed message of alternating concerns about human rights and security, and human rights violations were a particular embarrassment because Romero's government had such a weak claim on international legitimacy. The civil-military junta, by contrast, could temporarily sustain a high level of violence without becoming internationally isolated because it featured broadly based civilian participation. After the coup, the only concern was whether the violence was so provocative as to trigger a Nicaragua-style insurrection. Anything short of that level was acceptable, and human rights problems were viewed by the embassy as "behind us." Though U.S. policy later came to place greater emphasis on democratic practices, in 1979 even a nondemocratic change of regime, if it included a measure of civilian representation, could satisfy U.S. requirements and make human rights conditions irrelevant. There is no evidence that U.S. policy makers adequately weighed the consequences of post-coup state violence for the longer-term prospects of a political resolution to the crisis.

Beginning on 20 December, the embassy met with the junta, military leaders, and COPEFA to pressure them to adopt stronger measures against the left and to accept increased U.S. military assistance. In the first such meeting, Devine expressed concerns about increasing seizures of farms and agricultural processing plants, takeovers of industrial premises, taking and holding of hostages, and almost daily marches and demonstrations of a "threatening character." His concerns were so disproportionate that even Colonel Gutiérrez remarked that "he did not consider the overall situation as too alarming but that he viewed it as a prolonged effort to provoke GOES [the government of El Salvador] and its security forces into a renewal of repression." Devine told the junta members that he saw the most serious threat to the government coming from the left, while the rightist threat remained "incipient," depending on the nature of reforms that were implemented. Devine concluded his report: "Overall conversation was not reassuring. I am struck by extent to which [the junta] seems immobilized by fear of negative human rights image, by extent to which some of its members seem transfixed by idea of ultra-right as being greater threat than armed and militant left" (SS 7315, 20 December 1979).

The next day, the ambassador and a defense attaché met with the junior officers of COPEFA (SS 7327, 21 December 1979). According to a retired Salvadoran officer who was present at this meeting, the ambassador told COPEFA members that they should disband because the council posed a threat to the chain of command and the stability of the armed forces.[109] There is nothing in the declassified documents to corroborate this claim, but it is consistent with Devine's view of COPEFA. On 20 December, he had cabled Washington that COPEFA "has had side-effect of weakening normal military and governmental structure. In addition, inexperienced and somewhat immature officers of council have presented target for lobbying by various interest groups hoping to impose their views through this extralegal channel" (SS 7310).

On 23 December, Devine met separately with Majano and Gutiérrez to continue the pressure on them to accept greater U.S. military assistance—a step that Ungo and Mayorga feared would worsen the junta's relations with the left and reinforce hardliners within the military. Devine once again expressed his concerns that "if too much ground is given away to an enemy such as extreme left it may well prove impossible to recover it." Devine continued, "I then asked rather pointedly whether we would all still be around in January to move forward with any such program. Colonel Gutiérrez promised me that we would" (SS 7349, 23 December 1979).

Devine was apparently under orders from Washington to warn the junta about the leftist security threat. Secretary of State Cyrus Vance reported to President Carter: "We have already asked Ambassador Devine to increase his efforts as a catalyst in helping the Junta see the seriousness of the extreme left's challenge and the need for cohesion and decisiveness in maintaining its authority" (memorandum, 26 December 1979). The perceived need to pressure the junta to take stronger measures stemmed from a belief that "the proficiency of the security forces has deteriorated to such a degree that their ability to deal with a sustained guerrilla effort by the extreme left is in question." The document continues, "The Junta's most immediate threat is a determined and violent challenge from the groups which comprise the extreme left. Intelligence sources indicate that preparations to launch a concerted attack on the government are under way." At this point Washington still saw the threat from the right as "incipient."[110]

Collapse of the Junta

On 22 December, civilian members of the government met with officials of the high command. Following a heated debate about continued repression and the blockage of reforms, Defense Minister García introduced National Guard Director Vides Casanova to speak for the armed forces. Vides' comments were a powerful assertion of institutional military supremacy: "Colonel García is the man from whom we take orders, not the junta. We have put you into the position where you are, and for the things that are needed here, we don't need you. We have been running the country for 50 years, and we are quite prepared to keep on running it" (Bonner 1984, 162). This seems calculated to provoke, though it may have been merely a statement of fact, since the high command was probably already in touch with the Christian Democratic Party regarding the formation of a second junta.[111] Either way, Vides' remarks signaled a major shift in the balance of power within the government. The increasingly violent confrontation with the radical left, the high command's successful suppression of COPEFA, the mobilization of the private sector right, and pressures from the U.S. embassy had combined to weaken the position of the junior officers. Without that power base, the civilian government was in trouble.

An intense debate began within the government. Some advocated resigning, others favored staying in office, and still others wanted to turn to the junior officers for assistance. The third option won out. Rather than contacting the junior officers through quiet channels and attempting to foment a second movement against the high command, the majority of cabinet members issued a formal ultimatum to COPEFA calling for its support for a series of proposals. COPEFA was to be the sole representative of the armed forces before the junta; the junta would be recognized as the commander-in-chief of the armed forces; all transfers and command assignments within the armed forces would have to be approved by the junta; COPEFA would meet regularly with the junta and cabinet; and COPEFA would join the junta in engaging in dialogue with the popular organizations. The cabinet also asked COPEFA to publicly condemn the oligarchy and its use of economic, political, and social power to block reforms.[112]

After three days of deliberations, COPEFA responded on 2 January that it was an apolitical institution dedicated only to the preservation of the unity of the armed forces, and particularly to the exclusion from the military of any "extremist" influence that might interfere with its proper and professional conduct. COPEFA reaffirmed that the junta was the commander-in-chief of the military and had the power to review all promotions, transfers, and assignments, but declined to communicate directly with the junta, saying that the Ministry of Defense was the appropriate channel for communication between them.[113]

This rebuff confirmed that the junta's "power problem" was unresolvable. Ironically, the National Resistance and the United Popular Action Front, which had been unwilling to publicly support the junta, urged the government not to resign. Archbishop Romero made an unsuccessful last-ditch effort to convoke a dialogue between the high command and the civilian government, and to persuade Mayorga and Ungo to remain in the government (Anaya 1980a, 101).[114] Cabinet members from the Communist National Democratic Union were the first to resign, but most of the rest followed shortly. Only Colonels Gutiérrez and Majano remained on the junta, and only Minister of Defense García remained in the cabinet.[115]

The First Junta and the Protection Racket

The failure of the first junta, and the accompanying violence against popular organizations, reveal just how strongly the protection racket had been institutionalized and how difficult it would be to break. Although the military-led state could no longer conceal its essentially exclusionary nature, and although repression was proving to be less and less effective, there was, as yet, no basis of political power within civil society that was strong enough to replace the military regimes maintained since 1932. The left was fragmented into competing organizations that seemed almost as hostile toward one another as toward the state. Though they had organized small commando units, they lacked the military power to take over the state as their brethren in Nicaragua had. Their large popular organizations could demonstrate the depth of popular discontent, but little else. The civilian right was not well organized politically, and continued to depend upon the military to govern. Although it had strong ideological influence within the military, it could not be said to be hegemonic even within that institution, much less within society as a whole. Centrist political parties such as the Christian Democrats were organized around electoral strategies and therefore depended upon the indulgence of the military for opportunities to compete for political power.

Thus the only group in Salvadoran society capable of challenging the existing statist order came from within the state itself. Junior officers in the regular army were increasingly disenchanted with the protection racket and had the military capability, once organized, to challenge their senior commanders, defeat the security forces if necessary, and create a new order. Unfortunately, as political actors they had serious drawbacks. They were young and inexperienced, and were adapted to a hierarchical institution based on a chain of command. They did not easily go against established authorities. Moreover, they had been deeply indoctrinated in anticommunist thought and therefore easily became frightened of civilian political elites who espoused radical reform and were willing to enter into dialogue with the left.

While junior officers could organize a rebellion to throw out President Romero and maintain sufficient pressure on their superiors to ensure a radical proclamation and the selection of reformist civilians for the junta, they were singularly ill-equipped to verify and enforce subsequent compliance with their agenda. Since virtually their only tool was rebellion, they were vulnerable to the high command's salami tactics in which their agenda was removed a slice at a time.

Though disrupted in the immediate aftermath of the coup, the protection racket institutions proved hardy. The high command acted quickly to rebuild the domestic intelligence infrastructure, transferring files and intelligence networks from the defunct ANSESAL to the C-II intelligence section of the high command, and reviving the operational side of the death squads through the existing security forces, particularly the National Police. These efforts received political, rhetorical, and financial support from the civilian right, which once again found working through the armed forces to be the most expedient way to defend its interests.

The United States, a "client" of the protection racket at least since the 1960s, found it difficult to break out of that role. U.S. policy was in flux in the wake of the Nicaraguan revolution and other distractions. High-level inattention and the conservative and not particularly savvy personnel in charge of the embassy led the United States to miss a crucial opportunity to back the reformists and reinforce their challenge to the existing order. Instead, the United States hesitated, then backed the high command, despite the deep involvement of these officers in violating human rights. Concerned more about appearances than the substance of human rights, the Carter administration fell silent regarding the increasing abuses and pushed for stronger measures, playing into the hands of hardliners.

The reformist civilians who entered the government in October 1979 had little power of their own. Installed at the demand of the junior officers, they depended for their popular legitimacy on their ability to deliver substantive change quickly. They were thus extremely vulnerable to both obstruction of their reform program and ongoing repressive actions by the security forces. This made them an attractive and easy target for Machiavellian elements within the military, who increased violence in a deliberate and successful attempt to unseat them.

If they had made different decisions at various points, the reformist elite might have produced a different outcome. Former members of the junta, cabinet, and junior officers' movement all mentioned in interviews that they should have remained in closer contact with one another and challenged the high command in a more coordinated way when it stepped up repression and disregarded the formal authority of the junta. The decision to make a formal request to COPEFA, rather than contacting the junior officers and asking them for direct military backing for a challenge to the high command, may have been another mistake. As we shall see in the next chapter, the junior officers were still prepared to take drastic action against the high command: hundreds of them nearly rebelled following the resignation of the first junta. Had the junta found a means of harnessing that political will, it might have effectively defied the high command.

There were numerous obstacles to such an outcome, however, some of which are discussed in the next chapter. The closer the armed forces came to internal conflict, the more afraid they became of the left. Had the junta and the junior officers who supported them taken more radical action, the junior officers' movement might well have broken down altogether. The hardline factions of the military enjoyed the backing of a civilian elite who, though disorganized and unbalanced by the pace of events, had significant financial resources to contribute and whose strident anticommunism provided a simple, action-oriented formula for dealing with the left. Moreover, the United States was unprepared to back the reformist faction of the military if that meant destabilizing the high command; it might have shifted from passivity to direct opposition had the junta acted against the high command. Ultimately the most crippling obstacle was the capacity for violence that remained in the hands of hardliners. By attacking the popular left, hardliners could ensure that any kind of inclusionary strategy would fail. Without the capacity to gain legitimacy in the eyes of the populace, the reformist project was doomed. Chapter six examines how a series of last-ditch efforts by moderates to head off civil war were systematically scuttled by the violence of the security apparatus.

SIX

DESCENT INTO MASS MURDER

García used violence provocatively, yet was also a reformist. Hitler was a great reformist, as was Mussolini. That doesn't mean that they weren't repressive. There is a tendency to see these as contradictory. That is incorrect.

— Héctor Dada, member of the second Revolutionary Governing Junta

Chucho no come chucho ["Dogs don't eat dogs"]. Majano used to say that over and over again. So he was very shocked and surprised when they tried to kill him.

— Former cabinet member in the second Revolutionary Governing Junta

García was a smart, shrewd individual, who . . . kept his personal ambitions and feelings well concealed and had a subtle sense of humor which he often used to influence others. . . . He appeared to have a self-righteous streak, a sense of superiority, and probably had a capacity for vindictiveness, even cruelty, toward those who would thwart his plans and objectives. . . . He tended to view people as components of the environment to be organized, manipulated, and eventually controlled.

— Declassified CIA document

The year 1980 was probably the most tragic one in Salvadoran history. Some of the nation's finest leaders, individuals who sought to avoid a civil war through political compromise and negotiation, were assassinated. With each killing, prospects for reconciliation dimmed. In February, Attorney General Mario Zamora Rivas was shot in his home the day before a convention of the Christian Democratic Party at which he was expected to call on the party to resign from the government in protest over military violence. An outspoken critic of government violence, Zamora had been engaged in dialogue with the Popular Forces of Liberation—the most hardline of the guerrilla groups—regarding a negotiated political solution (United Nations 1993, 139–44). In March, Archbishop Oscar Romero, who had insistently urged both left and right to stop the violence, to the point of calling upon soldiers to disobey orders to kill, was shot in the back while saying Mass (United Nations 1993, 127–31). Dozens of mourners died amid detonating bombs and gunfire at his funeral. In November, the entire top leadership of the nonguerrilla left, the Democratic Revolutionary Front, were assassinated on the morning of a press conference at which, according to some reports, they were to announce their acceptance of Church-mediated negotiations with the junta.

These deaths were accompanied by almost twelve thousand others. Most were either captured and executed by the death squads or killed in wholesale massacres carried out by government forces in rural areas (Socorro Jurídico Cristiano 1984). With each major demonstration or labor strike, the popular movement lost dozens of supporters and key leaders. In a sense, the repression worked. Demonstrations grew smaller, and fewer people would outwardly identify themselves as being affiliated with leftist organizations. Yet the repressive state paid a high price: though the demonstrations and strikes gradually became smaller, there was a concomitant shift within the leftist opposition toward a military strategy. In May, the left began to move its militants into rural areas to develop a military structure; by September, this process was well advanced, though the groups still lacked arms; and by November, the left, now united as the Farabundo Martí National Liberation Front (FMLN), had begun obtaining sufficient weapons to form an army.

Ironically, the bloodbath of 1980 was accompanied by the long-awaited land reform, a redistribution of large land holdings far more sweeping in its scope than that envisioned by Molina or any previous military government. The reform resulted from the demands of the junior officers' movement and the exhortations of the United States, and it signaled a small breach in the relations between the Armed Forces of El Salvador (the FAES) and the landed elite. Yet the high command managed these civil–military frictions exactly as military presidents had in the past—by delivering state terrorism, with overt and symbolic references to Martínez' massacre of 1932. Like past military presidents, García's high command made policy decisions that were politically expedient but internally inconsistent. Though forced to implement the land reform decreed by the junta, the high command intensified its violent campaign against the radical left.

Some of the factors that weakened the first junta no longer applied. First, the second Revolutionary Governing Junta and cabinet were formed by the Christian Democratic Party (PDC), which had an established popular base of its own, something of a permanent party structure, contacts with Christian Democratic parties in Europe and South America, and the active and increasingly generous support of the United States. The PDC entered office on the basis of an explicit pact in which the armed forces agreed to support major structural reforms and improve human rights protections. Moreover, the United States became a more active player, now that it had a junta in place that it was comfortable supporting, and higher-level officials were involved in both making and implementing El Salvador policy. The United States sought what seemed at the time a reasonably coherent political formula of blocking the political aspirations of the far right, undercutting their economic base through land reform, and reinforcing moderate elements of both the military and civil society. It protected the PDC from being overthrown, and it promoted land reform, but it failed to reduce state violence. On the contrary, killings by state forces increased throughout 1980.

After the fall of the first junta, the junior officers' movement mobilized again. In January the young officers confronted the high command. Colonel Majano, who had acted with great caution during the first junta, began to exercise greater leadership on behalf of the reformist current, openly challenging the high command on two occasions, and bringing the FAES to the brink of internal armed conflict. He engaged in international diplomacy and negotiated with factions of the left to garner support for the military's reformist movement. He also continued his efforts to prevent human rights abuses and ordered the arrest of prominent rightist coup plotters, including Roberto D'Aubuisson and many of his closest associates. Yet the ability of the high command and hardline elements to carry out violence with impunity continued to undermine the authority of civilian and military reformers. The generalized killing, as well as the targeted assassinations of key moderate leaders, scuttled any chance of negotiation and reconciliation, preserving conditions congenial to the protection racket regime.

The high command proved adept at responding to the challenges posed by the reformist military. It used its power over personnel assignments to disperse the so-called *Majanista* officers, remove them from troop commands, and expose them to combat or personal involvement in human rights abuses. The security forces and officers of the high command took more direct actions as well: at least four *Majanistas* were assassinated, and attempts were made against several others, including three attacks on Majano himself. A final confrontation in September broke the *Majanistas* and removed the last internal constraint on state terror, setting the stage for even higher levels of violence in the final months of 1980 and the start of 1981. The high command's work was facilitated by the youth and inexperience of the junior officers, Majano's caution and unwillingness to rupture military unity, and the difficulties encountered by reformist officers in collaborating with the revolutionary left. After showdowns in May and September, junior officers lost confidence in Majano's leadership and became afraid that the left could take advantage of the military's internal strife.

The power and interests of the high command likewise account for the limited success of U.S. policy and its failure to reduce state violence. When U.S. policy coincided with the interests of the high command, it was successful; where interests clashed, it failed. García and his colleagues stood to benefit from having the Christian Democrats remain in office: it was convenient to have an internationally recognized civilian facade between the military and the world community. The land reform, too, augmented the power of the military, placated reformist officers, pleased the United States, and served the counterinsurgency project. In contrast, the measures required to reduce state violence, such as purging rightists from the security forces or trying and punishing officers who had committed violence, would directly undermine the political position of the high command. García depended upon leaders like Carranza, Vides Casanova, and López Nuila, as well as the entire rightist network within the military, as a counterweight to the reformists. Moreover, accountability for human rights abuses would inevitably lead back to García and his circle. In this context, virtually no inducement or threat available to the United States could outweigh his political interest in protecting the hardline faction of the military and permitting it to go about its business.

The weakness of U.S. leverage was compounded by two facts. First, the United States was providing little in the way of military assistance at this time, leaving the high command relatively unimpressed by threats to withhold hypothetical future aid if human rights conditions did not improve. Second, the United States did not speak with a consistent voice. Ambassador Devine gave human rights concerns lower priority than retaliating against the left. Though Devine told Salvadoran military leaders that there was no inherent conflict between a strong response to the left and protection of individuals' rights, in practice his emphasis on security was probably interpreted as a signal that human rights concerns were secondary. Subsequently, both Chargé James Cheek and Devine's successor, Ambassador Robert White, repeatedly pressured the FAES to curb abuses by the security forces, but their positions were undercut by U.S. military attaches, whose ongoing ties with right-wing sectors in and out of the military were perceived as signals of approval.[1]

Another handicap for U.S. human rights policy was its dependence upon the Christian Democrats. The PDC had the potential to curb military abuses if it could issue a credible threat to withdraw from government if the violence continued. The ambitions of some PDC leaders, however, led the party to ingratiate itself with the high command by helping the military avoid international political accountability.

Ironically, the areas in which the United States was successful—getting the Christian Democrats into the government and implementing land reform—stimulated greater political activism by the civilian right and, as a direct result, greater violence against opposition civilians. During 1980, the civilian right reached new levels of political mobilization. The land reform, and the presence in the government of the reformist Christian Democrats (for whom many members of the social elite harbored special contempt), spurred rightist efforts to obstruct state reformism and restore an exclusionary, repressive regime. Aside from the protest marches of December 1979, the right followed its historical pattern of working through conservative elements of the military. Conservative civilians also increased their financial sponsorship of death squads and conspired to overthrow the junta with the help of military sympathizers.

Besides contributing to thousands of civilian deaths, these activities had the political side-effect of helping the high command consolidate its position. The coup plots of the right were directed primarily against the Christian Democrats and the reformist elements of the military. García, Carranza, and their cohort would almost certainly have remained in their jobs even if one of the plots had succeeded. The plots forced both the U.S. embassy and the *Majanistas* to expend limited political resources to prevent coups, distracting them from advancing their own projects or from effectively blocking the on-going violence being carried out by the hardliners.

The only real antidote to increased state violence was the reformist sector of the military. Yet U.S. policy makers ignored the pleas of left-wing Christian Democrats and the State Department Bureau of Human Rights and Humanitarian Affairs that the United States side decisively with the reformist officers, even at the risk of fracturing the FAES. Instead, the United States became wedded to the existing high command, beginning a policy that would last throughout the 1980s of working with and hoping to reform a group of military leaders who were willing to kill tens of thousands to stay in power.

More than anything, the events of 1980 reflect the political skills of the military high command and the resilience of the institutions and practices of the protection racket state. Although land reform shook García's relationship with the civilian right, he was able to satisfy the extreme right's preference for bloodshed while manipulating actors like D'Aubuisson to rebuild the domestic intelligence apparatus and dismantle the reformist movement in the military. At no point did the machinations of the civilian right pose a serious threat to the tenure of the high command.

The high command owed its success to its superior understanding of intra-state factional politics. In contrast to both the Juventud Militar and the U.S. embassy, García and his colleagues were willing to encourage divisions within the military. They gave D'Aubuisson and his associates freedom of movement and access to military installations to plot against the PDC and Majano; at the same time, they used the rhetoric of institutional unity to discourage both the reformists and the U.S. embassy from challenging them or the far right within the military. By encouraging the murderous conduct of the far right, the high command helped to radicalize the left and make it appear more threatening. This, in turn, made the high command's appeals to military unity more compelling. In effect, the high command operated a protection racket against its own institution, creating a security problem for its subordinates in an effort to consolidate its own position.

The cost of this strategy was, of course, that the military catalyzed a civil war. From the point of view of the high command, this was not an altogether unwelcome outcome. Senior officers were confident in their ability to withstand the left's still rudimentary military forces. Although the FMLN later developed into a serious threat, in the short run the high command's strategy was consistent with longstanding practices of Salvadoran military elites. It allowed them to prolong their enjoyment of the perquisites of state power, regardless of the long-term inviability of the policy or the cost in human lives.

The Christian Democratic Junta

When the first junta collapsed at the beginning of January, José Napoleón Duarte, Adolfo Rey Prendes, Fidel Chávez Mena, and Abraham Rodríguez had already been in secret consultation with the U.S. officials and the military high command at the U.S. embassy. Assistant Secretary of State William Bowdler had taken the lead in pushing for a Christian Democratic government. Bowdler had been in El Salvador in 1972, knew the PDC well, and according to a former U.S. official, "thought the PDC was the only salvation."[2] Bowdler's successor, Viron Vaky, had spoken with Duarte in Caracas in August, and U.S. cable traffic from November onward mentioned Duarte frequently.[3]

To put the deal together, U.S. Deputy Assistant Secretary of State James Cheek conducted a kind of shuttle diplomacy between the military and the Christian Democrats, who were not accustomed to speaking with one another and harbored deep mutual suspicions. According to Cheek, both sides had to be convinced that the other was not the enemy.[4] In dealing with the PDC, he played up the "historic responsibility" that the party was shouldering and the "courageous" nature of the decision; apparently no ambition was thought to be involved (SS 0051, 4 January 1980). The approach to the military high command was more direct: U.S. officials made it clear that any possibility of future aid hinged on the military's accepting the PDC.[5] With little in the way of an aid program to work with, all leverage derived from promises and threats regarding future aid.[6]

The Christian Democrats were themselves seriously divided between a conservative leadership group associated with former San Salvador Mayor Duarte and a more left-wing group led by younger figures like Mario Zamora Rivas. The left wing of the party had gained ascendance during the years leading up to 1980, but Duarte's return in mid-1979 restored some of the power of the more conservative, anticommunist wing.[7] The Duarte faction was eager to go into the government even if this meant unsavory compromises with the military. After 20 years of struggling to gain power, the January 1980 crisis seemed like an opportunity. The left wing of the party was reluctant, in part because several of its leaders had held positions in the defunct first junta and distrusted the military. They eventually agreed to form the second junta largely because they were unwilling to break up the party after 20 years of unity and still hoped to avert an all-out civil war. The most radical elements of the party had a different reason for agreeing: they believed that the popular sectors were not ready for full-scale confrontation with the military and hoped, by going into the government, to provide some protection from repression while popular mobilization continued.[8]

The new junta included Antonio Morales Erlich and Héctor Dada Hirezi, representing the centrist and left-wing sectors of the party, respectively. The military members remained the same—Gutiérrez and Majano—and a political independent, José Ramón Avalos, was named as the fifth member, replacing Mario Andino. The Christian Democrats adamantly refused to include any representative of the private sector in the new government, a fact that enraged those portions of the business community that had collaborated in the first junta (SS 0051, 4 January 1980). The exclusion of the business community caused its few remaining moderate members to fall silent, enabling the hardliners to monopolize the discourse within the upper classes.

On the surface, the second junta seemed better positioned to carry out a reformist strategy than the first junta had been. In a pact signed on January 9, the Christian Democrats extracted from the military a public commitment to extend the nationalization of external trade to cotton, seafood, coffee, and sugar; carry out an integrated agrarian reform directly benefiting the rural poor; nationalize the banking system; initiate a constructive dialogue with the popular organizations aimed at including them in the process of structural changes; and guarantee the human rights of members of those organizations. The pact also required the military to recognize the authority of the junta as their joint commander-in-chief (Castro Morán 1989, 416–19). Yet the formation of the second junta created a configuration of elite politics that made greater violence likely. The military had entered into the pact under considerable international pressure, particularly from the United States. The first junta's cabinet had been correct in thinking that the military would be isolated and vulnerable, both domestically and internationally, without a legitimate civilian facade. Now, since a significant portion of the Christian Democratic leadership and most of its mass base were too left-wing and antioligarchic to be suitable partners in government, the high command and the security forces both had strong incentives to use their capacity for violence to "domesticate" the PDC, suppressing its mass base and leaving only the elite level as a facade.[9] As a result, 64 PDC members were assassinated during 1980, including Attorney General Zamora.[10]

The Revival of the Military Reform Movement

The collapse of the first junta magnified junior officers' misgivings about their superiors. Despite the early January pact between the Christian Democrats and the high command, on 11 January a petition circulated among all of the army barracks in the country demanding the immediate resignation of García and Carranza. The language of the petition implied that the Juventud would remove both if they did not step down. About fifty officers signed it.

A few days later, at an assembly of officers at San Carlos, 75 percent of those present voted to call for García's and Carranza's resignations. A second petition calling for their dismissal and addressed to the new junta was circulated the same day; 186 signed, including all 74 officers in the First Brigade, the Signal Corps, the Military Hospital, and the military academy (Montgomery 1982, 160). Each signatory was exposing himself to retaliation by the high command.

In votes taken throughout the military over the course of several days, García and Carranza generally had the support of officers in the National Guard, the National Police, the Treasury Police, and the Cavalry Regiment. They had partial support from the Artillery Brigade and the Third Brigade in San Miguel. Other barracks either supported the Juventud position or were divided, and it appeared by 14 January that the vote was coming out against García and Carranza.[11]

On 15 January, while votes were still being gathered, Juventud officers met at San Carlos to organize themselves. Angry and impatient, they decided to contact García and Carranza directly (Mena Sandoval 1992, 191). The high command sent in turn Chief of Staff Francisco Castillo, Colonel Gutiérrez, and air force chief Colonel Rafael Bustillo to try to calm the young officers and convince them that they should not challenge the chain of command.[12] Not relying entirely on diplomacy, the high command also deployed National Guard and National Police units to surround the First Brigade and Signal Corps barracks. The two opposing forces faced off through the night "with sabers half-drawn."[13]

As before, the junior officers fell victim to the greater experience and political skill of the high command. The senior emissaries argued that by challenging the high command, the junior officers were endangering the integrity of the armed forces while the radical left lay in wait.[14] They also offered to convey the young officers' grievances to the high command and obtained from García a verbal agreement to carry out the reforms called for in the 15 October 15 Proclama. Temporarily satisfied, the officers disbanded (Mena Sandoval 1992, 191).[15] In the end, the vote by the full officer corps was evenly divided, and García and Carranza remained in their posts. The young officers, having sent their petition to the junta, merely waited for the junta to act against García and Carranza.

The failure to follow up on the petition illustrates one of the central weaknesses of the junior officers' movement: they did not really have an organization. The movement was dispersed and spontaneous.[16] In certain settings, especially when large numbers of officers were able to meet in one place, they could become quite radical in their stance. Once they returned to their respective posts, however, they had no reliable means of monitoring government compliance with agreements, and no means, short of rebellion, to mobilize themselves and apply pressure.

The Popular Mobilization

While the high command was struggling to prevent the military from coming apart at the seams, the popular organizations of the left on 11 January announced their unification under an umbrella called the Revolutionary Coordinator of Masses (CRM). The question of how to respond to the first junta had divided the left. Once the members of the National Democratic Union and the National Revolutionary Movement resigned, there was no further obstacle to unification. On 22 January, shortly after the military had weathered its crisis, a massive leftist march catalyzed yet another confrontation within the military. Organizers of the march, which commemorated the 1932 *matanza*, found ways to transport at least two hundred thousand people to San Salvador, most of them peasants from the countryside, despite roadblocks and a strike by transportation workers. The turnout was all the more remarkable because for several days before it a media campaign by the Broad National Front had called on "patriots" to block the march (Dunkerly 1985, 145). It was a true show of force by the organized left, designed to protest against the ongoing violence by state forces, to counteract the marches organized by the Broad National Front during December, and, for some participants, to encourage the reformist military to act.[17]

National Guard and National Police troops fired on the march. Twenty-one people died and 128 were injured, some shot, others trampled by the crowd (NSA 1989a, 41). Organizers managed to redirect the route of the march, which was miles long, to avoid the area where the shooting occurred. Leaders of the left feared another massacre on the scale of the *matanza* of 1932. "Security" for the march, consisting of militia members armed with pistols and a few sub-machineguns, would have been no match for an all-out assault from the military had one taken place.[18] As the march ended, twenty-five thousand campesinos took refuge on the campus of the National University.

The reform-oriented commander of the First Brigade in San Salvador, Major José Francisco Samayoa, acting with Majano's approval, sent troops to surround the university and protect the demonstrators from massacre by the security forces.

> At 8:30 the next morning the junta met with the army high command, including the directors and other officers of the security forces. The latter wanted to invade the university. When the junta refused to give its permission, Major Roberto Staben from the National Police and Captain Arnoldo Pozo of the Treasury Police announced they would invade the university with or without orders. Héctor Dada demanded that Minister

of Defense García discipline these officers for insulting the junta and for insubordination. García responded that he did not have the power or authority to control the security forces. (Montgomery 1982, 162)

The troops of the First Brigade did have the power, however, and their cordon prevented the invasion.

During the early part of the year, guerrilla forces continued to be active: the Popular Force of Liberation, the People's Revolutionary Army, the Revolutionary Party of Central American Workers (PRTC), the National Resistance, and the nascent armed wing of the Communist Party, known as the Armed Forces of Liberation (FAL). They posed little military threat to the government because of their lack of armament, training, logistics, and military organization. The accelerated pace of events had caught the politico-military organizations somewhat by surprise: they lacked the military capability to take advantage of the high degree of popular mobilization. The guerrilla groups faced a perplexing strategic problem. The high population density of El Salvador had led them to doubt the feasibility of creating rural "fronts of war," yet the strong presence of the security forces in the cities made it infeasible to develop a large-scale, urban-based military movement.[19] They therefore retained, for the first half of 1980, an uncomfortable urban-based compromise in which they continued small-scale guerrilla operations while challenging the government continuously through demonstrations and strikes, actions that made their supporters vulnerable to state repression.

In effect, the left had to develop the military capacity to challenge the state before state forces could destroy its popular base. The different groups had different ideas of how to resolve this strategic problem. The Popular Forces of Liberation favored a long, protracted struggle based on peasants and the urban poor: it opposed the idea of an early insurrection, seeing the death toll of 1980 as just the beginning of an inevitably long and costly struggle. The People's Revolutionary Army favored a strategy of catalyzing an insurrection, as illustrated by its abortive uprisings following the October 1979 coup. The National Resistance also wanted to take advantage of the high degree of popular mobilization in 1980. It sought a quick remedy to the military weakness of the left by attempting to negotiate a coalition with the "progressive" and "honest" sectors of the military. In effect, the National Resistance was willing to settle for a Torrijos-style reformist military regime that the left could then influence or even control through popular action. RN representatives met several times during 1980 with Torrijos himself (as did Majano), seeking his help in motivating Majano to act more decisively.[20] The other groups rejected this strategy out of hand, arguing that the military as a whole was untrustworthy and would have to be destroyed. The RN continued its discussions with the military, but the lack of consensus on this question contributed to the reluctance of reformist officers to attempt joint action with the left.

Between January and August of 1980, the RN concentrated one to two thousand members of the United Popular Action Front, its mass organization, near *Majanista*-controlled army barracks at the end of each month. They were available to take arms in support of the Juventud Militar should the monthly general order issued by the high command transfer *Majanista* officers away from their troop commands.[21] To their disappointment, Majano never proved willing to give the young officers the order to act.

The Reaction of the Right

The right took for granted that the military could and would suppress the popular movement. Thus, the right really mobilized when the PDC and the military signed an accord. This action made the PDC an immediate threat to the right's interests.
—Héctor Dada

There is every reason for the ultra-right to strike. From their viewpoint, the current JRG has transformed itself from a joke to a real menace to their vital interests.
—U.S. embassy in San Salvador to State Department (SS 1336, 22 February 1980)

To say that the Salvadoran right was hostile to the new junta would be an understatement. The reaction seems irrational, given that the Christian Democrats were, despite their commitment to reform, less radical than the National Revolutionary Movement and the National Democratic Union, which had participated in the first junta. Yet by most accounts the private sector saw the PDC government as a real menace (SS 1336, 22 February 1980). Businessmen I interviewed confirmed that they had viewed the second junta as more threatening than the first.[22] One reason was that the Christian Democrats had obtained an explicit pact and commitment from the high command, reinforcing the private sector's previous suspicion that García and his colleagues would be willing to sell out private sector interests in exchange for continued power. Even during the first junta, the willingness of García and Gutiérrez to cooperate with radical civilians had enraged the private sector elite. The pact with the PDC—the last straw in a process of alienation that had begun with Molina's land reform attempt—forced the business elite to question a practice that had "left political positions in the hands of opportunists—that is, the armed forces."[23]

The Christian Democratic Party seemed all the more dangerous because it had the support of the United States. The U.S. embassy had spoken with private sector representatives "to impress upon them how much it is in their interests to dispel existing fears and doubts" about the PDC in government (SS 0046, 4 January 1980). Not surprisingly, this effort to encourage political unity between actors whose interests were diametrically opposed backfired. The announced commitment of the United States, combined with the military high command's public agreement to implement reforms, convinced the civilian right that the party might just carry out the substantive reforms described in the pact.

The Christian Democrats reinforced this impression by making it clear from the outset that they were going to govern without collaborating with the private sector. On 17 January they charged that the National Association of Private Enterprise exemplified exactly those oligarchic capital sectors which the promised reforms were designed to eliminate. Outgoing Ambassador Devine commented in a cable that the statement was "unlikely to improve the party's very strained relationship with conservative elements traditionally opposed to any kind of reform in this country" (ST 39992, 14 February 1980).

Roberto D'Aubuisson summarized the common view on the right when he said, "The Christian Democrats are communists," explaining that "communists are those or that which directly or indirectly aid Soviet expansionism." According to D'Aubuisson, the "collectivist" policies of the PDC fell into this category (Pyes 1983h). The historical basis for this thinking was the Salvadoran far right's perception that Christian Democracy in Chile had paved the way for the Marxist Popular Unity government.[24] Historical precedent aside, much of the hostility was personal. One businessman I interviewed commented, "The PDC are the worst creatures in politics. They are dishonest at base, because they do not have a clear ideology, and they are really trying to get rich while claiming to be working for the people. Their views are bullshit. I would rather talk with a communist. With a communist, I could have coffee and have an exchange of views, because we would disagree, but both would be being honest. With a PDC member, they are basically lying."[25] Asked whether the Christian Democrats were more of a threat than the leftists in the first junta, he responded, "Yes, in the sense that they lent more international 'legitimacy' to the government and its project, both U.S. and other international support. This made the reforms possible."

While the leaders of the Broad National Front (FAN) understood that the PDC was useful as an international face for the military, they were determined to destroy its popular base and halt the momentum toward reform. Pyes (1983a) claims that attacking the "rank-and-file Christian Democrats" became a primary goal for the death squads for which the FAN provided financial and logistical support: "D'Aubuisson's 'new ANSESAL' was moved under the army general staff and, until late 1981, operated as a political police against the Christian Democrats then in power and did little else, according to military officials from the United States and El Salvador." Beginning in February 1980, D'Aubuisson "waged a sophisticated, well-financed television campaign for several weeks pushing himself and a nationalist, anti-communist crusade that focus[ed] more on the reformist civilians in the junta than the leftist terrorists who are rocking the country to its foundations" (SS 1257, 20 February 1980). In these programs, videotaped at an air force base in Guatemala, D'Aubuisson denounced PDC members and reformist officers as communists. Some of the material used was pure fabrication; much of it, however, came from ANSESAL files, to which the Ministry of Defense had given D'Aubuisson access.[26]

In addition to direct violence against the Christian Democrats and public denunciations, the rightist political program from January onward focused on plots by the Broad National Front to unseat the party and the *Majanistas,* and organizing within the military to step up the violence against the popular movement and undercut the reformist military leadership. These were complementary activities that involved some of the same tools: alarmist propaganda about the threat posed by leftist radicals, enhanced by accusations that reformist military leaders were in league with them (Castro Morán 1989, 423–33). One informant with close ties to both the military and the civilian elite told me, "The acceleration of violence after January 1980 was predominantly a response to the prospect of land reform. With the military moving toward carrying out the reform, the right had to find a way to defend itself. So they put the D'Aubuisson group into action. The purpose of the violence was to stop the reforms by erasing the call for them."[27] The effectiveness of this strategy was illustrated by the almost complete failure of a PDC demonstration on 15 February at which Duarte spoke to a "small and ineffectually organized" gathering of around a thousand of the party faithful (SS 1180, 19 February 1980).

The first serious coup plot was slated for the end of February and involved basically the same cast of characters from the Broad National Front who had begun organizing in December 1979.[28] By mid-February, it was clear that the Christian Democrats were moving ahead with major reforms. The goal of the coup was therefore to create an all-military junta, replacing Majano, the PDC members, and the civilian independent Avalos with conservative officers.[29] The PDC cabinet was to be replaced with right-wing civilians (SS 1257, 20 February 1980). It is unlikely that García would have been removed, even though the FAN did not trust him. Without the Christian Democrats in government, there would be little momentum toward reforms, and García had proven cooperative in restoring the repressive apparatus.

This plot was taken very seriously by James Cheek, who met repeatedly during January and February with the high command and military junta members.[30] The U.S. delegation stated in unequivocal terms that a rightist coup would be completely unacceptable to the United States and would result in cessation of all current and future aid to the government and military.[31] These warnings were taken to heart by the high command, thanks in part to the leverage the United States had gained through the offer of roughly $50 million in aid, of which a small fraction was slated for military credits and training. On 20 February the Department of Defense gave preliminary approval to a plan to provide El Salvador with six helicopters, though delivery would be delayed to gain leverage (NSA 1989a, 43–45).

The high command's own political and military calculations were probably the most decisive factor in preventing the coup. Although Majano's removal might well have been convenient, the high command understood the international political advantages of having the Christian Democrats continue in the government. Thus, although it was willing to use D'Aubuisson to rebuild the domestic intelligence network and the FAN conspirators to help destabilize Majano and his supporters, in the end a rightist coup would not have advanced the high command's interests. The other main barrier to the coup, of course, was the Juventud itself, which was solidly in control of two army barracks in the capital, meaning that any coup would automatically mean open combat between military units there. Such a fight could have uncertain consequences at other barracks around the country where the high command and the far right were not necessarily popular. It is almost inconceivable that the reformist officers' movement would have permitted without a fight a rightist takeover of the kind planned.

Though it stopped the coup, the high command did not interfere with rightist killings. The Christian Democratic leader and Attorney General Mario Zamora was assassinated in his home soon after Roberto D'Aubuisson accused him in a television broadcast of membership in the Popular Forces of Liberation. Zamora in turn had charged D'Aubuisson with defamation before the criminal court.[32] A few days later two staff members of the attorney general's office were "riddled with bullets" while driving an official car. Two days after that, on 23 February (the day after the coup of the Broad National Front was to have taken place), six masked men carrying small arms with silencers entered Zamora's house through the roof late in the evening, ordered friends and family members to lie on the floor, and asked Mario Zamora to identify himself. He did so, and was taken to the bathroom and shot to death.

The United Nations Commission on Truth for El Salvador (hereafter the Truth Commission) declared that Zamora's killers were members of the intelligence section of one of the security forces. They were acting on the basis of a plan that had been drawn up with the approval of the C-II intelligence department of the high command, but, apparently, without specific authorization. The high command carried out an internal investigation, identified the unit involved, then protected its members from outside investigation (United Nations 1993, 139–41).

This sequence of events is consistent with the ambiguous nature of the security forces during this period—protected by the high command, but partly autonomous and heavily influenced by pressures and inducements from the Broad National Front and other rightist civilian organizations. As noted, D'Aubuisson assisted the high command in reconstituting ANSESAL's intelligence and death squad coordination functions under the intelligence department (C-II) of the Joint High Command of the military. A special investigative unit created within the National Police reputedly became the most active death squad in the country. Operated by Lieutenant Colonel Aristides Márquez, it operated clandestine jails in Santa Ana and in San Salvador, infiltrated the National Resistance guerrilla organization in the western departments of the country, and killed hundreds of people in close collaboration with D'Aubuisson's civilian squads. They jointly operated a clandestine jail in San Salvador, and National Police Major René Emilio Ponce provided logistical assistance for D'Aubuisson's private squad.[33]

Similar squads operated out of the National Guard, Treasury Police, and intelligence units within the army. One informant told a CIA official, "García and Carranza gave him [D'Aubuisson] their most suitable men in each part of the country for his death squads. . . . The goal was to make it seem that the revolutionary junta was incapable of governing, to create chaos so they could push Majano out."[34] In these units, the lines between private and state structures were similarly blurred.[35] The right's control was less secure within the regular army, which hardliners viewed as not reliable for "dirty" operations. However, all major army units had an intelligence department, known as S-II. In most army units, except those such as the First Brigade and the Signal Corps in San Salvador, where the senior officers were loyal to Majano, the S-II was integrated into the right-wing network at both the local and the national levels. These army intelligence departments typically assembled a relatively small group of officers and soldiers who were politically trustworthy to carry out captures and murders of people identified (often without corroboration) as belonging to the left.[36]

A key component of the rightist network was a group of officers from the academy class of 1966, the so-called *tandona* or big class, with close political ties to the Equipo Molina and to Roberto D'Aubuisson and other rightists. Key figures, including Aristides Márquez of the National Police, René Emilio Ponce (who would later become defense minister), Roberto Staben, Juan Orlando Zepeda, Denis Morán, and Joaquín Zacapa, are implicated in U.S. cables and in the documents captured by Majano at the Finca San Luis (see below) as participants in the rightist death squad network.[37] This parallel command structure was beginning to take shape by the end of 1979 and was well on its way to being consolidated by April or May of 1980.

The United States Confronts the Civilian Right

U.S. officials attempted to prevent a rightist coup by intimidating the private sector. Chargé James Cheek warned representatives of the National Association of Private Enterprise as well as operatives of the Broad National Front of the intensity of U.S. opposition to a rightist takeover. At one meeting, Cheek told ANEP members, "The American Government is not willing to support regimes directed by bastards such as Somoza or other dictators. Within that context, the U.S. can live with benign Marxist regimes in Central America."[38] At another meeting he said, "People like you are responsible for what's happening here."[39] Cheek succeeded in conveying to the private sector elite that the United States intended to break their economic and political power, yet there was early evidence that the elite's economic power might not be the most urgent problem: the FAN publicly threatened Cheek's life and that of embassy Political Officer Joseph Lee. These threats were taken very seriously in the wake of the Zamora assassination (SS 1358, 23 February 1980; SS 2611, 21 April 1980).

According to Ambassador Robert White, who replaced Devine on 11 March, Cheek needed to be blunt because the embassy had been sending messages that had encouraged the right to think that a right-wing coup would be acceptable to the United States (SS 1886, 13 March 1980). In February, U.S. defense attachés and military group officers had openly advocated right-wing strategies in cables to Washington, suggesting that a new coalition between civilian rightists and the military would result in lower levels of violence and would still permit "economically feasible reforms" (SS 0977, 12 February 1980). Most likely their support for right-wing solutions was not confined to secret cable traffic. According to a former U.S. State Department official, Cheek was sent to "run the embassy over Devine's shoulder" after Washington began to lose confidence in its envoy, in part because of Devine's lack of control over his staff.[40] Shortly after Ambassador White arrived in San Salvador, he cabled Washington:

> This is unquestionably the most undisciplined diplomatic mission I have ever seen and a good share of our problems in El Salvador arise directly out of the mixed signals we have been sending to the various political actors here, especially to the armed forces. I am morally certain that if Jim Cheek had not taken charge when he did and if he and Mark Dion had not engaged in a marathon effort to untangle the mass of miscues and misreadings about our position, notwithstanding the department's firm and public rejection of a rightwing coup, we would now have an intractable rightwing junta in place and good prospects for a civil war. . . . It would help if Washington agencies, specifically CIA and DIA [Defense Intelligence Agency, responsible for defense attachés], gave clearest and most forceful instructions to their representatives that U.S. policy does not countenance a rightwing solution. (SS 1886, 13 March 1980)

Cheek's confrontational posture toward the Salvadoran economic elite was part of a plan devised by an inter-agency task force on El Salvador that Cheek himself had headed in Washington. The plan assumed that the upheaval in El

Salvador was caused by the recalcitrance of the oligarchy and its power over the military, particularly the security forces. This was an erroneous assumption in light of the military's independence and internal incentives for violence, and the plan based on it had serious weaknesses. The long term goal was to undermine the oligarchy through successive land reforms while building up the regular army as a counterweight to the security forces, which the administration hoped eventually to see disbanded.[41] Such a plan would require a long gestation period. It underestimated the capacity of the right to catalyze a war in the meantime, and assumed that the violent far right of the military would be unable to gain control of the army. Moreover, it offered no mechanism to counteract the power and autonomy of the security forces. For instance, while U.S. officials threatened to abandon the private sector right to the mercy of the left, no comparably stern warnings were delivered against the military high command for orchestrating or tolerating the ongoing slaughter of civilians. This would prove to be a crucial failing of U.S. policy.

Reforms with Repression

The blockage of the late February coup shifted the power equation slightly and temporarily in favor of the Christian Democratic Party and the reformist current of the military, so that planning for the reforms proceeded rapidly in the final week of February. The high command appears to have accepted the idea of reforms, and Colonel Gutiérrez worked closely with U.S. agrarian reform advisers on revisions to the proposed decrees (AID/Latin American and Caribbean Bureau memo, 4 March 1980). Colonel Majano played a crucial role in pressing for the reforms, backed by the continued strength and growing impatience of the Juventud (Castro Morán 1989, 311). Sensing that the reforms were moving forward, the Broad National Front increased its media blitz against the Christian Democrats, invoking nationalism and anticommunism in its calls to the armed forces to oust the PDC and not be intimidated by the U.S. State Department (SS 1685, 6 March 1980).

On 6 March the reforms were implemented, expropriating properties of greater than 1,250 acres and turning them over to the permanent workforce as cooperatives. On the same day, major banks around the country were nationalized, as were remaining elements of foreign trade. The *way* the reform was implemented, however, illustrates the amount of influence the right had achieved within the military and the limited ability of the Juventud to constrain violence in rural areas. The reform decrees were accompanied by a state of siege and the militarization of the countryside: "The implementation of the Junta's agrarian reform program in March 1980 produced a new surge of refugees. National Guard and Army units ostensibly deployed to implement the program were allegedly involved in the disappearance, torture, and execution of hundreds of rural inhabitants of villages where the population included members of opposition labor organizations" (Americas Watch and ACLU 1982a, xliii). The greatest violence took place in the Morazan, Cuscatlán, Chalatenango, and San Salvador departments, where the workforces of the new cooperatives included members of popular organizations. Amnesty International reported that army, National Guard, and ORDEN forces virtually wiped out several hamlets in Cuscatlán on 13 March (Americas Watch and ACLU 1982a, 158). In at least one case, the new cooperativists were told to elect leaders, who were promptly executed by National Guard troops (Bonner 1984, 199–200).

The violence with which the military established the cooperatives appears to have been designed, in part, to prevent organizations of the left from gaining a new institutional base. During a stormy meeting with Vice Minister of Agriculture Jorge Villacorta about the military's role in implementating the reforms, Gutiérrez told him, "Doing it your way would be to establish guerrilla *cuartels* on every *finca*." U.S. military attaches received Salvadoran military reports from this period indicating that the Popular Forces of Liberation were planning to place cadre in each of the 376 expropriated farms to help build a popular militia.[42]

The reforms, and the way they were implemented, included something for everybody. The *Majanistas* got their long-awaited structural reforms, as did the U.S. embassy. The state of siege and the opportunity to occupy the cooperatives and surrounding countryside satisfied the demands of hardline elements within the military for decisive action against the mass opposition. Thus the private sector, though deeply disturbed by the reforms, was in a weak position to oppose them because its basis for organizing within the military—a putative commitment to anticommunism—seemed actually to be well served by them.

A representative of a federation of agrarian reform cooperatives pointed out that the reforms provided the National Guard and participating army units with a much clearer political context in which to engage in repression: "With the reforms, it made it easier and more legitimate to kill more people. If there is a reform, and people are still politically active, it must mean that they are leftists. Thus the army could kill more freely."[43] Former Vice Minister of Agriculture Villacorta concurred, pointing out that the formation of reform cooperatives provided the military with an opportunity to draw politically minded people and organizers out in the open.[44]

The manner in which the reform was carried out also had the effect of purging the left wing of the Christian Democratic Party from the government and the party itself. Junta member Héctor Dada resigned before the state of siege decree, unwilling to "continue providing an umbrella of progressivism for a regime that is immersed in a profound repression" (Castro Morán 1989, 299).

The PDC convention held on 9 March to choose Dada's successor "split the party wide open" (Montgomery 1982, 167). Duarte had handpicked most of the delegates, but all of the PDC ministers in the government opposed him. The Juventud Militar expressed their opposition as well, but Duarte won by a slim margin. With that, the PDC ministers of economy and education and the vice minister of agriculture resigned in protest, along with such prominent party figures as Rubén Zamora.[45] Just as the violence of December 1979 had driven the first junta from office, the violence of January and February, combined with the repressive implementation of the agrarian reform, triggered the resignations of the more popularly oriented elements of the party, leaving those who were willing to cooperate with the high command.

The Killing of Archbishop Romero

If they kill me, I will rise again in the Salvadoran people.
—Archbishop Oscar Romero

Three weeks after the implementation of the land, banking, and international commerce reforms, gunmen assassinated the archbishop of San Salvador, Oscar Romero, while he was saying Mass in the chapel of a small hospital. The assassin, who has never been definitively identified, shot him in the back from inside a red Volkswagen parked outside the chapel, using a high-velocity rifle and a fragmenting bullet. The Truth Commission concluded on the basis of testimony and documentary evidence that the killing was ordered by Roberto D'Aubuisson and planned by Captains Alvaro Sarávia and Eduardo Avila along with civilians Fernando Sagrera and Mario Molina. The unknown, bearded gunman was driven to the scene by Sarávia's driver, and both Sarávia and Avila arranged payment to the assassin. All but the unknown gunman belonged to the core of D'Aubuisson's security team and were active in death squad activities involving both the security forces and civilians (United Nations 1993, 127–31).

Romero's death was a watershed event. He had been one of the most consistent voices for peace, condemning the violence of both the left and the right. He was also an advocate for the poor, calling for socioeconomic reforms that would respond to the demands of the popular organizations of the left while rejecting the rigid organizational approaches and manipulation of the politico-military groups. His gestures of solidarity with the poor and oppressed, such as his peaceful retaking of the church in Aguilares in 1977, had earned him the devotion of hundreds of thousands of poor Salvadorans (Whitfield 1994, 107–9). In 1977 he had begun broadcasting his Sunday sermons and other commentaries over the archdiocesan radio station YSAX, and thousands throughout the country would drop what they were doing to listen. He used these homilies to condemn human rights abuses, basing his remarks on the reports of Socorro Jurídico Cristiano, the archdiocesan legal aid organization. He had, as noted earlier, taken an active role in the October 1979 coup, hoping to preempt civil war. As violence accelerated in 1980, he spoke out against proposed U.S. military assistance and, in his final broadcast homily, called upon soldiers to disobey their superiors if ordered to kill innocent civilians.

Until Romero's death, Washington had been frustrated by his persistent criticism of the junta for failing to curb violence. On 24 January, Assistant Secretary of State Bowdler wrote to Deputy Secretary of State Warren Christopher, "A weak archbishop, strongly influenced by an idealistic but naive Jesuit cadre, is paradoxically leading the Church into a position where its not inconsiderable weight favors the extreme left rather than its secular co-religionaires [sic] — the Christian Democrats." He suggested that "it would be helpful to have the archbishop travel to Europe for two purposes:

— to obtain a respite in Sunday homilies which have not been helpful to junta;

— to have Vatican invite him to Rome where Pope or other high officials could talk to him about role of the Church in El Salvador." (SS 0529)

Before Romero's trip to the Vatican, the State Department drafted a letter to be sent to the Pope by National Security Advisor Zbigniew Brzezinski (presumably because he was a Polish Catholic) complaining about Romero's failure to support the junta. Upon his return, Romero was quoted in the press as remarking that "the Pope has obviously been receiving bad information," that "El Salvador is not free of U.S. domination," and that "the U.S. has not significantly modified its past policies toward El Salvador."[46]

Whatever disagreements U.S. officials had had with Romero, there was little doubt that his assassination posed an even more imminent threat to the survival of the junta. Shortly after the killing, the embassy cabled Washington that the murder could trigger a massive popular revolt comparable to the one that followed the murder of Pedro Joaquín Chamorro in Nicaragua. Military forces went on alert (SS 2163, SS 2178, 25 March 1980). The ministers of education and economy and the vice minister of agriculture had resigned (SS 2274, 28 March 1980). Colonel Majano, whose enthusiasm for the junta had already declined, considered leaving the junta after Minister of Defense García refused to curb the security forces (SS 2283, 29 March 1980). Retired Colonel Roberto Santibañez later claimed that the civilian right had ordered the assassination "with the single idea of destabilizing the junta."[47]

Despite its vulnerability, the junta survived the assassination. One reason was that the left was unable to take advantage of the killing to spark an insurrection. Though there was clearly deep and widespread abhorrence of the killing, it was also an act that destabilized the popular left itself. Romero had been one of the most prominent spokesmen for the popular cause, and one of its few unifying forces. The willingness of the right to kill him, and their ability to do so with impunity, heightened the sense of terror. The Salvadoran left lacked sufficient arms, communications, and logistics to protect its supporters from the government and to have a plausible chance of defeating government forces. The guerrillas and the progressive sector of the military were not ready to act jointly (SS 2420, 4 April 1980). The fifty thousand people with the courage to attend Romero's funeral were sprayed with pesticide from crop-dusting aircraft during the procession. Later, in the plaza in front of the Cathedral, between 26 and 40 of them died when bombs exploded and gunfire erupted between armed members of the Revolutionary Coordinator of Masses and security force personnel (NSA 1989a, 52; SS 2296, 31 March 1980).

The other reason the junta survived was that the Christian Democrats felt that they had to stay in office. As Ambassador White remarked in a cable, "The PDC is shaken, but determined to continue as part of the government. At this point it has very little other choice. Having just invested its main resource, Napoleón Duarte in the JRG, the PDC cannot quit without severely damaging its future prospects in this country" (SS 2274, 28 March 1980). This observation summarizes the dilemma faced by the Christian Democrats—and by extension the United States—when confronted with the uncontrollable violence of the security forces. The party had been so damaged by failing to control the repression that its future political prospects depended almost entirely on a longer-term strategy of remaining in government and eventually moderating the security forces. Yet virtually its only leverage for influencing the military was to threaten to resign, something it was unwilling to do. The party had to depend upon the United States to apply financial leverage, and the low U.S. military aid levels of this period made that leverage very weak.

Majano Confronts the Broad National Front

Aside from the assassination of Romero, the months of March and April brought a series of setbacks for the far right. Not only had the junta gone ahead with the land reform, but the arrival of Ambassador White had brought a new direction in U.S. policy that threatened the right. In a pair of lengthy cables sent within a week of his arrival, White argued against Devine's view that the left posed an imminent threat. White claimed that El Salvador was not in imminent danger of being "lost," and that the greatest menace to U.S. interests came from the right. He predicted that it would be impossible for the junta to survive unless the right were reined in and security force killings halted. The right was attacking precisely those moderate elements of the "accessible left" from whom the junta most needed support:

> Each day the toll mounts with the brunt of violence falling on the left wing Christian Democrats, on the Socialists (MNR), orthodox nonvio-

lent Communists (UDN), and on the more moderate leaders of the popular blocs. The strategy of the right is clear: (1) destroy the accessible left, those who might be open to an appeal to reason from the JRG and could potentially be persuaded either to support or at least not violently oppose the junta's reform program; (2) demonstrate the impotence of the junta and the tolerance of the armed forces for savage reprisals by the ultra-right, thereby radicalizing the moderates and insuring denunciations of the government from the archbishop and other popular leaders; and (3) convince the armed forces that its only hope of survival as an institution is to return to its traditional alliance with the oligarchy, especially those who are bankrolling the rightwing violence. (SS 1886, 13 March 1980)

White perceived "a substantial group within the Armed Forces, especially in the high command, that will never accept civilian leadership and who will attempt to undermine all movement towards democracy. This group wields important power and several of its members not only tolerate assassinations and bombings but probably actively encourage the rightist terrorist squads."

In marked contrast to Devine's view that the reformist military represented a threat to U.S. interests, White claimed that the *Majanistas* were a crucial counterweight to the civilian right and the high command. White viewed the Christian Democrats as "a truncated version of the European species, whose leaders have been out of touch with the people for many years and who cannot make the proper political moves because they lack the power to end officially sponsored, encouraged or tolerated violence." Survival of the reformist project therefore rested squarely on the shoulders of the reformist officers and Majano. "In my judgment this is the sector that will decide whether we will win or lose the war. . . . The only way I see this whole crisis coming out in an acceptable fashion over the months ahead is as follows: Col. Majano succeeds in building up a corps of progressive officers who gradually acquire enough power to force out the commanders of the security forces, either into powerless retirement or prestigious posts abroad. At that point, the government would become acceptable not only to the left-leaning Christian Democrats (who quit last week) but to others of the moderate and non-violent left." Failing that, White predicted that the hardliners in the military would consolidate control, marginalize the reformists, and lead the country into civil war, which White predicted the government would lose. One of the key implications of White's analysis was that although military unity remained "an important desiderata," the U.S. could no longer afford to protect military unity "at all costs if a political solution, which is the only one possible, is to be found for El Salvador's political crisis" (SS 2038, 19 March 1980).

To signal his distrust of the high command, White requested that Washington delay the arrival of U.S. mobile training teams (MTTs). While Cheek had argued that the training teams were needed to retain some minimal level of leverage with the high command, White saw no reason for rewarding the Salvadoran military leadership for not overthrowing the government it was sworn to defend.[48] Moreover, he believed that "the arrival of the MTTs will be interpreted by the rightist officers as USG [United States Government] support for the armed forces as presently constituted. The right-wing terrorists will not be disciplined because we will have committed our support already without demanding action to end the assassinations and bombings. With the USG 'in the bag,' the right-wing officers will begin to press again for the ouster of Col. Majano and the PDC. In fact, we could easily find ourselves with a coup in progress while the MTTs are here" (SS 1886, 13 March 1980).

White began meeting regularly with Majano, coaching him on politics and encouraging him to strengthen the organization of his supporters. White's goal was to rebuild the army "around Majano," suppress the hardline officers and security forces, and orchestrate a political pact that would include enough of the left to preempt armed revolution. Toward this end, the embassy made secret contact with leaders of the Revolutionary Coordinator of Masses and with Ferman Cienfuegos (*nom de guerre* of Eduardo Sancho) of the National Resistance.[49] Since Majano and his supporters could not expect the high command and the security forces to give up easily, the reformists began preparations for a second coup which would draw on support from the RN and the United Popular Action Front. At the end of April, the RN and FAPU put their militia on alert to receive arms from units loyal to Majano. By the beginning of May, the plan was ready.[50]

While these negotiations and preparations were under way, Majano began to challenge more actively the high command's policies. After the "domestication" of the Christian Democrats in February, Majano felt that he and his supporters were virtually the only remaining obstacles to an all-out campaign to exterminate the radical left.[51] Acting as junta member and technical commander-in-chief of the armed forces (see below), Majano headed off plans by the high command to increase violence against civilians. Though his piecemeal approach was not really effective, it did present an obstacle to further escalation. Lower-level reformist officers were unwilling to participate in state terrorism and often interfered in the actions of their more hardline colleagues.[52]

Faced with the risk of a second reformist coup that seemed likely to enjoy the support of the U.S. embassy, the Broad National Front renewed its efforts to organize a coup to throw out the *Majanistas* and Christian Democrats and form a more conservative civil–military junta. D'Aubuisson and his allies in the military persisted in their public denunciations of the Christian Democratic Party and pursued their dual-purpose organizational work within the military. D'Aubuisson, though formally retired, continued to have access to military bases, where he met with officials and gave vitriolic talks about the communist threat within the military. On Beta-Max videocassettes and audio tapes circulated among the barracks, D'Aubuisson enumerated the supposed communist connections and commitments of Majano and PDC leaders.

In March, unknown agents fired on the reformist Captain Mena Sandoval at a crossroads near Santa Tecla. He had been warned that he was on a FAN death list (Mena Sandoval 1992, 193–94). In early April, hardline elements appear to have made an attempt on Colonel Majano's life. An aircraft sent to Guatemala to pick him up was delayed by inclement weather. It exploded in mid-air at about the time it should have been airborne with Majano on board. Three officers on board were killed (Castro Morán 1989, 316).

In early May, the Broad National Front, no doubt aware of the reformists' coup plans, tried to pull off a coup of their own. It failed to garner sufficient support and was called off. Majano had been aware of the plotting and had confronted García and Carranza with his information. They denied involvement but also refused to take any action against the conspirators, as was logical, given that the proposed coup was directed against Majano, not them. Majano went on television after the coup attempt failed, asserting that it had been fomented by "groups that do not want to see the extreme left lose its national and international support because of government reforms" (SS 3222, 7 May 1980). It was, in other words, an effort to keep the protection racket alive.

Two days later, Majano got wind of a meeting of right-wing civilians and officers at the Finca San Luis near Santa Tecla, a few miles west of the capital. Acting unilaterally, Majano sent troops from the Signal Corps and the First Brigade to surround the farm and arrest the conspirators. When Majano's men arrived, the dozen heavily armed men guarding the ranch house did not resist, though conspirators inside quickly tried to destroy evidence. D'Aubuisson tried to eat an incriminating document before being taken into custody (SS 3287, 9 May 1980). Majano's troops arrested a dozen other officers and a dozen civilians.[53] The officers included Jorge Adalberto Cruz Reyes, Roberto Mauricio Staben, Alvaro Sarávia, Victor Hugo Vega Valencia, Eduardo Avila, and Rodolfo López Sibrián, all of whom would soon become notorious for their role in important assassinations and death squad operations.

A notebook belonging to Captain Sarávia listed weapons, ammunition, night-vision devices, bulletproof vests, vehicles, and names of operatives used in death squad activities. Several entries regarding an "Operación Piña" appeared to relate directly to the Romero assassination. Other documents proposed members for a post-coup government, who would include several well-known rightists as well as D'Aubuisson himself.[54] Also mentioned as possible candidates were Colonel Nicolás Carranza (who as vice minister of defense had cooperated closely with the Broad National Front) and Colonel Gutiérrez, currently on the junta. A remarkable draft manifesto among the documents spelled out how President Carter and Secretary of State Cyrus Vance, as operatives of the Trilateral Commission, had "installed a revolutionary governing junta in our country with the participation of the Christian Democrats, international socialists, multinational corporations, communists, and military officers." The commission, working through its instrument U.S. Ambassador Robert White, had provoked the resignation of Héctor Dada Hirezi, replaced him with Napoleón Duarte (whom the Trilateral Commission viewed as the "Imam of the masses"), and was preparing to impose yet another junta dominated by the left as a first step toward turning Central America "into a Cuban paradise" (SS 3268, 8 May 1980). Notwithstanding its extremist language (see Appendix C), there was an element of truth in D'Aubuisson's proclamation: the U.S. embassy—or at least that part of it responsive to Ambassador White's leadership—was exploring the possibility of a deal with the left.

The prisoners were taken to the First Brigade headquarters, where at least some of the reformist officers wanted to have them shot for treason.[55] The arrests triggered a dangerous crisis for the junta and within the military. The PDC leadership met through the night and agreed to side with Majano in calling for the prosecution of those arrested and the removal of Colonels García and Carranza for their presumed complicity in the plot. Junta member Duarte asked Majano why he had acted without consulting the junta, to which the colonel replied that he had repeatedly warned of the danger and had acted to protect his own life and to secure irrefutable proof of the rightist conspiracy. A U.S. cable from the next morning remarked that during this conversation Colonel Gutiérrez "remained mute" (SS 3269, 8 May 1980).

The Third Brigade in San Miguel and the Sixth Military Detachment in Sonsonate sent word early on the morning of 9 May that if the prisoners were not released by noon, they would attack the Presidential Palace and the First Brigade. The First Brigade responded that it would kill all of the prisoners if the barracks were attacked. Majano took shelter in the First Brigade, while García, Carranza, and Gutiérrez went to the National Guard headquarters. The reformist junior officers, fed up with the high command, notified Majano that they were ready to go forward with a coup. They then awaited his orders, which never came.[56]

The U.S. embassy was also divided in its reaction. Some officials felt that Majano had acted rashly and risked dividing the military; others, including Ambassador White, felt that the divisions already existed and that Majano's actions had been appropriate.[57] White favored prosecuting the conspirators, whose "wild charges" against senior U.S. foreign policy makers made it clear that they were fanatics "who would willingly plunge this country into civil war" (SS 3269, 8 May 1980). Successful prosecutions would be a "body blow" to the far right, the ambassador thought, even though a serious investigation might uncover the involvement of senior officials in the Ministry of Defense, potentially destabilizing the already divided military (SS 3287, 9 May 1980).

In the end, the United States left Majano to fend for himself. Intensive negotiations followed. Majano was willing to permit leniency toward those officers who were still on active duty in the military, a position that was legally questionable but politically pragmatic (SS 3287, 9 May 1980). He insisted, however, that D'Aubuisson and the other retired officers and civilians be charged with "endangering state security," and ordered a pretrial hearing. The military judge who heard the case was associated with Majano's faction but was a member of D'Aubuisson's *tanda*. After a delay of a few days, and much wrangling and confusion throughout the military, the judge ordered D'Aubuisson and his associates released for "lack of evidence" (Christian 1986, 91–92).

Their release was costly for Majano and the reformist faction. Up to this point, there had been some ambiguity about who was the highest authority within the military. Within the junta, Majano had one year less seniority than Gutiérrez, but he was from the "arms" branch of the military while Gutiérrez was from the "services" branch, which made Majano the ranking officer according to Salvadoran military law. As the senior military member of the junta, he was the commander-in-chief of the FAES, superior to the minister of defense and all other officers. Majano had correctly exercised his legal authority in ordering the arrest and trial of D'Aubuisson and the other conspirators. In doing so, however, he was confronting head-on precisely the issue that had most divided the military since October—the willingness of the institution to punish officers who carried out politically motivated, illegal activities. He had also taken on a key player within the hardline sector of the military, thus inviting open conflict between his own allies in the army and the security forces.

By exercising his formal authority in this way, Majano inadvertently brought to the fore the question of who should command the military. As had happened during the January crisis, a poll was taken of the entire officer corps on the question of whether Gutiérrez or Majano should be the commander-in-chief. Because of the perception that he had put the institution at risk, a slim majority voted against Majano, going against formal military law and custom. This was, of course, a heavy blow to Majano's status within the institution. A U.S. embassy cable on 13 May commented, "Majano's pride is hurt and he is probably considering some action that will put a strain on the government" (SS 3337). This patronizing remark misses the point: the representative of the reformist, pro-civilian, human rights–oriented sector of the military had just been removed from his position as commander-in-chief and left as a figurehead on the junta. The substantive consequence of the vote was that Gutiérrez would be able four months later to issue a general order removing virtually all of Majano's supporters from the command of troops, effectively preventing the reformist faction from challenging increasing state violence.[58]

Many confidential informants criticized Majano for triggering a confrontation and then failing to carry through with the potentially violent action necessary to win. Alejandro Fiallos claims that if the reformist officers at the San Carlos and El Zapote barracks had taken action at this point, they could have won, because junior officers throughout the country were still sympathetic.[59] Other former military officers agreed. The National Resistance was still willing and able to provide support at this juncture, and members recall with bitterness Majano's failure to act. Majano claims that he backed down because he simply did not have enough forces to win and doubted the willingness of his troops to kill their fellows. He also feared that despite the support of the more moderate RN, the other guerrilla organizations might take advantage of the instability within the armed forces. In fact, the RN and the United Popular Action Front were harshly criticized by other groups on the left for negotiating with the government and contemplating participation in a "possible imperialist coup" (SS 3525, 19 May 1980). The precedents of the Cuban and Nicaraguan revolutions, during which government military forces crumbled from within, made it seem too hazardous to push the issue to the point of internecine combat.[60] Majano's inaction turned even officers who supported his political project against him: it was simply too dangerous to follow a leader who would bring them to the brink of confrontation, then back down, leaving all of them vulnerable to retaliation by the high command and the security forces.

The position of the *Majanistas* now deteriorated rapidly. Majano was portrayed by the high command as a threat to the unity and integrity of the armed forces.[61] His loss of command authority greatly weakened the position of reformist captains and lieutenants in most of the brigades, where they had to contend with brigade commanders—full colonels—who were loyal to García. Meanwhile, the May confrontation affirmed the political strategy of the Broad National Front and of the high command. By permitting the FAN plot to go forward even after the publicized attempt at the beginning of the month, the high command provoked Majano into a high-risk act of self-defense. It was then able to portray him as a threat to military unity, discrediting him in the eyes of many officers and undermining the solidarity of the Juventud Militar. In effect, the high command deliberately created divisions within the military, then manipulated the myth of military unity to make Majano bear all the costs. The risks to the high command were low throughout this episode, and though Majano prevented the coup from going forward, within a few months the FAN and the high command had achieved their goal of his removal.

Buoyed by the suppression of Majano, García was in a stronger position to resist human rights pressures from the United States. On 21 May, White met with García to demand reductions in state violence and to warn the defense minister that any future U.S. military assistance would be jeopardized by further coup plots from the right. White came away from the meeting disheartened: "This is the most discouraging and disappointing conversation I have had since my arrival in El Salvador. Col. García made no promise, implicit or explicit, to put an end to the official violence. . . . It was obvious that he would like nothing better than to drive Col. Majano out of the junta and rehabilitate D'Aubuisson. The reality is that the principal threat to the stability of this government comes from the officers of the high command who are secretly in the right's corner" (SS 3598, 21 May 1980).

The Road to War

While the junior officers' movement was unraveling and the government becoming increasingly conservative, the left was taking important steps toward unification. In April the popular organizations of the Revolutionary Coordinator of Masses (CRM) joined with dissident left-wing Christian Democrats, the National Revolutionary Movement, and a variety of progressive professional associations to form the Democratic Revolutionary Front (FDR), which was to serve as an umbrella organization for all the nonguerrilla components of the left. Many of the components of the FDR, such as the Popular Revolutionary Bloc, the United Popular Action Front, and the Popular Leagues of February 28, were closely affiliated with or even controlled by guerrilla organizations. But in a context in which the left lacked the military power to overthrow the state, nonviolent or at least nonmilitary forms of political struggle remained an important component of the left's strategy (Bonasso and Leyva 1993, 35).

These popular organizations continued to suffer a terrible death toll. According to the archdiocesan human rights office Socorro Jurídico, about twelve hundred civilians were killed by government forces and death squads during March and April (see Table 3).[62] The death toll more than doubled in May, in part because of a massacre that took place along the Sumpul River where it forms the border with Honduras. Combined forces of the National Guard, the First Military Detachment of the army, and former ORDEN members attacked a group of peasants who were attempting to flee into Honduras. Honduran military forces blocked the crossing, and the Salvadoran forces moved in to murder an estimated three hundred peasants, including many women and children (United Nations 1993, 123–24).

The left was losing key leaders and supporters at a terrible rate. Each time a labor union went on strike, it risked destruction. Moreover, the fluidity of the political situation and the pace at which popular organizations had grown during the past two years had allowed extensive penetration by government informants.[63] The reconstituted domestic intelligence network of the security forces, intelligence sections of regular army units, and various paramilitary structures were making highly effective use of both old and new sources of information to target the left. Nonviolent forms of struggle became increasingly pointless, since the government was not distinguishing between

Table 3

Political Killings during 1980

	Jan	Feb	Mar	Apr	May	Jun	Jul	Aug	Sep	Oct	Nov	Dec
Civilians Killed												
By state forces	320	293	584	634	1,424	963	1,077	869	1,818	1,389	1,360	1,164
By left	17	23	0	37	63	80	261	314	258	109	17	64

Source: Socorro Jurídico Cristiano (1984).

combatants and noncombatants anyway (Mason and Krane 1989). Although some elements of the left continued to advocate nonmilitary strategies and advance negotiated solutions, the center of gravity shifted decisively toward a military approach.

On 22 May the politico-military organizations of the left announced the formation of a Unified Revolutionary Directorate (DRU) to coordinate the military planning and operations of the different groups and began shifting personnel to rural areas, since it was impossible to organize and train forces of any size in the city. They did not completely abandon mass popular actions, however. General strikes in June and August were disrupted by the military with great loss of life, but the June strike shut down most of the businesses in the San Salvador area. The August strike was less successful. As the journalist Horacio Castellanos put it, "The massacre proceeded faster than the mobilization."[64] During a third strike later in August, the military broke one of the most strategically important unions of the left, STECEL, which represented electric power utility workers. Unionists attempting a series of rolling blackouts lost control of the grid and were unable to reactivate it. The military invaded the power stations and captured most of the leadership, removing one of the last effective nonmilitary tools of the left.[65]

From roughly June onward, the guerrilla organizations increased military action against the government, attacking smaller police and security force posts. They also set about murdering people they considered government informants and members of ORDEN. By the end of the year, they had eliminated ORDEN as a functioning organization in some areas of the country (Harnecker 1993, 174). According to figures gathered by the University of Central America, the guerrillas assassinated 1,488 civilians between June and the end of the year, an estimate that is most likely conservative. Most of the killing took place between June and September.[66] By September, the left was devoting itself to building logistical bases of support, training combatants, and preparing for an offensive (SS 6612, 24 September 1980). They also undertook a major effort to obtain arms through Panama and Costa Rica (SS 4156, SS 4169, 16 June 1980; SJ 3593, SJ 3606, 25 June 1980).

Finishing Off the Reformists

With Majano's formal command authority diminished, the high command found additional means to undermine his faction. Lower-ranking officers who were known to be loyal to Majano were transferred to hazardous locations, such as Chalatenango, where guerrilla organizations were beginning to operate. The idea was to put the young officers in a place where they would "take some fire" from the guerrillas and potentially be forced to draw blood themselves; it also put reformists under the authority of more hardline senior officers. The Defense Ministry would then offer them an opportunity to transfer back to a safer locale if they were willing to "stop being *Majanistas*."[67] These transfers were matched by relocation of more hardline officers into units in which the *Majanistas* had particularly strong influence, a measure designed to "dilute the influence of Colonel Majano over some military installations" (SS 4575, 3 July 1980).

Reformist junior officers were subject to increasing pressures to commit massacres against civilians, particularly in rural areas. Captain Amilcar Molina Panameño, who was among the most outspoken of the original reformist coup plotters, was transferred into the National Police and assigned to a unit in the core of the national death squad network.[68] Captain Mena Sandoval was repeatedly pressured to kill civilians and only narrowly managed to avoid doing so (1992, 196–207). His superiors warned him that he was being watched and regularly accused him of being a communist. Suspicion eased slightly when Mena led a successful combat operation against a group of guerrillas.

The deterioration of the *Majanistas*' position culminated in the general order of 1 September, signed by Gutiérrez and García, transferring the rest of Majano's loyalists away from troop commands. Majano countermanded the order, telling his officers to stay put. Once again, the barracks in the capital prepared for combat. Majano took shelter this time at the Signal Corps barracks, while Gutiérrez, García, and Carranza went to the National Guard barracks. Once again, Majano called upon his loyalists to confront the high command. By this time he no longer had the option of calling on the National Resistance for outside support: the disastrous consequences of the June and August strikes and the shift of resources to rural areas meant that the RN and the United Popular Action Front could no longer mobilize large numbers of people to support the reformist officers.[69] Once again, Majano backed down from an armed confrontation. He was unwilling to be the cause of open combat between Salvadoran military units, believed that he lacked sufficient forces to be successful, and feared that the left would take advantage of any instability within the military.[70] He agreed to permit the transfers to go through in exchange for a minor concession under which the high command allowed a few of his loyalists to retain their commands (NSA 1989a, 81).

The high command and the security forces were not satisfied with the removal of most of Majano's supporters from troop commands. So many officers throughout the military had originally supported him that the high command perceived a risk that some barracks and troops might yet rebel against their superiors and side with the left, especially in the context of the expected general offensive by the revolutionaries. After September, Majano continued his discussions with the left, as did a number of junior officers acting individually. Increased surveillance by the intelligence sections of their own units and by the security forces made it difficult for reformist officers to maintain contacts with the left, and made it less likely that they could pull off a large-scale, coordinated defection of military units to the guerrillas. With each officer having to make independent arrangements with organizations of the left, relatively few ended up doing so.[71]

In early November, a large bomb exploded near the central military headquarters just as Majano's vehicle was driving by. The dynamite was ignited from a remote location, and the timing was slightly off: although it blew an enormous hole in the pavement and destroyed Majano's car, the colonel himself emerged unscathed. He immediately proceeded to the military academy, where he confronted Vice Minister of Defense Carranza, who seemed extremely surprised to see him, blurting out, "Majanito, Majanito!" Captain Amilcar Molina Panameño was not so fortunate: in mid-November elements of the National Guard assassinated him in front of his home; as Captain Alejandro Fiallos put it, "They left him like a colander." An anonymous telephone call to reformist Captains Fiallos and Marcelo Cruz told them to go pick up their dead "comrade." Fiallos left the country shortly thereafter, while Cruz and Mena Sandoval proceeded with plans to join the revolutionaries (Mena Sandoval 1992, 206).[72] Ironically, the risks of discovery and assassination dictated that officers who wanted to maintain contacts with the left shifted away from the National Resistance, despite its ideological willingness to cooperate with the reformist military. Because its military apparatus was built upon a very large popular organization, the United Popular Action Front, the RN had been heavily infiltrated by the security forces. In contrast, the People's Revolutionary Army (ERP) was first and foremost an army, and it took tight security measures before admitting new combatants. Cruz and Mena Sandoval chose to collaborate with the ERP, as it was the safer organization to join.[73]

It is difficult to exaggerate the ideological gaps between Marxist-Leninist revolutionaries and FAES officers. Very few officers had sufficient exposure to radical ideas to be comfortable with the fairly severe discourse of the Salvadoran left during this period. They had spent their entire careers in an organization whose doctrine, training, and mission were dedicated largely to defending the country against communism. They had also been deeply inculcated with respect for military hierarchy, loyalty to the institution, and norms of secrecy and impunity. This was a difficult legacy for most officers to overcome, and even those few who joined one of the guerrilla organizations found the transition extremely difficult.[74] All of the officers who crossed the line were misfits in some regard. Mena Sandoval had been thrown out of the military academy twice for insubordination and was widely perceived as a maverick. Bruno Navarrete, Alejandro Fiallos, and Marcelo Cruz were medical practitioners who answered to a second set of professional commitments.

As late as 31 December 1980, the intelligence available to the high command indicated that the guerrillas were "weak and poorly led and that even with large supplies of new arms they could be contained by the armed forces" (SS 9078). The January 1981 general offensive would prove the accuracy of this assessment. Yet in discussions with junior officers, senior Defense Ministry leaders portrayed the threat from the left as imminent and argued against doing anything that might endanger military unity. As the repressive violence of the security forces radicalized the left and pushed it toward a military strategy, it became easier for the high command to make this argument. The irony, of course, was that the high command itself was responsible for creating internal divisions within the military, as well as for the polarizing violence of the security forces. By encouraging the development of an "uncontrollable" hardline network within the military, the high command was better able to control and suppress the reformists.

The Costs of Defeat

I don't think that García was inhumane. I never detected in him a shade of tolerance for human rights abuses.
  —General Fred Woerner, 1989[75]

When I meet tomorrow (Monday) with the four junta members (Majano is in the United States) and the Minister and Vice Minister of Defense plus the National Guard Commander . . . , it will be like facing murderers row with no infield or outfield behind me.
  —Cable from Ambassador Robert White to State Department, 30 November 1980

We must now make the difficult and deliberate choice of risking the cohesion of the armed forces in an effort to strengthen the democratic and moderate elements within both the JRG and the armed forces.
  —Deputy Assistant Secretary of State for Human Rights Patricia Derian to the Secretary of State, 4 December 1980

Once the high command checkmated Majano and his supporters, there was little to prevent an ongoing escalation of state violence. Notwithstanding an order issued by the junta on 19 October to members of the military to respect human rights and uphold the law, the archdiocesan human rights office Socorro Jurídico received reports of over one thousand civilians killed by government forces or death squads each month from September 1980 onward (SS 7217, 17 October 1980; Socorro Jurídico Cristiano 1984; see Table 3 above). Numerous labor and peasant leaders were killed during this period, including members of the Salvadoran Communal Union, a semiofficial peasant union formed under past military regimes, and beneficiaries of agrarian reform.[76] Not only did these death-squad-style killings increase, but in October the security forces and special army units began carrying out sweeps of rural areas in the north of the country where guerrilla units were being trained and where the population was thought to be sympathetic to the left. Following the model of the Río Sumpul massacre in May, these units committed indiscriminate violence against entire communities (NSA 1989a, 66). Rural people in targeted areas often attempted to flee, and in some cases fought back with whatever weaponry was available to them.[77] State violence in the city became more indiscriminate as well. The military began to outrun its intelligence system, resorting to crude target profiles based on age, sex, clothing, occupation, and geographic location.[78] An official with the American Institute for Free Labor Development, wrote, "The armed forces have been operating with the list system here: if your name happens to be on the list and you are taken prisoner your future life expectance [sic] is about one hour. Young people from 16 to 20 are indiscriminate victims of the security forces as these look upon most students as potential enemies."[79] The left responded in kind, killing people it identified as government informants and ORDEN members, though the "overwhelming majority of violence suffered by campesinos comes from security forces and, to a lesser extent, the army."[80] The U.S. embassy reported that 222 people were killed in the first week of November alone, a figure that tends to corroborate the reporting of Socorro Jurídico (SS 7853, 9 November 1980).

A series of important targeted assassinations followed. Two members of the Non-Governmental Human Rights Commission (CDHES) were killed in October, as was the rector of the National University, Felix Ulloa (NSA 1989a). On 14 November the secretary general of the union federation FESIN-CONSTRANS was killed. Two days later, the left assassinated retired Colonel Carlos Choto, along with his wife and children, using a fire bomb. Choto had headed the Armed Forces Reserve, a service responsible for maintaining rural paramilitary structures.

On 27 November about two hundred men belonging to combined security forces kidnapped, tortured, strangled, and then shot six top leaders of the Democratic Revolutionary Front (FDR): Enrique Alvarez Córdova, Juan Chacón, Manuel Franco, Humberto Mendoza, Enrique Barrera, and Doroteo Hernández. The six were preparing for a press conference at which they

were going to announce their willingness to participate in a process of negotiation with the junta, to be mediated by the Salvadoran bishops. The assassination effectively ended any serious hope of a negotiated solution to the ac-
celerating civil conflict. By killing the leaders of the nonguerrilla left, the
security forces closed off all political space and made arms the only viable
form of opposition. In retrospect, other leaders in the FDR marveled at the
willingness of the six who were killed to pursue open political activity and negotiations in such a violent climate. It was either a terrible miscalculation on
their part or a remarkable act of courage.[81]

It was immediately apparent to virtually all observers that one or more of the
security forces were responsible for the killings. The FDR leaders were killed
at the Externado San José Jesuit high school, which also housed the human
rights organization Socorro Jurídico. These facilities, located just a few blocks
from the U.S. embassy near the center of San Salvador, were under constant
surveillance by the security forces. Witnesses confirmed the presence of uniformed police and known security force vehicles at the scene. Within a few
hours of the killings, the deputy foreign minister confirmed to Ambassador
White that the six were in government custody (SS 8321, 28 November 1980).
The bodies later appeared near Lake Ilopango, east of San Salvador. Later that
day a statement was delivered to the leading San Salvador daily newspapers in
which the "Maximiliano Hernández Martínez Anti-Communist Brigade"
took credit for the "just executions" of the "FDR communists" for being "materially and intellectually responsible for thousands of assassinations of innocent people who did not want to be communists." It warned that it would kill
Catholic priests if they did not stop "poisoning the minds of Salvadoran Youth"
(SS 8301, 28 November 1980).

In a lengthy cable to Washington, Ambassador White wrote: "By killing the
leaders of the FDR the military have explicitly rejected dialogue and heralded
a policy of extermination." The killings could force the Christian Democrats,
Majano, or both to withdraw from the junta, he warned, or reformists in the
military, disorganized in the wake of the September transfers, might act
against the security forces or the high command. White argued that U.S. policy could be salvaged only if the Christian Democrats forced the military to
sack some of the most egregious offenders from the security forces in exchange
for an agreement to stay in the government: "The military leaders are worried
and off balance. They know they have been caught out and it is my best guess
that they will respond to properly applied pressures. Our objective is not to
fracture the military but to strengthen the hand of the civilian and military elements who back reform and a political solution to the problems of El Salvador" (SS 8321, 29 November 1980).

Declassified CIA documents paint a very different picture. One report,
dated 1 December ("Satisfaction of Many Military Officers with Assassination

of Leaders of the Revolutionary Democratic Front (FDR); Belief That the Same Tactics Should Be Used to Eliminate Other Leftist Leaders"), does not portray a senior leadership which has been "caught out." Rather, it reports that many mid-level and senior National Guard and army officers approved of the killings, and even more significantly, that "both García and Carranza indicated that they supported this line of thinking."

On 4 December, Assistant Secretary of State for Human Rights and Humanitarian Affairs Patricia Derian wrote a strongly worded memo to the secretary suggesting that the U.S. goal *should* be to fracture the military: the United States "must now make the difficult and deliberate choice of risking the cohesion of the armed forces in an effort to strengthen the democratic and moderate elements within both the JRG and the armed forces, or stand aside and with our silent complicity witness over the next several weeks an accelerated drift to the right, the result of which can only be the collapse of the JRG."[82] As it turned out, the junta survived, but Derian's point that halting the violence and preserving the unity of the military were incompatible goals was absolutely correct. By the time she wrote her memo, however, the reformist current in the military was so disrupted that it is unlikely that they could have taken control away from García and his circle.

As early as March, State Department documents discussed the importance of controlling the security forces, primarily by removing the heads of the offending agencies and replacing them with officers "responsive to the junta" (ST 83127, 29 March 1980). There was, of course, no reason for the minister of defense to cooperate with U.S. requests for such transfers. On the contrary, the security forces leaders were among Minister García's most important allies in opposing Majano and the reformist movement, his insurance against being overthrown by a coup from the right, and the most active forces against the left, a position that García clearly endorsed. Thus, while García was willing to placate the United States by implementing land reform in March, he was not willing to undermine his own political position by removing officers whom he depended on. It is difficult to escape the conclusion that the failure of the United States to act more decisively in support of Majano in May and June doomed its human rights policy, contributing to the deaths of tens of thousands of Salvadorans.

Virtually the only source of U.S. leverage after May was the limited economic and military aid package that had received preliminary approval earlier in 1980. It included six helicopters that Ambassador White hoped to use to persuade the high command to sack some of the worst human rights offenders. White proposed to arrange to deliver the helicopters within 60 days, begin flight training for Salvadoran pilots, and then condition eventual delivery of the aircraft on improvements in human rights performance: "It is a fair combination of carrot and stick, and may have a positive effect on the Sal-

vadoran military who are anxious to the point of desperation for the helicopters" (SS 4575, 3 July 1980). The embassy was particularly interested in the
transfer of Vice Minister of Defense Nicolás Carranza, "the principal
rightwinger among active duty officers," whose departure would signal an end
to toleration of hardline activities.

This strategy was not effective. As already noted, the senior officer corps
were well aware that the left did not pose an imminent threat. Therefore, although the high command would have been pleased to have the helicopters,
their value was far less than that of maintaining intact the repressive network
that the high command had reestablished after the October 1979 coup. Carranza in particular had played an instrumental role in establishing and managing this network, and was a crucial liaison between García and the civilian
right.

García might have considered removing Carranza and others if the Christian Democrats had made a credible threat to leave the government, thereby
isolating the military before the international community. However,
Napoleón Duarte was unwilling to take such a position. On the contrary, as
Ambassador White wrote in a cable to Washington, "It is Duarte's strategy to
increase his authority by continuing to cover up for the military's wave of
killings thereby winning their gratitude and confidence" (SS 8332, 30 July
1980). Foreign Minister Fidel Chávez Mena, for one, favored stronger measures, but Duarte dominated what remained of the party, and his ambitions
outweighed the concerns of his colleagues. This left the Christian Democrats
and the United States with only a longer-term strategy that consisted of increasing the size and budget of the army while freezing the security forces at
their current levels. This would gradually shift the military's center of political gravity in a more moderate direction.[83] Duarte's plan, which was essentially the same as that proposed by James Cheek at the beginning of the year,
was to use increased U.S. military assistance to arm and train special army
units for guerrilla warfare in the countryside, while withdrawing the security
forces to the towns and cities. This would theoretically reduce the frequency
of abuses while maintaining the effectiveness of the military against the left,
promoting what Cheek had called "clean counterinsurgency" (SS 8963, 23
December 1980).[84] This strategy had the virtue, from Duarte's point of view,
of offering the military something it had been unable to win on its own, without having to force it to hold its members accountable for human rights violations. But this strategy also had drawbacks. It was based upon the questionable assumption that the regular army, under rightist leadership, would be less
likely to commit abuses than would the security forces. (In fact, the special
antiguerrilla units created within the army, such as the Atlacatl Battalion,
would commit some of the worst atrocities of the war, including the El Mozote massacre and the assassination of Jesuit scholars in November 1989.) As

a practical matter, the strategy also depended upon major increases in U.S. assistance, a scenario that assassinations made improbable in the short run. After the FDR murders, the United States undertook measures to suspend future military aid, notwithstanding a private visit by Duarte to President Carter and representatives of the incoming Reagan administration to urge a resumption (NSA 1989a, 87).

Then, on the night of 2 December, a unit of the National Guard raped and murdered four U.S. churchwomen—three nuns and a lay worker—and buried their bodies in a shallow grave. This atrocity made it impossible for the Carter administration to contemplate increased military assistance, especially since there was almost immediate evidence of efforts by the military to obstruct any investigation of the case. The plan to deliver helicopters was promptly put on hold; then all economic and military assistance commitments were frozen (ST 322499, 6 December 1980). A high-level commission including former Assistant Secretary of State William Rogers and current Assistant Secretary William Bowdler was sent to assess the situation (ST 322251, 5 December 1980; NSA 1989a).

Yet the Carter administration failed to follow through decisively and drive out García and other hardliners. Minutes of an 11 December meeting of a high-level committee of the National Security Council (NSC) reveal reluctance to take a firm stand. Bowdler reported on his recent trip, and the committee discussed the possibility of insisting on the departure of García, Carranza, and Treasury Police Director Francisco Morán. Bowdler then remarked that "we shouldn't go into details," and Deputy Secretary of State Warren Christopher suggested that "we ought to say that if the PDC accomplishes its purposes, then we are prepared to go out in full support." Only Director of Latin American and Caribbean Affairs for the NSC Robert Pastor dissented, arguing that the United States should decide what its own interests were and insist on them in detail. Pastor was overruled, and National Security Advisor Zbigniew Brzezinski recommended to President Carter that the United States simply inform Duarte that if the Christian Democrats could reach a political arrangement with the military providing "a basis for political stability," then U.S. aid would resume.[85] In view of the Christian Democrats' past reluctance to confront the military, this decision amounted to little better than surrender.

In fact, right-wing officers in the Salvadoran military were feeling increasingly confident of their position, and the Christian Democrats would have had little leverage even if they had insisted on García's ouster. At the end of November, an informant told the CIA station in San Salvador that a strong movement of officers within the military wanted to replace the junta with an overtly military government headed by Carlos Eugenio Vides Casanova, who was at that point the head of the National Guard. The coup plan did not go forward because Vides, who had been considered for several years one of the most likely candidates to be the next military president, was not willing to endorse the movement.[86]

Events in the United States tended to encourage the right. As it seemed increasingly likely that Jimmy Carter would lose the November election, Salvadoran rightists realized that they might soon be free of the human rights criticisms and pro–Christian Democratic policies associated with his administration. Cletus DiGiovanni, a former CIA agent, visited San Salvador in September to meet with prominent conservatives and convey the foreign policy views of conservatives associated with the U.S. Republican Party (SS 7621, 31 October 1981). After Reagan was elected, a group representing themselves as members of his "transition team" visited El Salvador and Guatemala. According to former Ambassador Robert White, they conveyed the message that human rights concerns would soon be secondary to the primary task of defeating the left.[87]

Majano remained on the junta until early December, but the willingness of officers to support him deteriorated rapidly. Since there was no longer any reasonable chance that Majano could gain control of the military and unify it around a new agenda, it became too dangerous to associate with him. The officer corps' vote on whether Majano should remain on the junta coincided with the visit of the Bowdler and Rogers commission. Four supported him, and 300 voted against (Baloyra 1982, 111). After the assembly, Minister of Defense García made a derisive pun based on Majano's four votes, calling him a *quatrero*, or cattle rustler.[88]

In the end, the Christian Democrats extracted minor concessions from the military. A week after Colonel Majano was voted out, Napoleón Duarte became president of the junta. Vice Minister of Defense Carranza was transferred to the national telephone company, ANTEL, a traditionally lucrative post and one from which he could facilitate state intelligence-gathering activities.[89] In addition, Colonel Francisco Morán stepped down as head of the Treasury Police. The high command made a number of formal commitments to improve human rights conditions, but a CIA analysis of the situation as of 17 December predicted no reduction in state violence:

> The military's commitments to crack down on human rights abuses by security forces and to eliminate rightwing paramilitary terrorism—even if genuine—will at best only marginally effect [*sic*] the level of officially inspired or condoned violence. . . . The armed forces are set on eliminating the revolutionaries through indiscriminate warfare and probably would reject moves viewed as hampering that effort. . . . The military believe they have the left on the run and while they may temper their most excessive acts, they will not accept civilian control of their institutions and will not long relent from indiscriminate pursuit of the left.[90]

Hindsight

The political events of 1980 led to a civil war in which thousands died. There is reason to think that the war could have been avoided if the elite-level political struggles of this year had followed a different course—if Majano and his supporters had acted more decisively, if the left had been more willing to cooperate with the progressive sector of the military, and if the United States had been willing to risk a "fracture" of the military institution in order to break the power of the violent right. Yet in many ways these actors were structurally constrained by the institutions and political movements they represented. The reformist movement had many liabilities as a political actor, not the least of which was its lack of an organizational core. The alliance of the high command, the security forces, domestic intelligence organizations, and the civilian far right had far more organizational and financial resources to draw upon, and greater political experience. The leaders of the reformist movement tended to be somewhat idealistic individuals who lacked the political ambition and aggressiveness to take on the high command. In contrast to Guillermo García or Carlos Eugenio Vides Casanova, for instance, both of whom had been groomed to be president, Adolfo Majano was an academy professor with no history of personal ambition and a reluctance to wield authority. He was not a Torrijos. Unlike García, moreover, he was unwilling to risk internal divisions within the military to advance his own fortunes. Though he grew into the role in which the junior officers had placed him, Majano lacked the two decades of political experience possessed by his rivals.

It is also difficult to imagine how the two other protagonists—the left and the United States—could have conducted themselves differently. The Salvadoran guerrilla organizations and their mass movements became a major force largely because of the violence, corruption, and political fraud of the military. Given this history, it is remarkable that even one of the five politico-military organizations was willing to cooperate with elements of the military. Moreover, the ideological rigidity of most of the parties of the left during the late 1970s and early 1980s makes it difficult to imagine a scenario in which the measures taken by the reformist military would have been sufficient to persuade leftist leaders to accept peace. Although much of the popular base of the left wanted to avoid a conflict (as evidenced by pressures from the lower echelons of the Popular Revolutionary Bloc to give the first junta a chance), their leadership was interested in intensifying conflict in order to augment the militancy of their "masses" and hasten the arrival of a revolutionary moment (Harnecker 1993). It seems unlikely, for instance, that the Torrijos-style reformist military regime envisioned by the National Resistance would have satisfied Cayetano Carpio, the hardline leader of the Popular Forces of Liberation.

U.S. behavior was in general consistent with U.S. policies in Nicaragua in the two years leading up to 1980. In Nicaragua, the United States had sought to preserve the National Guard as an institution long after its disrepute among the Nicaraguan population made its survival unlikely. Similarly, the United States clung to the existing command hierarchy of the FAES, missing several opportunities to side with the reformist branch of the military. These decisions reflected the same anticommunist impulse, short-sightedness, and caution that led the United States to attempt to hold on to the Nicaraguan Guard. Although Ambassador White understood the importance of the reformist movement and was less devoted to military unity, he lacked support from Washington to intervene on Majano's behalf when things came to a head in May 1980. White's recommendations were simply out of step with the Washington mainstream. By the end of 1980, some senior officials considered him "excitable" and viewed his reports on the role of security forces in political killings with increasing skepticism.[91]

To recognize that the actors behaved in ways consistent with their political and institutional backgrounds does not diminish the importance of human agency in producing the tragedy of 1980. The path to war involved a series of maneuvers by the high command and the Broad National Front that could have been prevented had the actors better understood the game of factional politics that was being played. The reformist movement in the military, the left, and the United States were all, in their own ways, overly deferential to the myth of military unity. Majano and some of his followers were afraid to challenge the high command for fear of breaking the military; the left, with the exception of the National Resistance, dismissed the military as a single, monolithic enemy; and the United States, notwithstanding Ambassador White's efforts, shrank from siding with the reformist faction. U.S. policy makers at the time no doubt thought they were being pragmatic realists as they accommodated themselves to the unsavory high command; they were, in fact, being naive when they treated self-interested, skilled factionalists like García, Carranza, Gutiérrez, and Duarte as if they were national leaders.

The Salvadoran high command, in contrast, demonstrated a knack for Machiavellian maneuver, skillfully provoking and exploiting divisions within the military, playing the reformist and far-right factions off against one another, all the while appealing to institutional unity to reinforce their own position. At the core of the high command's strategy was the same protection racket logic that had informed military political leadership for half a century. They exploited the growing violence of the left to impose internal control within the military, to gain enough independence from landed elites to implement a major land reform, and to win the forbearance and even assistance of the United States. In the meantime, they oversaw a campaign of state terror that made a political solution impossible and guaranteed the existence of a leftist military threat that they and their successors would exploit for a decade.

SEVEN

BREAKING THE PROTECTION RACKET:
FROM WAR TO PEACE

From January 1981 until February 1992, El Salvador witnessed a brutal civil war fought mainly in rural areas. After an unsuccessful "final" offensive in January 1981, the Farabundo Martí National Liberation Front (FMLN) retreated to strongholds in the north and east of the country, rebuilt its forces, then attacked the government army in what became virtually a conventional war. After seriously threatening to defeat the FAES in late 1983, the FMLN took heavy losses from government air power and was forced to retrench. Thereafter, it shifted to a highly successful guerrilla strategy, extending its military and sabotage operations to all departments of the country and making its presence felt once again in the cities. In November 1989, the FMLN launched a major offensive in the capital city, proving that it still had significant military capability despite nine years of government counterinsurgency efforts. In 1990 and 1991, the bitter fighting would escalate, as the FMLN introduced anti-aircraft weapons and the FAES attempted to challenge the Front's de facto control over territory. By the beginning of the 1990s an estimated seventy thousand people, the majority of them civilians, had died at the hands of both sides. A deep war-weariness had taken hold within the population, yet the society was also bitterly divided. With both the government and the FMLN at the peak of their military capability, prospects for an early peace looked grim.

While the two armies fought, a transition took place to elected civilian rule, guided by the United States. Repeated elections were held, with the left excluded. The first election, in 1982, produced a majority for the rightist coalition of the National Conciliation Party (PCN, the old official party) and a new party of the right, the National Republican Alliance (ARENA) which had been formed by Roberto D'Aubuisson in 1981. Only heavy pressure from the United States prevented D'Aubuisson from being named provisional president. A compromise candidate, Alvaro Magaña, took office, presiding over a multiparty cabinet. In the mid-1980s, the Christian Democrats became the dominant party on the basis of a broad social pact to pursue peace and promote social equity. By the late 1980s, however, they had become discredited, and ARENA won the legislative elections of 1988. In 1989, Alfredo Cristiani of ARENA won the presidency.

By the end of the 1980s, therefore, El Salvador faced an intensified civil war and was governed by a party that had begun as an anticommunist, anti-reformist terrorist organization. To most observers, it did not seem to be a situation ripe for political resolution. Remarkably, just two years later, the ARENA government and the FMLN signed a final peace accord and the guns fell silent. Between January 1990 and the signing of the final accords on 16 January 1992, the government and the FMLN had negotiated a series of cumulative agreements that were to be verified by an observer mission of the United Nations and a multiparty Salvadoran peace commission. Taken all together, the accords provided for what U.N. Secretary General Boutros Boutros-Ghali called "a revolution achieved by negotiations."[1] Although the accords did little to rectify the socioeconomic inequities that contributed to the conflict in the first place, they fundamentally altered the functional and political role of the armed institutions of the state.

The agreements virtually eliminated the military's ability to operate a protection racket. The military was constitutionally excluded from internal security functions, replaced by a new civilian police force. Up to 20 percent of the new force was to be made up of members of the FMLN; 20 percent would be former National Police agents who could pass stringent admissions tests and would be screened for past human rights abuses; 60 percent were to be civilians who had played no role in the armed conflict. The civilian police would operate under a civilian ministry, would be well trained and highly regulated, and would work within a nonpartisan, nonideological legal framework that prohibited the use of deadly force except under extreme circumstances when it was required to protect citizens' lives (see Stanley 1995). Domestic intelligence activities were taken over by a new civilian agency, and the Constitution was changed to make the military more clearly subordinate to civilian authority. Finally, the government and FMLN agreed that the military would be purged of officers whose records suggested brutality or corruption, that a United Nations–sponsored Truth Commission would report on acts of violence by both sides during the conflict, and that a new state Human Rights Ombudsman's office would be created with powers to investigate abuses. Not surprisingly, there were numerous delays and flaws in the implementation of these agreements. The new civilian police force ended up containing fewer former FMLN members and more former National Police agents than originally envisioned. The military roundly rejected the findings of the Truth Commission. Nonetheless, in the end, 103 senior FAES officers were purged, including Defense Minister René Emilio Ponce and virtually all his senior commanders.

Along with these antimilitary measures, the government agreed to permit the FMLN to participate in future elections as a legal political party, abandoning six decades of excluding the left. By signing the accords, ARENA took on the obligation of winning political power through persuasion rather than force. The new legal and institutional constraints on the freedom of the state to use force essentially ruled out exclusionary strategies. In the process, the potential political power of the military was greatly diminished. Although the military continued to command a large budget, and initially resisted the implementation of some aspects of the accords, in the end it had no choice but to comply. By 1995, with ARENA firmly in charge and the new National Civilian Police force in place, it appeared that the military's future ability to manipulate political conditions and augment its own power through violence would be very limited.

What happened during the 1980s to make this breakthrough possible? Why did the protection racket, which resisted domestic and international challenges in 1979 and 1980, break down in the midst of a civil war, a context that should have been an ideal one for the military to assert its own importance? This chapter examines a series of factors that undermined the political basis for the military's protection racket. Probably the most important was the failure to defeat the FMLN—a failure that stemmed from internal factionalism, the propensity for indiscriminate violence, and the corruption and short-term vision that we have already examined.

The other key development was the emergence of a successful political party that directly represented the interests of the social elite. With the creation of ARENA, and its evolution into a successful electoral competitor, the upper classes and their political allies no longer needed the military to act as a political guarantor and interlocutor. Despite its militarist origins, ARENA came to reflect above all the interests of an increasingly diverse private sector. As a result of economic, generational, and institutional changes, the politically organized business elite became more moderate in its views and less interested in continued state repression. The failure to prevent FMLN sabotage to the economy contributed to a gradual distancing from the military, which was widened when elements of the military returned to the practice of kidnapping members of the social elite for ransom. This literal protection racket, combined with the failure to provide protection at the national level, made the military seem less and less useful to the upper classes. As ARENA developed confidence in its abilities to garner and maintain mass political support, and as international events made the left seem less threatening, it became less important to preserve the military institution in its current form.

State Violence and the Conduct of the War

The violence [in the early 1980s] was motivated by fear of losing, by the rapid acceleration of violence by the left, by the risk of complete chaos. The repression was excessive at times, certainly overly brutal, in terms of tortures, etc. But it's

probably a good thing that it happened. It saved the country from communism. I have no problem with the idea of identifying your enemy and going out and killing him.
—U.S. State Department official, San Salvador, October 1989

One Team, One Fight.
—U.S. Army slogan

The El Salvador National Military Strategy's dependence on the United States for materiel and training support, to an uncomforting degree, makes the actions of the Revolutionary Junta Government and its successor directly answerable to the American electorate. Care must be taken, as evil as this condition is, that it does not evolve into a condition of reverse dependency.
—Woerner Commission Report (1981)

In January 1981, the FMLN launched its long-awaited "final offensive," attacking military targets throughout the country and attempting to spark an urban insurrection in San Salvador and its surrounding communities. The goal was to present the incoming Reagan administration with a *fait accompli*—two Marxist revolutions in Central America. The offensive was unsuccessful. Although the FMLN managed to occupy many towns and launch attacks against military bases around the country, their assault did not trigger a mass insurrection in the cities as they had hoped. Of several planned barracks uprisings by army forces, only one company in Santa Ana rebelled, under the leadership of Captain Mena Sandoval. Overextended, ill equipped, inexperienced, and disorganized, the FMLN retreated, leaving the government intact.

The FMLN survived this tactical defeat. By challenging and stretching the resources of the military, it had forced the FAES into a more defensive posture. It was now able to consolidate areas of control in rural areas in the north and east of the country, as well as pockets near the capital city, where the rebels could stockpile supplies, train their personnel, and organize themselves for the war to come. These zones became a strategic rearguard, an unexpected phenomenon in a country so small and densely populated. Although the army frequently invaded these zones during the course of the war, it generally did so only in force and did not remain long. Army supply lines were vulnerable, and much of the population supported the FMLN, so that army forces were subject to ambushes or major attacks by concentrated insurgent forces who could quickly disperse. Two factors contributed to the consolidation of rebel zones of control. Areas along the Honduran border, the so-called *bolsones* or pockets, were disputed territory in which the Salvadoran and Honduran militaries were reluctant to operate. A more important factor was the support of the population, which was directly attributable to the military's own brutality. As early as 1980, as noted in the previous chapter, the security forces and special army units conducted sweeps in the areas where the FMLN was forming

rural-based guerrilla units. Survivors and people who heard about these extremely violent and indiscriminate operations often fled to remote areas along
the border. When the FMLN established a stronger military presence there
and was able to protect the local civilians, either by counterattacking or by organizing mass retreats known as *guindas*, it earned the loyalty of much of the
population. State violence also encouraged people to take arms in self-defense
or for revenge. Journalist Tom Gibb, who has surveyed former FMLN combatants, found that most gave government repression as their primary reason
for joining the rebels.[2]

Only in those parts of the country where the rebels could offer protection
were they able to turn the military's brutality to their own advantage. In the
cities, and in western departments of the country, state repression effectively
destroyed the FMLN's organization. In January 1981, the month of the
FMLN's final offensive, Socorro Jurídico reported the killing of 2,293 civilians
(see Table 4). Of these, 679 were killed in the western department of Santa
Ana, where the FMLN was heavily infiltrated by the security forces and, despite having considerable numbers of people under arms, was unable to protect its cadre from assassination (Comisión de Derechos Humanos de El Salvador 1981).[3] San Salvador and San Vicente had the next highest concentrations of casualties, at 544 and 248 respectively. This pattern continued:
in March, for instance, Santa Ana, San Salvador, and San Vicente departments together accounted for 63 percent of the 1,704 civilians reported killed.
Throughout 1981, the killing in Santa Ana was particularly methodical, as the
security forces used a meat packing plant to behead as many as 30 victims per
week.[4] The FMLN had difficulty recovering from the government's mass
murder in these areas. Although it maintained a presence in San Vicente, it
lost most of its political organization in Santa Ana and the capital. Only after
human rights conditions improved from 1985 onward was the FMLN able to
reestablish a substantial organized base in San Salvador; it never fully reestablished itself in the west.

According to Socorro Jurídico (1984), government forces killed an estimated
16,266 people during 1981, up from 11,895 in 1980. The University of Central
America gives a lower estimate of 11,727, and the U.S. embassy attributed 9,118
deaths to "unknown forces" (see Table 4). The differences in the reported death
toll result from varying methodology: Socorro Jurídico and the UCA, for instance, supplemented information from the national press with reports funneled
through Church and popular organization networks. They therefore included
in their counts reports of mass killings, such as the massacre at El Mozote in
northern Morazan in December 1981, which the U.S. embassy refused to acknowledge (Danner 1993; United Nations 1993). They also most likely included some unfounded reports, as well as FMLN combatants killed in action,
in their reports of civilians killed. All three sources probably underreported

Table 4

Estimates of Political Killings during 1981

	Jan	Feb	Mar	Apr	May	Jun	Jul	Aug	Sep	Oct	Nov	Dec
Socorro Jurídico Cristiano (1984)												
By state forces	2,293	1,402	1,704	3,038	712	730	819	654	498	975	1,295	2,146
By FMLN	12	49	21	33	33	10	22	11	22	7	12	21
University of Central America/Centro de Documentación e Información (1981)												
By state forces	2,333	1,402	1,622	841	547	685	667	592	400	731	617	1,290
By FMLN	25	49	21	33	33	10	—	—	—	—	—	—
U.S. Embassy ("Violence Week in Review" Cables and Summaries)												
By unknown forces	1,163	883	1,033	863	772	708	701	776	593	583	495	548
By FMLN	96	52	44	44	—	42	58	60	59	33	29	49
FMLN members killed in action	148	44	114	52	81	58	—	—	18	36	14	79

Note: These figures reflect apparently politically motivated killings reported to the archdiocese or announced in the public news media. They are likely to underreport violence outside the central area of the country.

rural violence, particularly in those parts of the country, such as La Unión, where the Church did not have extensive lay organizations and where much of the violence went unreported and uninvestigated. Given the clearly high levels of violence and the difficulties of obtaining information, it is striking that the reports of diverse sources are as consistent as they are.

The extreme levels of violence in 1981 reflected, in part, the dissipation of the reformist movement after Majano's expulsion. According to former Defense Minister García, 40 percent of the officers were forced out or had resigned by the beginning of 1981.[5] A U.S. military commission sent to evaluate the Salvadoran military in late 1981 observed, "The reassignment of Colonel Majano's followers to non-command positions and non-influential roles scattered their numbers and their ability to exercise further significant influence within the Armed Force institution. As a consequence, no countervailing force presently exists within the Armed Force to oppose the propensity of the more conservative officers to tolerate the use of excessive force and violence" (Woerner et al. 1981, 46).

In contrast to the *Majanistas*, the hardline structure within the military was intact. Although the FMLN had done considerable damage to the grassroots structure of ORDEN during its 1980 assassination campaign, the intelligence and death squad network within the security forces remained largely unscathed. A number of officers suspended from the service in the October 1979 coup—men whom general staff officers characterized as "brilliant"—were recalled to duty (Woerner et al. 1981, 102). Moreover, hardline officers had taken key command positions in the regular army, including intelligence units and the new Atlacatl Rapid Reaction Infantry Battalion (BIRI), freshly trained by U.S. special forces instructors.

Another factor contributing to increased carnage was that the FMLN's offensive provided the military with a great deal of information about who supported the guerrillas. Clandestine members of popular organizations exposed themselves while attempting to organize an insurrection. Hundreds of such people who failed to flee the country or escape to the mountains were killed in the aftermath of the offensive. This new intelligence played directly into the military's simple strategy: destroy the FMLN's political infrastructure wherever possible to prevent it from expanding into new areas, then carry out sweep operations through rural areas to prevent the rebels from consolidating a popular support base. For if the FMLN could claim to control territory, its members might receive international recognition as belligerents, which would undercut the government's claims to legitimacy (Woerner et al. 1981, 178). This concern probably helped to motivate Operation Rescue, an army sweep through northern Morazan in December 1981 in which the BIRI Atlacatl, under the command of Lieutenant Colonel Domingo Monterrosa, killed hundreds of civilians. In one mass grave in the village of El Mozote, U.N. investigators in 1992 found 143 skeletons, of which 85 percent belonged to children less than 12 years of age (United Nations 1993, 114–21). It is thought that several hundred other people were killed in El Mozote and surrounding communities. Most of them were *not* loyal to the FMLN and had therefore made the terrible mistake of not fleeing from the army (Danner 1993).

The strategy of mass murder enjoyed the tacit support of the highest levels of the U.S. government. The Reagan administration made its interests clear early on. Embassy personnel in San Salvador reported fairly accurately on the violence of 1981, but when they attempted to admonish top FAES officers, they found that they had little leverage, even in cases in which members of the armed forces murdered U.S. citizens. In early January, National Guardsmen gunned down two U.S. land reform advisors and the director of the Salvadoran land reform institute in the coffee shop of the San Salvador Sheraton Hotel. Neither the military nor the judiciary were willing to pursue the case, despite U.S. pressures. Part of the problem was that embassy officials lacked high-level support for challenging abuses. When the new U.S. ambassador, Deane Hinton, requested guidance from Washington following a Treasury Police massacre in Soyapango on 7 April 1981, Deputy Secretary of State William Clark instructed him: "You should meet immediately with Duarte, Gutiérrez, and García. You will be the best judge of tone to adopt, but in our view it should be non-confrontational and sensitive to their difficulties in controlling the Treasury Police and other Security Forces" (ST 089363, 9 April 1981). Clark's concern about avoiding confrontation was characteristic of U.S. policy throughout the 1980s: senior Salvadoran officers repeatedly warned that pursuing human rights cases too vigorously could destabilize the institution and lead to a rightist coup. Since the United States placed the highest priority on maintaining the stability of the military, these warnings led to caution and de facto tolerance of egregious abuses. When Ambassador Hinton had the temerity to say in a 1982 speech that "since 1979 perhaps as many as 30,000 Salvadorans have been MURDERED, not killed in battle, MURDERED" (emphasis in original), his statements were immediately repudiated by Clark, by then National Security Council chief (Arnson 1989, 99).

A related problem was the credulity of U.S. officials who had not dealt with the likes of Defense Minister García in the past. García and his circle had the advantage of continuity and familiarity with their own political environment. A pair of cables from Ambassador Hinton to Washington are illustrative of the problem. After a friendly, jocular meeting with García in which the defense minister admitted that there were human rights abuses within the military, Hinton wrote: "García is either one of the best liars in the world or he is what he says he is, a man who errs in saying what he thinks. In any case, we agreed that we should both continue 'the error'—which I asserted was no error—of telling each other what we think" (SS 5333, 14 July 1981). Just over six months later, as news of the El Mozote massacre filtered out of northern Morazan, a chastened Hinton wrote: "As I have said before we are hostage to malevolent forces seemingly beyond our control. While García talks a good game, I no longer trust him or believe him" (SS 775, 1 February 1982).

In July 1982, U.S. diplomats met with National Police chief Carlos Reynaldo López Nuila. The *Washington Post* had reported allegations that the National Police engaged in torture. López Nuila adopted an aggressive posture, accusing the embassy of being instruments of a leftist scheme to discredit the one security force that had achieved a good human rights record. Major Aristides Márquez, head of National Police intelligence and director of the most active death squad network in the country, sat beside him. Ambassador Hinton concluded the cable reporting this meeting: "López Nuila is an angry man, or at least in the presence of his subordinate he acted angry . . . . We think he was trying to impress Major Márquez, his DII [intelligence chief], with how seriously he took this slight on National Police honor, in the sure knowledge that Márquez would put this conversation into the officer corp [*sic*] rumor mill." Hinton also noted that charges of torture could easily lead the security forces to execute those they torture instead of releasing them, and he charged that those within the State Department who leaked discrediting information could bear some responsibility for subsequent deaths (SS 6316, 29 July 1982). Even the ability of the U.S. government to report on death squads was held hostage.

The Reagan administration approached the crisis in El Salvador as a military problem from the outset. In late 1981, junta president Napoleón Duarte asked for a team of specialists to help develop a national strategy. The administration sent a six-member team of U.S. military officers, plus a part-time CIA employee, to form an "El Salvador/U.S. Binational Team for Development of a Salvadoran National Military Strategy."[6] The U.S. team, led by General Fred Woerner, worked with Salvadoran counterparts to develop a combined strategy. They also wrote an unflattering, classified report on the current state of the Salvadoran military. Finally, they drew up a five-year plan that outlined the levels of assistance that would result in a loss, stalemate, and victory. The plan called for encouraging the Salvadoran military to go into action while U.S. advisors worked to improve it. For General Woerner, a veteran of Vietnam, the most important thing was for the FAES to adopt aggressive small-unit tactics that would take the war to the FMLN and prevent it from consolidating a strategic rearguard. The military would prove singularly resistant to this piece of advice.

Although the high command was willing to kill large numbers of civilians, it was not, in fact, very aggressive in fighting the war. Military units stayed close to their barracks, and there were few offensive operations in guerrilla-held areas. Those that were carried out were brief and so ponderously executed that the FMLN and its supporters had ample time to evade them. One problem was mundane: the troops had no field rations, so they could not stay out long. They refused to eat U.S. combat rations (Woerner et al. 1981, 127–28). The other problem was political. Defense Minister García told General Woerner that the military was dangerously divided and unstable, despite his having purged the reformists. He feared that significant tactical defeats and heavy losses might split the army wide open, so he kept units from venturing out too far. He devoted most of his forces to defending static positions that the FMLN might attack. As General Woerner put it, "They had two men on every bridge in the country. This wasn't security, it was a renewable arms supply for the guerrillas."[7]

This approach gave the FMLN considerable latitude to maneuver in the countryside. From mid-1982 through the end of 1983, the FMLN was almost constantly on the offensive. Smelling victory, its leaders abandoned political concerns to maximize their military potential. They forcibly recruited young people, requisitioned supplies and vehicles, and operated like a regular army, attacking in large units. A confidential state department briefing paper entitled "El Salvador: The Military Situation" (2 December 1983) states: "The guerrillas' primary tactic has been to concentrate a large force against lightly defended government outposts and then to ambush reinforcements. They use surprise well to multiply their force, and they have excellent intelligence. Ammunition and weapons capability on the ground often seem equal to the ESAF [El Salvador Armed Forces] and certainly sufficient for their operations" (NSA 1989b).

Faced with García's incapacity or unwillingness to pursue the war more aggressively, Ambassador Hinton, in a cable entitled "Saving El Salvador," suggested the possibility of sacking him. In the end, the United States decided against a radical move that involved a risk of destabilizing the military (SS 775, SS 796, ST 26083, 1 February 1982).[8] U.S. policy makers also had trouble identifying a substitute who would be markedly different from García, since most of the likely candidates were closely affiliated with the cluster of *tandas* known as the Equipo Molina. "No outsider will ever understand the levantine motives and intrigues that are part and parcel of this sick society," Hinton remarked (SS 824, 2 February 1982).

The one thing the United States could do was increase military aid. It provided rifles, squad automatic weapons, upgraded artillery, and vehicles. Probably the most important components were helicopters, reconnaissance and transport aircraft, and later A-37 ground attack jets. The increased mobility provided by helicopters, combined with the ability to attack large FMLN troop concentrations from the air, forced the guerrillas to abandon their all-out offensive and adopt a more traditional guerrilla strategy based on small units, mobility, geographic dispersion, emphasis on political work, and, above all, economic sabotage.

Ironically, the U.S. aid program may have forced the FMLN to abandon an unsustainable strategy for one that was, in the long run, more successful. The process of building a large rebel army and attacking the enemy head-on had taken a toll on the FMLN's political support. Their forcible recruitment drives had alienated many people whose support they needed, and the forced recruits had low morale, were reluctant to take risks, and deserted frequently (Byrne 1994, 211–12). In contrast, the guerrilla strategy the FMLN adopted in 1984 was one the organization could maintain to the end of the war. It solidified their connection to their political base and enhanced their ability to survive the improved air power, mobility, and technical intelligence available to the FAES. In the long run, it had the effect of driving a wedge between the army and the civilian elite, helping to create the political conditions for breaking the protection racket.

When the Reagan administration realized that much higher levels of military assistance would be needed to fend off the FMLN, it was forced to begin taking the human rights problem more seriously. Congress would be writing the checks, and many members were skeptical about the administration's military approach and appalled by reports of massacres. In July 1983 Congress had set a cap of $64.8 million as opposed to the $110 million requested by the administration, and tied 30 percent of the reduced figure to a trial and verdict in the case of the troops accused of murdering the U.S. churchwomen (Arnson 1989, 129–33). Anticipating the need to go to Congress for increased levels of assistance in the future, the administration began to put serious pressure on the Salvadoran military, focusing on the hundreds of noncombat assassinations being carried out by death squads.

Part of the death squad problem came from outside the military. D'Aubuisson, as president of the Assembly, had placed trusted men like Héctor Regalado in charge of Assembly security. Regalado, whose Boy Scout troop death squad had been disbanded after the October 1979 coup, assembled a band of former members of the security forces into a new death squad. They received intelligence from, and cooperated with, Aristides Márquez' operation in the National Police (Gibb and Farah 1989).[9] Despite the emphasis in press reports and even in U.S. documents on the private death squads, by far the greater part of the killing was being carried out by official agencies such as the National Center for Analysis and Investigations (CAIN) in the National Police, as well as the intelligence sections of the National Guard, the Treasury Police, and most major army units.[10] CAIN served as a clearinghouse, distributing intelligence to the other security forces just as ANSESAL had done before the October 1979 coup. CAIN is also widely reputed to have operated one of the most active security force death squads (Gibb and Farah 1989; Pyes 1983e).[11]

The U.S. embassy had noted an increase in death squad killings in May 1983, which were accompanied in the latter part of the year by threats against

U.S. Ambassador Thomas Pickering and Archbishop Arturo Rivera y Damas. If either threat had been carried out, it would have been impossible for the administration to maintain or increase military aid. Interestingly, human rights statistics from Tutela Legal, the new archdiocesan human rights office established in May 1982, do not show a marked increase in death squad killings during this period (Americas Watch and ACLU 1983b, 1984). The increase noted by the embassy involved attacks directed against members of what Washington hoped would be the centrist coalition for the 1984 elections: Christian Democrats, government officials, pro–Christian Democratic labor unions, the Church, and academics.

Washington sent its message through a variety of channels, starting with a "hard-hitting" speech in which Ambassador Pickering condemned death squad activities and called for prosecutions.[12] D'Aubuisson and other rightists associated with terrorism were put on a visa "watch list" and denied entry to the United States; the Federal Bureau of Investigation began an investigation into the activities of wealthy Salvadoran exiles in Miami.[13] The Salvadoran right responded with increased threats against U.S. personnel and Salvadoran moderates. This, in turn, brought a higher-level response from Washington, which dispatched Vice President George Bush to San Salvador in December with a list of individuals whom the United States wanted removed from command of forces and exiled. Among the names on the list were Nicolás Carranza (at this time head of the Treasury Police) and Aristides Márquez, director of CAIN, a tacit acknowledgment that the core of the death squad problem lay within the armed forces and involved high-level leaders.[14]

Bush made the trade-offs explicit: if the FAES cleaned up the death squad problem, the Reagan administration would seek enough money from Congress "to field 39 newly-organized, fully equipped countersubversion battalions, 2 immediate reaction battalions, and an engineering battalion. And you will receive A-37 aircraft, transport aircraft, helicopters, augmented artillery, and naval patrol and landing craft. . . . We are also taking steps to augment El Salvador's aero-medical evacuation capability, a critical area for troop morale" (SS 11567, 14 December 1983). Bush's mission was supplemented by a visit from Director of Central Intelligence William Casey, who similarly warned the Salvadorans to curb death squad killings. Casey's message was one that Salvadoran hardliners took seriously (Woodward 1987, 291).

Death squad killings fell during 1984, but the military compensated for reductions in targeted killings by increasing its indiscriminate violence in rural areas, both through attacks on communities thought to be FMLN supporters and through increased aerial bombardment of FMLN areas.[15] It was more difficult for human rights groups to monitor this kind of violence. Moreover, the U.S. embassy itself would have trouble gaining information on repression carried out in conjunction with military operations, since, as one U.S. embassy cable pointed out, "DAO [defense attaché officer] and MILGP [Military Group] personnel are prohibited from accompanying ESAF [El Salvador Armed Forces] on operations and therefore have no first-hand knowledge of army behavior in captured towns" (SS 2247, 29 February 1984). In February 1984 a delegation from the International Committee of the Red Cross observed that rural communities in contested areas would often be bombed by the FAES during or immediately after Red Cross visits to provide medical attention. They surmised that the military, which they routinely notified of their movements, was using them as a guide to pro-insurgent populations (SS 2247, 29 February 1984).

U.S. policy continued to be held hostage to purported threats to the internal stability of the military. Whenever the United States pressed for the arrest of individuals implicated in key assassinations such as those at the Sheraton, senior commanders would warn that arrests and prosecutions might destabilize the military, in part because any officer prosecuted would be able to name dozens of other officers guilty of equal or worse crimes.[16] Brigade-level commanders and right-wing junior officers routinely threatened to take action against senior leaders if prosecutions went forward. Since U.S. officials considered their policy to hinge on the survival of an elected civilian government and the tenure of military leaders with whom they had a working relationship, they held back from making aid flows contingent on a genuine break from military impunity. Not until 1990 was a FAES officer successfully prosecuted for an act of political violence.

Ironically, despite the theatrics and repeated threats of instability, the only forced command change to take place within the Salvadoran military during the 1980s was one instigated by the United States in 1983, when Colonel Sigifredo Ochoa, with the support of air force commander Rafael Bustillo, mutinied against Minister of Defense García for his failure to conduct the war effort properly. After some negotiations, President Magaña agreed to accept García's resignation after six months. He also demanded that the United States recall the head of the U.S. Military Group, John Waghelstein, whom he accused of planning the rebellion.[17]

Despite the many deficiencies of U.S. human rights policy during the 1980s, in the long run the conditionality of U.S. aid began to have a broad and positive effect on the conduct of the FAES. By 1985 and 1986, indiscriminate killings by government forces were fluctuating between a low of around 70 and a high of 232 per month, while targeted killings remained in the twenties and low thirties (Americas Watch 1986, 1987a, 1987b). Violence stabilized at these levels or slightly below until 1989—a dramatic improvement compared with the early 1980s, yet still slightly higher than the levels of violence seen in the last five months of Carlos Romero's administration in 1979, a period widely perceived at the time as extremely bloody. Even as the frequency of killing de-

clined, moreover, the security forces continued to practice forced disappearances, illegal detention, and torture against suspected collaborators of the left
(SS 5852, 8 May 1989; SS 5529, 5533, 5534, 2 May 1989).

The reduction in state violence had a major political effect. Popular organizations crushed during the early 1980s flowered again, allowing the FMLN to
reestablish a presence in the capital and other cities. It became possible for the
FMLN to return thousands of displaced people from camps in government-
controlled areas, and later refugees from camps in Honduras, repopulating
conflictive areas of the country and reestablishing communities that had been
abandoned earlier in the decade after military sweeps or bombardment. The
new communities strengthened the support base for the FMLN and attracted
extensive international assistance.

The FAES never fully rose to the task of fighting the guerrillas with less draconian tools. U.S. Military Group trainers became increasingly frustrated with
its failure to make use of intelligence. Too often, U.S. agencies would pass on
solid information (often obtained through infrared and other sensors aboard
U.S. surveillance aircraft) on the location of a rebel column, only to see FAES
forces turn in the other direction. U.S. officers began to suspect that the FAES
was not really trying to win; keeping the war going, after all, prolonged their
access to opportunities for graft.[18]

FAES field commanders, for their part, bitterly resented the repatriation of
refugees to rebel-held areas, which they felt had been forced upon them and
which greatly complicated their counterinsurgency operations. This resentment contributed to a number of attacks against these communities. FAES officers also felt that improvements in human rights protections had gained them
little, since they continued to be attacked in the press for those abuses that did
take place, and many concluded that the press was a tool of the international
structures of the left.[19]

Elections and Political Change

You are a subversive. You don't belong in our democracy.
—National Police sergeant to Salvadoran Green Cross volunteer Francisco Castro
(pseudonym) after crushing his testicles with a device known as "The Carter" (SS 4826,
10 June 1982)

Elections were a key component of U.S. policy, intended to achieve greater
legitimacy for the government both within El Salvador and abroad. The first
of these, for a Constituent Assembly, was scheduled for March 1982. The idea
of holding elections had a certain appeal to some sectors of the Salvadoran
right. As early as September 1980, a delegation representing a private sector organization, the Productive Alliance, traveled to Washington to promote an
election, inspired by distrust of the joint Christian Democratic–military junta,

fear that it might go forward with additional reforms, and confidence in their own ability to organize a grass-roots following after their largely successful effort to counterorganize against the August 1980 general strike.[20]

After yet another unsuccessful conspiracy to carry out a coup d'état in March 1981, D'Aubuisson and key associates from the Broad National Front quietly formed a new political party, the National Republican Alliance (ARENA), which publicly announced its existence in September 1981 (Baires 1994, 40–41). Mario Sandoval Alarcón, the leader of a Guatemalan rightist party, had told D'Aubuisson and company that they could not just be terrorists: they had to form a real party (Pyes 1983b). The resulting political organization was something of a hybrid. While clearly oriented toward the interests of the private sector elite, and funded largely by wealthy Salvadoran families, ARENA reflected from the outset the social elite's dependence on the military. It took Roberto D'Aubuisson, a man who had been deep inside the military's national security state, to form a party for the private sector elite. He brought to the project personal knowledge and control of the grass-roots network ORDEN, which had been established by the security forces under the guidance of General José Medrano in the 1960s and 1970s. ORDEN was the organizational core of the new party.

The new party was remarkably successful in the March 1982 Assembly elections, a clear indication of the organizational resources that D'Aubuisson brought to it. Although the Christian Democrats won a plurality of the vote, ARENA came in second ahead of the National Conciliation Party. With a majority between them, the two rightist parties were in a position to select Roberto D'Aubuisson as provisional president of the country. From the point of view of the United States, D'Aubuisson as president would cancel the public relations victory represented by the March elections. The international media had provided extensive coverage, focusing on the long lines of voters at the polls and the FMLN's failed efforts to disrupt the voting. (Most journalists did not report that voting was compulsory.) The United States applied heavy pressures on the political parties, and on the Salvadoran military itself, to prevent D'Aubuisson's election. The key actor appears to have been military. The United States sent General Vernon Walters to deliver the message that D'Aubuisson was out of the question. Soon thereafter the FAES held a meeting at which senior officers explained to D'Aubuisson that he would not be president and that he should not allow his ambition to undermine his loyalty to the armed institution. D'Aubuisson responded that his "little heart" was always with the armed forces.[21]

After considerable negotiation, the Salvadoran parties agreed upon Dr. Alvaro Magaña, a banker with close ties to military officers. At Magaña's farm in Apaneca the political parties negotiated a pact under which each of the parties in the legislature would have a share of ministerial posts in the provisional government. In recognition of its electoral strength and priority interests,

ARENA was granted control of the institutions responsible for implementing further land reform. As a further gesture, D'Aubuisson was elected president of the Assembly.

Having narrowly avoided an electoral disaster, the United States set about building up the PDC so that it would perform better in the 1984 presidential elections. Some $1.4 million was routed through covert channels to the Christian Democrats and, secondarily, to the National Conciliation Party, to enhance their organizational base and use of the media. Napoleón Duarte of the PDC won the presidential race, defeating D'Aubuisson in a runoff. U.S. aid and ARENA's own stridency had given Duarte an edge. A year later, the Christian Democrats swept the legislative elections, indicating strong popular support. The PDC's mass backing during this phase was based on a pact with the Popular Democratic Unity (UPD) in which the party committed itself to pursuing peace, democracy, and social justice (Byrne 1994, 262). Unfortunately for the PDC, the Duarte government could not deliver on its commitments. After a spectacular meeting with FMLN leaders at La Palma in northern Chalatenango, the military prevented Duarte from negotiating for anything other than the guerrillas' surrender. Dialogue with the FMLN quickly ground to a halt.

Duarte faced troubles on the economic front as well. Part of the U.S. aid package was conditioned on a devaluation of the colón and other measures to reduce the fiscal deficit. These measures alienated labor, leading to the formation of a new union federation, the National Unity of Salvadoran Workers (UNTS), which criticized and demonstrated against the government's austerity program.

Irreconcilable, conflicting demands from its various constituencies chipped away the Christian Democrats' popularity and legitimacy. Having distinguished itself from ARENA in part by proposing a progressive social pact, the PDC presided over austerity. Although some of its economic measures were favorable to some sectors of the business community, it never built a significant constituency within the private sector (Byrne 1994, 264–66). Rampant corruption within the government exacerbated these problems and undercut popular confidence. Faced with a stagnant economy, a stalemated war, and erosion of its political position, PDC prospects in the Legislative Assembly elections of 1988 were grim.

Change on the Right

While the PDC was enjoying, and dissipating, its moment in state power, a series of changes taking place within the civilian right were paving the way for negotiations with the FMLN. The key development was the gradual transformation of ARENA into a relatively broad-based party of Salvadoran private enterprise, the middle classes, and the conservative poor. Though initially formed by pro-militarist elements with funding from disgruntled Miami-based oligarchs, ARENA became an expression of a broader set of interests. The business community, frustrated by its lack of influence over state policy during the Duarte years, gradually united in support of ARENA. This was the first time the Salvadoran capitalist classes had united around a single party. Drawing on this broader constituency, a more moderate and modernizing image, and a free-market economic program developed by a private conservative think tank (see below), ARENA gradually transformed itself into a more serious electoral competitor, paving the way for its victories in the 1988 and 1989 elections. At the same time, the costs of the war combined with structural and generational changes within the private sector to prepare ARENA to negotiate with the FMLN.

Encouraging moderation was the ascendance within private sector associations of less wealthy entrepreneurs distinct from the oligarchic families that had dominated these associations in the past. This shift was a direct outgrowth of the war. Many of the wealthiest members of Salvadoran society fled the kidnappings of the late 1970s and early 1980s but managed to influence national affairs from the relative safety of Miami or Guatemala by funding and coordinating rightist death squad activities, plotting coups, and subsequently helping to finance ARENA. Their absence from the country, however, gradually undercut their influence within such organizations as the National Association of Private Enterprise (ANEP), the Salvadoran Industrial Association (ASI), and the Chamber of Commerce. In their place, the owners of smaller businesses who could not afford to leave the country began to play a greater role. They could also lay claim to greater political legitimacy and nationalist prestige because they had remained in the country during the years of kidnappings, sabotage, and warfare.[22]

Meanwhile, the younger people taking over some of the largest family concerns brought with them more cosmopolitan outlooks developed through education and experiences in the United States and Europe. Those who had been educated at the Externado San José high school had been influenced by their Jesuit teachers and by the social service projects in poor communities in which students had been required to participate. Their perspective was somewhat more humane and less violence-prone than that of their parents, for whom the events of 1932 had been a formative experience.[23]

The war itself and the reforms of 1980 created additional changes within the private sector elite. In general, landed producers of agricultural exports such as coffee, cotton, sugar, and beef became weaker, while families with primary interests in financial capital and export processing fared better. The owners of expropriated lands were compensated with bonds that quickly lost most of their face value, while intense fighting and the presence of the FMLN in some rural areas, particularly in the eastern half of the country, led some landowners to abandon their properties. In their absence, peasants, many of whom supported the FMLN, moved onto their estates and converted them to the production of basic grains. By 1984, 46.6 percent of coffee lands had been abandoned, and coffee production fell by half from 1980 through 1990 (Wolf 1992, 11–12).

Those growers who managed to maintain control of their operations in the east were often compelled to pay substantial "war taxes" to the FMLN, as well as higher wage rates imposed by the guerrillas. Those who refused suffered sabotage. The FMLN regularly destroyed coffee trucks loaded with harvest, as well as processing mills. The most vulnerable sector was the cotton industry: cotton crops burn easily when nearly mature, and the crop-dusting aircraft essential for cotton production in El Salvador's pest-prone climate made easy targets for the FMLN.[24] Not surprisingly, many growers shifted their energies and liquid capital into other activities in El Salvador or abroad, and the remaining undiversified agricultural producers as a group lost economic power relative to other sectors.

Ironically, these wartime conditions eventually produced incentives for political moderation, even among the notoriously hardline coffee growers. As Daniel Wolf (1992) points out, at the beginning of the war coffee growers had significant, ephemeral investments in coffee plants that they would lose unless stable (read "repressed") labor relations and secure conditions were quickly restored by strong military measures. By the latter part of the 1980s, however, it was clear that the military would be unable to deal with the left quickly. Meanwhile, coffee trees on abandoned lands had been neglected for so long that they needed to be cut down and replaced. Coffee growers from the less secure parts of the country, therefore, found that their interests now lay in the direction of a negotiated solution if this would allow them to regain access to their land or find buyers for lands that they no longer wanted. This shift was reflected in the internal politics of the coffee growers' association, ASCAFE: in early 1990, the reactionary old-guard leadership from Santa Ana was replaced by younger, more moderate growers.

The state's March 1980 hostile takeover of international trade in key agricultural commodities also undermined the economic strength of many growers. Once in control of agricultural commodity exports, the government manipulated producer prices in such a way as to effectively tax exports more heavily. While this hurt growers, agricultural processors fared well because they were able to pass the lower producer prices on to the growers. Moreover, the government, which now owned many *beneficios* and therefore shared common interests with private processors, mandated higher prices for the service of processing coffee (Johnson 1993, 209).

Financial capitalists also weathered the March 1980 reforms relatively well. In contrast to the landowners expropriated under the land reform, former owners of banks that were nationalized were relatively well compensated, thus providing them with liquid capital to invest in other activities.

The net effect of the reforms and subsequent management of prices was to shift the economic center of gravity away from agricultural producers and toward the processing and financial sectors. This shift had important, if gradual, political consequences. As we saw with reference to Costa Rica (see Chapter One), processing and financial elites are, as a rule, more insulated from labor costs and are therefore generally less interested in maintaining a heavy-handed labor-repressive system. Paige (1993) found in interviews with members of the Salvadoran coffee elite that those who belonged to the growers' association, ASCAFE, tended to be more pro-authoritarian than those associated with ABECAFE, the organization of coffee processors and exporters. As the processing and financial sectors became ascendant economically, their somewhat more moderate voice began to affect the political stances of ARENA.

Following the 1980 reforms, state economic policy remained relatively unchanged until Duarte took office in 1984. Duarte sought to use the power of the state to promote the development of small and medium businesses, and attempted to extract as much revenue as possible from traditional export activities in order to subsidize basic consumer goods. During the first two and half years of his administration, he maintained overvalued exchange rates that harmed export competitiveness (Rosa 1992, 6–8), and his government was unpopular with most of the private sector. Many entrepreneurs felt that credit from the nationalized banking sector was too often distributed according to political, rather than economic, criteria.[25] Yet many individual entrepreneurs fared well during Duarte's administration. Overall, state policies toward industry, commerce, agricultural processors, and the banking industry were relatively favorable between 1980 and 1988. The juntas, the provisional government of Alvaro Magaña, and Duarte's administration all maintained the protective tariffs favored by industrialists.

Another major source of structural changes in the economy was the flow of money sent home by Salvadorans living abroad. Migration to the United States began in the 1960s and accelerated in the 1970s. The 1980 U.S. census enumerated 94,447 Salvadorans, of whom 24,826 were legal residents (Massey and Schnabel 1983, 218; Peterson 1986, 72). In the early 1980s, the flow of Salvadorans increased dramatically in response to state terror, and, to a lesser degree, forced recruitment and violence by the FMLN (Stanley 1987). Even as state repression declined, mass emigration continued as both clandestine means of travel to the United States and Salvadoran communities in cities like Los Angeles, Washington, D.C., Houston, and Chicago became more fully developed. Those who fled from violence in the early 1980s became the vanguard of a mass diaspora. By 1987, roughly one million Salvadorans were living in the United States (Montes 1987).

By the late 1980s, remittances from Salvadorans abroad had become the life blood of the economy, matching or exceeding (depending on data sources) all other sources of foreign exchange, including export earnings and U.S. Economic Support Funds (ESF). Estimates vary from a low of $433 million per year to a high of $1.4 billion, the latter based on Montes' (1987) survey of households in El Salvador. The U.N. Economic Commission for Latin America and the Caribbean (Comisión Económica Para América Latina y el Caribe 1991) estimated remittances at over $1 billion for 1989. All studies agree that remittances increased the income of poorer families, sometimes by as much as a third, with important effects on the economy as the foreign exchange and domestic buying power generated by remittances helped buoy the commercial, transportation, and construction sectors.

During the first few years of the 1980s, the U.S. Agency for International Development (AID) focused on protecting agrarian reform by ensuring that sufficient financial and technical assistance were available to make the cooperatives viable. By 1984, AID's attention shifted to the economy as a whole. AID analysts believed that, quite aside from war damage, El Salvador's economic viability depended on breaking out of its dependence on traditional exports, combined with import-substitution industrialization. AID began advocating a restructuring of the economy toward production and export of nontraditional products, a process that would require extensive deregulation of financial markets and international commerce, as well as heavy devaluations of the currency. By withholding portions of the U.S. aid package, AID succeeded in pressuring Duarte to devalue the currency and implement the austerity measures that cost him much of his popularity by 1987 and 1988.

To advance its model for El Salvador's economy, AID provided extensive funding ($67 million between 1985 and 1987) for a free-market think tank known as the Salvadoran Foundation for Economic and Social Development (FUSADES) (Larmer 1989). The foundation's staff of professional economists produced extensive analyses of regulatory bottlenecks in the Salvadoran economy, while also offering seminars and technical assistance designed to promote nontraditional exports. For the first time the modernizing sectors of the Salvadoran business community had an institutional base, and FUSADES helped them develop a critique of the statist policies of the Duarte administration that was based on something other than anticommunist hyperbole and threats of violence (Johnson 1993, 213–74; Rosa 1992). The foundation's analysis, though economically conservative, also contained an ideological emphasis on the "social economy of the market"—the view that if a market economy was to be successful, a country must first develop a social consensus around the value of market mechanisms (Johnson 1993, 220). The apparent coherence of the FUSADES model and its prescriptions helped the modernizing sectors build a rough consensus, and a common project, within the private sector as a whole. This too produced political changes within ARENA.

By the end of the 1980s, Salvadoran business men and women could not avoid noticing that the war and associated violence were obstructing their interests. The FMLN had imposed over $2 billion in economic damages, virtually destroying the cotton industry and severely damaging most other areas of economic activity. It maintained a constant assault on the electrical grid, blowing down posts and even attacking generating facilities. Power cuts interrupted industrial production and imposed significant costs on business owners who had to invest in their own power plants. In the latter part of the decade, FMLN transportation stoppages became increasingly frequent and effective. In 1987, it declared seven stoppages of seven days each, during which "cargoes were dumped, trucks were burned, and buses were machine-gunned" (Byrne 1994, 282–83; Murray 1992, 108). Between 1979 and 1990, more than two thousand trucks and thirty thousand buses were damaged or destroyed. Combined with the damage to the electrical grid and to bridges, the FMLN actions imposed direct costs of $1.1 billion for repairs and replacement of equipment and infrastructure (Murray 1992, 107). Added to these direct losses were serious opportunity costs. With discussions of hemispheric free trade, the private sector perceived that foreign investment might increase in the near future *if* the war were to end.[26] The idea of a negotiated solution acquired greater appeal, regardless of the preferences of the military.

The reemergence of a literal protection racket further alienated many in the business community from the repressive agenda of the military and of ARENA hardliners. Elements of the military, and civilians associated with ARENA, returned to the practice of kidnapping members of the business elite for ransom, taking at least 11 prominent captives between 1983 and 1986.[27] There had always been a fine line between the structural protection racket, under which security forces and civilian mercenaries repressed labor organizers, leftists, and reformists in exchange for money and privileges, and specific operational protection rackets, in which members of the security forces kidnapped wealthy individuals for ransom. ARENA, having begun as a terrorist organization, included individuals prone to kidnapping, often in conjunction with members of the military.[28]

As in the 1970s, the operations of 1983–86 were made to appear to be the work of the FMLN, but testimony from individuals who were successfully ransomed suggested that military personnel might be involved. In 1985, when a prominent attorney was kidnapped, an ad hoc commission of private sector leaders encouraged Duarte to bring in the FBI and Venezuelan intelligence to investigate the kidnapping ring. By the time arrests were made in March 1986, an estimated $4 million had been paid in ransoms.[29]

Charged with overseeing the investigation was Vice Minister of Defense for Public Security Carlos Reynaldo López Nuila, who had headed the National Police from October 1979 until May 1984.[30] Although he had aligned himself with Duarte and cultivated the image of a reformer intent on cleaning up the security forces he commanded, he had been closely involved in the creation of the National Center for Analysis and Investigations (CAIN) within the National Police and cannot have been ignorant of the activities of his chief of detectives and intelligence, Aristides Márquez.

The ring turned out to be a direct outgrowth of security force death squad operations, and particularly of CAIN. Former operatives of the National Police had helped to carry out the kidnappings, and three of them were killed under suspicious circumstances. Former detective Edgar Pérez Linares had been a key operative in Márquez' death squad operation within the National Police, responsible for managing the highly effective police infiltration of the National Resistance and directing three assassins ("the Little Angels") who had infiltrated the guerrillas and systematically murdered clandestine guerrillas and collaborators in the early 1980s.[31] He had also collaborated with Dr. Héctor Regalado, who ran death squads for D'Aubuisson out of the National Assembly. Pérez Linares had been exiled, along with his boss, Márquez, after appearing on Vice President Bush's list in December 1983, but returned after a brief time abroad.

After the kidnapping case began to break, Pérez Linares was arrested in Guatemala by a special unit of the National Police. On the way back to El Salvador, he was riddled with bullets by the roadside, supposedly after trying to escape, while handcuffed, from the speeding van. A military investigator acknowledged that he had been executed, saying: "He had to die. There was no way that group could have let someone as knowledgeable as Pérez Linares live." Another key participant and potential witness was killed in a shootout with National Police; a third man reportedly hanged himself "from a four foot high bunkbed with his socks" while in National Police custody (Gibb and Farah 1989, 13). With remarkable credulity or cynicism, U.S. Ambassador Edwin Corr cabled Washington, "We are now increasingly confident that the armed forces will support a complete investigation of the kidnapping let the chips fall where they may." The next section heading in the cable read: "Key Suspect Found Dead in Cell" (SS 4789, 5 April 1986).

Among the masterminds implicated in the kidnapping racket was Colonel Roberto Mauricio Staben, who had been arrested with D'Aubuisson back in May 1980 and whose name appears repeatedly in declassified CIA documents as a death squad leader and benefactor. At the time of his arrest, Staben commanded the U.S.-trained Arce Rapid Reaction Infantry Battalion. Others arrested included former Lieutenant Rodolfo López Sibrián, Major José Alfredo Jiménez, and Orlando Llovera Balette, a businessman and ARENA member. Llovera and Jiménez "escaped" under suspicious circumstances; López Sibrián, who had ordered the assassination of two U.S. land reform advisors at the San Salvador Sheraton Hotel in January 1981, remained in custody, probably in order to satisfy the United States. Colonel Staben was released after his brethren in the *tandona* exerted heavy political pressure on the government. He returned to the Arce battalion and six months later received an award from U.S. Colonel James Steele, head of the U.S. Military Group, who remarked, "This battalion is one of the best in the fight against terrorism."[32] Several other current and former military officers who were implicated fled the country just prior to being arrested (Gibb and Farah 1989). Márquez was never charged.[33]

The kidnappings and the failure to successfully prosecute most of the perpetrators had a chilling effect within the business community. The involvement of military personnel, their obvious impunity, and the extrajudicial execution of suspects at the hands of the National Police all tended to deepen their distrust of the armed forces. The apparent involvement of ARENA members also created some embarrassment and helped undercut the hardline current within the party, raising the prestige of moderates like Alfredo Cristiani, who were more representative of the business community than of the party's militarist founders.[34]

During 1987 and 1988, hardline founders who wanted to preserve the party as an anticommunist extremist organization engaged in an intense debate with a growing faction of moderates who represented the increasingly pragmatic and organized modernizing business community. As Wolf puts it, "One vision was associated with D'Aubuisson's earlier hardline goal of restoring a mystical status quo ante, the other with moving on to constructing a social climate more amenable to business activity" (1992, 12). The turning point came when D'Aubuisson surprisingly threw his weight behind Cristiani, who was elected party president and soon became ARENA's candidate for the presidency. This paved the way for broader and more active business sector support and helped make the party acceptable to the United States.

This turning point was in many ways a culmination of the various economic, generational, and institutional factors discussed above that had helped mobilize the business community to seek political power. It also reflected a learning process within ARENA. Most of its early members had not participated in politics prior to the crisis of 1979–80. Their first experiences were therefore with street politics and confrontation. After participating in the provisional government of 1982 to 1984, and after two terms in the Legislative Assembly, they had begun to appreciate the advantages of negotiation, bargaining, and playing by (and exploiting) institutional rules (Wolf 1992, 13). After losing the 1984 presidential elections to Duarte, ARENA leaders recognized the advantages of building as broad a political base as possible, and of having at least the grudging acceptance of the United States.

Above all, however, D'Aubuisson's decision to pick Cristiani and thereby integrate into the party a broader range of business people and relative moderates was a pragmatic recognition of what the party needed to do to gain power. It in no way erased the "violent and primitive anticommunism and the identification of nationalism with the interests of class and party" that characterized many senior officials and much of the party's popular base (Whitfield 1994, 326). The replacement of Armando Calderón Sol by Francisco Merino as the vice presidential candidate signaled the tensions between the violent old guard (whom Merino represented) and the newcomers (Miles and Ostertag 1989, 22). The party nevertheless pulled itself together and demonstrated strengths that made victory in the 1988 and 1989 elections likely. The business community made handsome donations and provided logistical, technical, and communications skills that the Christian Democrats and National Conciliation Party lacked. ARENA had begun organizing among young people in the mid-1980s, a shrewd decision in a demographically young country. An array of civic organizations helped channel volunteers into the party structure. Far outshining its competitors in the use of television and radio, ARENA broadcast slickly produced spots that hit the PDC's most vulnerable points: the economy and corruption.

ARENA also made extraordinarily effective use of nationalism. D'Aubuisson was a master of this theme, reminding local-level party officials never to say "the country," but always "our country" (Miles and Ostertag 1989, 15). Much of the population saw the United States as managing the conduct of the war and as having imposed the PDC/military juntas and the discredited Duarte government. Anti-gringo rhetoric thus became a useful tool, not only for satisfying the party's traditional hardline constituency, but for attracting new supporters, along with unemployed workers and petty entrepreneurs angry over PDC corruption and the sinking economy. Together, these themes enabled the party to build a broader, more multiclass alliance than it had enjoyed in the past, supplementing the clientelist base that D'Aubuisson had organized around the remnants of ORDEN in the early 1980s (Miles and Ostertag 1989, 22–23).

In the 1988 Assembly and municipal elections, ARENA proved its vote-getting ability, winning an absolute majority of seats in the legislature and an overwhelming 70 percent of mayoralties.[35] With control of the legislature, ARENA could tie President Duarte down during his final year in office; with control of municipal government, it could use patronage to build strong local political machines. ARENA campaigned in the 1989 presidential race with an intensity and degree of mobilization never before seen in Salvadoran electoral politics. Cristiani and Merino held rallies in virtually every town in the country, accompanied by live music and cheerleaders, and an entourage of youthful party faithful outfitted in ARENA vests and windbreakers, tight jeans and Reeboks. For election day, the party mobilized almost three times the legally permitted number of poll watchers, as well as a nationwide motor pool of donated vehicles and volunteer drivers to get voters to the polls despite an FMLN transportation stoppage. In the end, ARENA won only slightly more votes than in the past, but in a context of declining turnout 54 percent of the vote was sufficient to gain ARENA 13 of 14 departments (Miles and Ostertag 1989, 24–25).

War and Peace during Cristiani's First Year

Even before Cristiani took office, there were early signs that the prospects for a negotiated settlement of the war might be improving. In May 1988, the top leadership of the FMLN had spent a month meeting with Latin American leaders abroad and visiting the Soviet Union and other socialist countries. Their travels gave them a new appreciation of the pace of international political change, of reforms in the USSR and eastern Europe, and of the lack of support among Latin American countries for a Marxist takeover in El Salvador. This development led to their proposal in January 1989 that the FMLN put down its guns and encourage supporters to vote for the Democratic Convergence, which was made up of the social democratic National Revolutionary Movement (MNR) and the Popular Social Christian Movement (MPSC), which Rubén Zamora and other disaffected Christian Democrats had formed in 1980. This proposal went nowhere, but it was seriously considered by the United States and sparked intense debate regarding the FMLN's sincerity and electoral prospects (Whitfield 1994, 322).

FMLN members were not alone in thinking about the possibility of peace. Speaking in November 1988 at the University of Central America, candidate Cristiani committed himself to a process of "permanent dialogue" with the FMLN. Before the elections, ARENA representatives carried out a discreet dialogue with the FMLN outside the country (Miles and Ostertag 1989, 21). Cristiani reiterated this commitment in his inaugural address. The rector of the university, Ignacio Ellacuría, used every opportunity and medium available to him to promote the idea that 1989 was the moment for dialogue. With a pragmatic rightist civilian government coming into office, the FMLN seeming to be open to the idea of negotiation, and the pragmatic new Bush administration in Washington, conditions for negotiations seemed more promising than they had been in nine years. Ellacuría publicly aligned the university with Cristiani by publishing in *Estudios Centroamericanos* an assessment of the administration's first 100 days that was so laudatory that Ellacuría's colleague Ignacio Martín-Baro called it "an ode to Cristiani" (Whitfield 1994, 321–42).

Yet getting the dialogue moving proved difficult. The FMLN hesitated, reluctant to commit itself to a process of dialogue with a president and party it deeply distrusted. Only after a meeting in Mexico at which the opposition parties strongly urged the FMLN to meet with a government delegation did the meetings go forward. The first meetings, held on 16–18 September in Mexico City, went better than most observers had expected. The FMLN arrived with proposals that were similar to, but in some ways less sweeping than, the eventual peace accords. The guerrillas recognized the existing executive and abandoned previous demands that FMLN combatants be integrated into the military. They called for judicial reform, prosecution of members of death squads, implementation of the agrarian reform, agreement to advance the 1991 municipal and assembly elections so that the FMLN could participate, reforms of the police, and a self-purging of the military. The proposal was intended to conform to the requirements of the Bush administration, which the FMLN thought to be open to a pragmatic, negotiated solution (Miller 1989).

The government responded cautiously. The delegation sent by the Cristiani administration was of a lower level than the panel of top commanders sent by the FMLN, and they made it clear that they wanted to talk more about procedures than about substantive proposals. When the two sides met again a month later in San José, Costa Rica, there was little substantive progress. Nonetheless, they agreed to meet again, and the joint statement issued at the end of the meetings included the key provision that the end of military confrontation would be linked to effective guarantees of the rights of citizens. This phrase signaled the government's recognition that the rebels could expect some substantive reform *prior* to putting down their weapons (Gruson 1989). It was too much for the military. At a high-profile press conference a few days later, Defense Minister Rafael Humberto Larios, surrounded by senior staff and the commanders of virtually all the major units in the country, expressed grave doubts about the negotiations. He vehemently rejected the idea that the military's "self-purge" would involve, a priori, the dismissal of all 16 active duty members of the *tandona* group, as well as the commander of the air force, General Bustillo.

The opponents of negotiations within ARENA, the military, and the FMLN, not surprisingly, expressed their dissent through violence. The period from April through October 1989—the period Ellacuría had identified as a window of opportunity for negotiations—was characterized by escalating violence by both sides. On 15 March, commandos of the FMLN assassinated Dr. Francisco Peccorini, a rightist intellectual and former Jesuit who had criticized the influence of the FMLN within the National University. On 14 April, someone detonated a bomb in the house of Vice President–elect Merino. On 19 April, FMLN assassins placed a bomb on the roof of Attorney General José Roberto García Alvarado's vehicle while it waited at a stop light, killing him. On 9 June, Dr. José Antonio Rodríguez Porth was killed by a lone gunman while leaving his home. Rodríguez Porth had just been installed as Cristiani's minister of the presidency (chief of staff). He had been a close advisor and friend of Cristiani and, as president of the Chamber of Commerce, helped pull together the coalition of diverse business interests and ideological currents that had allowed ARENA to win the Assembly and the presidency (Miles and Ostertag 1989, 18). These killings were followed in June and July by the assassinations of Edgar Chacón and Gabriel Payés, both well-known, hardline rightists, and of Colonel Roberto Armando Rivera Escobar, the national fire chief. The FMLN took responsibility for some of these acts but denied others, including the killing of Rodríguez Porth. There was speculation at the time, still not fully resolved, that some of the assassinations had been unauthorized actions by the Armed Forces of Liberation, the armed wing of the Communist Party.

Rightists carried out some violence of their own. Days before the March 1989 elections, the University of Central America was bombed for the first time since 1983. After the killings of prominent rightists, it was bombed again in April and July. The July bombing involved larger devices, placed to cause serious damage. A well-informed visitor told university rector Ellacuría that the attack had come from within the Treasury Police, and that he should interpret it as a serious warning.

As had happened in the past, Jesuits seeking to promote moderate solutions became the target of intense criticism and red-baiting in the right-wing press and paid advertisements. ARENA and the military paid for newspaper advertisements calling Father Segundo Montes "inhuman and immoral" for his "justification of the terrorist acts" of the FMLN. It was unusual and surprising for Montes to be singled out: as director of the university's Human Rights Institute and as a professor of sociology and political science, he had devoted himself to careful documentation of human rights violations and research on the conditions of El Salvador's displaced people and refugees while maintaining cordial relations with a handful of military officers. The offending statements had been sound, analytical observations: during a television interview, Montes predicted increased violence as both sides positioned themselves for negotiations (Whitfield 1994, 328–29). Other advertisements followed. The Crusade for Work and Peace, a right-wing civic association affiliated with ARENA, labeled Ellacuría and Montes terrorists and called for reinstatement of the death penalty and the capture and application of "justice" to those it named (Whitfield 1994, 331–32).

Tensions increased as the actual negotiations began. On 15 October, the FMLN organized a massive demonstration and nighttime vigil in support of the peace talks in front of the San Salvador Cathedral, the site of many violent incidents in the early 1980s. The organizers kept the nervous crowd seated to prevent stampedes, and inured the crowd to loud noises by detonating "celebratory" fireworks throughout the proceedings. Air force agents shot two people on the periphery of the crowd, and sporadic machine-gun fire broke out as the crowd retreated into the cathedral.[36] On 17 October, unknown gunmen assassinated the daughter of Colonel Edgardo Casanova Véjar, machine-gunning her as she returned home from an aerobics class. This killing seemed to violate the unspoken rule against assassinating members of the families of commanders on either side. (Parents and siblings of FMLN commanders had remained in the capital throughout the war.) The response came two days later, when satchel charges were tossed into the entry of Rubén Zamora's house, causing extensive damage but injuring no one.

On 22 October, Cristiani made a statement that seemed to foreclose negotiations. He rejected out of hand the idea that the government would allow "a minority group to give orders to change the Supreme Court of Justice and restructure the Armed Forces. All these absurd ideas have to come off the FMLN's agenda if they really want peace" (Whitfield 1994, 342). On 30 October, the FMLN attacked the military Joint Command headquarters with homemade catapult bombs that misfired, killing a civilian nearby. A pair of bombings, presumably by government forces, followed. The first, on the morning of 31 October, damaged the offices of COMADRES, an organization of wives and mothers of political prisoners, the disappeared, and the assassinated. Four people were injured. At noon, a second device exploded at the headquarters of the FENASTRAS union. This enormous blast, timed to coincide with the lunch hour and centered just outside an area that served as a canteen, killed 10 people and wounded 35. Among those killed was a charismatic and effective FENASTRAS leader, Febe Elizabeth Velázquez. As one witness put it, "This was getting like the early 1980s all over again. We are living the nightmare of the past" (Doggett 1993, 6).

The pure carnage of the FENASTRAS attack presented Cristiani with a serious political problem. He promptly called upon the Church, the United Nations, and the OAS to contribute representatives for an independent investigative commission. He also asked UCA rector Ellacuría to participate. Cristiani's efforts at damage control were too late. The FMLN was by this point committed to a major urban offensive. Unconvinced of Cristiani's sincerity and confident that it could, at a minimum, considerably advance its negotiating position, it chose to attack.

The FMLN had been planning a major offensive against the capital since 1986. By mid-1989, preparations were under way. The core strategy was to occupy poor neighborhoods in the eastern and northern parts of the capital, use them as a base for forays into parts of the city controlled by the government, and defend them against government attacks. By digging into densely populated areas, the FMLN hoped to trigger a mass insurrection. In any case their strategy would present the army with a dilemma: it would need heavy weapons and air power to dislodge the guerrillas, but their use would cause heavy civilian casualties, popular opposition, and international condemnation. During the weeks and months prior to the offensive, the FMLN brought in literally tons of weapons and ammunition, pre-positioning enough arms to supply an insurrection. The large stockpile enabled the guerrillas to use ammunition unsparingly and to discard weapons as needed to blend into the civilian population and move from area to area within the city.

The FAES was caught by surprise, even though they had received intelligence warning of a major offensive. The extent of the intelligence failure was remarkable. A week before the offensive, it was common knowledge within poor communities in San Salvador that something really big was about to happen. It was, as Frank Smyth puts it, "a national conspiracy; tens of thousands of people participated in preparations for the offensive. Truckloads of rice, beans, bullets, and medicine were stockpiled in poor barrios." Smyth interviewed a senior military official in the U.S. embassy on the morning before the offensive and was told that the FMLN did not have the capability for a major strike. A few hours later, guerrillas and soldiers were fighting to control the suburban neighborhood where the officer lived, and he was forced to barricade his family in his house (Smyth 1989). The chief of the National Intelligence Directorate, the chief of the air force, the head of the Civil Affairs Department of the Joint Command, and other senior officers were out of the country. President Cristiani, at his vacation home, had not been informed of the reports of an impending offensive.

The offensive shook the military high command. The FMLN attacked multiple targets around the city, creating confusion as to their objectives. Then military units pursuing retreating guerrillas began to encounter heavy resistance from the communities in which the FMLN had established fortified positions. Over the ensuing days, the military found it extremely difficult to push the FMLN out and resorted to fairly indiscriminate aerial strafing, rocket attacks, and bombing. The confidence of many military commanders was shaken, and the incapacity of many officers—promoted according to *tanda*, not ability—became particularly evident.[37] Senior commanders seriously considered the possibility that they might lose, or that San Salvador might become a divided city (Doggett 1993, 38).

Using air power, the military gradually pried the FMLN loose from its strongholds in the eastern part of the city. The guerrillas, having neglected to obtain antiaircraft weapons and having failed to destroy the air force on the ground at its base just east of San Salvador, realized that their continued presence would lead to heavy civilian casualties. They chose to withdraw, taking heavy losses in the process, and moved some of their forces into the wealthy Escalón neighborhood in the western part of the city. This strategy had an important political effect. Unwilling, for obvious reasons, to use artillery and aerial bombardment there, the military found it difficult to flush out the FMLN forces. Many of the wealthy residents of the zone felt that the military had failed in its duty to protect them. Others had surprisingly civil conversations with rebels who had occupied their homes, and began to rethink their assumption that the guerrillas were irrational fanatics.

The offensive brought to the fore the frustrations within the military about the manner in which the United States had forced them to conduct the war. The U.S. stipulation that the military discontinue the death squad–style killing of the early 1980s had allowed the FMLN to rebuild its urban organizational structure. The officers' frequent charge that the popular organizations of the left were merely a "facade" for the FMLN was essentially accurate. Under its policy of *"doble cara"* ("two faces") the FMLN encouraged the development of various kinds of civic groups in which it had a clandestine organizational presence. Many members of popular organizations joined the FMLN as combatants during the November offensive (and many, as inexperienced combatants in a difficult urban setting, were killed). Members of the military and the hardline sector of the civilian right felt that U.S. human rights concerns had forced them to abandon the most successful tools for counterinsurgency: terror and selective assassination of those who supported the left. By 1988 and 1989, it was common to hear calls for a "Guatemala solution," a "total war" against the left, unhindered by U.S. constraints (Miles and Ostertag 1989, 28–30).

The pressures of the offensive, frustration with human rights constraints, and strident demands from civilian rightists led the FAES to commit a grave error. On 15 November, members of the high command ordered the assassination of Ignacio Ellacuría and the other Jesuits in his household. In the pre-dawn hours of 16 November, members of the Atlacatl Battalion entered the grounds of the University of Central America and murdered Ellacuría, Martín-Baro, Montes, their colleagues Juan Ramón Moreno, Amando López, and Joaquín López y López, their housekeeper, Julia Elba Ramos, and her daughter, Celina. The soldiers had been ordered to kill Ellacuría and leave no witnesses. They then vandalized the priests' residence, detonated grenades and an antitank weapon, and wrote graffiti on the walls suggesting that the FMLN had been responsible. The details of the murders and subsequent cover-up have been carefully documented by the United Nations Truth Commission (1993), Martha Doggett (1993), and Teresa Whitfield (1994). No doubt remains that the killings reflected a collective decision by the minister of defense, the vice minister, and several other senior commanders.

These killings were so irrational as to seem inexplicable. Killing six priests, among them three internationally prominent scholars, could not help but cause international condemnation and jeopardize the U.S. aid program. In the two years following the murders, the U.S. Congress would gradually lose its willingness to pay for the war in El Salvador, forcing the military to accept a process of negotiation that would eventually lead to a drastic loss of power for the armed forces. In view of the predictably high costs, how could senior military leaders have decided that the Jesuit scholars were appropriate and important targets to pursue in the context of the FMLN's offensive? Notwithstanding the frequent rhetorical charges that the Jesuits were the intellectual authors of the FMLN's violence, it was obvious to any reasonable observer that the Jesuits were not part of the FMLN.

While the motivations of those who ordered the murders will never be known, the killings appear to have been an expression of internal struggles within the military and ARENA over the question of negotiations and the appropriate use of state violence. As already noted, many officers in the military were bitter about the constraints imposed by the United States and felt that U.S. support, though needed, had come at too high a price. The idea of negotiations was anathema. From the hardliners' point of view, negotiations would be unnecessary if the military were winning, and the military was so far not winning only because the gringos kept it from fighting as it should. For the far right of the military and ARENA, intellectuals like Ellacuría and Montes, as well as leftist politicians like Ungo and Zamora, symbolized what was wrong with the country and the U.S.-regulated counterinsurgency strategy. The fact that such ideological enemies were still in the country was a sign of weakness and a loss of sovereignty. Ideas and political agendas that should be excluded were being tolerated, and this gave succor to the guerrillas. Retired Colonel Sigifredo Ochoa, who had left the military and joined ARENA in the late 1980s, summarized the hardline position in an oral history interview taped in 1987:

> Well, I think it's important, for example, to maintain an intelligence apparatus, an apparatus that permits us to identify the real subversives. For example, we are shooting a lot and wasting a lot of ammunition out in the field, causing problems for the people as well. But the true leaders, the true thinkers are in the Universities. For example, Father Ellacuría, a Jesuit priest of the Central American University, is a Spaniard, who along with all his entourage of Spanish Communists from liberation theology are those who are here. They move around freely in El Salvador. In my opinion a law should be implemented in order to strengthen democracy, in the sense of expelling from the country all those foreigners who come to subvert order and implant the seeds of communism in the minds of the youth. If not, it will never end.[38]

Civilian rightists' hatred of Ellacuría and his colleagues had much in common with the right wing's traditional obsession with reformist members of the elite and priests. Rightists viewed poor people as incapable of effective, organized action and therefore blamed unrest on intellectuals and educated opposition figures—"traitors to their class," as the archconservative coffee grower Orlando DeSola put it.[39]

Killing the Jesuits became a litmus test for the military's willingness to defend upper-class interests and defeat the left. On the first night of the offensive, the army forced all radio stations in the country to broadcast a signal distributed by its own "Radio Cuscatlán." The signal originated from the National Information Center, which was the press office of the Presidential Palace. Throughout the night, the network broadcast a call-in program during which callers denounced FMLN front organizations and called for the deaths of Ungo, Zamora, Ellacuría, Archbishop Arturo Rivera y Damas, and Auxiliary Bishop Gregorio Rosa Chávez. Vice President Merino called the station and accused Ellacuría of "poisoning the minds" of Salvadoran youth. Only after the head of the armed forces press office returned to the country on the second day of the offensive, and after the United States exerted pressure, was the call-in program stopped. In the meantime, the right had made its wishes known (Doggett 1993, 39–40).

The high command no doubt had its own incentives. Shaken by the rebel offensive, it needed a way to show its resolve. The strength of the offensive made it instantly clear that the U.S.-designed strategy of the past five years was not succeeding. The military may have felt a need to strike a blow that would commit it to a more violent path, demonstrate its autonomy from the United States, and foreclose further discussions of negotiations. They may also have simply been following the well-established Salvadoran military tradition of expediency. In the early 1980s, at a time when he was afraid to commit his forces to battle, Defense Minister García oversaw tens of thousands of security force murders that held the promise of interfering with the guerrillas' plans while entailing little risk. The high command of 1989, faced with their own failure to prevent or blunt the FMLN's offensive, needed a way to fight back. Killing six unarmed priests was well within their means.

The Aftermath

As the FMLN retreated from San Salvador, many observers feared that the military would go on a rampage, implementing the long-feared "Guatemala solution." Although the military did search and destroy the offices of many popular organizations, and arrest hundreds of people, and although there were some incidents of summary violence, there was no bloodbath. Nor was the overall death toll from military bombardment of poor neighborhoods as high as many had expected. With more sophisticated weapons, communications systems, and tactics, the military was better able than in the past to control its application of force, even in a dense urban setting. An analysis by Americas Watch suggested that the military had exercised some discretion in its use of heavy weapons and that civilian casualties, though heavy, had been lower than the thousands of dead predicted in the press during the heat of the offensive (Americas Watch 1989a, 1989b).

The most important reason for the military's restraint was that despite its frustration with U.S. human rights constraints, the FAES still needed U.S.

assistance and was unwilling to jeopardize the flow of ammunition, weapons, spare parts, and fuel by going on a rampage. At rates of operation typical of 1989, the FAES had only one month of reserves in combat consumables (Miles and Ostertag 1989, 30). Given intense combat, like that of November and December 1989, their reserves would last a week or two. This dependence was structured into the force. The FAES had become heavily dependent upon helicopter mobility and close air support for its ground troops. The air force had been vital to driving the FMLN out of San Salvador, and continued to be the linchpin of FAES combat operations in the countryside. Aircraft require constant maintenance, spares, fuel, and munitions, none of which the Salvadorans could afford on their own.

The talk about emulating the Guatemalan military was just talk. The FMLN was a far more potent military force than the Guatemalan guerrillas had ever been. It had the capacity to protect its supporters at least in some parts of the country, and had so far prevented the FAES from establishing the kind of comprehensive civil defense network that existed in Guatemala. As FMLN commander Joaquín Villalobos had pointed out earlier in 1989, "Even the most desperate and recalcitrant rightist has noticed that it is not so easy to unleash repression. The correlation of forces will make a large-scale wave of repression very difficult. . . . Duarte carried out a total war in his first two years [1980–81], killed 50,000 Salvadorans and the Reagan administration paid for it. ARENA would like to wage a total war but they have no one to foot the bill" (Miles and Ostertag 1989, 30).

Avarice helped to avert a bloodbath. The FAES had always nurtured an elaborate system of corruption in which officers pocketed salaries paid to fictitious soldiers, and sold the food, weapons, and ammunition allocated to these phantoms. This system had become more elaborate, and larger in scale, as the military expanded from roughly 12,000 troops in 1980 to a supposed 57,000 by 1989. The flow of goods into these units, and therefore the opportunities for graft, depended on U.S. assistance (see Millman 1989).

The situation became more complicated in 1990 and 1991 as the FMLN introduced the use of heat-seeking antiaircraft missiles obtained from the Sandinista army and other sources. By downing just a few aircraft, the FMLN greatly reduced the effectiveness of the air force. To be safe from the missiles, aircraft had to fly at very low altitudes, making it far more difficult to locate and attack guerrilla targets and making airmen vulnerable to small arms fire from the ground. (A U.S. helicopter on its way to Honduras was among the aircraft shot down.) FAES ground forces, then, were essentially on their own during 1990–91, and they did not fare well. The absence of air support exposed them once again to the risk that the FMLN would mass its forces as it had in 1982 and 1983. The FAES began sending out larger forces, saturating rebel-held areas. When they failed to do this, they could be badly hurt, as happened when the under-manned Bracamonte rapid reaction battalion was surrounded by the FMLN in 1991 and forced to flee into Honduras with heavy casualties. When the military did move in large forces, the FMLN often avoided it. Although some FAES forces sucessfully engaged the FMLN in combat during 1990–91, the military's strategy failed to shift the balance of the war in its favor.

Time was not on the side of the FAES as an institution. With support for military assistance eroding in the U.S. Congress and ARENA pragmatists gaining the upper hand, the chance of a negotiated settlement and major institutional losses for the military grew stronger by the month. The popular left took advantage of the military's weakness by mobilizing a series of peasant land invasions in mid-1991, which coincided with intense military activity throughout the countryside. After a month of issuing threats to use force, the ARENA government ultimately negotiated with the peasant organizations, agreeing not to evict some of the peasants from lands already taken if they would agree not to carry out further invasions (*Proceso*, 12 June, 19 June, and 15 July 1991). This episode reinforced perceptions within the business community and ARENA that the military was incapable of protecting private interests and that some other means needed to be found.

International actors began to play an increasingly important role in encouraging a negotiated solution. Shortly after the November 1989 offensive, U.N. Secretary General Javier Pérez de Cuellar and his personal representative, Alvaro de Soto, stepped up their consultations with both sides. This process led to the Geneva Accords of April 1990, in which the parties agreed to bring about a definitive end to the armed conflict, reunify the country, promote democratization, and guarantee respect for human rights. They committed themselves to a process of secret negotiations in which the secretary general or his representative would play an intermediary role (United Nations 1992, 1–3). Keeping the negotiations secret would reduce the likelihood that hardliners on either side could organize themselves to block progress at the negotiating table. U.N. involvement helped advance the process. During subsequent rounds of negotiations, the U.N. representative and his staff prepared working papers based on separate discussions with both sides. By this mechanism, the United Nations was able to promote discussion of proposals on delicate issues that, if presented directly by one of the parties, would have been automatically rejected by the other.[40]

A month later, the parties met in Caracas, Venezuela, to establish an agenda for the subsequent negotiations. The agenda included language that foresaw a U.N. role in the verification of the accords, to compensate for the parties' mutual distrust and increased the international political cost to both sides of failing to reach an agreement.

In the first substantive agreement, reached in San José, Costa Rica, in July 1990, the parties accepted minimum standards for the protection of human rights, including an immediate end to night arrests, incommunicado detention, and torture. This agreement also envisioned the establishment of a U.N. human rights verification mission (ONUSAL) that would have broad powers and would demand the cooperation of all parties. The agreement paved the way for an important initiative: rather than waiting for a cease-fire to put the human rights mission in place, the United Nations opened an ONUSAL office in San Salvador in January 1991 and began verification operations six months later (United Nations 1991, 2–4). The presence of ONUSAL observers would prevent either side from escalating the war (Americas Watch 1992).

An agreement on constitutional reform, signed in April 1991, marked more serious progress. The reforms reduced the institutional powers of the armed forces, clarifying the power of civilian authorities, and excluding the military from internal security functions. These reforms were promptly approved by the ARENA-controlled Legislative Assembly, laying the groundwork for full implementation within the next two years.[41] The FMLN took the Assembly's cooperation as a sign of good faith on the part of the government and a sign of ARENA party discipline.

The next major breakthrough came in September 1991 in New York, where the parties agreed to carry out a definitive, single-phase cease-fire that would involve a progressive separation of forces, followed by the gradual but total demobilization of the FMLN. In a secret annex to the agreement, the FMLN agreed to forgo all demands to participate in the existing armed forces, accepting instead a guarantee that its personnel would be allowed nonprejudicial access to participation in a new national civilian police force, the PNC. The New York accord also established the National Commission for the Consolidation of Peace (COPAZ), which would possess the power to verify all aspects of the implementation of the accords.[42]

With the New York talks, U.S. diplomacy weighed heavily in favor of a definitive agreement and an end to the war. The United States had increased its direct contacts with the FMLN during the latter half of 1991 and had become convinced that the rebels were serious. Once the FMLN agreed not to demand incorporation of its forces into the military, U.S. policy makers felt that U.S. concerns were being met. In New York, U.S. officials prodded the high-level Salvadoran delegation to accept the terms and attempt to close the deal.[43] Although the Salvadoran military was resistant, it had little choice. With declining U.S. aid levels, and the FMLN as strong as ever, the military was not in a position to argue.

International factors hastened the final agreement. The rapid breakup of the socialist bloc reduced the Salvadoran right's perception of threat. During the FMLN offensive in November 1989, the Berlin wall had come down. In February 1990, the Sandinista regime in neighboring Nicaragua was voted out of office and complied. And in August 1991, the failed coup in the USSR signaled the death throes of the Soviet system. Since the Salvadoran right had always been convinced that revolution in their country was externally inspired, these events made the idea of legalizing the FMLN and diminishing the strength of the national military more palatable.

Another international factor was the impending departure of Pérez de Cuellar, whose personal commitment to the peace process had raised the stakes for all those involved. His term as secretary general was to end on New Years Eve. Working against this deadline, the government and the FMLN entered into a marathon series of negotiations leading to final agreements completed four minutes before midnight on 31 December and incorporated into the formal accords signed on 16 January 1992 in Mexico City.[44]

Shutting Down the Racket

From 1980 through 1983, the conduct of Salvadoran government forces can only be characterized as a campaign of terror. Yet despite the fact that the FMLN became consistently stronger and defied efforts to destroy it during the 1980s, state violence actually diminished. By the late 1980s, El Salvador was no more dangerous for active members of the left than it had been in the years immediately prior to the war, though people who participated in the activities of popular organizations, or belonged to social democratic political parties, ran a risk of being imprisoned, tortured, or killed.

With the peace accords in 1992, El Salvador entered a radically different phase in which human rights conditions improved further and institutional changes to the state made it likely that the state would use coercion far less frequently. Remarkably, these changes took place under the auspices of a government controlled by ARENA, a party that had stood for "total war" against the left during its early years.

The reductions in state violence during the 1980s are quite simple to explain: the U.S. executive found that it could not sustain congressional support for an expanded aid program unless the killing was reduced. With hundreds of millions of dollars at stake, the FAES high command had an incentive to cooperate and a strong argument to use within the ranks. Serious military pressures from the FMLN during 1982–83 reminded the FAES that it needed U.S. help to survive — in contrast to their Guatemalan colleagues, who did without U.S. aid, and without U.S. human rights pressures, during the crucial first years of their guerrilla war in the late 1970s and early 1980s. U.S. leverage proved limited, however. Washington was unable to move the military to hold its officers accountable for violent acts, even when these included the murder of U.S. citizens. The high command's threats to lose control of the institution if forced to act too strongly were merely an extension of the internal protection racket that García used against the *Majanistas* in 1980. U.S. policy makers, saddled with the Cold War imperative of preventing a leftist takeover and concerned that a rightist coup could undermine the entire counterinsurgency project, allowed themselves to be manipulated by the high command's claims of vulnerability.

The peace accords, and the resulting transition to a post–protection racket state in the midst of a civil war, are more surprising and more difficult to explain. The key lesson of this process is that a protection racket state can function only when there is no civilian political class capable of establishing political legitimacy through inclusionary means. Until the evolution of ARENA into an effective party of the entrepreneurial classes, the landowners, bankers, merchants, and industrialists of El Salvador remained merely a social and economic elite, without sufficient political coherence, organization, and vision to put forward a project that could achieve popular and electoral legitimacy. As such, they were vulnerable to the ability of the coercive agencies of the state to polarize the political climate, maintaining conditions in which repressive strategies seemed the only means of maintaining order.

This is not to absolve the civilian social elite from responsibility for the protection racket—we saw throughout the past four chapters how members of the upper classes financed and promoted state violence and exclusion. Yet in so doing they were acting in defense of a social order, and an ideological perspective, that were themselves products of Hernández Martínez' *matanza*. Moreover, the political dynamics of the 1980s make it clear that despite the contributions of some civilian rightists to perpetuating hardline policies, the military was by no means a simple instrument of an "oligarchy." The military high command took advantage of private sector contributions and organizing when it was useful to do so, but acted with considerable autonomy from the interests of the landed elite. It carried out a land reform, prevented rightist coups, continued to consort with the Christian Democratic Party, and tailored its use of violence to the exigencies of U.S. congressional politics.

The evolution of ARENA into a successful electoral machine changed the dynamics. After the electoral victories of 1988 and 1989, and faced with the economic costs of permitting the military to continue the protection racket, the new entrepreneurial political class opted to rely on their own legitimacy, rather than military force, to defend their interests. International factors played an important role in this outcome. Had the United States not insisted on elections as a condition for aid, El Salvador's transition to elected government and the first steps toward transforming the social elite into a political class would have come later, if at all. The result would likely have been something akin to the situation in Guatemala, where no party, as yet, enjoys the near-hegemonic political capacity of ARENA. The decline of the socialist bloc also played an important and timely role, making it easier for an intensely anticommunist business elite to contemplate allowing the domestic left—now no longer a Trojan horse for international communism—to compete in elections.

The most important factor in ARENA's evolution toward accepting pluralism was the war. Simply put, the FMLN's ability to resist the military's violence broke the protection racket. By surviving, sabotaging the economy, and then demonstrating their potency and resilience with the November offensive, the FMLN drove a wedge between much of civil society and the military. The military high command collaborated in its own ruin by managing the war more to make money than to win, and by indulging in terrorist strategies that limited the FMLN in some ways but strengthened it in others. State terrorism in the 1980s, as in the previous decade, was a policy of short-term expedience practiced by an institution and leadership group who were unwilling to take the risks associated with strategies that were more likely to succeed in the long run. In the end, the costs of allowing the military to continue to play its game forced the diverse sectors and strata of the propertied classes to mobilize, take power, and eventually negotiate a new order in which the military would play a less prominent role.

CONCLUSION

The details of El Salvador's protection racket state are no doubt unique, but many of its features are found elsewhere. Certainly other state elites have justified their power by protecting social elites from their class enemies. As discussed in the Introduction, the Brazilian, Argentine, and Uruguayan militaries have at times used violence in ways that seemed calculated to create an image of greater opposition than actually existed, or to polarize politics in order to create an ongoing need for powerful coercive institutions. The Salvadoran case teaches us that we cannot assume, as domestic realist theories do, that state violence is a proportionate response to opposition. Nor can we assume that states are either apolitical arenas for competition among interest groups or simply the instruments of dominant classes. Rather, states are semi-independent agents with powers distinct from those of other groups within society. Their most important power is coercion, and they can use it to create a climate beneficial for state elites. For those members of the elite who work in the agencies of coercion, the most congenial or profitable environment is not necessarily one of political stability. On the contrary, the most repressive agencies and leaders can demand more resources when conditions are polarized and violent. The less legitimate the existing order, the greater the opportunities for these leaders.

Whether this logic translates into actual violence and manipulation of the political arena by state elites depends on the political and institutional context. Several features of the Salvadoran case made the formation and maintenance of a protection racket regime more likely. First, the society was highly stratified, a situation that was itself a product of Liberal state policies during the nineteenth and early twentieth centuries. The social elite had good reason to be afraid of their landless workers, which made it easier for the military to claim state power by killing supposedly rebellious peasants. Second, the social elite was politically weak, making the costs of mobilizing to challenge the military takeover relatively high. Thus, even though members of the elite organized to oust the Martínez regime, they quickly accommodated themselves to a new military regime rather than incurring the costs of organizing and maintaining a viable political party of the right.

The political weakness of the social elite could have provided an opening for the military to create a more inclusionary corporatist regime, using the power of the state to rectify social inequities and attracting broader political support for the regime. This did not occur largely because the military was very porous to elite interventions. The military's mechanisms for selecting political candidates were poorly institutionalized and subject to outside manipulation. Furthermore, some agencies of the military, particularly the security and intelligence services, were heavily influenced by their financial links to the private sector. Blurring of private and public functions had characterized these forces from the outset. They were essentially mercenaries of the agrarian elite, yet were also able to manipulate and prey on members of that elite through protection racketeering and outright extortion. The willingness of these forces to serve as political agents of the agrarian elite within the military made it impossible for military presidents to carry out reform projects that might have boosted the regime's legitimacy. By blocking reforms, the hardline institutions also served their own interests, since in the process they created a more polarized climate in which their services became all the more necessary. Even when the top military leadership finally agreed to reforms under the Revolutionary Governing Junta of 1980, the measures were accompanied by so much violence as to prevent them from depolarizing the political situation.

The entire protection racket was premised on the legal impunity of the military. Since the officers who ordered violence were doing so primarily to advance their own political and financial fortunes, they were extremely sensitive to risks of accountability. Whenever there appeared to be risks associated with state terrorist activities—as during November 1979, when reformists nearly had the upper hand, or after Vice President Bush's December 1983 visit—conspicuous state terrorist activities fell markedly. We can see the same dynamic in Romero's curbing of security force abuses to avoid international criticism and sanctions. Conversely, as reformists lost power during 1980, making prosecution of abuses less likely, hardliners found the courage to kill more unarmed civilians.

The importance of impunity to the entire system is evident in the extreme ·resistance of the FAES to nearly constant U.S. pressures to prosecute officers for murders committed during the 1980s. Until the Jesuit case, no successful prosecutions were ever carried out except against enlisted men. To do otherwise would have paralyzed the coercive apparatus. Obviously this points to the importance of effective judicial reform, nonmilitary control over criminal investigations (recall that the National Police criminal investigations division *was* a death squad during the early 1980s), and the repeal of military immunity (*fuero militar*) in the case of crimes against civilians.

One of the key lessons of the Salvadoran case is that if we wish to apply a rational actor model to explain decisions to use repression, we must select the correct level of analysis. The role of the FAES high command in orchestrating the campaign of terror after the October 1979 coup is illustrative. The security of the Salvadoran state, and even of the military institution, might have been better served during this moment by a more accommodative stance toward the popular movement. If we treat the state as a unit, the campaign of terror launched by García and Carranza seems ill-considered and irrational.

If we consider their personal and factional political position, however, the use of terror is rational, if obscene and cold-blooded. They were faced by a reformist challenge from within the military that required them to align themselves with its most hardline components. Moreover, in a context in which the military was being pressured to hold elections and transfer power to civilians, the power of the Ministry of Defense could best be protected and even augmented by escalating the conflict with the left.

Obviously we cannot generalize from El Salvador in 1979 and 1980 to any other case or time period: this particular configuration of intra-state politics was unique. The generalization we can make is that intra-state politics can be a crucial determinant of how states actually behave. Exactly what the effect will be in a given situation depends upon the specific features of the case. This is not a popular argument to make in a discipline like political science that rewards simple, parsimonious explanations. Yet chances are good that a model of internal political violence that ignores intra-state politics and elite state–society relations will spawn inaccurate predictions about the timing, intensity, and targeting of violence in a given case and historical moment. When policy makers apply such models, as elements of the Salvadoran left and the U.S. embassy did during the 1979–80 crisis, the consequences can be disastrous.

Despite the appeal of simplicity, we have to accept that some of the most important determinants of internal state violence may be factors that are difficult to generalize. This is analogous to the increasing attention international relations scholars are giving to the specifics of how substate institutions and domestic politics determine international policies of states. The resulting theoretical perspective is not tidy, but it is more likely to produce adequate explanations for what actually happens.

Protection Rackets and Democratization

El Salvador's violent history demonstrates the difficulty of replacing a protection racket state with one based on broad political legitimacy. Not only did members of the upper class consider themselves generally well-served by the military-led state of 1932 through 1982, but conservative factions of the military itself demonstrated great capacity to defend the coercive character of the regime. Neither reformist initiatives from within the state nor mass opposition from civil society could overcome the violent countermeasures available to hardline individuals and institutions within the military.

The shift away from repression and coercion as the primary means of governing El Salvador, and the institutionalization of a less powerful and privileged role for the military, were possible only because the social elite consolidated greater political power, to the point of ideological and cultural hegemony in the Gramscian sense. Moreover, El Salvador achieved peace and demilitarization in a unique moment. The political party representing elite interests was at the peak of its electoral strength. The ideological challenge represented by the FMLN was waning because of the crumbling of socialist states in eastern Europe. The coercive strategy embodied in the armed forces was discredited as a result of the military's failure to defeat the rebels by force. Moreover, the military had become almost completely dependent upon U.S. aid. The international diplomatic blunder of killing the Jesuits hastened the deterioration of its prospects for ongoing military assistance and made it unable to resist ARENA initiatives to negotiate an end to the war at the military's expense.

Ironically, the FMLN, called totalitarian terrorists for most of the 1980s, ended up being a powerful force for political liberalism. Their unsuccessful effort to overthrow the military regime catalyzed a combination of U.S. intervention and political class formation among the upper and middle classes. The left forced the conservative upper and middle classes to stop depending on the military to govern for them. In the process, conservative civilians had to overcome (or set aside) their internal differences and build a political and ideological machine. Only when these forces were assembled were the privileged classes willing to depend on their own political legitimacy, rather than force, to protect their interests. Their incentive for making this effort, something they had never bothered to do in the past, was the FMLN's ability to deny them economic opportunities for the foreseeable future.

The outcome in El Salvador suggests an extension and modification of the views of Gramsci and Althusser regarding the use of force by subordinate classes. They both argued that "war of maneuver" or "frontal strategies"—the use of force to defeat the state—would not consolidate a revolution. Lasting change would come through "war of position"—that is, the development of an alternative counterideology and its dissemination and development within the subordinate classes, breaking the ideological hegemony of the upper classes (Carnoy 1984, 97). The success of the FMLN in breaking the upper classes' reliance on coercion, though it has had the immediate effect of consolidating hegemony for the upper classes, at least forced the now dominant classes to engage with the subordinate classes on ideological and political terms, rather than by shedding blood.

In the short run, things look bleak for the popular classes in El Salvador. The peace accord resulted in minimal socioeconomic reform, most of it targeted to benefit people directly involved in the struggle as combatants or civilian supporters of the rebels. Overall poverty, unemployment, and maldistribution of land and capital remain virtually unchanged from their prewar levels. Although the ARENA government seems likely to be able to generate rapid aggregate economic growth, the prospects for greater distributional equity remain uncertain, since much of the growth is premised on low-cost labor and highly mobile light industries. Migration to urban areas and abroad has eased rural unemployment, and the large flow of remittances from the Salvadoran diaspora has improved income distribution somewhat (Seligson 1994). However, these changes could prove temporary if large numbers of Salvadorans are forced to repatriate from the United States.

Despite these uncertainties, it seems likely in the long run that the poor in El Salvador will challenge the upper classes more effectively in the ideological and political arena than through violence. The state has always had the upper hand when it comes to coercion. In an ideological struggle, the popular classes will be disadvantaged by the current dominance of neo-liberal thought within the international community, but they will benefit from the prevailing emphasis on electoral democracy, international rejection of authoritarian governments, and increasingly dense monitoring and international sanctioning of human rights abuses. In such a climate, and with no Leninist strategic enemy for the United States to engage, the left in El Salvador may yet find an opportunity to challenge the ideological hegemony of the wealthy and play an important role in shaping the material realities of the country.

The fact that the peace accords and accompanying demilitarization were achieved under extraordinary circumstances raises questions about their longevity. What will happen as ARENA loses its electoral dominance, as most incumbents eventually do? The Salvadoran upper classes have in the past chosen the path of expedience, turning to the military to secure political protection that they were unwilling to earn for themselves. There remains a risk that they will do so again when their electoral fortunes decline, but there are strong reasons to expect that this will not happen. First, the political experiences of the 1980s militate against a return to the old repressive system. The members of the social elite who called for hardline solutions and financed death squads in the 1970s were still drawing upon the legacy of the *matanza* and its ideological dimensions. They believed that reformism and political openness paved the way to revolution, and that extreme measures by the state could restore a social order that would benefit them. A decade of civil war, the failure of the military to restore the status quo ante through force, the collapse of Leninism as an international threat, and the evident willingness of the FMLN to participate in an institutional political process all make it very clear that *Martinismo* is no longer a relevant political model for El Salvador. Even though ARENA leaders still feel the political need in public speeches to genuflect toward the military and the image of Roberto D'Aubuisson, the reality is that by the end of the 1980s D'Aubuisson himself no longer believed in or advocated *Martinismo*.

This process of learning has been reinforced by generational change. Most of the current and emerging leaders in ARENA and private sector peak associations were born after 1932. Their most formative experience with revolution and state repression was the civil war of the 1980s, in which coercion and political exclusion proved ineffective and costly. Although both the private sector and the military no doubt harbor individuals and groups who are still personally invested in the idea of a hardline state, they no longer dominate.

The current hegemony of neo-liberalism in the international economic system, as well as the increasing openness of the Salvadoran economy, may help preserve post–protection racket institutions. Even if a coalition of the left or center/left won the presidency or a majority in the legislature, it would be very constrained by international financial realities. No government could afford to attempt radical measures that might cause massive capital flight or suspension of international credits. Thus the private sector elite represented by ARENA would most likely choose to be a critical but loyal opposition, rather than soliciting the support of the military. Should ARENA be voted out of office, the social elite, having twice won the presidency and a majority in the legislature, will be unlikely to risk the opportunity of reclaiming that power in exchange for the short-term expedience of knocking at the barracks door.

Perhaps more importantly, military hardliners no longer have an adequate institutional base to advance an extortionist project, even if they were to find a receptive audience. The peace accords have virtually excluded the military from internal security duties. There is, of course, a risk that the new civilian police force will develop the same mercenary relationship with local elites as its predecessors. However, its recruitment, training, and disciplinary mechanisms, if properly implemented, should provide constraints on the use of violence and repression (Stanley 1995). Moreover, it is controlled by civilians and, in contrast to the military, has no historical tradition of claiming the right to govern. There is little likelihood, therefore, that it will be able to construct a national political protection racket of the kind maintained by the military for half a century.

The military itself has undergone additional changes that make it unlikely to reestablish the protection racket. The officers who are now reaching the senior ranks have spent at least half their career in a context in which army officers did not aspire to the presidency. The *tanda* system, infamous for reinforcing the legal impunity of officers and the advancement of undeserving men to positions of command, is likely to break down over the next decade. Large numbers of officers were hastily trained and commissioned in the 1980s under conditions that reduced opportunities for them to form bonds with academy classmates.[1] With the rapid shrinkage of the military after the end of hostilities, and the virtual end of U.S. aid, the officer corps presides over a very much reduced pie. Institutions like the military's social provision fund (IPSFA) are in financial turmoil as a result of earlier corruption and mismanagement.[2] In this climate, the leadership has largely accepted the military's reduced mission and is dedicated to promoting a narrower vision of military professionalism focused on national defense and emergency preparedness.[3] (Whether this trend continues depends on the success of the new civilian police force in dealing with the postwar increase in crime—as of late 1995, there were alarming signs that public outcry over crime might allow the military to reclaim, in practice if not in law, a portion of its historical role in public security.)

Unfortunately, the conditions that made this particular kind of transition possible in El Salvador are not likely to be reproduced in other countries, such as Guatemala, where the military retains a powerful role in government. Guatemala's National Revolutionary Unity (URNG) has not been able to hold the economy hostage as the FMLN did. The Guatemalan military is not as dependent on U.S. aid as the FAES was, and therefore is less vulnerable to international pressures to accept a reduced role. Nor has the Guatemalan elite confronted the kind of U.S.-imposed economic reform process implemented in El Salvador in 1980. They therefore have no incentive to undergo the process of political class formation that led to the moderate and broad-based ARENA party of the late 1980s and early 1990s. As a result, the Guatemalan military remains extremely powerful and still has the capacity to regulate political conditions through its use of repression. Until a powerful political counterweight to the military takes shape, Guatemala is unlikely to escape the pattern of violence and exclusion that has characterized its politics for four decades. Such a counterweight is more likely to form on the right than on the left, but since the Guatemalan elite has not experienced the overt failure of coercion that the Salvadoran elite did, its members probably would lack the political will to limit the military's role, even if they developed the formal political power to do so.

Another important lesson of the Salvadoran experience is that would-be reformers should not place their hopes in what Dermot Keogh (1983) has called "the myth of the reformist coup." A corporatist state in which elements of the state are operating a protection racket is unlikely to reform itself. The hardline agencies proved far better at shaping the political arena, and controlling the internal politics of the military through factional maneuvers and intimidation, than most observers of El Salvador understood in the 1970s and 1980s. This internal dynamic within the state, not merely the regime's lack of public legitimacy, is what Stepan (1978, 86) refers to as the "birth defect" of corporatist regimes. In light of this, the Mexican corporatist system's capacity to reform itself would seem to be vulnerable to internal resistance from within the state and Mexico's wave of political assassinations may reflect such resistance.

Lessons for International Actors

The United States was appallingly ineffective in defending human rights in El Salvador. Although the Reagan administration eventually succeeded in imposing a less bloody strategy of counterinsurgency on the FAES, by the time it did so at least 40,000 people had been murdered. More than 14,000 of these people died during the Carter administration, which claimed a commitment to defending human rights. In those days Cold War geostrategic interests made human rights protection secondary, so one of the main determinants of international failure to curb FAES abuses is no longer relevant. Yet some more general lessons may be applicable to future efforts by the United States and other international actors to intervene against state institutions that are murdering people.

First, the United States dramatically underestimated the internal pressures and incentives for state violence. During the Romero administration, for instance, the United States was incredibly casual about restoring aid to the Romero administration whenever it showed the least signs of moderating its abuses. Romero's almost instantaneous response to any relaxation of aid conditionality was, of course, to fulfill the demands of his *other* constituency, the domestic right. Similarly, the U.S. effort to use the promise and delay of new helicopters to encourage moderation on the part of García and Carranza in 1980 was astonishingly naive: a few aircraft did not compare to their factional and institutional incentives to move ahead with the terror campaign. The inconsistency and mildness of U.S. sanctions made them almost totally ineffectual. Only when serious money was involved, in a context of growing military danger, did the FAES cooperate, and then only to the degree absolutely required. In the meantime, the FAES was allowed to commit tens of thousands of murders with essentially no sanctions.

Just as the United States overlooked the incentives for violence presented by the internal politics of the military, it failed to recognize the opportunities internal divisions presented for changing state policy. In late 1979 and early 1980, the reformist movement within the military, though diffuse, represented an important potential counterweight to the growing power of the right wing within the force. The hundreds of junior officers and the troops they commanded represented a far more compelling force for moderating hardline conduct than did the U.S. promise of six helicopters. Yet the United States, which was willing to intervene in heavy-handed ways for purposes such as land reform or preservation of the Christian Democratic junta, stood by passively while the high command systematically picked apart Majano and his backers. A year later, General Fred Woerner's commission would bemoan the fact that there was no internal counterweight to the military's murderous right wing.

Part of the failure to appreciate the potential significance of the internal politics of the military was that portions of the U.S. embassy were not interested in providing Washington with this information. The contrast between Ambassador Devine's and Ambassador White's reports on the junior officers' movement is striking: Devine described them almost exclusively as a threat to stability, effectively denying Washington information that might have led to a different political strategy during the brief moment when the junior officers were still strong. White saw them as the key to a successful political solution to the conflict; yet by the time he arrived, the *Majanistas* were already weakened, and White's arguments were insufficient to sway Washington from its support for the high command.

Another contributing factor was the way U.S. personnel are rotated in and out of foreign assignments. In the Byzantine world of intra-military politics, senior FAES officers had 20 or more years of experience, while U.S. officials were still trying to figure out who was who. As a result, Defense Ministers Guillermo García, Eugenio Vides Casanova, and René Emilio Ponce were able to manipulate, sweet-talk, mislead, and betray their U.S. patrons with panache and impunity.

The relative inexperience of U.S. officials in the political environment of El Salvador was probably unavoidable. What was avoidable was the astonishing failure of the U.S. embassy to keep track of information about the key actors they were dealing with. Declassified State Department and CIA documents make it clear that by the late 1980s U.S. officials considered officers like Ponce and López Nuila to be among their allies and agents of influence within the military. Perusal of earlier cables regarding these individuals would have made it clear that each had been extensively involved in death squad activity and should not be trusted. The U.S. assessments seem to have been driven too much by the images that these officers chose to present.

Factional divisions within the U.S. foreign policy apparatus were nearly as significant as those within the Salvadoran military. Central Intelligence Agency and Defense Intelligence Agency operatives in El Salvador in 1979 and 1980 were virtually as dedicated to hardline anticommunist policies as their Salvadoran counterparts. The political solutions sought by the first junta and by Ambassador White ran counter to the ideology and self-perceived missions of these agents. While there are always differences of opinion within a government apparatus, and while hardliners in the embassy had every right to voice their views through proper channels, it is alarming that U.S. intelligence operatives, like their hardline Salvadoran colleagues, appear to have taken matters into their own hands to shape political events in ways consistent with their political views (SS 1886, 13 March 1980).

The U.S. role in El Salvador yields two positive lessons. For all of its flaws, the U.S. policy of promoting elections helped create a climate in which the most powerful political levers were obtained through the vote. This, combined with U.S. funding for the right-wing think tank FUSADES, contributed to the process of rightist political party formation that eventually permitted a negotiated solution and substantial demilitarization of the political system. Whatever one may think of ARENA, its role in government is considerably less likely than the military's protection racket regime to create incentives for state terrorism. This outcome was not foreseen by U.S. officials, who devoted themselves until the late 1980s to promoting the Christian Democrats.

The other lesson is that the separation of the military from public security functions achieved in the peace accords seems likely to minimize opportunities for protection racketeering. By aiding the development of the National Civilian Police, the U.S. has helped create an institutional counterweight to the military. Other countries could benefit from similar measures. Unfortunately, only in rare instances when militaries have become discredited (El Salvador and Argentina) or have been dismantled through foreign intervention (Panama and Haiti) have civilian governments had the political will and power to carry out such sweeping reforms.

Finally, the officials of protection racket regimes and agencies commit serious crimes for the ignoble purpose of personal advancement. Much of the violence they commit involves little personal risk. Victims are generally unarmed and lack powerful allies. The intellectual authors of the crimes order subordinates to do the dirty work, then have the perpetrators killed if they get caught and seem likely to talk. State-level protection racketeering is a cowardly business. This has important implications for international policy. International agencies must use their information and resources to hold *individuals* responsible for their crimes or at least create a climate in which individuals perceive some degree of risk in perpetrating them. It does not take much.

International technical assistance to investigations of death squads, even if ultimately unsuccessful in bringing individuals to justice, nonetheless increases the risks for the criminals. In most cases, their operations depend upon freedom of movement and confidence that they have protection and backing at high levels of police and military institutions. (Recall, for instance, that D'Aubuisson and his minions were *writing down* the details of their operations in a notebook in the midst of the political turmoil of 1980.) Any remotely serious investigation inhibits violent activities. Thus the work of the Joint Group for the Investigation of Illegal Armed Groups—which was sponsored by the United Nations and the Salvadoran government and which investigated death squad activities in 1993 and 1994—had a chilling effect on remaining assassination squads, even though it was unable to present sufficient evidence for legal actions. The earlier participation of U.S. and Venezuelan experts in investigating the military kidnappings during the Duarte presidency similarly unnerved the far right within the military. Even where domestic police and judicial institutions are weak and compromised, therefore, the international community can play a constructive, if transitory, role in preventing, if not punishing, violent crimes by state agents.

The international community can make a more lasting contribution through support for judicial reform. As with the civilianization of police, for judicial reform to be effective, the incumbent government must have the political will to implement the program. Such political will is rare, and without it international funds and technical assistance are likely to be largely wasted. Yet protection racketeering as a system depends on essentially air-tight impunity for those who commit the crimes. Even a modest degree of independence by investigatory and judicial institutions could significantly dampen the willingness of state elites to attempt such practices, and the willingness of civilian elites to sponsor them.

Unfortunately, the international community cannot transplant functional police and judicial institutions to a society that lacks political support for such changes. Ultimately, the ability of El Salvador or any other country to move beyond a protection racket state depends upon the desire and capacity of an internal political coalition to promote and defend alternatives to the old institutions. In a most basic and literal way, El Salvador's state was a criminal organization, and much of the nation's elite accepted that arrangement as necessary to ensure the state's capacity to deal with their political enemies. Organized criminals and anticommunist conservatives have made common cause, just as leftists became kidnappers, bank robbers, terrorists, and international arms traffickers to advance their political causes. While the peace accords mark a significant step toward establishing a system of individual accountability, it remains to be seen whether enough people believe strongly enough in reducing impunity to prevent state protection racketeering from taking root again.

APPENDIX A

Proclamation of the Armed Forces
of the Republic of El Salvador, 15 October 1979

A. The Armed Forces of El Salvador are fully conscious of their sacred duties toward the Salvadoran People and sympathize with the clamor of all of the people against a government that has

1. violated the Human Rights of the population;
2. fomented and tolerated corruption in public administration and the justice system;
3. created a veritable economic and social disaster;
4. profoundly discredited the country and the noble armed institution.

B. The Armed Forces are convinced that the problems mentioned are the product of antiquated economic, social, and political structures that have prevailed traditionally in the country, which do not provide the majority of inhabitants with the minimal conditions necessary for them to realize themselves fully as human beings. Moreover, the corruption and incapacity of the regime have caused mistrust on the part of the private sector, resulting in millions of colones in capital flight, intensifying the economic crisis at the expense of the popular sectors.

C. The Armed Forces are well aware that recent governments, products as they were of scandalous electoral frauds, have adopted inadequate programs of development. Those timid programs of structural change that have been attempted have been obstructed by the economic and political power of conservative sectors, which have consistently defended their ancestral privileges as dominant classes, endangering in the process the more socially progressive and conscious sectors of capital, which have shown an interest in achieving a form of economic development that would be more just toward the population.

D. The Armed Forces are firmly convinced that the conditions mentioned are the fundamental cause of the economic and social chaos and of the violence that we are suffering at the moment. These conditions can only be overcome through the arrival in power of a government that will guarantee the installation of a genuinely democratic regime.

Toward that end, the Armed Forces, whose members have always been identified with the people, hereby, on the basis of the Right of Insurrection that all peoples have when governments fail to uphold the Law, depose the Gov-

Source: Castro Morán 1989, 412–15. Translated from the Spanish by William Stanley.

ernment of General Carlos Humberto Romero and will immediately form a Revolutionary Governing Junta, composed in its majority of civilians whose honesty and competency is beyond all doubt. Said Junta will assume State Power with the goal of creating the necessary conditions under which all Salvadorans can have peace and live with the dignity that befits human beings.

While establishing the conditions necessary for the holding of genuinely free elections in which the people can decide its future, it is an unavoidable necessity, in view of the chaotic political situation in which the country is living, to adopt an Emergency Program containing urgent measures aimed at creating a climate of tranquility and at establishing the basis that will sustain the profound transformation of the economic, social, and political structures of the country.

The elements of this Emergency Program are the following:

I. STOP THE VIOLENCE AND CORRUPTION

A. Dissolving ORDEN and combating extremist organizations that violate Human Rights;

B. Eradicating corrupt practices in public administration and the justice system.

II. GUARANTEE THE PROTECTION OF HUMAN RIGHTS

A. Creating a propitious climate for the holding of genuinely free elections within a reasonable time frame;

B. Permitting the formation of political parties representing all ideologies, in a manner which will fortify the democratic system;

C. Granting a general amnesty to all political prisoners and exiles;

D. Recognizing and respecting the right of laborers to organize and form unions;

E. Stimulating free expression of thought in accordance with prevailing ethical standards.

III. ADOPT MEASURES CONDUCIVE TO AN EQUITABLE DISTRIBUTION OF NATIONAL WEALTH, INCREASING AT THE SAME TIME THE GROSS NATIONAL PRODUCT

A. Creating a solid basis for initiating a process of Agrarian Reform;

B. Furnishing greater economic opportunities for the population by means of reforms in finance, the tax system, and foreign trade;

C. Adopting measures for the protection of consumers, counteracting the effects of inflation;

D. Implementing special development programs designed to increase national production and create additional sources of employment;

E. Recognizing and guaranteeing the basic right to housing, food, education, and health of all inhabitants of the country.

IV. PURSUE A CONSTRUCTIVE FOREIGN POLICY

A. Reestablishing relations with Honduras as quickly as possible;

B. Strengthening ties with the people of Nicaragua and their government;

C. Tightening our ties with the peoples and governments of our fellow republics Guatemala, Costa Rica, and Panama;

D. Establishing cordial relations with all countries that are disposed to aid the struggles of our people and respect our sovereignty;

E. Guaranteeing the fulfillment of existing international commitments.

To achieve the accelerated implementation of these measures which the Salvadoran people has, with all justice, demanded, the Revolutionary Governing Junta will assemble a cabinet, formed by honest and capable individuals, representing diverse sectors of society, who will apply all of their patriotism to the performance of their vital roles.

In this moment of genuine national emergency, we make a special appeal to the popular sectors and to socially progressive sectors of private capital to contribute to the creation of a new epoch for El Salvador, guided by the principles of peace and respect embodied in the human rights of all citizens.

APPENDIX B

Statement of the Martínez Anti-Communist Brigade

The following statement was given to newspapers after the assassination of six leaders of the Democratic Revolutionary Front (FDR) on 27 November 1980:

We make known to the citizenry in general: today we, a squadron of the General Maximiliano Hernández Martínez Anti-Communist Brigade, make known our responsibility for the just execution of the communists of the FDR: Enrique Alvarez, Juan Chacón, Enrique Barrera, Manuel Franco, and Humberto Mendoza, for being materially and intellectually responsible for thousands of assassinations of innocent people who did not want to be communists. We also warn the priests who have an affinity for the terrorist Marxist bands that they will have the same fate if they insist in their sermons on poisoning the minds of Salvadoran youth. The Brigade will continue the just executions of the traitors to our country.

APPENDIX C

Draft Manifesto by Major Roberto D'Aubuisson for Use in Aborted Right-Wing Coup of May 1980

In our country, the influence of the Trilateral Commission began with the coup d'état of October 15, 1979, which was promoted by Carter and Cyrus Vance (head of the Department of State and creature of the Trilateral Commission). They installed a revolutionary governing junta in our country with the participation of the Christian Democrats, International Socialists, multinational corporations, communists and military officers. This shrimp salad, together with its cabinet of guerrilla fighters, was never able to reach any agreement and the first JRG resigned.

Wednesday, January 9, 1980, a second Revolutionary Governing Junta was formed. The military and the communists remained in this government and the Trilateral Commission thereby retained its power and they believed that by putting Christian Democrats in the second JRG they might be able to gain popular support. When this proved false and the Trilateral Commission was on the verge of losing its control of El Salvador, it provoked the resignation of Dada Hirezi and replaced him with Napoleón Duarte, whom they regarded as the Imam of the masses. They also decided it was necessary to send a loyal spy to the country and thus on Tuesday, the 11th of March 1980, Robert White, a left-wing socialist, arrived in the country. Robert White quickly analyzed the studies prepared by the Department of State of the JRG No. 2 and the political career of Napoleón Duarte and understood that neither could count on popular support. The program of the Trilateral Commission was thus in danger and another alternative would have to be found to achieve popular support. Therefore it was necessary to undermine the prestige of the second and reformed JRG No. 2. On the 24th of March 1980, only 13 days after Robert White's arrival, Cuban communists were hired to assassinate Monsignor Oscar Arnulfo Romero. The JRG was left tottering. The first week of April Robert White left for Washington, where he argued that the survival in power of the Trilateral Commission in El Salvador necessitated a government with enough popular support to avert a civil war. He calls an invasion of mercenary communists operating from a base in the territory of our Nicaraguan brothers "civil war". Robert White returned to El Salvador the 6th of April and only 12 days afterward the Frente Democrático Revolucionario,

Source: SS 3268, 8 May 1980.

social democratic coalition, was formed as a last alternative for installing a communist regime in the country.

The Revolutionary Democratic Front, which is nothing but the conversation carried on among Robert White, Col. Arnoldo Majano, Juan Chacón and Pichinte, produced the required results, and the FDR merged with the Coordinadora Revolucionaria de Masas (CRM). This is the new alternative that is being prepared for El Salvador. This alternative was presented to FENAPES the 29th of April by an emissary of Robert White, who asked the FDR to support the naming of Juan Chacón to the Revolutionary Governing Junta. This proposal was rejected.

Lacking approval for this scheme, the campaign of destabilization against the second Revolutionary Governing Junta (reformed) was planned by Robert White, who used the CRM to secure the resignations of various ministers in order to bring down the second JRG (reformed) and to put the Frente Democrático Revolucionario and the Coordinadora Revolucionaria de Masas in power. For them this was the last alternative because, as is publicly well known, the National University and AGEUS [General Association of Salvadoran University Students] are in the hands of the communists and have supported the coalition of the FDR and CRM.

The plan is to turn Central America into a Cuban paradise. Salvadoran military officers: these are to be your new rulers and this is to be the *golpe d'estado politico* [political coup d'état]. Salvadoran military officers: the people are depending on your intelligence and on the integrity of the Armed Forces. We know how small communist penetration has been in your ranks. The people and the Armed Forces will stop the communist advance. Long live the Armed Forces. Long live liberty. Death to communism.

ABBREVIATIONS AND ACRONYMS

ABECAFE	Asociación Salvadoreña de Beneficiadores y Exportadores de Café (Salvadoran Association of Processors and Exporters of Coffee)
AD	Acción Democrática (Democratic Action)
AID	United States Agency for International Development
AIFLD	American Institute for Free Labor Development
ANDES	Asociación Nacional de Educadores Salvadoreños (National Association of Salvadoran Educators)
ANEP	Asociación Nacional de Empresa Privada (National Association of Private Enterprise)
ANSESAL	Agencia Nacional de Servicios Especiales de El Salvador (Salvadoran National Special Services Agency)
ANTEL	Asociación Nacional de Telecomunicación (National Telecommunications Company)
ARENA	Alianza Republicana Nacional (National Republican Alliance)
ASCAFE	Asociación Salvadoreña de Café (Salvadoran Coffee Association)
ASI	Asociación Salvadoreña de Industrias (Salvadoran Industrial Association)
ATACES	Asociación de Trabajadores Agropecuarios y Campesinos de El Salvador (Salvadoran Association of Agricultural Workers and Peasants)
BIRI	Batallón de Infantería de Reacción Inmediata (Rapid Reaction Infantry Battalion)
BPR	Bloque Popular Revolucionario (Popular Revolutionary Bloc)
CACM	Central American Common Market
CAEM	Centro de Altos Estudios Militares (Center for Higher Military Studies)
CAIN	Centro de Análisis e Investigaciones Nacional (National Center for Analysis and Investigations)
CDHES	Comisión de Derechos Humanos de El Salvador—No Gobernamental (Non-Governmental Human Rights Commission of El Salvador)

CEL	Comisión Ejecutiva Hidroeléctrica del Río Lempa (Lempa River Hydroelectric Power Commission)
CEPAL	Comisión Economica para America Latina y el Caribe (Economic Commission for Latin America and the Caribbean)
CGTS	Confederación General de Trabajadores de El Salvador (General Federation of Salvadoran Workers)
CIA	Central Intelligence Agency
COMADRES	Comité de Madres de Detenidos, Desaparecidos y Asesinados (Committee of Mothers of the Detained, the Disappeared, and the Assassinated)
CONAPLAN	Consejo Nacional de Planificación (National Planning Council)
CONDECA	Consejo de Defensa Centroamericano (Central American Defense Council)
CONFRAS	Confederación de la Reforma Agraria Salvadoreña (Salvadoran Agrarian Reform Confederation)
COPAZ	Comisión para la Consolidación de Paz (Commission for the Consolidation of Peace)
COPEFA	Consejo Permanente de la Fuerza Armada (Permanent Council of the Armed Forces)
CRM	Coordinadora Revolucionaria de Masas (Revolutionary Coordinator of Masses)
DRU	Dirección Revolucionaria Unificada (Unified Revolutionary Directorate)
ERP	Ejercito Revolucionario del Pueblo (People's Revolutionary Army)
ESF	Economic Support Funds
FAES	Fuerzas Armadas de El Salvador (Salvadoran Armed Forces)
FAL	Fuerzas Armadas de Liberación (Armed Forces of Liberation)
FALANGE	Fuerzas Armadas de Liberación Anticomunista de Guerras de Eliminación (Anti-Communist Armed Forces of Liberation by Wars of Elimination)
FAN	Frente Amplio Nacional (Broad National Front)
FAPU	Frente de Acción Popular Unificada (United Popular Action Front)
FARC	Fuerzas Armadas Revolucionarias de Colombia (Revolutionary Armed Forces of Colombia)
FARN	Fuerzas Armadas de Resistencia Nacional (Armed Forces of National Resistance)

FARO	Frente de Agricultores de la Región Oriental (Agriculturalists' Front of the Eastern Region)
FDR	Frente Democrático Revolucionario (Democratic Revolutionary Front)
FECCAS	Federación Cristiana de Campesinos Salvadoreños (Christian Federation of Salvadoran Peasants)
FENAGH	Federación Nacional de Agricultores y Ganaderos Hondureño (Honduran National Federation of Growers and Cattlemen)
FESINCONSTRANS	Federación de Sindicatos de Construcción, Transportes y Similares (Federation of Construction, Transport and Allied Trade Unions)
FMLN	Frente Farabundo Martí de Liberación Nacional (Farabundo Martí Front for National Liberation)
FNOC	Frente Nacional de Orientación Cívica (National Civic Orientation Front)
FPL	Fuerzas Populares de Liberación—Farabundo Martí (Popular Forces of Liberation—Farabundo Martí)
FTC	Federación de Trabajadores del Campo (Federation of Rural Workers)
FUAR	Frente Unido de Acción Revolucionaria (United Revolutionary Action Front)
FUDI	Frente Unido Democrático Independiente (United Independent Democratic Front)
FUSADES	Fundación Salvadoreña de Desarrollo Economico y Social (Salvadoran Foundation for Economic and Social Development)
FUSS	Federación Unitaria Sindical Salvadoreña (Salvadoran Unitary Trade Union Federation)
IDB	Inter-American Development Bank
INSAFI	Instituto Salvadoreño de Fomento Industrial (Salvadoran Institute for Industry Promotion)
ISTA	Instituto Salvadoreño de Transformación Agraria (Salvadoran Institute for Agrarian Transformation)
JRG	Junta Revolucionaria de Gobierno (Revolutionary Governing Junta)
LP-28	Ligas Populares de 28 Febrero (Popular Leagues of 28 February)
MJM	Movimiento de la Juventud Militar (Military Youth Movement)
MNR	Movimiento Nacional Revolucionario (National Revolutionary Movement)

MNS	Movimiento Nacionalista Salvadoreño (Salvadoran Nationalist Movement)
MPSC	Movimiento Popular Social Cristiano (Popular Social Christian Movement)
MTT	Mobile Training Team
OAS	Organization of American States
ONUSAL	Misión de Observadores de las Naciones Unidades en El Salvador (United Nations Observer Mission in El Salvador)
ORDEN	Organización Democrática Nacionalista (Democratic Nationalist Organization)
PAR	Partido de Acción Renovadora (Renovating Action Party)
PCN	Partido de Conciliación Nacional (National Concilation Party)
PCS	Partido Comunista Salvadoreño (Salvadoran Communist Party)
PDC	Partido Demócrata Cristiano (Christian Democratic Party)
PN	Policía Nacional (National Police)
PNC	Policía Nacional Civil (National Civilian Police)
PPS	Partido Popular Salvadoreño (Salvadoran Popular Party)
PRAM	Partido Revolucionario Abril y Mayo (April and May Revolutionary Party)
PRI	Partido Revolucionario Institucional (Institutional Revolutionary Party)
PRTC	Partido Revolucionario de Trabajadores Centroamericanos (Revolutionary Party of Central American Workers)
PRUD	Partido Revolucionario de Unificación Democrática (Revolutionary Party of Democratic Unification)
PUD	Partido de Unión Decocrática (Democratic Union Party)
PUSD	Partido de Unificación Social Demócratica (Unification Social Democratic Party)
SIE	Sección de Investigaciones Especiales (Special Investigations Section)
SJC	Socorro Jurídico Cristiano (Christian Legal Aid)
STECEL	Sindicato de Trabajadores de la Empresa Comisión Ejecutiva Hidroeléctrica del Río Lempa (Union of Workers of the Lempa River Hydroelectric Power Commission)

UCA	Universidad Centroamericana José Simeón Cañas (University of Central America José Simeón Cañas)
UCS	Unión Comunal Salvadoreña (Salvadoran Communal Union)
UDN	Unión Democrática Nacional (National Democratic Union)
UGB	Unión Guerrera Blanca (White Warriors' Union)
UN	United Nations
UNO	Unión Nacional Opositora (National Opposition Union)
UNT	Unión Nacional Trabajadores (National Workers' Union)
UNTS	Unidad Nacional de Trabajadores Salvadoreños (National Unity of Salvadoran Workers)
UP	Unión Patriotica (Patriotic Union)
UPD	Unidad Popular Democrática (Popular Democratic Unity)
URNG	Unidad Revolucionaria Nacional Guatemalteca (Guatemalan National Revolutionary Unity)
UTC	Unión de Trabajadores Campestres (Union of Rural Workers)

NOTES

Introduction

1. Many sources cite a figure of 70,000 without stating exactly how it was arrived at. It may well be close to the truth, since human rights organizations faced considerable difficulty in documenting and counting deaths in rural areas. Organizations such as Tutela Legal and Socorro Jurídico have documentation for closer to 50,000 cases for the period 1978–1990.

2. The human rights organization Socorro Jurídico Cristiano reports that in 1978 government forces and death squads killed 687 civilians; in 1979, this rate more than doubled to 1,792. During 1980, which was a turning point, government forces murdered at least 11,895 people. The peak year was 1981, with over 16,000 civilians killed. During 1982 and 1983, government forces killed over five thousand civilians per year (Socorro Jurídico Cristiano 1984).

3. The journalist Tom Gibb learned of the use of the meat packing plant from sources formerly with the National Police, as well as survivors of National Police interrogation (personal communication, January, February, August 1994; see also U.S. Department of State cable SS 6390, 26 August 1981, U.S. Embassy, San Salvador: "Violence Week in Review August 15–22," in National Security Archive collection 1989b).

4. The verb "to disappear" is used in Central American Spanish as a transitive verb—that is, a verb with an object, as in "death squads disappeared dozens of people during 1979." This usage began in Guatemala.

5. State violence was far more intense in Guatemala and El Salvador than in any of the more notorious episodes of state violence in the hemisphere. For example, secret cells of the Argentine military "disappeared" at least 8,960 people during the "dirty war" from 1976 through 1979. Some estimates run as high as 20,000 killed, out of a population of 28.2 million (Sloan 1984, 87). Even using the high-end estimates of killings, in per capita terms the Argentine dirty war was less than one-tenth as violent as the 1978–1983 period in El Salvador. According to an investigative commission, the military regime of Augusto Pinochet in Chile killed or disappeared 2,115 people (Comisión Nacional de Verdad y Reconciliación 1991). Beginning in September 1973, the Pinochet government also arrested an estimated 60,000 people from a population of around 10 million, in the process of taking and consolidating power (Sloan 1984, 86). In per capita terms Chilean state violence was roughly one-hundredth as intense as that of El Salvador. The Brazilian military used deadly force far less than the Argentines or the Chileans, disappearing over a hundred people and imprisoning and torturing thousands for political reasons beginning in the late 1960s. The Uruguayan government arrested and tortured tens of thousands (one in every fifty by one estimate) in a crackdown between 1973 and 1977, but killed no more than two hundred (Amnesty International 1979, 5, 10; Remmer and Merkx 1983, 13). The only countries that approach the Central American levels of violence in per capita terms are Peru and

Colombia, which are both currently experiencing high levels of political violence, some of which is state terrorism against suspected regime opponents.

6. Greater intensity and randomness tend to go hand in hand, largely because intensity is achieved at the expense of good intelligence. As more units and individuals become involved in repressive activity, targeting tends to be based increasingly on hunches, crude profiles of probable subversives, and geographic proximity to suspected guerrilla activity. See Chapter Six.

7. I cite documents from three collections. The first is *El Salvador: The Making of U.S. Policy, 1977–1984*, assembled by the National Security Archive (hereafter NSA 1989b.) This microfiche document collection includes a two-volume hardcopy guide and index, and is published by Chadwyck-Healey of Alexandria, Virginia. Most of the documents were obtained by various journalists under the Freedom of Information Act. Many are heavily redacted. The second collection, entitled *El Salvador: Human Rights, 1980–1993*, includes documents declassified by the Department of State, the Department of Defense, and the Central Intelligence Agency. These documents were identified in response to requests by the United Nations Commission on Truth for El Salvador for information regarding a series of human rights cases and are organized according to these cases. Additional documents were identified by an internal evaluation panel set up by the Secretary of State. Under pressure from Congress, the Clinton administration released the collection to the public in November 1993. The State Department documents are remarkably free of censorship, while the Defense and CIA documents tend to be more heavily redacted. At the time I conducted my research, the State Department volumes were available for public viewing through the State Department Office of Freedom of Information and Privacy. The Department of Defense and Central Intelligence Agency documents were held in the Periodicals Reading Room of the Library of Congress. A third collection released to the public in August 1994, entitled simply "El Salvador II," includes documents from the Department of State, the Department of Defense, the Central Intelligence Agency, and the National Security Council. This collection resulted from a request from congressional Republicans that focused on the Carter administration and on U.S. intelligence regarding the FMLN guerrillas. At the time I conducted my research, these documents were available to the public through the House International Relations Committee.

Chapter One

1. The total for battlefield deaths is 38.5 million. Rummel uses the term "democide" for government mass murder of noncombatant civilians, either through direct action or through policies that create conditions that can be reasonably expected to be lethal. He distinguishes between democide and genocide, which as commonly used includes such nonlethal actions as removing children from the care of a particular ethnic group, potentially destroying the group but not killing the individual human beings (1994b, 31–43).

2. Studies of totalitarian regimes were among the few writings to focus primarily on state violence: see, for example, Dallin and Breslauer 1970; two major studies — Hibbs 1973 and Duff and McCamant 1976 — examined the interactions of opposition and state violence.

In the 1980s a series of edited volumes focused on internal violence by states: Stohl and Lopez 1984, 1986; Lopez and Stohl 1989; Bushnell et al. 1991. There were also a few books: McClintock 1985a, 1985b; Moreira Alves 1985; Pion-Berlin 1989; and Rummel 1990, 1991, 1992, 1994a, 1994b; and some articles and papers: Banks 1986; Bollen 1986; Goldstein 1986; Mitchell and McCormick 1988; Mason and Krane 1989; and Lauria Santiago 1991.

3. Protest and Internal War are variable names and thus capitalized in the original.

4. Some versions of this argument, including that of O'Donnell (1978), adopt the structural view that the state will defend the capitalist order, but not necessarily the interests of capitalists. In other words, the state may carry out policies that hurt entire sectors of the capitalist classes, but will use coercion as necessary to prevent challenges to capitalism as a system.

5. Baloyra adapted the term "reactionary despotism" from Giner (1979).

6. Some believe that land privatization affected indigenous communities in Guatemala. Pérez-Brignoli argues, correctly, that the Mayan communities in the highlands were little affected by these changes in land tenure, though they were affected by subsequent vagrancy laws and other labor-coercive measures (1989, 84–85).

7. Corporatism is a form of government in which political participation is channeled through a limited number of official parties and organizations, rather than through the plethora of independent parties and interest groupings characteristic of pluralism. Exclusionary corporatist regimes differ from pure authoritarian regimes in that there are at least the forms of popular consultation and incorporation, though these may be so tightly controlled from above as to be effectively meaningless. Inclusionary corporatist regimes differ from populist regimes in that the latter generally lack formal, state-sponsored mechanisms of interest mediation such as official unions or party structures. Although Stepan is writing specifically about corporatism, his distinction between inclusionary and exclusionary strategies can be applied to any nondemocratic regime.

8. Bueno de Mesquita and Lalman, for instance, argue that from a realist point of view, with full information states should never go to war (1992, 60).

9. Other factors that can affect the ability of a leadership group to take power include how well known it is, whether it is seen as having international support, and whether it has good access to military or organizational resources.

10. Although the Argentine, Uruguayan, and Salvadoran states have literally harbored organized crime activity against wealthy citizens such as kidnapping for ransom, theft, and killing for hire, there is a broader analogy to be drawn about the political relationship between the state and civilian economic elites.

Chapter Two

1. The urban police force at this time was called the Policía de Línea. The name was later changed to Policía Nacional, though the institution remained continuous until it was replaced by a civilian force in 1994. For simplicity, I have used the term National Police throughout.

2. Kenneth Grieb (1971, 42–43). This description is based on interviews with Robert Gregg, then a resident of San Salvador.

3. Hernández Martínez is always referred to in Salvadoran histories as Martínez, contrary to the usual emphasis on the paternal surname in Spanish. According to Grieb (1971, 153), the American minister in San Salvador was sufficiently uncertain of the military's attitude toward the 1931 elections that he requested that a warship be held in readiness in Panama for hasty deployment to El Salvador should a revolt take place.

4. Under the provisions of the 1922 loan, El Salvador retained control of its own customs houses, though the U.S. fiscal representative, William Renwick, was empowered to allocate a substantial share of the revenues to bondholders abroad. Renwick made his presence as benign as possible through his tact, low profile, and evident love and respect for the country. Nonetheless, his role raised questions about Salvadoran sovereignty, and it was widely expected that the next loan could involve direct foreign control of customs houses or other heavy-handed fiscal intervention (Astilla Carmelo 1976, 27).

5. Secretary of State Henry Stimson "was very disappointed with the way his Minister had acted during the emergency. . . . Curtis had served as American Minister in Santo Domingo, where, according to Stimson, 'he had done badly.' His tenure in El Salvador was disappointing as well, prompting Stimson to write in his diary that 'It only shows that when you have a man who isn't quite up to snuff, the lightning is sure to strike wherever you put him'" (Astilla Carmelo 1976, 45).

6. Some observers have argued that Martínez' belief in the transmigration of souls made him less concerned than most leaders about taking human lives, but I would argue that these views merely facilitated what he already had powerful political incentives to do.

7. These included Alfonso Rochac, auditor of the Treasury, Margarito González Guerrero, chief of the legal staff of the Treasury; Manuel López Harrison, undersecretary of public works; Hermógenes Alvarado, undersecretary of government; David Rosales, undersecretary of public instruction; Max Patricio Brannon, undersecretary of finance; and Agustín Alfaro Morán, auditor general of the Republic (Parkman 1988, 30–31).

8. Even though the Meléndez-Quiñónez families had controlled the presidency for three terms, no *individual* had served more than one consecutive term, thus observing the constitutional prohibition on *continuismo*.

9. By the 1970s it was common for academy-trained army officers to serve for a time in the security forces. Many security forces officers, however, were promoted from the ranks and served only in the security forces. In the 1930s and 1940s, the forces were even more separate.

10. Castro Morán (1989, 177–78). Mariano Castro Morán, then a lieutenant, was among those sentenced.

Chapter Three

1. One of the three, Fabio Castillo, later ran for president as the candidate of the Renovating Action Party (PAR) after it had been taken over by the Communists.

2. *Foco guerrillero* refers to the model of revolutionary struggle that was successful in Cuba—namely, use of military action, rather than mass organizing, to destabilize and ultimately overthrow a vulnerable regime. For this brief period, the PCS focused its energies on developing a military capability rather than expanding on its traditional union organizing activities.

3. ORDEN's mission statement included the following goals: "1) promulgate the ideas of the organization; 2) maintain a positive image for the organization; 3) contribute to the formation of public opinion favorable to the policies of the nationalist government; 4) persuade others to follow the line of action of the movement; 5) combat antidemocratic practices of individuals and organizations; 6) inform the public regarding the programs of the organization; 7) collect, interpret, and transmit public opinion" (Cabarrús 1983, 260). As Sara Gordon (1989, 142) observes, ORDEN's methods were hardly democratic: to "collect, interpret, and transmit public opinion," it engaged in espionage; to "combat antidemocratic practices," it used armed violence.

4. Most of the early migrants were recruited by foreign-owned plantations in Honduras' north coast banana enclave, which valued Salvadorans as particularly efficient and diligent workers. The role of Salvadorans on the banana plantations diminished after a series of Honduran-led agricultural labor strikes in 1954 led to laws excluding foreign nationals from plantation jobs (Anderson 1982, 58). These laws appear to have been ineffectively enforced; in the 1960s, 30 percent of all workers on the plantations were Salvadorans (Durham 1979, 124). Salvadorans were also recruited to work in the mines in central Honduras. In 1906 the Honduran government had actually offered free land, unencumbered by taxes, for Salvadoran immigrants willing to help colonize and cultivate remote areas of the north coast lowlands (Anderson 1982, 71–72).

5. Interviews with Salvadoran army officers, August–September 1989.

6. Interview with Salvadoran army general, September 1989.

7. Though the left committed this murder, it was widely thought in San Salvador at the time that it had been committed by the right. The London-based *Latin America Weekly Report* recounted these suspicions: "Although no direct link has been established between the PCN and the unknown kidnappers, it is widely believed in San Salvador that the murder was a desperate attempt by the right-wing of the party [PCN] to arouse the country to the dangers of left-wing terrorism and to stampede the party into choosing a hardline candidate—preferably General Alberto Medrano, former head of the National Guard and until recently the government's strong man. The accusation that the Left was responsible lacked credibility even among those who would have liked to believe it. Observers argue that a left-wing group would have claimed responsibility for such an action as a victory, and would anyway have collected the ransom money" (cited in McClintock 1985a, 167). These rumors of rightist involvement give some indication of the divisions within the military, as well as the strains between the top military leadership and leading civilian sectors.

8. Interview with Salvadoran army colonels, September 1989.

9. The officer in question was Sigifredo Ochoa, who, despite his initial support for the 1972 coup, later emerged as a prominent hardliner within the military and subsequently as an ARENA deputy in the legislature (Mena Sandoval 1992, 97). Another source charges that Ochoa actually notified the minister of defense, General Fidel Torres, enabling him to evade the rebel forces and assemble other senior officers. Interview with retired senior officer, October 1989.

10. Interview with retired senior official with direct knowledge of events of 1972, September 1989.

11. This volatility is amplified by the particular ideological formation of military officers, for whom certain issues of institutional tradition often outweigh political issues

such as reformism, democracy, or repression. A former senior government official told me that an important contributing factor to the collapse of the 1972 movement was the fact that Colonel Mejía permitted the civilian member of the "Revolutionary Junta," Manuel Rafael Reyes Alvarado, to dress in a military uniform at the rebels' headquarters. A photo was taken of the three junta members, including Reyes, holding G-3 rifles. Word spread throughout the rebel units that "the civilian" had been photographed in uniform, causing a number of officers to defect with their troops. Interview with retired senior official, September 1989.

12. Interview with Ambassador William Walker, who served as political officer in the U.S. Embassy in San Salvador from 1974 to 1977, July 1992.

13. Among those who resigned were Benjamín Noyla, executive secretary of CONAPLAN; Enrique Alvarez Cordova from the Ministry of Agriculture, who played an important role in subsequent land reform efforts and was murdered by the security forces in November 1980; and Salvador Sánchez Aguillón of the Ministry of Economy (Gordon 1989, 168).

14. Between 1971 and 1975, the government had to provide tax credits amounting to more than 50 percent of an average worker's salary *per job created* in the industrial sector. The percentage rose during this period to 84 percent of an average industrial salary. In effect, the industrial sector, though ostensibly private, was hardly more efficient than direct public employment (Gordon 1989, 161).

15. Interview with Leonel Gómez, March 1989.

16. The ERP at this point focused on military preparations rather than forming mass organizations.

17. Pelupessy points out, for instance, that banks made 25 percent of their loans to traditional agricultural crop production, which generated only 10 percent of the Gross Domestic Product. These figures suggest a bias in lending practices toward the agrarian oligarchy (1987, 73).

18. Interview with journalist Tom Gibb, February 1994. Gibb learned about the use of the Customs service by ANSESAL through members of the National Resistance who killed a Customs Police agent in the late 1970s and recovered extensive documents linking him to ANSESAL and to other Customs officials.

19. Confidential interviews with military officers, 1989, 1992 and 1993.

20. "1er. Pronunciamiento de ANEP," *Estudios Centroamericanos* 31, no. 335/336 (September–October 1976): 611–12.

21. "1er. Respuesta del Gobierno," ibid., 615–16.

22. Several members of the private sector elite and the ARENA party whom I interviewed in 1989 used the same argument, as had several Reagan administration officials interviewed during 1987.

23. *Estudios Centroamericanos* 31, nos. 335/336 (September–October 1976) 614.

24. "2a Respuesta del Gobierno," ibid., 617.

25. Ibid., 618.

26. "3a Respuesta del Gobierno," ibid., 618–620.

27. Interview with retired senior official, August 1989.

28. Interview with former senior official with direct knowledge of these decisions, September 1989.

29. Interview with former advisor to President Molina, August 1989.

30. Interview with retired senior official, September 1989.

Chapter Four

1. The contrast in the level of official violence is telling: whereas under Molina the government assassinated 37 people and disappeared 69, under Romero these numbers increased to 461 and 131 respectively. The Romero government also made four times as many political arrests (López Vallecillos 1979b, 871).

2. Interview with Ambassador William Walker, July 1992.

3. The use of horsemanship to build political contacts with the elite was not confined to Carlos Romero. Another officer, Sigifredo Ochoa, in exile after his participation in and betrayal of the 1972 coup, taught equestrian arts to the daughters of wealthy Costa Rican families. This led to a similar role upon his return to El Salvador, and Ochoa, who had initially sided with the *juventud militar* in 1972, became rehabilitated as a hardliner. Interview with retired senior officer, August 1989.

4. Although not especially competent, Romero had training and experience consistent with his hardline political orientation. He had taken a three-month U.S. "Counter-Insurgency Course" in the Canal Zone during the early 1960s and, as an intelligence officer during the mid-1960s, worked closely with U.S. Military Group advisors and Office of Public Safety advisors on the restructuring of El Salvador's intelligence apparatus (McClintock 1985a, 192–93).

5. The U.S. citizen was Ronald James Richardson, who was arrested by the Salvadoran Immigration Police on the basis of theft complaints against him in Nicaragua. He was tortured and killed while in custody. Confidential interview with former Salvadoran government official, April 1989. See also U.S. Department of State Cables SJ 1091, SJ 1092 from San José, Costa Rica, 8 March 1978.

6. Mark Schneider was particularly effective in getting Salvadoran human rights issues on the Washington agenda. As a former Peace Corps volunteer in El Salvador, he had in-depth knowledge of the country and its political system. His expertise, combined with his bureaucratic skills, enabled him to push the State Department toward taking more account of human rights issues in El Salvador than the professional diplomatic corps might otherwise have preferred. Following the collapse of the Somoza regime, however, security concerns became the focus of attention, and Schneider lost much of his influence. Interview with Ambassador Viron Vaky, April 1990.

7. September's actions included the kidnapping of the wife of a prominent U.S. businessman, the assassination of the rector of the National University, attacks by the Popular Forces of Liberation on a National Guard post and seizure of 15 radio stations to broadcast proclamations, and the invasion of a high school (NSA 1989a, 14).

8. In his book, Devine (1981) questions the motives of human rights monitoring groups, offering as counterevidence the denials made by the armed forces. He cites uncritically the claims of Salvadoran military officials that the "disappeared" had generally gone into hiding to be guerrillas or had gone to Cuba to receive training. He refers to the "traditions" of "frontier justice" meted out by the security forces, implying that much of the killing was justified.

9. *Diario de Hoy*, 16 November 1977, quoted in Dunkerly (1985, 113).

10. *Diario de Hoy*, 24 November 1977, quoted in Dunkerly (1985, 113).

11. Frank Smyth is a journalist who covered the war in El Salvador from 1986 through 1990. Interview, September 1989.

12. Interviews with Salvadoran businessmen, July and August 1993; interview with former U.S. intelligence official, April 1990. Major Guillermo Roeder was arrested in 1982 for crimes ranging from embezzlement to murder. He was acquitted of all charges. See declassified Central Intelligence Agency document, "El Salvador: Controlling Rightwing Terrorism—An Intelligence Assessment," Directorate of Intelligence, Office of African and Latin American Analysis, February 1985.

13. Interviews with former senior government officials and business association leaders, August 1993; interview with U.S. diplomat, August 1992. The claim of extensive military involvement in kidnapping was corroborated by a former Salvadoran government official with close ties to the military in an interview conducted in July 1989. See also "Un relato histórico" (Anonymous 1994).

14. A leading cotton grower from the eastern part of the country confirmed in an interview that in the late 1970s the National Guard had repeatedly attempted to kidnap him and on one occasion almost captured his mother. Interview, July 1993.

15. Former officers and enlisted men from the security forces consistently told me about the casualties their forces had suffered at the hands of the guerrillas during the 1970s.

16. Interview with a businessman, July 1993; interview with a former official of the University of Central America, April 1990. Other business, political party, and Catholic Church informants confirm that such meetings were held. See also Guido Véjar (1980b), cited in Gordon (1989, 255).

17. Interviews with members of the Salvadoran industrial and commercial elite, July–August 1993.

18. Interview with Luis Cardenal, July 1993.

19. Interview with a prominent merchant, July 1993.

20. Interview with journalists Tom Gibb and Douglas Farah, August 1989, October 1989. See also Gibb and Farah (1989).

21. Interviews with peasant organization leaders from Usulután, August 1989, October 1989.

22. See Gibb and Farah (1989); interviews with Gibb and Farah, August 1989, October 1989.

23. Interview by Elizabeth Wood with longtime resident of Santiago de María, 1994, personal communication.

24. This according to Elizabeth Wood, who has studied rural social and political relations in Usulután in detail. Personal communication.

25. See Gibb and Farah (1989); also interviews with Gibb and Farah, August 1989, October 1989.

26. Interviews with Gibb and Farah, August 1989, October 1989. Their account comes from a senior military officer present at the meeting who declined to be identified. This informant's descriptions of other events have proven accurate in the past.

27. Interview with former Captain Marcelo Cruz, October 1994.

28. Interview with former U.S. intelligence official, March 1990.

29. Interview with former U.S. intelligence official, March 1990. Actually, the labor movement became more radical because the Communist Party had *lost* control of it, displaced by the more radical leadership of the Popular Forces of Liberation and the National Resistance.

30. See "Sitreps" 1–8, 13 March–22 March 1979, in National Security Archive collection (1989b).

31. Interview with Héctor Dada, July 1993.

32. Interview with Salvadoran army colonel, September 1989; interview with retired Salvadoran army major, July 1993; interviews with business leaders, July 1993.

33. Interview with one of the founders of the Salvadoran National Movement, October 1989.

34. Interview with a retired senior official who was involved in this plot, September 1989.

35. (See n. 34). Ironically, the existence of the reformist officers' movement helped *prevent* Romero from being overthrown in April or May of 1979.

36. Interviews with Carlos Asencio (Eduardo Solórzano), member of the National Resistance, November 1992.

37. Interview with Lieutenant Colonel Mauricio de Jesús Chávez Cáceres, September 1989.

38. An interviewee who was involved in planning for the García/Vides Casanova coup claims that Romero called him on the phone and accused him of plotting against him. Interview, September 1989.

39. "Crónica del Mes," *Estudios Centroamericanos* 34, no. 367 (June 1979): 451.

40. Adolfo Majano participated in the National Conciliation Party legislative and municipal election campaign in 1976 and the presidential campaign of 1977 as a member of the presidential staff of Arturo Molina. Interview, March 1990.

41. Interview with Salvadoran army colonel, September 1989. Romero also had extremely frank conversations with Abraham Rodríguez, a leading Christian Democrat, but was unwilling to implement the political opening that Rodríguez recommended. See Memorandum of Conversation, "Former Christian Democratic Party (PDC) Candidate Analyzes National Political Scene," 15 June 1979, in Part 22B, "Additional Human Rights Records 1979–1981 (1979)," in El Salvador II document set.

42. Interviews, Ambassador Viron Vaky, April 1990; interviews with Salvadoran civilian right leaders, August–September 1989.

43. See Frank Devine to Vaky, San Salvador, 9 August 1979, classified Official—Informal, in U.S. Department of State, El Salvador II document set, Part 1: "Trip to El Salvador by Vaky and Bowdler—1979."

44. See Vaky to Devine, classified Confidential Official—Informal, 16 August 1979, in U.S. Department of State, El Salvador II document set, Part 1: "Trip to El Salvador by Vaky and Bowdler—1979."

45. Personal communication from journalist Tom Gibb, who has interviewed more than 200 former combatants of the Farabundo Martí National Liberation Front about their motivations for joining the organization.

46. Interviews with Tom Gibb, January–February 1994. According to Gibb's research, the National Police began infiltrating the guerrilla groups in the mid-1970s and successfully used the intelligence they gathered to attack their urban cells beginning in 1980. Such work was highly labor-intensive, however, and much of the violence carried out by the security forces was based on little intelligence.

47. Interview with a Salvadoran army colonel who participated in Taiwanese political warfare training, September 1989; interview with Colonel Adolfo Majano, former member of the Revolutionary Governing Junta, also trained in Taiwan, March 1990.

Chapter Five

1. Interview with Adolfo Majano, April 1990.

2. Interview with a retired senior government official, September 1989.

3. Interview with a former official of the National Association of Private Enterprise, August 1989.

4. See Central Intelligence Agency, "Final Phase of Coup Planning by Moderates within the El Salvadoran Army (DOI: 2 October 1979)," 3 October 1979. The name of the source for this document is excised, but the informant is identified as a colonel who is leading a coup plot, and his position is described as "chief of logistics, finance and support for the El Salvadoran military"—that is, the head of Maestranza, Gutiérrez. Moreover, in the third paragraph, his surname inadvertently appears: "Gutiérrez stated that planning for the coup has been under way, in one form or another, for more than a year." His name appears in a similar way in another CIA document, "Final Stages of Coup Planning by El Salvadoran Military (DOI: 10 October 1979)." This documentary evidence is consistent with the widespread belief among participants in the coup that Gutiérrez was working for the CIA.

5. Memorandum, Secretary of State Cyrus Vance to President Carter, "El Salvador: Prospects for the Junta and U.S. Policy," 26 December 1979.

6. Interview with former army Captain Marcelo Cruz Cruz, October 1994.

7. Interview with Lieutenant Colonel Carlos Avilés, September 1989.

8. Interview with Colonel Román Barrera, October 1989.

9. The officers were prepared to hold a military tribunal and execute President Carlos Romero, General Ramón Alvarenga, former president Arturo Molina, and a second lieutenant named Francisco Antonio Castillo, who had committed atrocities during the Romero administration (Mena 1992, 15).

10. Interview with a retired government official, August 1989.

11. Interview with a retired U.S. intelligence official, April 1990.

12. This according to a retired senior official who was involved in the Vides/García plot. Interview, September 1989.

13. Interview with a Salvadoran army officer who played an important role in planning the October 1979 coup.

14. Interview with a former army captain who participated in the October 1979 coup. He probably tends to minimize the junior officers' support for a more conservative agenda.

15. These vote tallies are from Keogh (1983, 168), who appears to have gotten them from René Guerra. Other sources, including Mena Sandoval (1992, 180) and Mariano Castro Morán (interview, August 1989), indicate that Gutiérrez, García, and Vides Casanova, got no votes at all. I suspect that Castro Morán got his information from Mena Sandoval, with whom he consulted regularly during the conspiracy. The specificity of Guerra's numbers, and the consistency of the vote tallies he reports with what

most of my sources told me about support for García within the movement, lead me to believe his account. Majano (1989, 38) indicates that García got a significant share of the votes, though he was not present at the meetings and does not provide specific counts.

16. Interview with Adolfo Majano, April 1990. See also Keogh (1983, 167–69) and Mena Sandoval (1992, 180).

17. See also Department of State Briefing Memorandum, undated, to the Deputy Secretary from ARA—Viron P. Vaky, "El Salvador: Situation Update." The document is apparently from early October, as it reports violence in "late September and early October."

One former U.S. intelligence official I interviewed provided a feel for how raw intelligence was transmitted. From roughly August onward, Salvadoran coup plotters paid social visits to him at his home. Sometimes representatives of opposing movements happened to drop by at the same time and would contrive various excuses to have a moment alone with him, usually in the kitchen or garden. They would tell him, in private, the status of their preparations, fishing, as he put it, for some sign of support.

18. Briefing Memorandum, 6 October 1979, to the Deputy Secretary from ARA—Viron P. Vaky, "U.S. Policy in El Salvador," classified secret. The same memo, with revisions, was forwarded to the National Security Council on 12 October. Apparently no action was taken before the coup on 15 October. From El Salvador II collection.

19. Department of State memorandum, 6 October 1979, classified secret, to ARA—Ambassador Vaky from ARA/CEN [excision], Subject: "Military Coup in El Salvador—Contingencies." From El Salvador II collection.

20. Interview with a former U.S. intelligence official, April 1990.

21. Interview with a former U.S. intelligence official, April 1990.

22. The captains drove the colonel to San Salvador a few days after the coup and dropped him off, in uniform, in the middle of a major leftist demonstration. He survived. Interview with U.S. intelligence official, April 1990.

23. Interviews with military officers who participated in the coup, August–October 1989, June–July 1995.

24. Several officers who participated in the rebellion said that Majano's tardiness undercut his credibility among some officers.

25. Domingo Monterrosa later made a name for himself as one of the most brutal officers in the military, overseeing the slaughter of hundreds of civilians at El Mozote in Morazan province in December 1981. He was later assassinated by the People's Revolutionary Army (ERP). See Danner (1993).

26. Both former Ambassador Robert White and an anonymous former U.S. embassy official described Carranza in interviews (April 1990) as the operational head of the armed forces; García played more of a political role.

27. This according to a former Juventud officer who was present in the San Carlos barracks on the day of the coup and a few days afterward.

28. Interview with a former U.S. intelligence officer, April 1990.

29. Interview with Román Mayorga, April 1990. Mayorga told the junior officers that he was not in a position to name those who should be purged from the military, but he assumed that young officers themselves knew who they were and would expel them.

30. Ungo led the National Revolutionary Movement, affiliated with the Socialist International. He had been the successful vice presidential candidate of the National Opposition Union coalition in 1972.

31. This assessment was shared by several of the officers I interviewed, including some who were captains and majors at the time of the coup and supported the idea of reforms, if not the specific civilians chosen to implement them.

32. Untitled document, dated 8 March 1984, in CIA documents, vol. 3. Other sources, including Salvadoran military officers, deny that Alvarez was a Communist.

33. Interview, August 1989.

34. A former senior member of the post-coup government who must remain anonymous described some of the means of obstruction in detail, suggesting that this is not an empty charge. Interview, April 1990.

35. Interview with Douglas Farah, September 1989.

36. ANSESAL agents routinely used stolen cars to pick up suspects they had identified for capture or execution. Interview with a former U.S. embassy official, April 1990.

37. Interview with a retired army colonel who specialized in military intelligence and worked closely with D'Aubuisson before and after the coup. Carranza continued to work closely with D'Aubuisson in subsequent years, passing him intelligence from military sources even after he began to devote himself more to the work of the ARENA party. See State Department cable SS 7437, 9 September 1982.

38. The other prominent member of this group, Colonel Vides Casanova, had been head of INSAFI, the state-run industrial promotion board. To my knowledge no specific information implicates Vides in noteworthy corruption, though other officers assigned to INSAFI, such as Major Guillermo Roeder, led lifestyles that suggested high levels of corruption. Interviews with a former U.S. embassy official, July–August 1992.

39. Interview with a retired Salvadoran military colonel, December 1989.

40. Interview with Rubén Zamora, October 1989. Zamora was an important leader in the left wing of the Christian Democratic Party in the 1970s, served as secretary of the presidency under the first junta, and later returned to politics as a prominent deputy for the social democratic Democratic Convergence coalition and subsequently as the presidential candidate for the FMLN/Democratic Convergence coalition in 1994.

41. Interview with a former U.S. embassy official, April 1990.

42. Interview with a former senior government official with close ties to these officers. My informant may tend to overstate the esteem in which the Equipo Molina were held within the military, but Majano (interview, March 1990) and other reformist officers (interviews, June–July 1995), who should have no such bias, corroborate the general view that they were widely recognized within the military as a key leadership group.

43. Interview with Adolfo Majano, March 1990. Mena Sandoval (1993) confirms that *tandona* members were frequently sheltered from disciplinary action. See his chapter 4.

44. Interview with a U.S. military advisor based in El Salvador, April 1990.

45. Interview with an active-duty military officer who participated in the October coup and supported the Juventud agenda, October 1989. This officer sees this concern about COPEFA as valid.

46. Confidential interview with a former government official who obtained his information from reformist junior officers who claimed that García was obstructing COPEFA's ability to meet, April 1990.

47. Interview with a former U.S. embassy official, April 1990.

48. Interview with a retired military officer who was present at these discussions, April 1990.

49. Interview with Lieutenant Colonel Mariano Castro Morán, September 1989.

50. Interview with Román Mayorga, April 1990.

51. Interview with Rubén Zamora, October 1989.

52. Interview, April 1990.

53. Interviews, March–April 1990.

54. Interview with a former cabinet member, April 1990.

55. Interview with Román Mayorga, April 1990.

56. Interview with Rubén Zamora, October 1989.

57. Interview with a former member of the post-coup government, April 1990.

58. See "Por que el pueblo no cree en la junta militar," *Estudios Centroamericanos* 34, nos. 372–73 (October–November 1979): 1028–29.

59. Interview, April 1990.

60. Interviews, March–April 1990.

61. Interviews with Alberto Ramos, former secretary general of the United Popular Action Front (FAPU), October 1994, and with retired army colonel Benjamín Ramos (July 1995), who negotiated with Alberto Ramos and other FAPU leaders.

62. Interview, April 1990.

63. Interview with official of the Revolutionary Governing Junta, April 1990.

64. Interview with Marcelo Cruz, an army captain who joined the People's Revolutionary Army (ERP), October 1994. The junior officers held meetings with all the groups on the left. Relations were most difficult with the Popular Forces of Liberation (FPL).

65. Interview, October 1994.

66. Interview with Rubén Zamora, October 1989.

67. Interview with Adolfo Majano, March 1990; interviews with private sector leaders, September 1992, July 1993.

68. Interviews with business leaders, September 1989, July 1993.

69. Interview, August 1989. This view failed to make some important distinctions among forces of the left. It was true that some affiliates of the post-Medellín Catholic Church were involved with revolutionary movements. Many priests, Jesuits and others, had become deeply involved in helping poor communities organize themselves, and many of the organizations founded, as well as the priests who had been involved, became incorporated into the more explicitly revolutionary mass organizations such as the Popular Revolutionary Bloc. A number of priests left their orders to join the guerrillas. Yet the Jesuits at the University of Central America remained aloof from these activities and were critical of opposition violence, as was Archbishop Romero. Opposition parties like the National Democratic Union, the Christian Democrats, and the National Revolutionary Movement were hardly the vanguard of revolution: organizations like the Popular Revolutionary Bloc, the United Popular Action Front, and the Popular Leagues of February 28 criticized their moderation and reformism, which the

radicals saw as a barrier, rather than an aid, to revolution. Thus it was a considerable distortion on the part of the private sector elite (and many in the military) to see the reformist efforts of the party and university elites in the government as part of a coordinated leftist plan to take power.

70. Interview, October 1989.

71. Interview, April 1990.

72. Interview with a former government official with close ties to the Salvadoran private sector, June 1989.

73. Interview with Ernesto Rivas Gallont, July 1993. "Gordo" planned to attack Rivas while he was jogging, but Rivas had taken the precaution of jogging against the flow of traffic, making the snatch more difficult. Rivas was unaware of the attempt until Pyes told him about it.

74. As noted, businessmen who spoke out in favor of structural reforms during the later months of the Romero administration received death threats. At least one pro-reform businessman suffered an attempt on his life. Interviews with business leaders, July 1993. See also State Department Cable SS 0096, "Millionaires' Murder Inc.?" (6 January 1981).

75. Four members of the private sector elite interviewed for this book claimed that there was strong distrust of these leaders, and of the military in general. This is consistent with Jeffery Paige's finding (1993) that the Salvadoran business elite continues to mistrust the military.

76. Two members of the private sector elite insisted to me (September–October 1989) that their own efforts, and the election of Ronald Reagan, prevented the victory of the left. While praising some military officers, they were reluctant to credit the military as an institution with having prevented a "communist" takeover.

77. Interview, October 1989.

78. Interview, October 1989.

79. The Broad Nationalist Front was converted into a political party with the founding of the National Republican Alliance (ARENA) in 1981.

80. Interview with a former U.S. intelligence official. Salvadorans commonly refer to the top stratum of the upper classes as "the 14 families."

An additional incentive for rightist mobilization against the high command in December was the launching by the popular organizations of increasing numbers of wage-related labor actions at agricultural facilities at the beginning of the harvest season, just as they had in December 1977. According to an embassy cable (SS 6976, 4 December 1979), about 50 coffee plantations, 25 cotton farms, and 15 cattle ranches were occupied by organized workers at the beginning of December. These figures came from Salvadoran private sector sources and may be exaggerated, but they reflect the growing alarm on the part of the agrarian elite about the level of activism in the countryside. As they did in late 1977, agrarian interests responded with a major newspaper advertisement campaign calling upon the government to restore "law and order," a position that struck a sympathetic chord with the U.S. embassy (SS 2150, 6 December 1979).

81. Interview with a former member of the first post-coup government, April 1990.

82. The "Woerner Commission" was a high-level U.S. military mission sent to El Salvador from 12 September until 8 November 1981 to evaluate the military situation

and assist the Salvadoran military in developing a national strategy to combat the Farabundo Martí National Liberation Front. It was led by Brigadier General Fred F. Woerner, Jr., and composed of two full colonels and four lieutenant colonels, plus staff. A heavily redacted copy of the report was obtained under the Freedom of Information Act (FOIA) by the National Security Archive, Washington, D.C.

83. A former National Guard corporal remarked nostalgically, "Before the agrarian reform, we were invited to *fincas*. They would give us food and a place to sleep, and at the end of the week, money." Interview, August 1989.

84. Interview with Leonel Gómez, April 1989.

85. Personal communication from Professor Tommie Sue Montgomery, June 1991. Montgomery was in San Salvador at the time and was monitoring information on human rights conditions through the press and Church sources.

86. Interview with a former reformist military officer, September 1989.

87. Interview with a former senior government official, September 1989.

88. Interview with a Salvadoran military officer formerly associated with the reformist current, October 1989. He was critical of Majano's approach, though not of his intentions.

89. Interview with Luis de Sebastian, August 1989; interview with Guillermo Ungo, September 1989; interview with Rubén Zamora, October 1989.

90. D'Aubuisson told a U.S. intelligence official that he was "on assignment" for the high command when he returned from Guatemala. This view was shared by senior Salvadoran military and civilian officials, one of whom identified Carranza as D'Aubuisson's handler.

91. Interview with a U.S. intelligence official. See also "Biographic Sketch, Roberto D'Aubuisson Arietta," Defense Intelligence Agency, May 1982, p. 3. Released under FOIA.

92. "Existence of Rightist Death Squad within the Salvadoran National Police; Location of Clandestine Prison Used by the Death Squad." CIA document, dated 19 March 1983, CIA, vol. 2.

93. According to Tom Gibb, the National Police were extraordinarily effective in infiltrating leftist groups, and killed hundreds of their members. Personal communication.

94. Interview, September 1989.

95. Interview, September 1989.

96. Interview with a military officer who was a major in 1979–80, September 1989. The officer claimed to disapprove of what was done but agreed with the perception within the security forces that the first junta was dangerous.

97. Interview, April 1990.

98. Interview, October 1989.

99. Interview, March 1990. A U.S. embassy official remarked that this might have reflected nothing more than the poor chain of command, but Majano felt that he was having to countermand signals, if not direct orders, that increased violence was required.

100. Interview with a military officer who was a captain at the time of the coup. October 1989.

101. Interview, April 1990.

102. Interview, former senior official of the first junta, April 1990.
103. Interview with Román Mayorga, April 1990.
104. Interview, April 1990.
105. Interview, April 1990.
106. Cable traffic from the period expresses alarm over the prospect that the new government might establish diplomatic relations with Cuba and the USSR (SS 5889, 16 October 1979).
107. Untitled document, dated 8 March 1984, in CIA documents, vol. 3.
108. Interview with FAPU leader Alberto Ramos, October 1994.
109. Interview with a retired colonel who was a COPEFA member, July 1995.
110. Memorandum, Secretary of State Cyrus Vance to President Carter, 26 December 1979, "El Salvador: Prospects for the Junta and U.S. Policy."
111. Interview with former Christian Democrat Juan José Martel, October 1989.
112. See "El Gabinete de Gobierno, Magistrados de la Corte Suprema de Justicia y funcionarias de instituciones autónomas, se dirigen a las Fuerzas Armadas por intermedio del COPEFA," *Estudios Centroamericanos* 35, nos. 375–76 (January–February 1980): 117–19.
113. See "El COPEFA responde al Gabinete, Magistrados y otros funcionarios del Gobierno," *ECA* 35, nos. 375–76 (January–February 1980): 119–20. Even after García's reported restructuring of COPEFA in mid-December, the officers still took three days to decide to reject the cabinet's ultimatum. It is probably safe to assume that COPEFA members were aware that the Christian Democrats were waiting in the wings. The long deliberation suggests that considerable division remained, particularly at the level of the military units with which the COPEFA delegates consulted. A U.S. military officer who was permitted to listen in on some of the debate said that even officers who supported the Proclama were unwilling to break with the military hierarchy by increasing COPEFA's authority. Interview, April 1990.
114. Interview with Román Mayorga, April 1990.
115. Some returned to posts in the second junta formed by the Christian Democrats.

Chapter Six

1. Interview with a former U.S. intelligence official, April 1990.
2. Interview, March 1990.
3. Interview with Viron Vaky, April 1990.
4. Interview with James Cheek, March 1989.
5. Interview with a former U.S. embassy official, April 1990.
6. Cheek commented that in negotiating with the military, he was working with "a shoeshine and a smile—nothing but my good looks" and conditional promises of future assistance (interview, March 1989).
7. Interview with Juan José Martél, October 1989. Duarte was exiled following the unsuccessful 1972 coup and remained in Venezuela until 1979.
8. Interview with Juan José Martél, October 1989; interview with Antonio Morales Erlich, August 1989. Morales represented the Christian Democratic Party on the junta from January 1980 through the inauguration of Magaña in 1982.

9. Interview with Rubén Zamora, October 1989; interview with Juan José Martel, October 1989; interviews with Eduardo Molina, August–September 1989; interview with an anonymous source formerly with the Christian Democratic Party.

10. Mario Zamora was killed at his home during a meeting of Christian Democratic leaders, under circumstances that point to high-level connivance. His telephone service was cut off about an hour before the assassination and restored shortly afterward. According to the United Nations Truth Commission, the murder was committed by one of the security forces (National Guard, National Police, or Treasury Police -- the commission did not specify), apparently without authorization from the high command. The security force involved may have contracted with one or more foreigners to carry out the execution. Interview with Rubén Zamora; United Nations 1993, 139–44.

11. Given the relative size of the security forces and the partial support enjoyed by García and Carranza in a few army units, it appears that at least some officers in the security forces voted against the high command.

12. Interview with former Captain Alejandro Fiallos, October 1989.

13. Interview with a retired U.S. military officer assigned to El Salvador in 1979–80 who observed these events.

14. Interview with a military officer who was present at this meeting.

15. Interview with former Captain Alejandro Fiallos, October 1989.

16. Interview with former Captain Marcelo Cruz Cruz, October 1994.

17. Interview with Alberto Ramos, October 1994. Ramos was secretary general of the United Popular Action Front.

18. Interview with Alberto Ramos, October 1994.

19. Interview with Alberto Ramos, October 1994.

20. Interviews with Alberto Ramos, October 1994; interview with Adolfo Majano, March 1990.

21. Interview with Alberto Ramos, September 1994; interview with retired military officer who negotiated with Ramos, July 1995.

22. Interviews, August–September 1989.

23. Interview with a military officer who belonged to the reformist current, August 1989.

24. Interview with Eduardo Molina, September 1989. Molina helped found the Christian Democratic Party.

25. Interview, September 1989.

26. Interview with a retired senior official, September 1989.

27. Interview with a former government official, June 1989.

28. Interview with businessman who helped organize the Broad National Front during 1979–1980, October 1989.

29. Interview with a retired senior military officer who was involved in these events.

30. The usual lineup for the United States was Chargé James Cheek, Deputy Chief of Mission Mark Dion, Defense Attaché Jerry Walker, the U.S. milgroup leader, and the political officer. The Salvadoran military was represented by García, Carranza, Vides Casanova, Majano, and Gutiérrez. Interview with former U.S. embassy official, April 1990.

31. Interview with James Cheek, June 1989.

32. This was the first attempt in El Salvador to use the courts to contain the actions of the radical right. Ironically, since the peace accords in 1992, rightists have used defamation suits to attack anyone who makes public charges against them regarding past human rights abuses, as in the case of Joaquín Villalobos versus Orlando DeSola.

33. See declassified CIA documents: "Briefing Paper on Right-Wing Terrorism in El Salvador," 27 October 1983; "Existence of Rightist Death Squad within the Salvadoran National Police: Location of Clandestine Prison Used by the Death Squad," 19 March 1983; "Members and Collaborators of the Nationalist Republican Alliance (ARENA) Paramilitary Unit Headed by Héctor Regalado," 13 July 1984. Other information was supplied in a personal communication from Tom Gibb, who has investigated National Police infiltration of FMLN organizations.

34. Declassified CIA document, untitled, 5 March 1984.

35. See declassified CIA documents: "File Summary Ricardo Sol Meza," 4 May 1985; "Responsibility of 'Death Squad' Run by Businessman Ricardo Sol Mesa [sic] and National Guard Major Denis Morán for murders of Rodolfo Viera and U.S. Citizens Michael Hammer and Mark Pearlman; Use of the Death Squad to Conduct Bombings in San Salvador," 30 May 1981; "El Salvador: Right Wing Death Squads, A Selective Study on Structure and Organization," 27 October 1983; and "File Summary Victor Manuel Santo Martínez," 27 April 1985. See also declassified State Department documents: "Avila Case," SS 3664, 23 March 1985; and "Interview with Lt. Col. Morán, Director of the Treasury Police," SS 2746, 10 April 1981.

36. Personal communication from Tom Gibb. According to a former member of an army intelligence section who spoke with Gibb, the special units operated by S-IIs and the security forces did most of the killing well into the 1980s.

37. See declassified CIA documents: "Briefing Paper on Right-Wing Terrorism in El Salvador," 27 October 1983; "Travel to El Salvador by Captain Eduardo Avila Avila Alleged Conspirator in the 1980 Assassinations of Two U.S. Citizens in the San Salvador Sheraton Hotel," 19 May 1983; "El Salvador: D'Aubuisson's Terrorist Activities," 2 March 1984. See also declassified State Department document, "Document Captured at Time of D'Aubuisson's Arrest," SS 4275, 20 June 1980.

38. Interview with former ANEP official, August 1989.

39. Interview with Salvadoran businessman, October 1989.

40. Interview with former State Department official, April 1990. Ambassador Robert White was appointed in February, but his Senate confirmation was delayed by North Carolina Senator Jesse Helms. For discussion of problems with personnel in the El Salvador mission, see National Security Council, 14 February 1980, "Memo for Zbig [Zbigniew Brzezinski], David Aaron, Henry Owen," from [Robert] Pastor, Subject: SCC Meeting on El Salvador, Friday, February 15, 1980—4:00 p.m. See also National Security Council, minutes of Special Coordination Committee Meeting, 15 February 1980, 4:25–5:10 p.m., White House Situation Room, "U.S. Policy to El Salvador and Honduras."

41. Interview with James Cheek, March 1989; interview with Ambassador Robert White, April 1990.

42. Interview with a former U.S. intelligence analyst; untitled 13 March 1980 Defense Intelligence Agency document obtained under the Freedom of Information Act.

43. Interview with Miguel Alemán, director of CONFRAS (Salvadoran Agrarian Reform Confederation).

44. Interview with Jorge Villacorta, September 1989.

45. This dissident group later formed the Popular Social Christian Movement (MPSC) outside the country. By November 1981, over 60 percent of party members had resigned, most of them becoming members of the MPSC (Montgomery 1982, 168).

46. National Security Council memorandum, undated (apparently early 1980), "Subject: Status Report on the State Department's Efforts to Encourage Vatican Officials to Try to Influence Salvador's Archbishop Romero to Support Moderate Change through the New Junta." The document remarks, "The archbishop apparently sees the hand of the U.S. in his being called to Vatican." See also National Security Council memorandum, 31 January 1980, for Secretaries of State and Defense, Director of OMB [Office of Management and Budget], Chairman JCS [Joint Chiefs of Staff], DCI [Director of Central Intelligence], "Subject: U.S. Policy to El Salvador and Central America." See also secret, undated State Department document, "Status Report on the State Department's Efforts to Encourage Vatican Officials to Try to Influence Salvador's Archbishop Romero to Support Moderate Change through the New Junta," El Salvador II set, part 5.

47. Colonel Santibañez was interviewed at length in Alan Francovich's 1985 documentary film *Short Circuit*. Santibañez was the director of ANSESAL under the Romero government and maintained close contacts with hardline sectors of the military after being forced into retirement by the October 1979 coup. See also State Department cable ST 263494, 14 August 1992.

48. See Briefing Memorandum, 13 March 1980, to the Secretary of State from John A. Bushnell, Acting Assistant Secretary for American Republic Affairs (ARA), "Situation in El Salvador and MTTs."

49. Interview with Robert White, March 1989; interview with Tom Gibb, who got his information from extensive interviews with current and former members of the FMLN and associated popular organizations, August 1995.

50. Interview with Alberto Ramos, September 1994; interview with Marcelo Cruz Cruz, former army captain and member of the Popular Revolutionary Army, October 1994; interview with retired army officer who participated in planning a second coup, July 1995.

51. Interview with Adolfo Majano, March 1990.

52. Ibid.

53. Interview with Adolfo Majano, March 1990. The officers included Major Jorge Adalberto Cruz Reyes, Major Roberto Mauricio Staben, Captain Alvaro Rafael Sarávia, Captain José Alfredo Jiménez, Captain Victor Hugo Vega Valencia, Captain Eduardo Avila, Lieutenant Federico Chacón, Lieutenant Miguel Francisco Bennet, Lieutenant Rodolfo López Sibrián, Lieutenant Carlos Hernan Morales, Lieutenant Jaime René Alvarado. The civilians included Amado Antonio Garay, Nelson Enrique Morales, Andrés Antonio Córdova, Herbert Romeo Escobar, Fredy Salomon Chávez, Marion Antonio Quintanilla, José Joaquín Larín, Julian García Jiménez, Antonio Cornejo, Ricardo Valdivieso, and Roberto Muyshondt. See CIA, "Arrest of Rightist Coup Plotters," 9 May 1980.

54. Other civilians mentioned included Miguel Muyshondt, Ulises Gonzalez, and Nelson García. See CIA, "Arrest of Rightist Coup Plotters," 9 May 1980. See also United Nations (1993, 129).

55. Interview with a retired U.S. military officer, April 1990.

56. Interview with a retired army officer who participated in these plans, July 1995; interview with Alberto Ramos, October 1994; interviews with army officers, September–October 1989. More conservative officers avoided answering specific questions about these events, responding instead with general comments to the effect that the military may come close to "divorce" but always manages to stay together. The former reformists' account of preparations for armed conflict is more consistent with documentary evidence.

57. See CIA, "Arrest of Rightist Coup Plotters," 9 May 1980; interview with Robert White, April 1990.

58. Of Majano's supporters, only Mena Sandoval remained in his post, largely because he threatened to take over the barracks if the high command tried to remove him, and had sufficient loyalty among the lieutenants to make his threat credible. He later mutinied and sided with the FMLN guerrillas (Mena Sandoval 1992, 209–17).

59. Interview, October 1989.

60. Interview with Adolfo Majano, March 1990; interview with Antonio Hernández, Politico-Diplomatic Commission of the FMLN, August 1989.

61. Interview with Robert White, April 1990.

62. Socorro Jurídico's figures are not particularly precise. They depended for reporting on Church and popular organizations, and it is likely that some of the civilians reported killed were actually leftist combatants. In some cases, the numbers may be exaggerated. On the other hand, the difficulty of collecting information, particularly outside San Salvador, may bias these figures downward, compensating for the risk of over-reporting by some affiliates. I have compared data collected by Socorro Jurídico, the University of Central America, and the U.S. embassy for late 1980 through 1983, and the three time series, though reflecting different absolute levels, are highly correlated, suggesting a degree of inter-source reliability, if not true validity. I therefore use these figures to indicate trends.

63. Personal communication from Tom Gibb, who has been studying infiltration of the FMLN by the National Police.

64. Interview, August 1989.

65. Interview with Alberto Ramos, October 1994.

66. See "Balance Estadística," mimeographed tables published by the University Center for Documentation and Research (CUDI) at the University of Central America.

67. Personal communication from Professor José Z. García, April 1991. García was in El Salvador from late 1979 through 1980 and had an opportunity to travel to Chalatenango, where he met with officers who were receiving the described treatment from the high command.

68. Declassified CIA document, "Existence of Rightist Death Squad within the Salvadoran National Police; Location of Clandestine Prison Used by the Death Squad," 19 March 1983. The document describes Molina as having led the death squad, which seems unlikely, given his previous left-wing political proclivities and prominence within the reformist movement. He was, however, posted to the National Police and may have been compelled to participate in repressive activities. Apparently he was not fully cooperative, for he was subsequently assassinated by the security forces for being a leftist.

69. Interview with Alberto Ramos, October 1994.

70. Interview with Adolfo Majano, March 1990.

71. Interview with Carlos Asencio (Eduardo Solórzano), member of the National Resistance, December 1993.

72. Interview with Captain Alejandro Fiallos, October 1989; interview with Adolfo Majano, March 1990; interview with Luis de Sebastian, former professor of the University of Central America, August 1989.

73. Personal communication from Tom Gibb. Although the ERP had been skeptical about working with the military as an institution, its leaders were willing to accept individual soldiers and officers who were willing to leave the military. The FPL, like the RN, had expanded by drawing on its popular base organization, the Popular Revolutionary Bloc. It maintained a greater separation from the popular organization, however, and was therefore not as heavily infiltrated in the early years of the war.

74. Interview with ERP member who knew Mena Sandoval during his first few years with the organization, March 1990.

75. Interview, July 1990.

76. American Institute of Free Labor Development (AIFLD) memoranda: Richard V. Oulahan to William C. Doherty, "Situation Report," 16 October 1980; Richard V. Oulahan to Bill Hallman, "Arming Canton Patrols," 23 October 1980, with attachments; and Richard V. Oulahan to William C. Doherty, "Violence against Agrarian Reform Beneficiaries and Workers Pertaining to Real Properties," 12 November 1980. All in NSA collection (1989b).

77. Interview with Alberto Ramos, October 1994.

78. Interview with Dagoberto Campos, El Salvador Human Rights Commission—Non-Governmental, September 1989.

79. AIFLD memorandum from Richard V. Oulahan to William C. Doherty, "Situation Report," 16 October 1980.

80. Ibid.

81. Interview with a former leader of the Revolutionary Democratic Front, July 1989.

82. Declassified secret memorandum from HA [Bureau of Human Rights and Humanitarian Affairs]–Patricia Derian to the Secretary of State, "U.S. Response to Assassination of FDR Leadership," 4 December 1980.

83. Interview with James Cheek, March 1989.

84. Interview with James Cheek, March 1989.

85. Minutes of Special Coordination Committee meeting, Thursday, 11 December 1980, 3:00–3:45 p.m., Situation Room, The White House, "Subject: U.S. Policy to El Salvador."

86. Declassified CIA document, "Strong Movement among Rightist Military Officers to Overthrow the Revolutionary Governing Junta (JRG) and Replace It with a Government Headed by Col. Eugenio Vides Casanova," 1 December 1980.

87. Interview with Robert White, April 1990.

88. Interview with a former leading member of Christian Democratic Party with close ties to the military, August 1989.

89. In fact, transferring Carranza out of the Defense Ministry may by this point have been in García's interest, as Carranza was beginning to compete for power. Declassified CIA document, "Extreme Rightist Activity," 1 December 1985.

90. Declassified CIA document, "El Salvador: Military Attitude toward Compromise," 17 December 1980.

91. See White House Memorandum of Conversation, "Summary of the President's Meeting with the Special Presidential Mission to El Salvador and U.S. Policy to El Salvador," 11 December 1980, Oval Office. See also undated National Security Council document, "El Salvador: Background Paper," apparently December 1980.

Chapter Seven

1. Speech by U.N. Secretary General Boutros Boutros-Ghali, "La larga noche ha llegado a su fin" (Mexico City, 16 January 1992), included in the collection *Acuerdos hacia una nueva nación* (San Salvador: FMLN, 1992), p. 151 (author's translation). The most important accords were constitutional reforms agreed upon by the FMLN and the government and ratified by the Legislative Assembly in April 1991; the agreement on the formation of a civilian police force to which FMLN candidates could be admitted, signed in New York in September 1991; and the final agreements of 16 January 1992, signed at Chapultepec Castle in Mexico City.

2. Personal communication. Gibb conducted a survey of more than two hundred combatants from various organizations and parts of the country. See also Mason and Krane (1989).

3. Tom Gibb has conducted research into the destruction of the FMLN's infrastructure in the west and found that the National Resistance, the main group in Santa Ana, was heavily infiltrated, leading to hundreds of deaths at the hands of the security forces. Personal communication.

4. U.S. Department of State cable SS 6390, 26 August 1981, U.S. Embassy, San Salvador, "Violence Week in Review August 15–22," in National Security Archive collection (NSA 1989b). While 34 in one week was the highest rate I found for Santa Ana, large numbers of decapitations were routine in that department. The embassy determined that the security forces were using the equipment of a meat packing plant because of the "cleanness of the cuts." Tom Gibb has interviewed survivors of the National Police jail in Santa Ana who were present (some blindfolded, others not) when police executed people with a garrote, beheaded them with a guillotine, chopped their bodies up, ran them through an industrial grinder, and washed them down the drain. These sessions were referred to as "the lesson." The National Policemen were advised by an unidentified Asian man known as "the professor," who communicated through an interpreter (Gibb 1995, chap. 8).

5. Interview with retired General Fred Woerner, July 1990. After Colonel Leonel Alberto Alfaro and Major José Francisco Samayoa, who were Majano loyalists, were forced out of the country, their names, along with that of Mena Sandoval, were expunged from the lists of graduates of the military academy. Interview with FAES colonel, October 1989; interview with retired Colonel Samayoa, July 1995.

6. Interview with retired General Fred Woerner, July 1990.

7. Interview with retired General Fred Woerner, July 1990.

8. The cited cables were entitled "Saving El Salvador."

9. Declassified CIA document, "Existence of Rightist Death Squad within the Salvadoran National Police; Location of Clandestine Prison Used by the Death Squad," 19 March 1983.

10. According to a former army intelligence official who spoke with Tom Gibb, the intelligence sections of most army installations operated special units that systematically assassinated civilians suspected of belonging to or collaborating with the FMLN. According to a declassified CIA document entitled "Members and Collaborators of the Nationalist Republican Alliance (ARENA) Paramilitary Unit Headed by Héctor Regalado," 13 July 1984, an informant told the CIA that the National Center for Analysis and Investigations (CAIN) was far more active than Regalado's unit. Tom Gibb's extensive interviews with former FMLN combatants indicate that they viewed the security forces, rather than private squads, as the primary threat to them. Despite the emphasis on private organizations in Craig Pyes' excellent 1983 series on the death squads, the one individual he cites as having killed large numbers of people was a member of CAIN. See Pyes (1983e).

11. Confidential interview with a former security forces officer. A cable from the U.S. embassy in Mexico City, No. 17359, 6 November 1983, entitled "Block Piece on Death Squads," summarizes a Reuters news story by Robert Block on the role of CAIN.

12. Declassified Department of State Briefing Paper, "El Salvador: Death Squads," 29 November 1983, in NSA (1989b).

13. The Carter administration had looked carefully at the possibility of deporting wealthy Salvadorans residing in Miami who were suspected of funding the death squads. This idea lay fallow once Reagan took office because, in the opinion of one State Department official, the administration was unwilling to incur the wrath of the very conservative Cuban community in Miami (interview, March 1989). See declassified San Salvador embassy cable "Millionaires' Murder Inc.?" SS 0096, 6 January 1981, regarding the role of Salvadoran expatriates in Miami in funding death squad operations involving the military. For 1983 investigations, see declassified memorandum from L/LEI–Jeffrey H. Smith to ARA–James H. Michel, entitled "Investigation of Domestic Support for Violence in El Salvador," 8 December 1983; also declassified memorandum from S/SE–Todd Greentree to ARA–Jim Michel, Amb. Richard Stone, and Constantine Menges entitled "Meetings in Miami with Salvadoran Oligarchs," undated.

14. Interview with a Salvadoran official who saw the list, September 1989.

15. William Bollinger made these findings by charting data from Tutela Legal for this period. By using Tutela's original reports and then eliminating all cases for which Tutela lacked the name of the individual victim, Bollinger found that although targeted killings declined, indiscriminate rural killing by the military increased markedly after the Bush and Casey visits. The findings are even more compelling if aerial bombardment (which also increased markedly during this phase) is included. Personal communication.

16. See, for instance, cable from U.S. embassy, San Jose, SJ 0526, 21 January 1984, entitled "Avila case." The reporting officer writes that no one has seriously interviewed Avila, who was implicated in the Sheraton killings and the assassination of Archbishop Romero, because of "justified fear that he will not limit the scope of his revelations." Minister of Defense Vides was reluctant to order the interview.

17. Interview with a Salvadoran official, October 1989.

18. Interviews with U.S. Military Group and embassy officials, January 1987, August 1989, September 1989, March 1991; interviews with Salvadoran army officers, July–

August 1995. Criticism of the conduct of the war is common among Salvadoran officers from *tandas* junior to the *tandona* (the academy class of 1966), which dominated the military in the late 1980s. Non-*tandona* officers obviously have incentives to criticize their former superiors. Unfortunately, such expressions of opinion by interested parties and circumstantial evidence are the best we can hope for on this question.

19. Interview with FAES colonel, October 1989.

20. Interview with Juan Vicente Maldonado, former executive director of the National Association of Private Enterprise and member of the Productive Alliance, August 1989.

21. Interview with a senior Salvadoran government official who was present at this meeting, September 1989.

22. Interview with Luis Cardenal, July 1993.

23. Ibid.

24. Interview with a prominent coffee grower, July 1993; interview with Rafael Montalvo, president of Land Bank, July 1993.

25. Interview with Francisco Castro Funes, Chamber of Commerce, July 1993.

26. Interviews with Salvadoran business leaders, July 1993.

27. El Rescate, "Kidnappings for Ransom: Background and Chronology of Events Surrounding the Military-Civilian Kidnapping Ring," document presented to the U.N. Truth Commission for El Salvador, 30 October 1992. Includes a "chronology of events 1986–1992."

28. Interview with a founding member of ARENA who quit the party as a result of threats to kidnap him, October 1989.

29. Ibid.

30. "Biographic Sketch, Colonel Carlos Reynaldo López Nuila," September 1986, Defense Intelligence Agency. Released under FOIA.

31. In their earlier writings on the "Little Angels," Gibb and Farah (1989) describe them as former guerrillas who were captured and tortured and who then turned against their former comrades. Gibb has since learned through additional research that they were loyal to the National Police from the outset and had successfully infiltrated the National Resistance during the 1970s.

32. El Rescate, "Kidnappings for Ransom" (1992).

33. Ibid.

34. Interview with a prominent Salvadoran businessman, July 1993.

35. ARENA was initially one seat short of an absolute majority and engaged in a prolonged dispute with the Christian Democrats over a seat that ARENA claimed, with some justification, the PDC had won through fraud. Thereafter a deputy from the National Conciliation Party (PCN) crossed over to ARENA, guaranteeing it a majority vote without the need for cooperation from the PCN as a party (Miles and Ostertag 1989, 20).

36. The author was present during these events.

37. Interviews with Salvadoran and U.S. military officers, March 1991, September 1992, July 1995.

38. From interview with Ochoa taped 14 October 1987, in BDM Management Services, Research Data, "Oral History of the Conflict in El Salvador 1979–Present," vol. 1, 14 March 1988, p. 29. Ochoa's description of Ellacuría and other Jesuits as "Spaniards" is inaccurate: the six Jesuits slain were all Salvadoran citizens, either nat-

uralized or by birth. After the killings, Ochoa told reporters for *Sixty Minutes* that the decision to kill the Jesuits had been made at the top levels of the Ministry of Defense. Ochoa is known to have had a bitter personal rivalry with members of the *tandona*, including then army Chief of Staff Ponce.

39. Transcript of interview with Orlando DeSola by Tommie Sue Montgomery, January 1980.

40. Interviews with United Nations officials, November–December 1992, San Salvador.

41. Constitutional amendments in El Salvador require the approval of two consecutive Assemblies. Quick passage of these measures made it possible for constitutional reforms to be in place prior to a cease-fire.

42. COPAZ was to be made up of two representatives each from the Salvadoran government and the FMLN, plus representatives from each of the political parties in the Legislative Assembly.

43. Interview with a U.S. State Department official, July 1993.

44. Interview with a U.S. State Department official, July 1992.

Conclusion

1. Although some *tandas* are attempting to create group identity through such devices as newsletters, the very large number of officers in the middle ranks and the dramatic reduction in available spoils make it less likely that the system will endure, at least in its current form. Interviews with Salvadoran captains, June 1992, October 1992.

2. Interview with FAES officer, October 1992.

3. Interviews with senior FAES officers, October–November 1992.

REFERENCES

Ahumada, Eugenio, et al. 1989. *Chile: La memoria prohibida—Las violaciones a los derechos humanos, 1973–1983*. 3 vols. Santiago de Chile: Pehuén Editores.

Allison, Graham. 1971. *Essence of Decision: Explaining the Cuban Missile Crisis.* Boston: Little, Brown.

Americas Watch. 1985. *Draining the Sea . . . : Sixth Supplement to the Report on Human Rights in El Salvador.* New York: Americas Watch. March.

———. 1986. *The Continuing Terror: Seventh Supplement to the Report on Human Rights in El Salvador.* New York: Americas Watch. September.

———. 1987a. *Settling into Routine: Human Rights Abuses in Duarte's Second Year.* Eight Supplement to the *Report on Human Rights in El Salvador.* New York: Americas Watch. May.

———. 1987b. *The Civilian Toll, 1986–1987.* Ninth Supplement to the *Report on Human Rights in El Salvador.* New York: Americas Watch. 30 August.

———. 1988a. *Human Rights in El Salvador on the Eve of Elections, 1988.* New York: Americas Watch. March.

———. 1988b. *Nightmare Revisited, 1987–1988.* Tenth Supplement to the *Report on Human Rights in El Salvador.* New York: Americas Watch. September.

———. 1989a. *Carnage Again: Preliminary Report on Violations of the Laws of War by Both Sides in the November 1989 Offensive in El Salvador.* New York: Americas Watch. 24 November.

———.1989b. *Update on El Salvador: The Human Rights Crisis Continues in the Wake of the FMLN Offensive.* New York: Americas Watch. 16 December.

———. 1990. *A Year of Reckoning: El Salvador a Decade after the Assassination of Archbishop Romero.* New York: Americas Watch.

———. 1992. "El Salvador: Peace and Human Rights: Successes and Shortcomings of the United Nations Observer Mission in El Salvador (ONUSAL)." New York: Americas Watch. 2 September.

Americas Watch Committee and American Civil Liberties Union. 1982a. *Report on Human Rights in El Salvador.* New York: Random House.

———. 1982b. *Supplement to the Report on Human Rights in El Salvador.* Written by Cynthia Brown. Washington, D.C.: Center for National Security Studies.

———. 1983a. *Second Supplement to the Report on Human Rights in El Salvador.* New York: Americas Watch Committee. 31 January.

———. 1983b. *Third Supplement to the Report on Human Rights in El Salvador.* New York: Americas Watch Committee. 19 July.

———. 1984. *As Bad as Ever: A Report on Human Rights in El Salvador.* New York: Americas Watch Committee. 31 January.

Americas Watch Committee and Lawyers Committee for International Human Rights. 1984. *Free Fire: A Report on Human Rights in El Salvador.* New York: Americas Watch. August.

Amnesty International. 1979. *Political Imprisonment in Uruguay*. London: Amnesty International Publications.

————. 1983. "El Salvador: A Gross and Consistent Pattern of Human Rights Abuses." Information Packet. New York.

————. 1988. "Colombia: Amnesty International Briefing." AI document index AMR 23/14/88.

Anaya, Eugenio C. h. 1980. "Crónica del mes: Enero 1980." *Estudios Centroamericanos (ECA)* 35, nos. 375–76 (January–February):101–8.

Anderson, Thomas P. 1971. *Matanza: El Salvador's Communist Revolt of 1932*. Lincoln: University of Nebraska Press.

————. 1981, *The War of the Dispossessed*. Lincoln: University of Nebraska Press.

Anonymous [Oficiales anónimos de inteligencia de la Fuerza Armada]. 1994. "Un relato histórico de los escuadrones de la muerte y estudios de caso." In *Los escuadrones de la muerte en El Salvador*, 228–62. San Salvador: n.p.

Arnson, Cynthia J. 1989. *Crossroads: Congress, the Reagan Administration and Central America*. New York: Pantheon.

Astilla Carmelo, Francisco Esmeralda. 1976. *The Martínez Era: Salvadoran–American Relations, 1931–1944*. Ph.D. dissertation, Louisiana State University. Ann Arbor: UMI.

Aubey, Robert T. 1969. "Entrepreneurial Formation in El Salvador." *Explorations in Entrepreneurial History* 15:268–85.

Baires Martínez, Yolanda. 1994. "Orígenes y formación del partido ARENA (1979–1982)." In *Centro América entre democracia y desorganización*, ed. Gilles Batallon, 29–50. Guatemala: Facultad Latina americana de Ciencias Sociales (FLACSO).

Baloyra, Enrique. 1982. *El Salvador in Transition*. Chapel Hill: University of North Carolina Press.

————. 1983. "Reactionary Despotism in Central America." *Journal of Latin American Studies* 15:295–319.

Banks, David L. 1986. "The Analysis of Human Rights Data over Time." *Human Rights Quarterly* 8:654–80.

Barham, Brad. 1991. "Migration, Remittances, and Central American Economic Development: A Household Level Approach." Paper presented at Latin American Institute, University of New Mexico, Albuquerque 1 November.

Becklund, Laurie. 1983. "Death Squads: Deadly Other War." *Los Angeles Times*, 18 December.

Blake, Andrew. 1990. "A Second Salvadoran Confesses." *Boston Globe*, 16 March.

Blaufarb, Douglas S, and George K. Tanham 1984. "Counterinsurgency: A Framework for Analysis." Fort Lewis, Wash: BDM Corporation.

Bollen, Kenneth A. 1986. "Political Rights and Political Liberties in Nations: An Evaluation of Human Rights Measures, 1950 to 1984." *Human Rights Quarterly* 8:567–591.

Bonasso, Miguel, and Ciro Gómez Leyva. 1993. *Cuatro minutos para las doce: Conversaciones con el Commandante Schafik Handal*. Puebla, Mexico: Periodistas Asociados Latinoamericanos/Síntesis.

Bonner, Raymond. 1984. *Weakness and Deceit: U.S. Policy and El Salvador*. New York: Times Books.

Bowen, Gordon. 1987. "Prospects for Liberalization by Way of Democratization in Guatemala." In *Liberalization and Redemocratization in Latin America*, ed. George A. Lopez and Michael Stohl, 33–56. Westport, Conn.: Greenwood Press.

Brewer, Anthony. 1980. *Marxist Theories of Imperialism*. London: Routledge and Kegan Paul.

Brockett, Charles D. 1990. *Land, Power and Poverty*. Boulder, Colo.: Westview Press.

———. 1991. "Sources of State Terrorism in Rural Central America." In *State Organized Terror: The Case of Violent Internal Repression*, ed. P. Timothy Bushnell, Vladimir Shlapentokh, Christopher K. Vanderpool, and Jeyaratnam Sundram, 59–76. Boulder, Colo.: Westview Press.

Bronstein, Phil. 1990. "U.S. Officials Reverse View on Salvadoran Army." *San Francisco Examiner*, 6 May.

Brown, Richard Maxwell. 1979. "Historical Patterns of American Violence." In *Violence in America*, ed. Hugh Davis Graham and Ted Robert Gurr, 19–48. Beverly Hills: Sage.

Browning, David. 1971. *El Salvador: Landscape and Society*. Oxford: Clarendon Press.

Buchanan, Paul G. 1989. "State Terror as a Complement of Economic Policy: The Argentine Proceso, 1976–1981." In *Dependence, Development, and State Repression*, ed. George A. Lopez and Michael Stohl. Westport, Conn.: Greenwood Press.

Bueno de Mesquita, Bruce, and David Lalman. 1992. *War and Reason: Domestic and International Imperatives*. New Haven: Yale University Press.

Bulmer-Thomas, Victor. 1987. *The Political Economy of Central America since 1920*. Cambridge: Cambridge University Press.

Byrne, Hugh G. 1994. *The Problem of Revolution: A Study of Strategies of Insurgency and Counter-Insurgency in El Salvador's Civil War, 1981–1991*. Ph.D. dissertation, University of California, Los Angeles. Ann Arbor: UMI.

Cabarrús, Carlos Rafael. 1983. *Génesis de una revolución: Analysis del surgimiento y desarrollo de la organización campesina en El Salvador*. Mexico City: La Casa Chata.

Cardenal, Rodolfo. 1987. *Historia de una esperanza*. San Salvador: UCA Editores.

Carleton, David. 1989. "The New International Division of Labor: Export-Oriented Growth and State Repression in Latin America." In *Dependence, Development, and State Repression*, ed. George A. Lopez and Michael Stohl, 211–350. Westport, Conn.: Greenwood Press.

Carnoy, Martin. 1984. *The State and Political Theory*. Princeton: Princeton University Press.

Castro Morán, Mariano. 1989. *Función política del ejército salvadoreño en el presente siglo*. San Salvador: UCA Editores.

Centro de Documentación e Información (CUDI). 1980–81. *Balance estadística*. San Salvador: Universidad Centroamericana José Simeón Cañas.

Ching, Erik. 1995. "Una nueva apreciación de la insurrección del 32." *Tendencias*, no. 44 (September): 28–31.

Chomsky, Noam, and Edward S. Herman. 1979. *The Washington Connection and Third World Fascism*, vol. 1. Boston: South End Press.

Christian, Shirley. 1987. "El Salvador's Divided Military." In *El Salvador: Central America in the New Cold War*, ed. Marvin E. Gettleman, Patrick Lacefield, Louis Menashe, and David Mermelstein, 90–103. New York: Grove Press.

Cienfuegos, Fermán. 1993. *Veredas de audacia.* San Salvador:Editorial Arcoiris.

Cohen, Bernard. 1984. "Political Death and Homicide in El Salvador." Manuscript, Department of Sociology and Criminology, Graduate Center, City University of New York.

Colindres, Eduardo. 1977. *Fundamentos económicos de la burguesía Salvadoreña.* San Salvador: UCA Editores, Universidad Centroamericana José Simeón Cañas.

Comisión de Derechos Humanos de El Salvador (CDHES). 1981. "Violaciones a los derechos humanos en El Salvador, Enero–Abril 1981." San Salvador: CDHES.

Comisión Económica para América Latina y el Caribe (CEPAL). 1991. "Remesas y economía familiar en El Salvador, Guatemala, y Nicaragua." Guatemala City: CEPAL.

Comisión Nacional sobre la Desaparición de Personas. 1984. *Nunca mas.* Buenos Aires: CONADEP.

Comisión Nacional de Verdad y Reconciliación. 1991. *Informe.* Published in special three-volume edition of *La Nación,* Santiago. Undated.

Corradi, Juan, Patricia Weiss Fagen, and Manuel Antonio Garretón Merino. 1992. *Fear at the Edge: State Terror and Resistance in Latin America.* Berkeley: University of California Press.

Dallin, Alexander, and George W. Breslauer. 1970. *Political Terror in Communist Systems.* Stanford: Stanford University Press.

Danner, Mark. 1993. "The Truth of El Mozote." *New Yorker,* 6 December, 50–74.

Devine, Frank. 1981. *Embassy under Attack.* New York: Vantage.

Dickey, Christopher. 1985. *With the Contras.* New York: Simon and Schuster.

Diskin, Martin. 1991. Typescript.

Doggett, Martha. 1993. *Death Foretold: The Jesuit Murders in El Salvador.* New York: Lawyers Committee for Human Rights.

Doyle, Michael W. 1983. "Kant, Liberal Legacies, and Foreign Affairs." *Philosophy and Public Affairs* 12:205–35.

Duff, Ernest A., and John F. McCamant. 1976. *Violence and Repression in Latin America: A Quantitative and Historical Analysis.* New York: Free Press.

Duhalde, Eduardo Luis. 1983. *El estado terrorista argentino.* Buenos Aires: Ediciones El Caballito.

Dunkerly, James. 1985. *The Long War: Dictatorship and Revolution in El Salvador.* London: Verso Editions.

Durham, William H. 1979. *Scarcity and Survival in Central America: Ecological Origins of the Soccer War.* Stanford: Stanford University Press.

Eckstein, Harry. 1975. "Case Study and Theory in Political Science." In *Handbook of Political Science,* vol. 7, ed. F. I. Greenstein and N. W. Polsby, 79–138. Reading, Mass.: Addison-Wesley.

Elam, Robert Varney. 1968. *Appeal to Arms: The Army and Politics in El Salvador, 1931–1964.* Ph.D. dissertation, Department of History, University of New Mexico, Albuquerque.

———. 1989. "The Army and Politics in El Salvador, 1840–1927." In *The Politics of Antipolitics,* ed. Brian Loveman and Thomas M. Davies, Jr. 2d ed., Lincoln: 82–88. University of Nebraska Press.

Ellacuría, Ignacio (Tomás Campos, pseudonym). 1979. "El papel de las organizaciones populares en la actual situación del país." *Estudios Centroamericanos* 34, nos. 372–73 (October-November): 923–45.

Evans, Peter B. , Dietrich Rueschemeyer, and Theda Skocpol. 1985. *Bringing the State Back In*. New York: Cambridge University Press.

Fagen, Richard. 1987. *Forging Peace: The Challenge of Central America*. New York: Basil Blackwell.

Farah, Douglas, and Don Podesta. 1989. "Salvadoran Killings Cited." *Washington Post*, 27 October.

Forché, Carolyn. 1980. "The Road to Reaction in El Salvador". *The Nation*, 14 June 712–16.

Francovich, Alan. 1985. *Short Circuit*. Documentary film. New York: First Run/Icarus Films.

García, Jose Z. 1978. "Military Factions and Military Intervention in Latin America." In *The Military and Security in the Third World: Domestic and International Impacts*, ed. Sheldon W. Simon, 47–75. Boulder, Colo. Westview Press.

———. 1982. "Origins of Repression and Moderation in the Militaries of El Salvador and Honduras." Manuscript, New Mexico State University, Las Cruces.

———. 1983. "Political Conflict within the Salvadorean Armed Forces: Origins and Consequences." Manuscript, New Mexico State University, Las Cruces.

Gibb, Tom. 1995. Manuscript.

Gibb, Tom, and Douglas Farah. 1989. "Death Squads in El Salvador." Manuscript.

Gibb, Tom, and Frank Smyth. 1990. *El Salvador: Is Peace Possible?* Washington, D.C.: Washington Office on in Latin America.

Giner, Salvador. 1979. "Political Economy and Cultural Legitimation in the Origins of Parliamentary Democracy: The Southern European Case." Paper presented to the Roundtable on "The Transition from Authoritarianism to Democracy in Southern Europe and in Latin America," Madrid, cited in Baloyra 1983.

Gleijeses, Piero. 1991. *Shattered Hope: The Guatemalan Revolution and the United States, 1944–1954*. Princeton: Princeton University Press.

Goldstein, Robert Justin. 1986. "The Limitations of Using Quantitative Data in Studying Human Rights Abuses." *Human Rights Quarterly* 8:607–27.

Gordon, Sara. 1989. *Crísis política y guerra en El Salvador*. Mexico City: Siglo Veintiuno.

Grieb, Kenneth J. 1971. "The United States and the Rise of General Maximiliano Hernández Martínez." *Journal of Latin American Studies* 2:151–72.

Gruson, Lindsey. 1989. "Salvador Epilogue: At Least They're Still Talking." *New York Times*, 20 October.

Guido Véjar, Rafael. 1979. "La crísis política en El Salvador (1976–1979)." *Estudios Centroamericanos* 35, nos. 369–70 (July–August): 507–26.

———. 1980a. *El ascenso del militarismo en El Salvador*. San Salvador: UCA Editores.

———. 1980b. "La crísis política en El Salvador," *Revista Mexicana de Sociología* 42, no. 1 (January–March):235–66.

Gurr, Ted Robert. 1971. *Why Men Rebel*. Princeton: Princeton University Press.

———. 1986. "The Political Origins of State Violence and Terror: A Theoretical

Analysis." In *Government Violence and Repression*, ed. Michael Stohl and George A. Lopez, 45–72. Westport, Conn.: Greenwood Press.

Harnecker, Marta. 1993. *Con la mirada en alto*. San Salvador: UCA Editores.

Hibbs, Douglas. 1973. *Mass Political Violence*. New York: John Wiley and Sons.

Hoffmann, Stanley. 1968. *Gulliver's Troubles: Or The Setting of American Foreign Policy*. New York: McGraw-Hill.

Huntington, Samuel. 1968. *Political Order in Changing Societies*. New Haven: Yale University Press.

———. 1984. "Will More Countries Become More Democratic?" *Political Science Quarterly* 99:193–218.

Institute for Policy Studies. 1980. "Background Information on the Security Forces in El Salavdor and U.S. Military Assistance." Prepared by Cynthia Arnson. Washington, D.C.:IPSO.

Jackson, Steven, Bruce Russett, Duncan Snidal, and David Sylvan. 1978. "Conflict and Coercion in Dependent States." *Journal of Conflict Resolution* 22:627–57.

Jervis, Robert. 1976. *Perception and Misperception in International Politics*. Princeton: Princeton University Press.

Johnson, Kenneth Lance. 1993. *Between Revolution and Democracy: Business Elites and the State in El Salvador during the 1980s*. Ph.D. dissertation, Tulane University. Ann Arbor: UMI.

Joseph, Paul. 1987. *Cracks in the Empire: State Politics in the Vietnam War*. New York: Columbia University Press.

Kant, Immanuel. 1983. *Perpetual Peace and Other Essays on Politics, History and Morals*, trans. Ted Humphrey. Indianapolis: Hacket.

Karl, Terry. 1986. "Imposing Consent: Electoralism versus Democracy in El Salvador." In *Elections and Democratization Latin America*, ed. Paul Drake and Eduardo Silva, 9–36. San Diego: Center for Iberian and Latin American Studies, University of California.

Keogh, Dermot. 1983. "The Myth of the Liberal Coup: The United States and the 15 October 1979 Coup in El Salvador." *Millennium: Journal of International Studies* 13:153–183.

Koch, Katherine. 1980. "Carter Throws the Dice on El Salvador." *Los Angeles Times*. 23 December.

Krueger, Chris, and Kjell Enge. 1985. *Security and Development Conditions in the Guatemalan Highlands*. Washington, D.C.: Washington Office on Latin America.

Larmer, Brook. 1989. "U.S.-Funded Think Tank Sways New Government." *Christian Science Monitor*, 28 August.

Latin America Bureau. 1979. *El Salvador under General Romero*. London: Latin America Bureau.

Lauria Santiago, Aldo. 1991. "The Social-Historical Construction of Repression in El Salvador." Paper presented at the research conference on "Central America in the 1990's: Domestic and International Change," New York University, 26 April.

Lenin, V. I. 1970. *Imperialism, the Highest Stage of Capitalism*. Peking: Foreign Languages Press.

Lietes, Nathan, and Charles Wolf. 1966. *Rebellion and Authority: Myths and Realities Reconsidered*. P-3422. Santa Monica, Calif.: RAND Corp.

Lopez, George. 1986. "National Security Ideology as an Impetus to State Violence and State Terror." In *Government Violence and Repression*, ed. Michael Stohl and George A. Lopez, 73–96. Westport, Conn.: Greenwood Press.

López Vallecillos, Italo. 1979a. "Fuerzas sociales y cambio social en El Salvador." *Estudios Centroamericanos* 34, nos. 369–70 (January–February):557–90.

————. 1979b. "Rasgos sociales y tendencias políticas en El Salvador (1969–1979)." *Estudios Centroamericanos* 34 nos. 372–73, (October–November):863–84.

Majano, Adolfo. 1989. *El golpe de estado de 1979: Una oportunidad perdida.* Manuscript.

Martin, Lisa L., and Kathryn Sikkink. 1993. "U.S. Policy and Human Rights in Argentina and Guatemala, 1973–1980." In *Double-Edged Diplomacy: International Bargaining and Domestic Politics*, ed. Peter B. Evans, Harold K. Jacobson, and Robert D. Putnam, 330–62. Berkeley: University of California Press.

Marx, Karl. 1940. *The Civil War in France.* New York: International Publishers.

————. 1963. *The Eighteenth Brumaire of Louis Bonaparte.* New York: International Publishers.

Mason, T. David, and Dale A. Krane. 1989. "The Political Economy of Death Squads: Toward a Theory of the Impact of State-Sanctioned Terror." *International Studies Quarterly* 33:175–98.

Massey, Douglas, and Kathleen M. Schnabel. 1983. "Recent Trends in Hispanic Immigration to the US." *International Migration Review* 17:212–44.

McCamant, John. 1984. "Governance without Blood: Social Science's Antiseptic View of Rule; or The Neglect of Political Repression." In *The State as Terrorist: The Dynamics of Governmental Violence and Repression*, ed. Michael Stohl and George A. Lopez, 11–42. Westport, Conn.: Greenwood Press.

McClintock, Michael. 1985a. *The American Connection: State Terror and Popular Resistance in El Salvador.* London: Zed.

————. 1985b.*The American Connection: State Terror and Popular Resistance in Guatemala.* London: Zed.

Mena Sandoval, Francisco Emilio. 1983. "La conspiración del 15 de Octubre." Annex no. 19 in Mariano Castro Morán, *Función política del ejército salvadoreño en el presente siglo*, 441–52. San Salvador: UCA Editores.

————. 1992. *Del ejército nacional al ejército guerrillero.* San Salvador: Ediciones Arcoiris.

Midlarsky, Manus I., and Kenneth Roberts. 1985. "Class, State, and Revolution in Central America." *Journal of Conflict Resolution* 29:163–93.

Miles, Sara, and Bob Ostertag. 1989. "D'Aubuisson's New ARENA." *NACLA Report on the Americas* 23, (July):14–38.

Miller, Marjorie. 1989. "Salvador Rebels Demand Major Reforms for Peace." *Los Angeles Times*, 14 September.

Millman, Joel. 1989. "El Salvador's Army: A Force unto Itself." *New York Times Magazine*, 10 December, 46, 95–97.

Mitchell, Neil J., and James M. McCormick. 1988. "Economic and Political Explanations of Human Rights Violations." *World Politics* 40:476–98.

Montes, Segundo. 1985. *Desplazados y refugiados.* San Salvador: Instituto de Investigaciones, Universidad Centroamericana/José Simeón Cañas.

————. 1986. *El Salvador 1986: En busca de soluciones para los desplazados.* San Salvador: Instituto de Investigaciones, Universidad Centroamericana José Simeón Cañas.

————. 1987. *Salvadoreños refugiados en los Estados Unidos.* San Salvador: Instituto de Investigaciones, Universidad Centroamericana José Simeón Cañas.

Montgomery, Tommie Sue. 1982. *Revolution in El Salvador.* Boulder, Colo.: Westview Press.

Moore, Barrington. 1968. *Social Origins of Dictatorship and Democracy: Lord and Peasant in the Making of the Modern World.* Boston: Beacon Press.

Moravcsik, Andrew. 1993. "Integrating International and Domestic Theories of International Bargaining." In *Double-Edged Diplomacy: International Bargaining and Domestic Politics,* ed. Peter Evans, Harold K. Jacobson, and Robert D. Putnam, 3–42 Berkeley: University of California Press.

Moreira Alves, Maria Helena. 1985. *State and Opposition in Military Brazil.* Austin: University of Texas Press.

Movimiento de la Juventud Militar. 1976. "Al Ejército." Open letter to armed forces, mimeographed. Archives of Centro de Documentación e Información, Universidad Centroamericana José Simeón Cañas, San Salvador.

Murray Meza, Roberto. 1992. "The State of the Economy," in *Is There a Transition to Democracy in El Salvador?* ed. Joseph S. Tulchin with Gary Bland, 105–24. Boulder, Colo.: Lynne Reinner.

Nairn, Alan. 1984. "Behind the Death Squads." *The Progressive* 48, no. 5 (May): 20–29.

National Security Archive (NSA). 1989a. *El Salvador 1977–1984: The Making of U.S. Policy.* Draft chronology. Photocopy. References to microfiche collection of U.S. government documents.

————. 1989b. *El Salvador: The Making of U.S. Policy, 1977–1984.* Microfiche document collection with two-volume guide and index. Alexandria, Va.: Chadwyck-Healey.

O'Donnell, Guillermo. 1978. "Reflections on the Patterns of Change in the Bureaucratic-Authoritarian State." *Latin American Research Review* 13, no. 1: 3–38.

————. 1979. *Modernization and Bureaucratic-Authoritarianism.* Berkeley: Institute of International Studies, University of California.

O'Donnell, Guillermo, and Philippe C. Schmitter. 1986. *Transitions from Authoritarian Rule: Tentative Conclusions about Uncertain Democracies.* Baltimore: Johns Hopkins University Press.

Osiel, Mark. 1986. "The Making of Human Rights Policy in Argentina: The Impact of Ideas and Interests on a Legal Conflict." *Journal of Latin American Studies* 18:135–78.

Packenham, Robert A. 1973. *Liberal America and the Third World. Political Development Ideas in Foreign Aid and Social Science.* Princeton: Princeton University Press.

Paige, Jeffery M. 1975. *Agrarian Revolution: Social Movements and Export Agriculture in the Underdeveloped World.* New York: Free Press.

————. 1991. "Coffee, Class and Class Fraction: Revolution and the Agrarian Bourgeoisie in El Salvador." Paper presented at the Meetings of the Latin American Studies Association, Washington, D.C., 6 April.

————. 1993. "Coffee and Power in El Salvador." *Latin American Research Review* 28, no. 3:7–40.

————. 1994. "History and Memory in El Salvador: Elite Ideology and the Insurrection and Massacre of 1932." Paper presented at the Meetings of the Latin American Studies Association, Atlanta, Georgia, 11 March.

Parkman, Patricia. 1988. *Nonviolent Insurrection in El Salvador: The Fall of Maximiliano Hernández Martínez.* Tucson: University of Arizona Press.

Pastor, Robert. 1987. *Condemned to Repetition: The United States and Nicaragua.* Princeton: Princeton University Press.

Pelupessy, Wim. 1987. "El sector agroexportador de El Salvador: La base económica de una oligarquía no-fraccionada." *Boletín de estudios latinoamericanos y del Caribe,* no. 43 (December): 53–80.

Pérez Brignoli, Héctor. 1989. *A Brief History of Central America.* Berkeley: University of California Press.

Peterson, Linda. 1986. "Central American Migration: Past and Present." Washington, D.C.: Center for International Research, U.S. Bureau of the Census. CIR Staff Paper no. 25, November.

Pion-Berlin, David. 1989. *The Ideology of State Terror: Economic Doctrine and Political Repression in Argentina and Peru.* Boulder, Colo.: Lynne Reinner.

Poulantzas, Nicos. 1978. *State, Power, Socialism,* Trans. Patrick Camiller. London: Verso.

Pye, Lucian. 1971. "The Legitimacy Crisis." In *Crises and Sequences in Political Development,* ed. Leonard Binder, James S. Coleman, Joseph Lapalombara, Lucian W. Pye, Sidney Verba, and Myron Weiner, 135–58. Princeton: Princeton University Press.

Pyes, Craig. 1983a. "Right Built Itself in Mirror Image of Left for Civil War." *Albuquerque Journal,* 18 December.

————. 1983b. "D'Aubuisson's Fledgling Party Finds a Mentor in Guatemala." *Albuquerque Journal,* 18 December.

————. 1983c. "A Dirty War in the Name of Freedom." *Albuquerque Journal,* 18 December.

————. 1983d. "A Chilling Plan Maps a Terror Road to Rule." *Albuquerque Journal,* 19 December.

————. 1983e. "A Policeman's Initiation: 'We Put Two Bullets in His Head.'" *Albuquerque Journal,* 19 December.

————. 1983f. "Two Dinner Parties Meet, and Two Americans Die." *Albuquerque Journal,* 19 December.

————. 1983g. "'The Doctor' Prescribes Torture for the Hesitant." *Albuquerque Journal,* 20 December.

————. 1983h. "To the Brotherhood, Reds Infect Every Niche of El Salvador." *Albuquerque Journal,* 20 December.

————. 1983i. "The Businessmen Invest in the Murky Side of War." *Albuquerque Journal,* 21 December.

————. 1983j. "'A Regular Americano' Joins the Kidnappers." *Albuquerque Journal,* 21 December.

————. 1983k. "The New American Right Cooks Up a Hot Potato." *Albuquerque Journal,* 22 December.

Remmer, Karen. 1993. "The Political Economy of Elections in Latin America, 1980–1991." *American Political Science Review* 87:393–407.

Remmer, Karen, and Gilbert Merkx. 1982. "Bureaucratic-Authoritarianism Revisited." *Latin American Research Review* 17, no. 2:3–39.

Rojas, H. F. 1981. "Estado capitalista y aparato estatal." In *Estado y política en América Latina*, 133–71. Mexico City: Siglo Veintiuno.

Rosa, Herman. 1992. "El papel de la asistencia de AID en el fortalecimiento de nuevas instituciones del sector privado y en la transformación global de la economía salvadoreña: El caso FUSADES." Paper presented at the 17th Congress of the Latin American Studies Association, Los Angeles, 27 September.

Rouquié, Alain. 1987. *The Military and the State in Latin America*. Berkeley: University of California Press.

Rueschemeyer, Dietrich, Evelyne Huber Stephens, and John D. Stephens. 1992. *Capitalist Development and Democracy*. Chicago: University of Chicago Press.

Ruhl, J. Mark. 1984. "Agrarian Structure and Political Stability in Honduras." *Journal of Interamerican Studies and World Affairs* 26, no. 21 (February):33–68.

Rummel, Rudoph J. 1990. *Lethal Politics: Soviet Genocide and Mass Murder since 1917*. New Brunswick: Transaction.

———. 1991. *China's Bloody Century*. New Brunswick: Transaction.

———. 1992. *Democide: Nazi Genocide and Mass Murder*. New Brunswick: Transaction.

———. 1994a. "Power, Genocide and Mass Murder." *Journal of Peace Research* 31, no. 1 (February): 1–10.

———. 1994b. *Death by Government*. New Brunswick: Transaction.

Salazar Valiente, Mario. 1981. "El Salvador: Crisis, dictadura, lucha . . . (1920–1980)." In *América Latina: Historia de medio siglo*, ed. Pablo Gonzalez Casanova, 87–122. Mexico: Siglo Veintiuno.

Samayoa, Salvador, and Guillermo Galvan. 1979. "El movimiento obrero en El Salvador ¿Resurgimiento o agitación?" *Estudios Centroamericanos*. 35, nos. 369–70 (July-August): 591–600.

Schmitter, Philippe. 1974. "Still the Century of Corporatism?" In *The New Corporatism: Social-Political Structures in the Iberian World*, ed. Fredrick B. Pike and Thomas Tritch, 85–131. Notre Dame: University of Notre Dame Press.

Schwartz, C. Michael, and Harry R. Targ. 1989. *Dependence, Development, and State Repression*, ed. George A. Lopez and Michael Stohl. Westport, Conn.: Greenwood Press.

Seligson, Mitchell A. 1980. *Peasants of Costa Rica and the Development of Agrarian Capitalism*. Madison: University of Wisconsin Press.

———. 1994. "Thirty Years of Transformation in the Agrarian Structure of El Salvador." Typescript.

Seligson, Mitchell A., and James M. Malloy. 1987. *Authoritarians and Democrats: Regime Transition in Latin America*. Pittsburgh: University of Pittsburgh Press.

Shafer, D. Michael. 1988. *Deadly Paradigms: The Failure of U.S. Counterinsurgency Policy*. Princeton: Princeton University Press.

Sheahan, John. 1980. "Market-Oriented Economic Policies and Political Repression in Latin America." *Economic Development and Cultural Change* 28:267–92.

Sikkink, Kathryn. 1993. "Human Rights, Principled Issue-Networks, and Sovereignty in Latin America." *International Organization* 47:413–39.

Simon, Jean-Marie. 1987. *Guatemala: Eternal Spring, Eternal Tyranny*. New York: W. W. Norton.

Singer, J. David. 1981. "Accounting for International War: The State of the Discipline." *Journal of Peace Research* 18, no. 1:1–18.

Sloan, John W. 1984. "State Repression and Enforcement Terrorism in Latin America." In *The State as Terrorist: The Dynamics of Governmental Violence and Repression*, ed. Michael Stohl and George A. Lopez, 83–98. Westport, Conn.: Greenwood Press.

Smith, Peter. 1980. "Argentina: The Uncertain Warriors." *Current History* 78 (February): 62–65.

Smith, Tony. 1994. *America's Mission: The United States and the Worldwide Struggle for Democracy in the Twentieth Century*. A Twentieth Century Fund Book. Princeton: Princeton University Press.

Smyth, Frank. 1989. "Caught with Their Pants Down." *Village Voice*, 5 December.

Socorro Jurídico Cristiano. 1981. "Sobre los refugiados salvadoreños." Mimeographed. San Salvador.

———. 1984. "Informe no. 11, año IX." Mimeographed. San Salvador.

Stanley, William. 1987. "Economic Migrants or Refugees from Violence? A Time-Series Analysis of Salvadoran Migration to the United States." *Latin American Research Review* 22, no. 1:132–54.

———. 1995. "International Tutelage and Domestic Political Will: Building a New Civilian Police Force in El Salvador." *Studies in Comparative International Development* 30, no. 1 (Spring): 30–58.

Stepan, Alfred. 1971. *The Military in Politics: Changing Patterns in Brazil*. Princeton: Princeton University Press.

———. 1978. *The State and Society: Peru in Comparative Perspective*. Princeton: Princeton University Press.

———. 1988. *Rethinking Military Politics: Brazil and the Southern Cone*. Princeton: Princeton University Press.

Stohl, Michael, David Carleton, George Lopez, and Stephen Samuels. 1986. "State Violation of Human Rights: Issues and Problems of Measurement." *Human Rights Quarterly*. 8:592–606.

Tilly, Charles. 1985. "War Making and State Making as Organized Crime." In *Bringing the State Back In*, ed. Peter Evans, Dietrich Rueschemeyer, and Theda Skocpol, 169–91. New York: Cambridge University Press.

———. 1990. *Coercion, Capital, and European States, AD 990–1990*. Oxford: Basil Blackwell.

Ugarte, José Manuel. 1990. *Seguridad interior*. Buenos Aires: Fundación Arturo Illia.

United Nations. 1991. *First Report of the United Nations Observer Mission in El Salvador*. U.N. Document A/45/1055; S/213037. New York: United Nations. 16 September.

———. 1992. *Acuerdos de El Salvador: En el camino de la paz*. U.N. Document DPI/208–92615. New York: United Nations. June.

———. 1993. *From Madness to Hope: The 12-Year War in El Salvador*. Report of the Commision on the Truth for El Salvador. United Nations Document S/25500. New York: Department of Public Information. 1 April.

Universidad Centroamericana (UCA). 1981. *Violación de los derechos humanos en El*

Salvador: Documentos y testimonios. Document collection. Photocopy. San Salvador: Universidad Centroamericana José Simeón Cañas.

Villalobos, Joaquín. 1991. "A Farewell to Arms." *El Salvador Perspectives* 1, no. 15 (11 February).

Wallerstein, Immanuel. 1984. *The Politics of the World-Economy.* Cambridge: Cambridge University Press.

Webre, Stephen Andrew. 1979. *José Napoleón Duarte and the Christian Democratic Party in Salvadoran Politics, 1962–72.* Baton Rouge: Louisiana State University Press.

Weeks, John. 1986. "An Interpretation of the Central American Crisis." *Latin American Research Review* 21, no. 3:31–54.

Weiss Fagen, Patricia. 1984. *Applying for Political Asylum in New York: Law, Policy, and Administrative Practice.* New York Research Program in Inter-American Affairs Occasional Paper no. 41. New York: New York University.

Wellmer, Albrecht. 1981. "Terrorism and Social Criticism." *Telos,* no. 48 (Summer): 65–78.

White, Alastair. 1973. *El Salvador.* New York: Praeger.

Whitfield, Teresa. 1994. *Paying the Price: Ignacio Ellacuría and the Murdered Jesuits of El Salvador.* Philadelphia: Temple University Press.

Wickham-Crowley, Timothy P. 1988. "Failure and Success among Latin American Guerrilla Movements: The Forms and Reforms of the State." Paper prepared for the Meetings of the Latin American Studies Association, New Orleans, 17–19 March.

———. 1990. "Terror and Guerrilla Warfare in Latin America, 1956–1970." *Comparative Studies in Society and History* 32, no. 2:201–37.

———. 1992. *Guerrillas and Revolution in Latin America: A Comparative Study of Insurgents and Regimes since 1956.* Princeton: Princeton University Press.

Williams, Robert G. 1986. *Export Agriculture and the Crisis in Central America.* Chapel Hill: University of North Carolina Press.

———. 1994. *States and Social Evolution: Coffee and the Rise of National Governments in Central America.* Chapel Hill: University of North Carolina Press.

Williams, William Appleman. 1972. *The Tragedy of American Diplomacy.* New York: Dell.

Wilson, Alan Everett. 1970. *The Crisis of National Integration in El Salvador, 1919–1935.* Ph.D. dissertation, Stanford University. Ann Arbor: UMI.

Woerner, Fred E., et al. 1981. "Report of the El Salvador Military Strategy Assistance Team (Draft)." Released by the Department of Defense to the National Security Archive, Washington, D.C, under the Freedom of Information Act.

Wolf, Daniel H. 1992. "ARENA in the Arena: Factors in the Accommodation of the Salvadoran Right to Pluralism and the Broadening of the Political System." *LASA Forum* 23, no. 1 (Summer):10–18.

Wolf, Eric R. 1969. *Peasant Wars of the Twentieth Century.* New York: Harper and Row.

Wolpin, Miles. 1986. "State Terrorism and Repression in the Third World: Parameters and Prospects." In *Government Violence and Repression: An Agenda for Research,* ed. Michael Stohl and George A. Lopez, 97–164. Westport, Conn.: Greenwood Press.

Woodward, Bob. 1987. *Veil: The Secret Wars of the CIA, 1981–1987.* New York: Simon and Schuster.

Zamora, Rubén. 1976. "¿Seguro de vida o despojo? Análisis político de la transformación agraria." *Estudios Centroamericanos* 31, nos. 335–36. (September–October):511–33.

INDEX

Agrarian Code of 1907 (Ley Agraria), 48

Agriculturalists' Front of the Eastern Region (FARO), 103, 107

Aguirre y Salinas, Osmín, 66–67

Andino, Mario, and connections to the elite, 149, 184; and the Revolutionary Governing Junta, 134, 149, 156

ANEP. *See* National Association of Private Enterprise

ANSESAL. *See* Salvadoran National Special Services Agency

anticommunism in El Salvador, 69, 72, 76, 95, 103, 114, 123, 219; among civilians, 43; among the elite, 73, 86, 88, 105, 118, 124, 131, 237, 241; in the military, 43, 54–55, 73, 92, 131, 176, 195, 217; and the Salvadoran Communal Union (UCS), 95

April and May Revolutionary Party (PRAM), 75

Araujo, Arturo, 45–49, 51

ARENA. *See* National Republican Alliance

Argentina, 18

Armed Forces for Anti-Communist Liberation (FALANGE), 101

Armed Forces of El Salvador (FAES), 3–4, 180, 208, 218–19, 246–47, 249–51, 263; and the chain of command, 203; and the elite, 179; and the FMLN, 221, 228; U.S. support for, 181–82, 226, 229–31, 249, 253, 257, 262, 264

Armed Forces of Liberation (FAL), 187, 244

Armed Forces of National Resistance (RN), 99, 122, 187, 216, 239; cooperation of, with labor unions, 97; and the coup plot of 1980, 204, 207–8; guerrilla tactics of, 115–18; infiltration of, 192, 208; and the junior officer corps, 118, 188; as a military threat, 96–97, 118, 157–59, 200; and the National Trade Union Federation of Salvadoran Workers (FENASTRAS), 96; and the October 1979 coup, 135; political tactics of, 118, 125, 135, 200, 208; and the Revolutionary Governing Junta, 159, 175; secret meetings of, with the U.S. embassy, 200; and support for

Majano, 204, 207; and the United Popular Action Front (FAPU), 157, 159, 200, 208

ASI. *See* Salvadoran Industrial Association

Association of Private Enterprise. *See* National Association of Private Enterprise (ANEP)

Atlacatl Rapid Reaction Infantry Battalion (BIRI), 224, 247

Avalos, José Ramón, 184

Banco Central de Reserva, 59

Banco Hipotecario, 59–61;

Barrera, Román, 139–41, 146

Bosque, Pío Romero, 45, 47

Bowdler, William (U.S. assistant secretary of state), 183, 197

BPR. *See* Popular Revolutionary Bloc

Brazil, 19, 28, 36–37

Broad National Front (FAN), 163, 186, 204, 217; and the coup plot of 1980, 189–92, 200–201; and D'Aubuisson, 164, 189–90, 200, 232; and the National Republican Alliance, 232; opposition of, to the PDC, 189, 194; and the United States, 193

Brzezinski, Zbigniew (U.S. national security advisor), 197, 214

Bush, George, 242; visit to El Salvador, December 1983, 229, 239, 257

Bustillo, Rafael, 185, 230

Calderón, José Tomás, 50–51, 55

Carranza, Nicolás, 150, 163, 181–82, 185, 212, 217, 257, 263; and the CIA, 144; and the coup plot of 1980, 201–2; and death squads, 151, 192, 229; and the Equipo Molina, 151; and the October 1979 coup, 213; and the Revolutionary Governing Junta, 148; and the security forces, 164; transferred to ANTEL, 215; as vice minister of defense, 208

Carter, Jimmy, 40, 108–9, 112–13, 123, 137, 173, 201, 214–15

Casey, William, 229